Baseball Beyond Our Borders

In memory of Bill Kirwin, friend and mentor, who created a community of baseball scholars, an annual event to bring them together, and an academic journal for their work.

—*George Gmelch*

and

For Allan Winkler, historian, adventurer, mentor, and friend, who sent us to Finland. And SBZ, always.

—*Daniel A. Nathan*

Contents

Illustrations

Figures

Graphs and Table

Acknowledgments

The idea for this book developed out of conversations George had with the late Bill Kirwin, the founder and editor of NINE: A Journal of Baseball History and Culture. Others who contributed to the shaping and development of the first edition were Ted Gilman, Dan Gordon, Bill Kelly, Alan Klein, Marty Kuehnert, Tim Wiles, Franklin Otto, Robert Whiting, and Rob Wilson. When considering a new and expanded second edition of the book in 2015, George invited Dan Nathan to be his coeditor, which he says is "one of the best publishing decisions I have ever made." Dan was pleased to be asked and honored to work with George on this project.

We owe many thanks to the participants and the organizers of the Baseball and American Culture symposium in Cooperstown, New York; the NINE Spring Training Conference held in Arizona; and the North American Society for Sport History. These annual gatherings of scholars have helped incubate many of our ideas about baseball culture and history.

Special thanks go to Rob Taylor, Courtney Ochsner, and Ann Baker at the University of Nebraska Press and our agent, Rob Wilson, for their wise counsel and for shepherding the manuscript through the publication process. We also thank our all-star copy editor, Annette Wenda. We have benefited from frequent discussions on all matters of sport and writing with Robert Elias, Dan Gordon, Sharon Gmelch, Kenji Tierney,

Howard DeNike, Diane Royal, Greg Pfitzer, Beck Krefting, Amber Wiley, Erica Bastress-Dukehart, Matthew Hockenos, John Brueggemann, Pat Oles, Beau Breslin, Jeff Segrave, and Peter von Allmen.

Thanks are also due to numerous Union College, University of San Francisco, and Skidmore College librarians and student assistants. The former group—Donna Burton, Bruce Connolly, Dave Gerhan, Mary Cahill, and Sandie Brown—for helping us track down all manner of information, sources, and loose ends. The latter—Emily Laing, Sandra Vega, Amy Bell, Nevon Kipperman, Hannah Doban, Tessa Kalinosky—for carefully reading the chapters that constitute this book, asking good questions, and offering valuable feedback.

We are grateful to our institutions—the University of San Francisco, Union College, and Skidmore College—for their generous financial support of this book.

Most important, we thank all of the authors in the volume for their responsiveness and commitment and for the quality of their contributions. Their essays have enriched our appreciation of baseball beyond U.S. borders. The book is a testament to their expertise, hard work, and patience.

Finally, we are thankful for the intellectual and moral support of Sharon Gmelch and Susan Taylor, both of whom understand the importance of an expansive worldview and the need to get up and go.

Introduction

Around the Horn

George Gmelch and Daniel A. Nathan

The way baseball is played in Cuba, Japan, and Australia looks much like
how the game is played in the United States. The players use the same
gloves and bats, wear similar uniforms, and play by the same basic rules.
But beneath the outward similarity there is usually a very different history and culture influencing the sport's nuances. Even how players and
their fans think about the game and what they value are not the same.
As journalist turned baseball executive Joseph A. Reaves notes about
baseball in Asia, "It can look so similar and somehow feel so different."[1]
Like others, we are interested in those similarities and differences,
about how the game is played and what it means around the world.

This book is an updated and expanded version of the first edition
of *Baseball without Borders*. It examines the game's history and current
status in six more countries than its predecessor. There are new chapters
about baseball in Finland, Israel, Mexico, New Zealand, South Africa,
Venezuela, and the Australian state of Tasmania. Many of the original
chapters have been significantly revised.

The essays in this new and expanded collection explore baseball in
nineteen nations, Tasmania, and Puerto Rico (a U.S. territory). The
essays are diverse not only in the settings and cultures they describe,
but also in the perspectives adopted by their authors, who range from
anthropologists to historians, from journalists to English professors,
with a few independent scholars and a coach as well. The essays are also

diverse because we placed few restrictions on what the contributors chose to write about. We suggested some topics, such as the origins of baseball in the country they examined, its development, how local versions of the game differ from that played in the United States, and how the World Baseball Classic (WBC) has impacted baseball in the countries about which they are writing. In the main, though, the contributors were free to write about whatever aspects of the sport they thought American baseball fans (the intended audience) would find interesting. Some of the essays deal exclusively with the professional game abroad, while some, especially where there is not a strong professional league, also look at amateur baseball.

As before, we have organized the essays geographically. The countries in each region—the Americas, Asia, the Pacific, the Middle East, Africa, and Europe—share similarities in history and culture that have resulted in some parallels in the origins, development, and local versions of baseball found within them.

The collection begins with the Americas, with a chapter by writer Tim Wendel about Cuba, where baseball is widely loved and "has been closely linked with the causes of national independence and revolution since the days of José Martí."[2] Baseball arrived in Cuba in the 1860s, introduced by students returning from the United States. Folklore credits Nemiso Guillo for bringing the game to Cuba, when he returned from Springfield College in Mobile, Alabama, with a bat and baseball in his trunk. American sailors helped spread the game by playing with locals in Cuban ports. The game also got a lift from visiting American barnstormers in the 1870s. Just as the Japanese were responsible for spreading the game through Asia, Cubans became the apostles of baseball in parts of the Caribbean.

In "Cuba: The Curtain Begins to Fall," Wendel takes us on a personal journey across the island's baseball landscape. Along the way he examines the inflated claims that Fidel Castro was a genuine prospect (he wasn't) as well as the Cuban revolution's considerable impact on the island's national pastime. Thanks to Wendel's interactions with local fans, we learn about their thirst for information about the Major Leagues, particularly what American baseball looks like, as few Cuban fans have access to TV or other images of American games and ballparks. He also reflects on the pride that many Cubans take in their countrymen—such as Yoenis Cespedes and Aroldis Chapman—who have made the arduous journey to the United States and succeeded in the Major Leagues, just before the Obama administration announced a renewal of diplomatic relations with the island nation.

The next chapter is by anthropologist Alan Klein and is about the Dominican Republic, where baseball is sometimes described as "a national fever." No other aspect of Dominican life, except perhaps merengue, has provided as much joie de vivre in this Caribbean country as has baseball.[3] As Klein ably documents in his books *Sugarball: The American Game, the Dominican Dream* (1991) and *Dominican Baseball: New Pride, Old Prejudice* (2014), the development of Dominican baseball is closely tied to sugarcane. Early on baseball became a diversion for cane workers during their breaks from the sugar fields, and sugar factory managers organized many of the first leagues. In "Dominican Republic: From Paternalism to Parity," Klein explores the Dominican Republic's impressive rise to international baseball prominence. After a brief review of the history of baseball in the country, Klein turns to the ways talented local youths are developed into pro prospects. These center on the baseball academies set up by Major League Baseball (MLB) teams to train Dominican youths and the network of *buscónes*, or amateur scouts, who locate, nourish, instruct, and then place young prospects with a Major League organization (in exchange for a slice of the prospect's signing bonus). Klein also examines the transnational relationships between Dominican and American baseball. Where some observers have viewed this relationship in mostly exploitative terms,[4] Klein shows that while North American interests dominated Dominican baseball in the 1950s and 1960s, severely crippling the local Dominican professional league, relations have become more reciprocal, approaching parity.

In "Puerto Rico: A Major League Stepping-Stone," Franklin Otto and Thomas E. Van Hyning write from the perspective of fans who grew up on the island watching Puerto Rico Winter League baseball in its heyday. They survey the early development of Puerto Rican baseball (Cubans probably brought the game to the island, and soon thereafter U.S. military and civilian personnel helped it thrive) and then turn to the PRWL, where many fine U.S. and Caribbean Major League players spent their winters in the six-team league. In operation since 1938, the PRWL was in danger of folding in the early 1990s, in part because many homegrown stars no longer wished to return home to play—as Major Leaguers they had large salaries and didn't need the money, and their American teams didn't want them to risk injury. Today, a new generation of Puerto Rican stars is playing in the former PRWL, which is now a five-team league called the Liga de Béisbol Profesional Roberto Clemente (Roberto Clemente Professional Baseball League). They want to honor their country and let their fans, many of whom will never travel to the United States, see their heroes in person.

Not all baseball-playing nations in the Americas trace the game back to the United States. In "Canada: Internationalizing America's National Pastime," historian Colin Howell cites evidence that baseball in Canada may have developed on its own, independent of the United States. After World War II the game was widely supported by Canadians. Earlier, though, baseball's reputation for rowdiness, gambling, and drinking turned away members of the Anglo-Saxon bourgeoisie, whose class, race, and nativist prejudices caused them to prefer curling, cricket, tennis, and golf. It is notable that Howell is the only one in this volume to discuss women and baseball. Canada had its own organized women's baseball leagues, and about 10 percent of the women who played in the All-American Girls Professional Baseball League (1943–54), the wartime creation of Chicago Cubs owner Phil Wrigley, were Canadian. Wide ranging, Howell's chapter also discusses Canadian Major League Baseball teams and players and the country's successes and failures in international competition.

Baseball has a long tradition immediately south of the U.S. border, too. In his chapter "Mexico: From Humble Beginnings to Budding Competitor," historian Jorge Iber demonstrates that while *fútbol* (soccer) is the national game, baseball's place in the country's sporting life is significant. As is true of many places around the world, Iber writes that baseball's "earliest proponents came from the United States (military personnel and individuals associated with corporations) and exiled Cubans." Likewise, the game became entwined with "the development of Mexican nationalism" and signified "modernity during the *Porfiriato* era." Probably no single individual contributed more to Mexican baseball's rise than impresario Jorge Pasquel, who in the 1940s and early 1950s elevated professional baseball in Mexico and aggressively pursued Cuban and Negro League players, and later white Major Leaguers, with mixed results. "While Pasquel's raid on Major League players did not break the infamous reserve clause or overcome the *yanqui* owners," Iber asserts, "his endeavors set in motion trends that would eventually help open the door to African Americans and Latinos and to free agency in the United States." In the more than half century since then, scores of Mexicans have played in the Major Leagues (including the iconic pitcher Fernando Valenzuela, who inspired "Fernandomania" in the United States in 1981), the Mexican League has survived, and the Mexican national team has become competitive in international competition.

The latter cannot be said of baseball in Nicaragua, which has experienced many social and political upheavals and changes since writer Dan Gordon first visited it in 1988. In his significantly revised chapter, "Nicaragua: In Search of Diamonds," based in part on his return trip to the impoverished country in 2003, Gordon finds that baseball's popularity in Nicaragua has ebbed and flowed and varies according to place and region. By some measures, soccer has eclipsed baseball. Unlike in the past, Gordon observes, "sports bars broadcast European soccer games, and it is more common to see people in the street wearing Lionel Messi and Cristiano Ronaldo jerseys than donning baseball gear. The pickup game of preference has also been soccer because in congested barrios it is less complicated and less expensive to play." Nevertheless, Gordon demonstrates that baseball has retained much of its cultural resonance in the formerly war-torn country, which is now one of the poorest in the Western Hemisphere. Drawing on interviews (including with former Major League pitcher Dennis "el Presidente" Martínez) and reportage, Gordon examines the game at its highest and grassroots levels, as well as its long history. Importantly, Gordon illustrates how baseball is inseparable from Nicaraguan society and politics. In Nicaragua, he explains, "the tentacles of *Pinolero* politics and sports are wrapped so tightly around one another that it's challenging at times to distinguish one from the other."

Arturo J. Marcano and David P. Fidler's chapter suggests the same is true in Venezuela, a country in the throes of political and socioeconomic crises. In "Venezuela: The Passion and Politics of Baseball," Marcano and Fidler note that, while Venezuelans are passionate, the game's history and contemporary status are complicated, especially in light of MLB's aggressive policies and practices and the wide-ranging effects of and responses to globalization. In the past twenty-five years, the number of Venezuelan Major and Minor Leaguers has greatly increased, and "Venezuela was integrated into MLB's increasingly globalized business model, which involved securing cheap foreign talent and expanding consumer interest in MLB's products (for example, broadcast games and team merchandise)." What is good for MLB, however, may not be so good for Venezuelan baseball, Venezuelans, and the country itself. Marcano and Fidler, and others, are concerned about MLB teams violating the human rights of children and that MLB has dictated and restricted the terms of MLB player participation in Venezuela's Winter League in ways that potentially hurt the teams' quality, performance, fan support, and revenue. These and other developments have weakened Venezuela's "baseball institutions, economy, and culture," write Marcano and Fidler. "In Venezuela," they argue, "baseball is becoming more than a way to escape poverty; it has become a way to get out of the country entirely." Long term, this kind of talent drain does not bode well for Venezuela.

Brazil is the southernmost nation in the Western Hemisphere to play baseball. Yet Brazilian baseball is unique not because of its geography but because of who plays it. Although introduced by visiting American workers in the early 1900s, baseball was actually developed by Japanese immigrants. For many years, the Brazilian Japanese community has embraced the sport, and the style of Brazilian play is closer to the Japanese game than to the Latin or North American game. In "Brazil: Baseball Is Popular, and the Players Are (Mainly) Japanese!" Brazilians Carlos Azzoni and Tales Azzoni, an economist and journalist, respectively, and American Wayne Patterson, a computer scientist and university administrator, examine this anomaly in baseball demography as well as baseball's place in a country much better known for its soccer dominance. Thanks in part to the leadership of Jorge Otsuka and MLB's support and input, Brazil has started to produce Major Leaguers—such as Yan Gomes, Andre Rienzo, and Paulo Orlando—and has competed in the World Baseball Classic.

Part 2 comprises five essays about baseball in Asia, with two on the Japanese game, both of which are significantly different from those in the first edition of this book. In Japan baseball is not a postwar General MacArthur–inspired American import, as some American baseball fans think. It was introduced in 1867 by a young American teaching at a Tokyo university. Baseball became popular among schoolboys and eventually won recognition from the government for its educational and health benefits.

In "Japan: 'No Matter What Happens, Stand Up,'" Dan Gordon reveals the unique characteristics of Japanese high school baseball and the all-Japan national tournament at Kōshien. Far more than a mere sport, Japanese high school baseball is a philosophy and an educational tool. It is considered a spiritual discipline that teaches many of the values that define the Japanese *Bushido* tradition of teamwork, dedication, discipline, and respect. Gordon also notes an unhealthy side to Japanese high school ball, which sometimes includes hazing, corporal punishment, and excruciating and occasionally abusive training methods—activities that would not be tolerated in an American high school. Revisiting Japan after the devastating 2011 Thoku earthquake and tsunami, Gordon finds that Japanese high school baseball, like some of the country itself, has undergone changes, yet many Japanese simultaneously yearn for the stability and comfort afforded by one of its most cherished sporting traditions.

In "Japan: Professional Baseball Enters the Twenty-First Century," Yale University anthropologist William W. Kelly examines Nippon Professional Baseball, which has two leagues, the Central League and the Pacific League. He considers the NPB's history and current organizational structures and practices, its place in Japanese society, and the ways in which it differs from Major League Baseball. Some of the differences are significant. Infields in most Japanese stadiums are composed solely of dirt, the games are slower, players' careers are shorter, the salary range is more compressed (with a smaller income gap between superstars and journeymen), and the rosters are larger because teams do not have much of a minor league system. It is this version of the game, and not the great American game, that has diffused across Asia. Yet even in Japan, where baseball obviously has deep roots, the game is facing serious challenges. Kelly notes that Japan's "rapidly aging and shrinking national population, a digital media revolution, the rising popularity of soccer, the threat of asset stripping from MLB, and the demands of the World Baseball Classic" have had a deleterious effect on NPB. "Baseball has yet to be displaced as the center sport in contemporary Japan," Kelly explains, "but the domestic professional leagues are under serious assault by baseball elsewhere, by soccer and other sports, and by the inexorable dynamics of an aging and shrinking society and troubled economy."

In "Korea: Straw Sandals and Strong Arms," Joseph A. Reaves, who covered Asia for the *Chicago Tribune* for many years and later covered the Chicago Cubs for four seasons, charts the development of Korean baseball. Although a U.S. missionary first introduced baseball to Korea in the 1870s, it was the Japanese occupiers who spread the game. The colonial authorities promoted baseball as part of their plan to indoctrinate Korean youth with Japanese ways. Much like in Taiwan, Koreans first adopted the game as a way to peacefully challenge the oppressors, but it later became a way to impress outsiders. Reaves also shows how a government, threatened by a restive population, used baseball as an opiate. Indeed, one of the primary objectives of the Korean Baseball Organization in the 1980s was to divert the public's attention from politics to sports—to find an outlet for its restless and often rebellious young men.

In "China: A Century and a Half of Bat Ball," Reaves recounts the erratic history of baseball in China. Surprisingly, baseball was played in China as early as 1863, a decade before the first game in Japan. However, the game did not take root until much later. In nineteenth-century China, baseball was best known for the role it played in the cancellation of China's first and most ambitious educational exchange with the United States. Many of the 120 Chinese students sent to the United States in 1872 to learn the best of Western science and engineering developed a fondness for baseball, along with some other Western habits. When Chinese conservatives reported the students' transgressions back to the Imperial Court, the mission was canceled and the students were called home. Baseball then languished until the early 1900s, when many Chinese students began studying in Japan and became reacquainted with baseball, Japan's major collegiate sport. Baseball then gained a small following in China until the Cultural Revolution (1961–74), when the game was dismissed as a symbol of Western decadence. Across China zealous Red Guards ridiculed and sometimes persecuted players and coaches, and international competitions were no longer held. After the Cultural Revolution the game made a comeback and was even extolled by Chinese leaders for its benefits in military training (for example, it teaches soldiers how to throw hand grenades more accurately). At times reviled, at times exalted, baseball survived these upheavals.

Baseball arrived in Taiwan in 1897, shortly after the Japanese colonized the island. First played by Japanese youth, mostly at school, it was later adopted by Taiwanese boys and was an acceptable setting in which Taiwan's colonized population could interact and compete with the Japanese. "Taiwan: Baseball, Colonialism, Nationalism, and Other Inconceivable Things" is by historian Andrew Morris, who lived two blocks from the baseball stadium in Taizhong while doing research for his doctoral dissertation. He became a die-hard fan of the President Lions and eventually became interested in questions of colonialism, nationalism, and ethnic identity in Taiwan's national game, questions he addresses in his essay.

Many American readers will recall Taiwan's unparalleled Little League success (ten Little League World Series titles between 1969 and 1981 and seventeen altogether). Morris examines the role of these championships in developing national pride and promoting nationalism. Morris is particularly interested in the interplay between local and international dimensions of Taiwanese baseball. The popularity of the Chinese Professional Baseball League, for example, has depended on maintaining a balance between respect for local Chinese tradition and the international (for example, allowing foreigners to play in its league). The league lost much of its fan support in the 1990s, when it allowed so many foreign players (up to ten per team) that the native Taiwanese players were pushed out of the starring roles.

Part 3 is about baseball in the Pacific, specifically in mainland Australia, Tasmania, and New Zealand. In his chapter "Australia: Baseball's Curious Journey," Rick Burton, a professor of sport management, considers baseball's history in the Land Down Under, which can be traced to the late nineteenth century. Over the years Americans, such as the famed (and well-traveled) sports equipment entrepreneur Albert G. Spalding, tried to promote baseball in Australia, with mixed results. The game has long had Australian devotees, Burton explains, yet it has always had a difficult time competing with already entrenched Aussie sports such as cricket, soccer, rugby, swimming, and Australian

Rules football. Still, baseball in Australia has endured, and the country has produced more than two dozen MLB ballplayers (including a few All-Stars), hosted MLB games in Sydney, and competed in the World Baseball Classic.

One of Australia's six states, Tasmania is an island south of mainland Australia, with a population of just over a half million. In his chapter "Tasmania: Baseball Struggles to Survive," George Gmelch, who has directed anthropology field schools in Tasmania, observes that historically the game has experienced "short periods of enthusiasm among a small group of followers, followed by waning interest and decline." The baseball Tasmanians play is decidedly grassroots, never having become ingrained in the culture. There are few playing fields, and the talent, at best, does not exceed that of U.S. high school baseball. Major League Baseball holds little interest to Tasmanians. As Gmelch notes, Tassie baseball is more social than competitive, and "having fun rather than beating your opponent is what counts." At the same time, the mainstay Hobart Summer Baseball League is doing its best to promote the game and bring institutional stability to Tasmanian baseball.

Much smaller than Australia, New Zealand shares a similar Anglo-influenced history, yet the two island nations have notably different cultures, including sporting traditions and preferences. In "New Zealand: Baseball between British Traditions," historian Greg Ryan documents that baseball has been played in New Zealand since the 1880s. It has never, however, been widely popular. As in Australia, in New Zealand British games such as cricket and especially rugby were well established and incorporated into the local culture before baseball arrived. But this did not deter some Kiwis from embracing the game and establishing the Wellington Baseball Club in 1888. Over the next century, Ryan shows, baseball, always a minor sport, persisted in small pockets of Aotearoa (the Màori name for the country). For reasons that are unclear, softball took hold in the 1930s, and New Zealand has consistently done well in international softball competitions. Since the 1990s, partly due to "globalization and diversifying sport and leisure patterns," some New Zealanders have become "more receptive to American and other non-British sports," baseball among them. The establishment of Baseball New Zealand, the national governing body for the sport, is one example of this increased interest. So, too, is the fact that the national team's world ranking has dramatically improved and several New Zealanders have played professionally in the U.S. Minor Leagues.

Part 4 is about the Middle East, where baseball has barely taken root, other than in Israel, which has close links to the United States, has pioneered numerous irrigation technologies, and has three main baseball fields.[5] In "Israel: From the Desert to Jupiter . . . and Beyond," marketing and communications scholar William Ressler focuses on the values that baseball represents to many Israelis and how the Israel Association of Baseball administers and promotes the game. Still in its infancy (the first real baseball field in Israel was built in 1979), Israeli baseball represents *chevreman* culture, Ressler argues, that is, it embodies connections between and among people, collaboration, and good cheer. To many Israelis, even those on the 2012 Senior National Team—which included several "heritage players," such as then Minor Leaguer Joc Pederson—who competed to qualify for the wbc, baseball is still primarily a game, rather than a big business or a lucrative profession to which one might aspire. Clearly an admirer, Ressler is impressed with the "resilient and rejuvenating character of baseball in Israel" and is hopeful about the game's future in Eretz Yisrael.

Part 5 also deals with a single country but in the vast region of an entire continent. Marizanne Grundlingh's "South Africa: The Battle for Baseball" considers several aspects of the game: its historical origins in South Africa (which are not exclusively American, for Japanese sailors were responsible for introducing baseball in the Eastern Cape), its racially bifurcated development during the turbulent apartheid years, and its contemporary struggles in a multicultural nation whose sporting passion is primarily devoted to rugby, soccer, and cricket. As is the case in many countries, baseball is "a minor sport in South

Africa," Grundlingh acknowledges, yet for many of its thousands of players, coaches, administrators, and fans it is nonetheless meaningful. An anthropologist, Grundlingh has done fieldwork with the Bothasig Baseball Club in Cape Town that highlights how the game contributes to local community identity. Internationally, the South African national team has competed in the Olympics (2000) and the World Baseball Classic (2006 and 2009), without much success, as one would expect considering the elite competition. Yet as Grundlingh demonstrates, "Baseball offers those who play the game in South Africa an athletic identity and sense of belonging to a small but growing and passionate" baseball community.

Part 6 contains essays on four European countries. Peter Carino, a former English professor, views the Italian game from the vantage point of a fan in the stands in "Italy: No Hot Dogs in the Bleachers." He usually doesn't have a lot of company, though, because, as elsewhere in Europe, Italian baseball is not popular outside its small coterie of devoted followers. In the *bel paese*, Carino writes, baseball is "a 'boutique sport,' about as popular as professional lacrosse in the United States," appreciated by those with discerning taste. Most regular-season games draw fewer than a thousand spectators. Italy is considered the strongest European baseball country, although the Netherlands has won more European Championships. Carino reports that the gap between the strongest and the weakest teams and players is considerable. The teams at the bottom, for example, can go an entire season without winning a single game, while league champion teams often win 80 percent of their contests, often thanks to former professional ballplayers from the United States.

In "Holland: An American Coaching *Honkbal*," Harvey Shapiro describes the baseball scene in the Netherlands from a perspective unique in this volume. Shapiro, a veteran American college baseball coach, was hired to manage a club team in the Dutch National League (the Amstel Tigers) and later became the head coach of the Dutch National Team. Shapiro gives us a good sense of how Dutch amateur baseball games and players are different from those in the United States. In recounting his experiences as manager of the Dutch National Team, he reveals much about international competition, particularly the European and World Baseball Championships.

In Britain, the birthplace of baseball pioneer Henry Chadwick, baseball must compete with its distant relative, cricket, for attention. In "Great Britain: Baseball's Battle for Respect in the Land of Cricket, Rugby, and Soccer," writer and former ballplayer Josh Chetwynd charts the rocky development of the sport, beginning with Spalding's 1889 exhibition game at Kennington Oval in London, through the twentieth century (when several baseball leagues were established, all of which failed), and up to the present. Even more so than in Italy and Holland, baseball is a minor sport in Great Britain, sometimes dismissed by Brits as a glorified American version of rounders, a children's game. Still, Chetwynd demonstrates that, while the phrase *British baseball* may be oxymoronic, the sport does in fact have a long (but not glorious) history in Great Britain.

Finland's version of baseball is certainly unique, as historian and archivist Mikko Hyvärinen explains in "Finland: *Pesäpallo*, Baseball Finnish Style." An early-twentieth-century creation of a politically conservative Finnish sports educator, Lauri Pihkala, *pesäpallo* was inspired by American baseball. There were of course Finnish bat-and-ball-game precursors to *pesäpallo*. Yet on a 1907 trip to the United States, Pihkala attended a Boston Red Sox game, which he found engaging, if too slow. Years later, after much innovation, Pihkala introduced *pesäpallo*, which for many years was widely considered the Finnish national sport. People familiar with baseball will immediately grasp some features of *pesäpallo*. It has a pitcher, a batter, and fielders. There are bases (well, areas called bases) to which a batter must run after he or she puts the ball in play. Runs are scored. Baseball gloves are used. Yet some of the differences are stark. The pitcher, for one, stands *next to the batter*, not sixty feet and six inches away on a mound, and then tosses the ball skyward, which the batter hits on its descent. Hyvärinen notes other differences between the games, in addition to *pesäpallo*'s ideological roots, its recent history, and why the game is especially meaningful to Finns from small towns.

The last chapter is by political scientist Robert Elias, author of *The Empire Strikes Out: How Baseball Sold U.S. Foreign Policy and Promoted the American Way Abroad* (2010). In "The World Baseball Classic: Conflicts and Contradictions," Elias critiques Major League Baseball's attitudes toward and policies regarding other baseball-playing nations. He begins by asking: "Does the WBC serve the sport's best interests?" It is a good, tough question. After surveying different ways in which MLB has maintained its status as an international baseball hegemon, often pursuing profit and its primacy at the expense of evenhandedness and the game's global well-being, Elias concludes that the WBC primarily served and serves American interests. "To pursue any sort of *real* baseball globalization and development of the sport," Elias argues, rather than just a rapacious, self-serving version of globalization, "MLB will have to do more than maximize its profits." It is unclear, however, what would persuade MLB and its many stakeholders to change their modus operandi. In 2014 MLB generated approximately nine billion dollars in revenue, a record-setting amount and a 13 percent increase from the year before.[6]

A few words about our own involvement in baseball and why we produced this anthology are appropriate. As an anthropologist, George has spent a good deal of his career over the past forty years living in other cultures. And as a former professional baseball player who devoted his youth and early adulthood to the game, he was naturally interested in knowing what local versions of baseball were like. In some of the countries in which he has taught and done research—Austria, Barbados, and Vietnam—there isn't any baseball to speak of, which in itself is intriguing. Why in Vietnam, for example, where hundreds of thousands of U.S. troops had been deployed over nearly two decades, had baseball not caught on? Or why in Barbados, where there had been a small U.S. naval station where Americans played baseball and softball, was the sport never taken up by local villagers? In other places he has lived—notably Japan, Ireland, Britain, and Australia—baseball has taken root, though with wildly varying levels of interest.

George's interest in "foreign" baseball also stems from having spent several seasons in the 1960s playing in a professional league outside the United States—in the independent Quebec Provincial League. And after having been selected to play on a Canadian team that was to barnstorm in Cuba, he looked forward to the trip with much anticipation, only to be dropped from the squad because he held a U.S. passport. Even before that, while still a Minor League first baseman in the Detroit Tigers' farm system, he had fantasies of someday playing in Japan. Editing this anthology has allowed him to explore what might have been.

Like George, Dan played baseball as a boy and in high school (though not well) and then again in his thirties in the local Roy Hobbs amateur recreation league (again, not well). Beginning in the early 1970s, while living in suburban Washington DC, he rooted enthusiastically for the Baltimore Orioles, like his father and grandfather. Many years later he realized that the game was worthy of scholarly study. Since then he has been writing baseball history, most notably about the Black Sox scandal and the Negro Leagues. His interest in international baseball and the game's globalization can be traced to his experiences as a Fulbright scholar at the Tampereen yliopisto in Finland in 2001–2.

Living and working in Tampere for almost a year with his wife—who gave birth to their son there—was remarkable. He learned a great deal about Finnish culture and history, as well as about how many Finns and others understood and imagined the United States and Americans. Stumbling upon *pesäpallo* was a revelation. "Is this baseball?" he wondered, watching ballplayers attired in a what looked to him like a bewildering combination of softball gear, NASCAR driver jumpsuits (with corporate logos all over their loosely fitting jerseys), and minimalist bicycle helmets. It was baseball, of a sort. Partly due to his Finnish experience (and the September 11, 2001, terrorist attacks), Dan became increasingly interested in transnational studies of American culture and globalization.

We are hopeful that readers will learn and better appreciate several things from this collection. First, the remarkable heterogeneity of baseball history, of how the game was and is played and experienced, and what it meant and means to people around much (but not all) of the world. Obviously, what baseball signifies to many Cubans and Dominicans is different from what it does to, say, even die-hard Italian and Aussie baseball players and fans. For many good reasons, different places have different investments in the game: financial and emotional investments, but also historical and cultural. Second, we hope readers appreciate what these essays tell us about globalization, which is multivalent, often asymmetrical, and ever in flux. Baseball is inorganic; it does not grow or spread naturally. It evolved in the United States (and perhaps Canada) and was then exported and dispersed around the world, but not always by Americans. How the game was introduced to different places matters, as does how it continues to circulate in different cultural networks. The ways in which the game sometimes travels back and forth across international borders are often amazing. Third, we are also hopeful that readers will learn something about the many countries and cultures examined here *through* baseball. Doing so might promote a kind of cosmopolitanism and a sense of global citizenship. We also hope that readers simply enjoy learning about how baseball is played and thought about in places near and far. One might think of the book as a baseball adventure narrative and of our contributors as knowledgeable guides.

Finally, as some readers may know, the first edition of this book was titled *Baseball without Borders: The International Pastime*. The title was partly inspired by the humanitarian aid organization Doctors without Borders, which was founded in the late 1960s and provides free medical aid to people all over the world. Only after the book was published did we begin to think that the title was somewhat misleading. After all, baseball does have borders, and the nations examined here do, too. In his review of *Baseball without Borders*, historian Joel S. Franks notes that the book "shows vividly that baseball has proven the permeability of national borders. But, for good or ill, those borders still exist and still shape baseball's history."[7] Franks is correct. The geopolitical and baseball worlds clearly have borders that divide nations and continents. They are often contested and traversed, but they do exist and they have myriad effects on people and their cultural practices and institutions, including baseball. In recognition of this, we have changed the title of this new edition.

NOTES

1. See Joseph A. Reaves's fine history *Taking in a Game: A History of Baseball in Asia* (Lincoln: University of Nebraska Press, 2002), 6.
2. Bruce Brown, "Cuban Baseball," *Atlantic*, June 1984, 109.
3. Rob Ruck, *The Tropic of Baseball: Baseball in the Dominican Republic* (Westport CT: Meckler, 1991).
4. See, for instance, Arturo J. Marcano Guevara and David P. Fidler, *Stealing Lives: The Globalization of Baseball and the Tragic Story of Alexis Quiroz* (Bloomington: Indiana University Press, 2002).
5. Iraq and Iran do have national baseball teams, and, remarkably, in Iran the game seems to be becoming more popular. See Jason Rezaian, "America's Pastime Finds Some Fans in Iran," *Washington Post*, July 18, 2014, A6.
6. Maury Brown, "Major League Baseball Sees Record $9 Billion in Revenues for 2014," *Forbes*, December 10, 2014, http://www.forbes.com/sites/maurybrown/2014/12/10/major-league-baseball-sees-record-9-billion-in-revenues-for-2014/.
7. Joel S. Franks, review of *Baseball without Borders*, edited by George Gmelch, *Journal of Sport History* 34 (Summer 2007): 320.

Part 1 The Americas

1

Cuba

The Curtain Begins to Fall

Tim Wendel

Between innings at the ballpark in Havana, we fell into a candid conversation with a Cuban baseball official.

"What would happen if the United States lifted the embargo tomorrow?" we asked. "Maybe a freighter, a big one from Rawlings or Wilson, docked in the harbor and they began to unload all kinds of equipment. Baseballs, gloves, bats—everything that could be used down here?"

Miguel Valdes, then the technical director for the Cuban national team, looked out toward the game, seemingly ignoring my traveling partner, Milton Jamail, and me.

"What would happen?" he finally answered.

Yes, we replied. What if such a ship rolled past the Old World fortress that marked the entrance to the Havana harbor and tied up to the ancient piers?

"What would happen?" Valdes repeated, his voice low and serious. "The world as we know it would change forever."

This world began to change forever a week before Christmas 2014 when President Barack Obama and President Raúl Castro announced that they would reestablish diplomatic relations, ending more than a half century of animosity between the two Cold War foes.[1]

The move has been criticized in some quarters—labeled as a capitulation to the Castro brothers. In the short term, it may empower the current government in Havana. But in the long run, it could lead to real progress and change on the island. The Cuban people are fascinated by our culture, sports, and entertainment. This move allows more of those passions to come into everyday play.

On a corner of the main park in Havana, at the famed Esquina Caliente, or "Hot Corner," they gather almost daily under the royal palm trees to discuss nothing but baseball. To political hard-liners, such a get-together is nothing more than a curiosity. But if table tennis helped open China, baseball could now play a similar role in the relationship between the two nations.[2]

Those at Esquina Caliente know the statistics of the big-time stars as well, perhaps even better, than most American baseball fans. They take pride that Yoenis Cespedes, Aroldis Chapman, and Yasiel Puig—all Cuban born—have taken center stage in the U.S. Major Leagues. Yet the borders can blur in Cuba, often about small things that Americans frequently take for granted.

On a trip to Havana's Central Park in 1999, I took along copies of USA Today Baseball Weekly. The cover story was about players nearing the end of their careers—Paul Molitor, Dennis Eckersley, and Cal Ripken Jr. Once again, I was reminded of one of the major contradictions about Cuba: they may hear what is going on elsewhere in the world, but they are rarely afforded a good look. In the United States we may not care about the latest Hollywood or sports celebrity. But, like it or not, we know enough about Brad Pitt or Jennifer Lopez or Cal Ripken to probably pick them out of a crowd.

For a half century, due to the embargo and the highly politicized tone, the relationship between the United States and Cuba has been like a giant black curtain. The kind of barrier found in an old-style theater. The kind that always muffles the sound and allows only a rare glimpse to what's going on on the other side. In 2014 the curtain of discontent and dysfunction between the United States and Cuban began to part.

In 1999 the Cuban national team played the Baltimore Orioles. On the return flight home, I ended up sitting next to Stan Kasten. Major League Baseball's charter jet rose to maybe twenty thousand feet out

1. *Esquina Caliente* (Hot Corner) in Havana where fans come to discuss baseball seven days a week. (Photo by Tim Wendel.)

2. Pitching in the park in Havana. (Photo by Tim Wendel.)

of Havana before beginning to descend for our approach to Miami. As American soil appeared below, the Florida Straits already well behind us, I asked Kasten, "How tough would it be, Stan? To put a professional ball club, a U.S. one, in Havana?"

Kasten is one of the sharpest guys in professional sports. He was part of the ownership group that purchased the Los Angeles Dodgers, and before that he was in the front office with the Atlanta Braves, Atlanta Thrashers, and Atlanta Hawks—all at the same time. While with the Hawks he led his National Basketball Association team on an unprecedented trip to the Soviet Union for an exhibition tour. In other words, he knows, perhaps better than anybody else in professional sports, what it takes to turn a socialist country toward capitalism with sports.

"A team in Havana?" Kasten replied.

"Sure, either Minor League or even someday a Major League franchise."

"Turn around the politics," Kasten smiled, "and it would be a piece of cake."

Of course, even the Kastens of the world have a ways to go before a Minor League team sets up shop in the old stadium in Havana, where we once talked with Miguel Valdes. (Valdes eventually left Cuba and works for the New York Mets.) But in the weeks after the December 2014 announcement between Washington and Havana, a group formed that wanted to transform the Cuban league into the premier winter-ball format in the world. It would be a league that would once again welcome U.S. players to the island.

In the months after the announcement, Major League Baseball (MLB) found itself in the same boat with American tourism interests. With Republicans in control on Capitol Hill, the Cuban Embargo was still in place, but change was certainly in the air. At least initially, the new relationship with Cuba meant better banking relationships and easier imports of Cuban rum and cigars. As for the rest of it? As trade attorney Robert Muse told the *Washington Post*, for many American companies the sanctions look "like a scary forest with monsters."[3]

What this means for professional baseball has yet to be determined. While MLB issued a statement saying it was "closely monitoring" matters,[4] many experts felt the new developments would only accelerate the movement of Cuban players to play professionally in the United States. At the very least it would end a deteriorating situation that had players going to great lengths, sometimes making deals with drug cartels and crime syndicates, to leave the island.

Almost a quarter century ago pitcher René Arocha ducked into a waiting car outside the Miami International Airport and left Cuba forever. In doing so he became the first baseball star from that country to defect. Many of those who followed in his footsteps—José Contreras, the Hernández brothers Liván and Orlando—still speak of him in reverential tones.

"He was the one who opened the door for the rest of us," Orlando "El Duque" Hernández said.[5]

In demonstrating that Cubans could play in America, if they had the courage and guile to get away, Arocha wrote the script that has been followed until now. A player could slip away while the Cuban national team played in another country. This was often more difficult than it seemed. On the road Team Cuba brought its own security detail to keep any eye on everyone. To be caught usually meant being excluded from the roster for the next international tournament or Olympics. A player could also be blackballed from playing in the Cuban leagues.

To try to leave directly from Cuba was even more dangerous. Since the early 1960s, as Castro's grip tightened, thousands of everyday Cubans took to rafts and tried to cross the Florida Straits. An estimated sixteen thousand died trying to do so. And any rafter knew that he had to step foot on American soil to fully escape. If apprehended at sea, the U.S. Coast Guard could return him to Havana to face the consequences.

As the curtain began to fall, Cuban ballplayers were among the top stars in the game. Nobody generated more excitement or debate than outfielder Yasiel Puig of the Los Angeles Dodgers. Nobody enjoyed the spotlight more than outfielder Yoenis Cespedes, a Home Run Derby champion. And nobody threw harder than fireballing relief pitcher Aroldis Chapman. Yet few of these stars followed the same exit strategy as Arocha or even the Hernández brothers took to play on baseball's biggest and most lucrative stage. This new path often involved high-dollar promises, plenty of cloak-and-dagger, and deals with dangerous crime syndicates. The parade of new stars coming out of Cuba reads like something from a Graham Greene novel.

Yasiel Puig was caught repeatedly and sent back to Cuba before finally making it to Southern California. In December 2014 a South Florida businessman pleaded guilty to taking part in a conspiracy to smuggle Puig out of Cuba. In return Puig promised him a cut of his multimillion-dollar salary. Court documents detailed how Gilberto Suarez was one of the Miami-based financiers of the 2012 smuggling venture in which Puig was taken by boat from Cuba to a village near Cancún, Mexico. The baseball star eventually crossed into the United States at Brownsville, Texas.

Aroldis Chapman has been sued under the Torture Victims Protection Act in Florida after somebody who tried to help him get out of Cuba ended up in prison there. According to *Yahoo! Sports*, Chapman served as a government informant to stay in the good graces of Cuban baseball officials.[6]

Yoenis Cespedes also found himself in court, where a judge eventually ruled that he needed to pay eight million dollars of the thirty-six-million-dollar deal that he originally signed with the Oakland Athletics to the gambling-hall proprietor who helped get him off the island.

Perhaps the most original escape from Cuba belonged to Yoan Moncada, a nineteen-year-old shortstop prospect. He avoided the smugglers and contract deals entirely by filing for a visa in Havana to travel to Guatemala. For some reason the Cuban authorities gave it to him, and Moncada legally left the country and never looked back. After establishing residency in Guatemala, which allowed him to avoid baseball's amateur draft, he began shopping his services to Major League teams.

But there is more to the story of Moncada's departure. After all, this is Cuba we're talking about. According to VICE *Sports*, Nicole Banks, a California sports agent, aided Moncada. While nobody is certain of the particulars of Banks's role, she reportedly became romantically involved with Moncada.

Such is the power of baseball in Cuba. It can break through any rules and regulations, especially in today's changing climate, and it can cause people to dream of the impossible. That's the way it has been for more than a century on the island. In the United States the national pastime will always be the game of red, white, and blue bunting and Mom's apple pie. In Cuba, from its very beginnings, the game was deemed dangerous and radical. So much so that it allowed Cubans to turn their backs on the old colonial ways, never more so then when Spain controlled the island, and demonstrate their preference for a new, independent nation.

"For many years, baseball in Cuba was a sport encased in amber," author S. L. Price said. "That's changing now. It had to change, sooner or later, for the game and the country itself to move ahead."[7]

More than a half century after Fidel Castro's revolution, the debate still rages about him and baseball. Is he a national hero or the devil incarnate? It often depends on which side of the Florida Straits you have that conversation. But any student of history concedes that Castro's decision to play baseball and form a ragtag barnstorming company from his rebel army called Los Barbudos (the Bearded Ones) was a stroke of genius. Castro knew how important baseball was and will always be for Cubans.

Los Barbudos played a series of exhibitions in the months after Castro took control of the island in 1959. The new president sometimes took the mound to show off his loopy curve ball for cheering baseball aficionados. That Fidel Castro has outlasted several U.S. administrations (Kennedy, Johnson, Nixon, Ford, Carter, Reagan, Bush, Clinton, Bush, and Obama) and counting is a credit to his understanding of his country's soul more than any success in national health or education.

Was Castro a legitimate baseball prospect? Again, it depends upon whom you talk to or what you choose to believe. According to Tad Szulc's acclaimed biography *Fidel: A Critical Portrait* (1986), Castro was an impressive athlete before enrolling in Havana University's law school in 1945. While attending Belen College, a preparatory school, he was the institution's top athlete, starring in track, table tennis, basketball, and baseball.

While researching his book Szulc had full access to Castro and his closest associates. Szulc says that Castro was so determined to be Belen's best pitcher that he often practiced "until eight o'clock in the evening at the school's sports grounds. Long after the catcher got tired and left, Castro would go on throwing the ball against the wall."[8]

Whether such effort attracted the attention of big-league scouts has never been confirmed. While researching my novel *Castro's Curveball* (2000), I spoke with several scouts and players from the old Cuban winter-ball league. Some dismissed such speculation about Castro's prowess, while several insisted that Castro was pretty good and had even pitched batting practice for them. Legend has it that the Washington Senators and New York Giants were interested in signing Castro in the waning years of World War II. At that point Castro was not overly politically active and had not fully aligned himself with the growing revolutionary factions in Cuba.

Searches at the National Baseball Hall of Fame in Cooperstown, New York, turn up a *Sport* magazine article from 1964. In it Don Hoak, who spent eleven years in the Major Leagues and several winters playing in Cuba, details a strange evening at the old ballpark in Havana, the same place we spoke with Miguel Valdes decades later. The year was 1951, Hoak said, and it was not unusual back then for students to come out of the stands and interrupt games to protest the government or the hold that such corporations as United Fruit had on their country. Once again, baseball was seen as a path to an independent nation.

On this night, Hoak recalled, a tall, skinny student wearing a white shirt, black pants, and suede shoes took the mound. Hoak was the next batter due up. To his dying day Hoak maintained that the interloper was a young Castro.

"Left-handers as a breed are eccentric, but Castro, a right-hander, looked kookier than any southpaw I have known," Hoak later told *Sport*.[9]

Hoak fouled off two Castro pitches before the field was cleared of demonstrators.

So the question remains: Was Castro a legitimate prospect? Probably not. But right when you're ready to dismiss such notions, somebody steps out of the past.

On another trip to Havana we were talking with several fans at the Esquina Caliente, and one of them, an old man, claimed to have played baseball with Castro as a boy on the eastern end of the island, where they both grew up. We asked about that part of the world, trying to catch the old-timer in a fib. But he fielded all of our queries flawlessly.

Finally, we asked, "What did Castro throw?"

"So-so fastball, sneaky slider at the knees," the old man answered. "But his best pitch was a curve ball. Castro had a great curve."

So appropriate for all that happened over the past half century when it comes to the rocky relationship between the United States and Cuba, don't you think?

As we are witnessing once again, affairs of state can remain locked in place until one event causes a major upheaval. It has happened before in Cuba, and it is beginning to happen again.

In 1949 Orestes "Minnie" Miñoso broke in with the Cleveland Indians and spent much of that season and the next in the Minor Leagues. Early in the '51 season he was traded to the Chicago White Sox, where he had to confront racial discrimination as well as opposing batters.

"First you had Jackie Robinson. Then Larry Doby and then you had me," Miñoso said. "I was the first black-skinned ballplayer to play in the city of Chicago."[10]

To make the leap, Miñoso explained, he had "to be strong in the mind." That required him to remember that Cuban players such as the great Martín Dihigo had not gotten a chance to play in the Major Leagues. Also, star players such as Ted Williams told Miñoso that he had talent. That he could hit in this league. He just had to stick it out.

"I cannot tell you how good that made me feel," Miñoso said. "How I remembered that when I was going through difficult times, on and off the field."[11]

Between 1951 and 1961 Miñoso scored more than one hundred runs four times and was among the leaders in hits. But such accomplishments were often overlooked because the first wave of Latino ballplayers was routinely marginalized. They were often given nicknames they didn't want. "Orestes Miñoso, with his proud classical name, became 'Minnie' Minoso in the United States," Yale scholar Roberto González Echevarria wrote.[12]

Yet such struggles paled in comparison to the decision Miñoso made regarding his homeland of Cuba. When Castro's armies took control of Havana in 1959, they were greeted as conquering heroes. Huge crowds lined the streets, cheering their arrival. Few of Castro's countrymen realized what the new leader had in store for the island as his tanks and soldiers streamed into the capital. But at least one ballplayer had a feeling that things were not as they seemed.

Miñoso sat in his trademark Cadillac as the military parade tied up traffic in Havana soon after the Batista regime fell. Passing rebels recognized him and called for Miñoso to join them. The ballplayer left his car and was about to climb aboard one of the military trucks when something stopped him in his tracks. Something didn't feel right about the whole situation. Miñoso claims that from that moment on, he never trusted the Castro government. Despite the cheering crowds, he hung back.

Soon after that day Miñoso made plans to leave the island and re-settle permanently in the United States. It would prove to be a costly process, as he owned several apartment buildings and a fleet of taxis. By pulling out of Cuba, he knew he would lose a lot of money.

Of course, Miñoso wasn't the only one to make such a decision. The exodus began in earnest as Castro destroyed the old social order and moved Cuba toward a socialist way of life. Soon after taking power, Castro abolished the professional winter-ball teams that had existed for decades on the island. Cubans would be amateurs and amateurs only, with the country's new president questioning the national team coaches about game strategy and roster moves.

The Cuban Revolution and the subsequent events had a profound on the U.S. baseball community. The Minnesota Twins, for example, had already released Tony Oliva when the Bay of Pigs debacle took place. All flights back to Cuba were canceled, so the Twins decided to keep him. Oliva went on to become the only player to win batting championships in his first two years in the Majors.

George Genovese was managing the Giants' Minor League affiliate in El Paso soon after the revolution. On his roster was José Cardenal, a Cuban who was listed as an infielder. "José hadn't shown much in spring training and he was about to get released," Genovese remembers. "So I decided to take him along with me to El Paso and make an outfielder out of him. . . . I knew if he went back to Cuba, he would never get out."[13]

The move paid off. As a right fielder Cardenal homered in his first game for El Paso and went on to hit thirty-six home runs that season. He played eighteen seasons in the Major Leagues, including appearances in the 1978 National League Championship Series and the 1980 World Series. He became a confidant to many of the Cuban players who followed him to the United States.

In 1999 the Baltimore Orioles and the Cuban national team played a two-game exhibition series; the first game was in Havana and the second a few weeks later in Baltimore. The first game was an extra-inning affair, with the Major Leaguers barely winning. In the rematch the Cubans trounced the Orioles.

Even though protesters came on the field, eerily reminiscent of Don Hoak's tall tale, the most memorable moment that night in Baltimore belonged to Andy Morales, a journeyman for the Cuban squad. His home run drove in Team Cuba's final runs in the 12–6 victory. As the infielder rounded the bases, he almost broke into a dance. He raised his arms in the air and nearly stumbled as he rounded second base.

After the game was over several Orioles grumbled that Morales had shown them up. After all, you're not supposed to exhibit so much emotion in baseball, at least not in the Major Leagues.

Back home in Cuba Morales was feted by Castro himself. So why did he try to defect a year after that exhibition game? Why, when he was sent back to Cuba, did he try again sixteen months later and this time make it to South Florida?

Some would say he simply wanted a better life. He had seen firsthand the luxurious existence of a Major Leaguer and the riches that can be earned for hitting a ball with a bat and sending it soaring into the night sky. But perhaps it wasn't all about the money. In America, as in much of the world, you can compete against the best. Have a head for stocks? Go to Wall Street. Ready to lead a nation? Try to fix Washington.

But if you have played ball for the past half century in Cuba, one had to often risk everything to play against the best. That is what the Baltimore Orioles, even many of the politicians, never fully understood.

It has been said that the real Cuba lies in the shadows and alleyways of Old Havana—anywhere baseball is played. The essence of the land rides the night air like a piece of music that grabs your attention, only to dissolve when you stop and try to determine where the tune is coming from.

In Havana they like to say that maybe tonight the world will sink into the earth. The waiting for something better might come to an end. The prayers may be answered.

Perhaps now, with Washington and Havana formally recognizing each other, the curtain that has long hung between the two nations is finally coming down.

NOTES

1. Peter Baker, "U.S. to Restore Full Relations with Cuba, Erasing a Last Trace of Cold War Hostility," *New York Times*, December 17, 2014, A1.
2. DeVoss, "Ping-Pong Diplomacy."
3. Quoted in Joshua Partlow and Nick Miroff, "U.S. Businesses Face Maze of Obstacles in Cuba," *Washington Post*, January 12, 2015, http://www.washingtonpost.com/world/the_americas/despite-changes-us-businesses-still-face-a-minefield-of-sanctions-in-cuba/2015/01/10/c7533fc4-96af-11e4-8385-866293322c2f_story.html.
4. "MLB Says It's 'Closely Monitoring' U.S.-Cuba Relations," *USA Today*, December 17, 2014, http://www.usatoday.com/story/sports/mlb/2014/12/17/mlb-statement-usa-cuba-relations/20544731/.
5. Orlando "El Duque" Hernández, interview by the author, Miami Beach, March 2010.
6. Passan, "10 Degrees."
7. S. L. Price, interview by the author, Washington DC, April 2010.
8. Szulc, *Fidel: A Critical Portrait*, 120.
9. Hoak, with Cope, "Day I Batted against Castro."
10. Orestes "Minnie" Miñoso, interview by the author, Chicago, June 2007.
11. Miñoso, interview.
12. González Echevarria, *Pride of Havana*, 8.
13. George Genovese, interview by the author, Los Angeles, March 2006.

BIBLIOGRAPHY

Arangure, Jorge, Jr. "The Weirdest Cuban Baseball Defector Story You'll Ever Read." *Vice Sports*, December 4, 2014.
Augenbraun, Harold, and Ilan Stavans. *Growing Up Latino*. Boston: Houghton Mifflin, 1993.
DeVoss, David A. "Ping-Pong Diplomacy." *Smithsonian*, April 2002, 58–64.

Dickson, Paul. *The New Dickson Baseball Dictionary*. New York: Harcourt Brace, 1999.

Fainaru, Steve, and Ray Sanchez. *The Duke of Havana: Baseball, Cuba, and the Search for the American Dream*. New York: Villard, 2001.

González Echevarria, Roberto. *The Pride of Havana: A History of Cuban Baseball*. New York: Oxford Press, 1999.

Hoak, Don, with Myron Cope. "The Day I Batted against Castro." In *The Armchair Book of Baseball*, edited by John Thorn, 161–64. New York: Charles Scribner's Sons, 1985.

Jamail, Milton H. *Full Count: Inside Cuban Baseball*. Cardondale: Southern Illinois University Press, 2000.

Miñoso, Minnie, with Herb Fagen. *Just Call Me Minnie: My Six Decades in Baseball*. Champaign IL: Sagamore, 1994.

Passan, Jeff. "10 Degrees: Cuban Trafficking Grows into MLB's Ugly Secret." April 20, 2014. http://sports.yahoo.com/news/10-degrees--cuban-trafficking -grows-into-mlb-s-ugly-secret-034704407.html.

Price, S. L. *Pitching around Fidel*. 2000. Reprint, Gainesville: University Press of Florida, 2014.

———. "Season of Change." *Sports Illustrated*, December 29, 2014.

Regalado, Samuel O. *Viva Baseball!* Urbana: University of Illinois Press, 1998.

Rucker, Mark, and Peter C. Bjarkman. *Smoke: The Romance and Lore of Cuban Baseball*. Kingston: Total Sports Illustrated, 1999.

Szulc, Ted. *Fidel: A Critical Portrait*. New York: William Morrow, 1986.

Wendel, Tim. *Castro's Curveball: A Novel*. New York: Ballantine, 2000.

2

Dominican Republic

From Paternalism to Parity

Alan Klein

There is little question that America's youth are abandoning baseball for other sports or passive forms of leisure time. Or so it seems to Kevin Roche, president of the Westwood, New Jersey, Little League, who laments, "Nowadays, kids have so many more options. Baseball is boring to them."[1] Roche was concerned because enrollments in his league were down 20 percent over the past five years, forcing towns to merge leagues.

The nostalgia-laden informal versions of baseball, so dominant in American life for a century, are beginning to fade. "If there isn't a scheduled practice or game, kids aren't playing baseball. They are playing PlayStation and Xbox. Heck, they aren't even playing catch with their dads," declares University of Virginia baseball coach Brian O'Conner.[2]

Linking boredom to baseball, or expunging baseball's ability to link fathers and sons, may reflect contemporary American concerns, but couldn't be further from the sport's position in the Dominican Republic (DR). This island nation (shared with Haiti) of approximately ten million has produced more professional players per capita than any place on earth. Of all Major League Baseball (MLB) players appearing on opening-day rosters in 2014, 9.7 percent were Dominicans.[3] The almost–10 percent figure of Dominicans leads all other countries (besides the United States) and has since 1995, when these numbers were first tallied. To get the full sense of just how many Dominicans play the game professionally, we have to note that 25 percent of all Minor League players are also Dominican.[4] Fully appreciating these numbers requires an understanding of the conditions and system that created this tidal wave of talent.

Grasping today's Dominican baseball success begins with understanding Dominicans and baseball separately, together, and, most important, as a system. Dominicans took the game as brought to them and made it their own. They were able to develop a rich and coherent baseball tradition in large part because Major League teams either had no interest in them or did not know that they existed. When, at midcentury, they finally realized that baseball talent might be mined there, Major League teams formed a relationship with Dominican baseball that reflected the quasi-colonial relationship between the two nations. Comprehending Dominican baseball, then, requires a view of it as a changing system of politics, economics, and culture.[5]

Appreciating the game developed by Dominicans also entails an understanding of classic colonial brutality. The Dominican Republic has been the fount for our images of corruption, brutality, and grinding poverty, but what formed and fueled it was combined Spanish and American interventions. By the time the Dominican Republic threw out Haitian invaders in 1844, it had already been "discovered," hailed, and abandoned by Spain for 250 years. Independence brought little relief, as Haitians continued to invade several times in the nineteenth century, and political factionalism in the fledgling republic kept it politically weak—so weak, in fact, that in 1861 the DR did something no other Latin American nation has ever done: Dominicans requested that Spain allow it to revert to colonial status! Even that failed to produce stability, as a few years later Dominican presidents sought to have their nation incorporated into the United States as a U.S. territory (a move that was rejected by the U.S. Senate in 1870).[6]

Cuban sugar planters fleeing the Ten Years' War in Cuba moved their operations to the DR, where they modernized that industry. Dictatorships continued, however, resulting in increased borrowing from European powers. With a chronically weak economy ravaged

3. Scoreboard in La Romana's stadium shows a little of the face of Dominican baseball. Soldiers and kids leisurely hang out at a game. (Photo by Alan Klein.)

by factionalism and corruption, the D R was despairingly bankrupt by 1905 and facing intervention by European powers. The Theodore Roosevelt administration arranged a U.S. Customs receivership in Santo Domingo, but when the French and German governments sent ships to strong-arm the Dominicans into paying, President Woodrow Wilson decided to move militarily, sending in troops and invoking the Monroe Doctrine. U.S. Marines occupied the country for eight years (1916–24), securing Dominican stability but incurring widespread resentment in all quarters of that country. That schizophrenic response of Dominicans toward the United States, more or less equal parts gratitude for stability yet resentment of American influence, persists.[7]

Early Baseball

Two Cuban brothers (Ignacio and Ubaldo Alomá) are credited with introducing baseball to Dominicans sometime in 1891.[8] According to widely accepted accounts, the sport first took hold in the capital, Santo

Domingo, but quickly spread to the east in San Pedro de Macorís and to the north in Santiago. At first, the sons of affluent Dominicans in Santo Domingo supplemented teams of Cubans, but the game rooted quickly, spawning teams in other cities. In Santo Domingo Licey was the first truly successful Dominican team. Assembled by a group of players from the city's Zona Coloniál in 1907, Licey dominated opponents for more than a decade until another group of players made up of rivals—called Escogido (the Chosen)—was formed 1918.[9] These two teams from the capital city continue to form the core of Dominican professional baseball.

Meanwhile, in San Pedro de Macorís—the key port city for sugar production—the game was also taking root. Two kinds of baseball were evolving. San Pedro had teams that soon rivaled those of the capital, the most successful one, Estrellas Orientales, becoming in 1911 that city's champion and representative in intercity competitions. Twelve refineries ringed San Pedro. They were composed of fields and living quarters for workers and American managers, and they soon developed an impassioned set of baseball rivalries between refineries.[10]

In the northern city of Santiago, the Aguilas Cibaoenas became its ball-playing representative in 1931. These four city-based teams formed the nucleus of Dominican professional baseball in the first half of the twentieth century. Over the years the Dominican Professional League changed its composition slightly (for example, Licey and Escogido were merged for a period by Dominican strongman Rafael Trujillo in the late 1930s, and two teams were added in the 1970s), but the nucleus remained and rivalries were legendary.

Major League Baseball ignored Dominican baseball until the early 1950s, and then warmed up to it only slowly. Cuba had been, early on, the primary venue for Latin players who could, if light-skinned enough, evade the racist restrictions against players of color that were in place before 1947. In the first three decades of the twentieth century, seventeen Cubans played in the Major Leagues, all being able to prove that they were white. Once Jackie Robinson of the Brooklyn

Dodgers broke the color barrier, MLB continued to mine talent in Cuba, only now unhampered by race restrictions. For teams such as the Washington Senators and New York Giants, who relied on their Cuban connections, there was no incentive to go to the neighboring Dominican Republic. It was really only when Fidel Castro's successful revolution was in place that relations between the countries ceased. Following the Cuban Revolution in 1959, teams looking for Latin talent began to turn to the Dominican Republic. Fortunately, Dominicans hadn't waited around, but instead had developed a caliber of play that was second to none. Relying upon constant competition with other Caribbean countries (for example, Puerto Rico, Cuba, and Mexico) and with games against Negro League teams as well as black players who regularly played in the DR, the Dominican brand of baseball was sophisticated and deep.

Formal relations between the Dominican Professional League and MLB began around 1951, when the first "working agreement" between them was set in place. In this informal accord MLB provided its expertise (coaches and training) to Dominicans, in return for which Dominicans allowed their teams to function as "holding pens" for various Major League teams that had signed players or were interested in doing so. Dominicans were also made to change the season when they played so as not to conflict with MLB. Ever arrogant, MLB representatives assumed ownership of the summer. This act of hubris sums up the relationship that exists between the two nations.

The first Dominican to play in the Major Leagues was the Dominican-born, U.S.-raised Ozzie Virgil, who in 1956 debuted with the New York Giants. It was Felipe Alou, however, who was the first player from the island to play in the Major Leagues. He debuted with the New York Giants in 1958 and went on to play seventeen seasons in the Majors, eventually becoming a successful manager with the Montreal Expos and the San Francisco Giants. By the 1980s the occasional Dominican player became fairly routine, and the country produced the most players of any country outside the United States.

Every decade the numbers of Dominicans grew, and while most fans and front-office people took note and even grew to look forward to it, very few if any understood the events and system that had grown up to provide the labor.

Dominicans in the Major Leagues by decade

1960s: 15
1970s: 34
1980s: 62
1990s: 162
2000s: 280

Structurally, the U.S.-Dominican relationship retained its quasi-colonial character for its first thirty-five years (1951–85). Only a handful of teams had a real presence in Latin America (the New York Giants, Washington Senators, and Pittsburgh Pirates) and then only because one of their scouts had pressed the issue. Veteran Pirates scout Howie Hack, for instance, had long known the caliber of play in the Caribbean. A network of part-time scouts in Cuba and the DR would alert him of a potential player, and he would fly there for a tryout. Ralph Avila, the man who built the modern system of player development in the DR, described the early days: "We called them 'bird dogs,' and they were there for the [Major League] teams that came into the country. [Teams] would come to Santo Domingo and contact their bird dogs to organize a tryout for them. They would pay these guys something to bring the players, and more if they signed the players."[11] The operative words in this manner of finding talent are *haphazard* and *opportunistic*. But as the flow of players increased through the mid-1990s, the interest and effort of teams grew as well.

Dominican Baseball Migrants

Dominicans who were fortunate enough to sign with American teams were simply cast into a new world: quite young, torn from all that was familiar, and thrown into a society where they couldn't speak the language and didn't share the culture or values of the host nation. Many succumbed to the cultural foreignness, as did Chico Contón, who played Minor League ball in Florida in the early 1960s. His racial identity quickly became an issue. Contón identified himself as mulatto, distinct from black. His racial education commenced:

> The manager said, "They [fans] gonna yell a lot of things at you. Put cotton in your ears." They took me to the black section [to live]. I introduced myself as a ballplayer, and the people said, "Where you gonna play?" When I told them where they said, "No, no, you made a mistake. No black ballplayers ever played here." . . . Yes, the racism was a problem. I couldn't eat with my teammates. I couldn't live with them. When I went home [to the Dominican Republic] they couldn't believe what I told them. I had to take over [news] papers to show them.[12]

Contón wound up leaving professional baseball in the United States and returning home to play. His decision was quickly and powerfully formed by these racist social conditions, which, combined with culture shock, made the move back quite simple. He is by no means alone in this, for while the worst of these responses has passed, the foreignness of moving to another world is still a daunting process.

The Academy System
The Los Angeles Dodgers weren't the first team to focus attention on the Dominican talent flow (Epy Guerrero working on behalf of the Toronto Blue Jays is credited with this), but it is the organization that first successfully turned the corner into the modern academy system.

Chico Contón's experience with racism was symptomatic of the larger issue of culture shock that confronts people ill prepared to deal with the travails of migration to other places. Ralph Avila saw this early:

I was scouting international tournaments [in the early 1970s]. . . .
It was clear that they [Dominicans] had really good ballplayers. . . .
Then I saw some of those Dominicans come to the United States
and get released. How could these guys have tools like that and get
released? So, I started taking notes and talking to players, and we
decided that 99% of the time [a player gets released] . . . because
he lacked education and work habits. We made a report and that's
when I came up with the idea of a baseball academy to teach them
and prepare them to go to spring training and a different culture.[13]

It took him several years to convince the Dodgers ownership that
it should invest in a baseball hinterland. So Avila put his own money
into developing a rudimentary academy that would house and train
prospects. His message eventually took hold, as Campo las Palmas—
the first modern baseball academy in a developing nation—was born
in 1986. For the next fifteen years this facility was the most lavish, complete baseball complex outside of the United States. Amplifying Avila's
view of cultural remediation, Campo las Palmas sought to instill new
values (work ethic, punctuality) in addition to language instruction
and learning how to behave in the United States. Word of this academy
spread throughout the country, and the Dodgers attracted much of
the best talent on the island for the next decade (among them Pedro
Guerrero, Alfredo Griffin, brothers Raul and Pedro Martínez, and
Raul Mondesi). Until other Major League teams adopted the Dodgers'
model, their players were not as prepared to succeed in climbing the
Major League Baseball ladder.

By the turn of the twenty-first century, Campo las Palmas had become
the standard that others sought to eclipse, and ultimately did. At present
all thirty Major League teams have built or lease state-of-the-art facilities
that develop players both as baseball prospects and in social and cultural
terms. Upon signing their professional contracts, players are assigned to
that team's Dominican academy for a period of up to three years, during
which they are boarded and their baseball education ensues.

The Dominican rookie ballplayer is given instruction from a range of coaches, some of whom fly down from the United States. The instruction extends to physical conditioning and even to expectations for behavior. Each day is filled with scheduled activity, instruction, and baseball-related information.[14] French scholar Michel Foucault's notion of disciplining comes to mind, but in this instance it is most certainly conscious and intentional. Team administrators tend to feel strongly that cultural remediation enhances the possibility of climbing the MLB ladder. This very deliberate system of altering the social psychology of young prospects has more to do with sociologist Pierre Bourdieu's sense of "habitas," or inculcating ways of handling the body as well as the mind. This is wrapped up in the sense of teaching prospects that come from looser environs about "responsibility." One academy head put it this way: "We do a lot of different things. We teach them about time—how to be on time for lunch [for example]. . . . If they're a few minutes late, they miss it. Also, they have to clean their tables after they eat. We take them to the mall. That's one of the first things we do. We teach them how to behave, how to treat their money, how to treat people there: girls, cashiers. We have good feedback from people who had our guys in Rookie and A ball. We had no problems."[15]

The academies all belong to a collective body of teams that form the Dominican Summer League. The DSL plays a seventy-two-game summer season and forms an important part of the rookie's time in the academy because it represents the most meaningful formal evaluation he will receive. The players refer to the DSL as "Vietnam," a reference to the hypercompetitive nature of the season and all that's at stake. Baseball statistics form the core of this evaluative process. Batting averages, earned run averages, home runs, strikeouts, and so on are telling statistics around which there is consensus. Team administrators responsible for bringing players up through the ranks look closely at such things. Because Dominican youth have so little opportunity to play organized baseball, they have no "body of work" that scouts or coaches can consult to help make a decision as to whether to sign them. The DSL is the first official stat line for these young men. Together with qualitative write-ups that detail the player's attitude and comportment in areas outside of the field, coaches and others select players to go to the next level.

Making the move to play in the United States is, then, a significant change for all concerned, especially for the players. They are nervous, not only because they are now competing at a higher level, but also because they've entered a world that they imperfectly understand. Stories abound. One young Dominican rookie, who was playing in a small U.S. town and was put up in a boardinghouse, "was so culturally paralyzed that he would not venture down the hall to the bathroom. Instead, he relieved himself out the window."[16] When he was finally caught, the team had to intervene with local authorities. Players refuse to undress in the locker room, thinking that the ceiling sprinklers are cameras. Simple things like eating in restaurants can embarrass Dominican ballplayers, and their inclination is to shut down. Some players just order items that they can pronounce, while others say nothing and point to pictures of food on the menu. To lessen the cultural impact the ballplayers will face, academies include a modicum of English-language acquisition. MLB now makes it mandatory for academies to require their rookies to take language courses. They also instruct rookies in what cultural issues they'll face in the United States. However, these remedial interventions are never enough to forestall the culture shock, which is often acute. By the time Dominican players spend two to three years working their way through the Minor Leagues, most have learned enough of life in the United States to function.

The MLB academies in the Dominican Republic have now become a system that is so pervasive that it has changed the way baseball operates in the country. Dominican superstars like Albert Pujols and Robinson Canó came of age in a world that was changing but had not yet been defined by the Major League academy. Certainly, by 2010 it was clear that the academy had not only become a standard for Major League player production: players coming into it were being groomed for the academy and getting signed, interest in local baseball was no longer an end in itself, and new economic opportunities had come into existence, while older ones had been redefined.

Consequences: Seen and Unseen

Dominican baseball had evolved into a system of amateur, semiprofessional, and professional play that was complete and self-sustaining. Talented youth were funneled into the best amateur programs in the country, and from there the best were signed to play professional Dominican baseball or were signed by U.S. teams. Major League academies created a physical presence in which young talent sought them out to hopefully get signed and in so doing increasingly bypass the amateur ranks. The result was that amateur baseball in the country began to whither in direct proportion to the intensification of the academy system.

For decades—beginning in the 1940s—Dominicans had a vibrant brand of baseball that centered on the ad hoc competition between sugar refineries around San Pedro de Macorís and teams in the capital; the Dominican Winter League and amateur leagues produced fantastic players such as Tony Fernandez, Rico Carty, and Juan Marichal. Local baseball was the stuff of legends, and children grew up on their fathers' stories of kings like Tetelo Vargas and rivalries between teams that were brimming with excitement and fisticuffs. "Wild Ball" is what locals in the eastern part of the country called it back then.[17] That kind of baseball was as pulsating and flamboyant as it was somewhat disorganized, and it was this kind of Dominican game that withered in the wake of the academy system.

To take advantage of the increasing numbers of Major League administrators who sought to keep tabs on their prospects, the academies began concentrating around the Boca Chica area. They now form a critical mass fostering all sorts of increased communication between, and intensified competition among, themselves. Economic opportunity—in the form of jobs and small businesses—has mushroomed in this area, inadvertently creating a baseball version of a "free-trade zone" (*zona franca*), industrial parks built by foreign interests that dot the country. The area has now become a hub of baseball, drawing every talented young player in the country.

Lending coherence to these independent and competing academies is the Dominican Summer League. Not only does this integrate the academies, but the DSL also represents the very first time in the life of these players when they generate statistics that form their baseball résumés, as they've had no Little League, high school, or college play to offer teams a rich array of statistics and highlight reels.

The Rise of *Buscónes*

The rise of the academy system created a void in Dominican player development at the same time that it increased MLB's appetite for talent. In this weakened climate where would Major League teams find the talented fifteen- or sixteen-year-olds? Old-school Dominican scouts whose role it was to locate talent and contact Major League scouts stepped up. Because they had always searched for and found these players, they were referred to as *buscónes* (Spanish for "one who searches"—usually for ores—or "one who is a thief," connoting a pimp or procurer). *Buscónes* were, in this changing climate of talent finding, locating younger players (thirteen- to fifteen-year-olds) and training them for the tryouts at MLB academies. Between the early 1990s and early 2000s, *buscónes* took over the entire process of developing talent, but it was no longer for Dominican baseball; rather, it was for signing with Major League teams that were by this time investing considerable sums on building or leasing state-of-the-art academies. The goal had changed. The DR was being acknowledged as *the* major source of foreign talent, and both the cost and the value of finding, developing, and signing that talent had shot up. Whereas in 1995 a legitimate prospect might cost ten thousand dollars to sign, by 2005 that cost might be five hundred thousand. Million-dollar signings began around 2000 and became fairly common. Even small-market and low-budget teams like the Tampa Bay Rays signed their number-one prospect for three million dollars in 2014, a move that had many in- and outside of the organization shaking their heads in disbelief.

Because *buscónes* are unregulated, they cannot be controlled by MLB, a situation that has been at the center of MLB-Dominican relations for the past fifteen years. At first, Major League teams' international scouts would speak of them derisively, as in, "Believe me, you don't want to have dinner with these guys" or "They're just pimps" or "We don't let them in the clubhouse."[18] The North American media took its lead from these scouts and portrayed *buscónes* as corrupt exploiters of naive players. When these disparaging attacks failed to rid the landscape of *buscónes*, MLB moved to a more aggressive stance: creating policies that would limit their growing power. What MLB failed to see was that some of these *buscónes* were politically savvy and fearless. Astín Jacobo is one of the most outspoken of this group. Born in the DR but raised in New York City by a father who was a community organizer in both countries, Astín was well equipped to confront the commissioner's office. Most of the policy moves from MLB were designed to reduce the cost of player development, bringing it back to "the good ol' days" when Latin talent meant "signing on the cheap" (for example, Hall of Fame pitcher Pedro Martínez was signed by the Dodgers for seven thousand dollars in 1988). That meant corralling these Dominican player developers.

Dominican "Pride" Turns into Dominican Power

Jacobo and his cohort understood the economics of the situation. They had witnessed MLB clear-cutting the forest that was Dominican talent to ensure its continued profitability. Jacobo and his mates responded to this openly:

> [Sandy Alderson, MLB's second in charge at the time] said that MLB was bringing about $40 million to $50 million into the country [DR] and all these jobs, and I said, "Thank you for that, but you're making $7 billion, and we're the principal guys helping make that for you."

I've been telling MLB that we're baseball's best partners, and they look kind of surprised. So I said, "Why do you look surprised? For the past 20 years, the minor leagues have existed because of Dominicans. You survive because of the cheap labor you get from us."[19]

Jacobo and others also grasped the intricacies of MLB's manipulation of cultural remediation to stem the rise of Dominican signing bonuses. Recall that the need for extra time to prepare Dominicans to pursue their careers in the United States grew out of a genuine concern for their success. This resulted in Major League teams signing the players earlier to accommodate for their adjustments. The minimum age that a Dominican may sign a contract with a Major League team is sixteen and a half years of age, but that minimum age has also become a de facto maximum age. Major League teams reinterpreted the remedial period as subtracted from a prospect's overall career, with the result that his value begins to decrease from what is really a premature signing age. A player seventeen and a half years of age is worth less, and by eighteen or nineteen his value on the market has decreased that much more. Compared with signing in the United States, one quickly notes that players are routinely signed upon graduating high school and in college in the range of eighteen to twenty-one years of age.

With an artificial market that targets sixteen-and-a-half-year-olds and penalizes players a year or two older, Dominicans began to pass themselves off as younger. This necessitated falsifying documents, in violation of U.S. State Department laws. Dominicans were routinely getting caught, and MLB and the U.S. media took this as further proof of Dominican corruptness and their penchant for criminality. Completely overlooked was the fact that the entire Dominican baseball market was fashioned by MLB to foster attempts by Dominicans to position themselves at the optimum point to take advantage of economic opportunity. Prizing and paying for sixteen-year-olds and penalizing them as they age results in people passing themselves off as sixteen.

July 2 is the date that teams can bid on the players they most covet.

As these bidding wars escalated through the 2000s, MLB ratcheted up its vetting process. Each bid on a Dominican rookie had to be examined in detail to make certain that the identity and birth dates were legitimate—a process that ate up time. Time, however, was the enemy of Dominicans in the market, as their price was being driven down: "MLB is manipulating the investigations so that the guys get less money," asserts Jacobo. "I need to have player okayed by MLB, but they make it difficult to get their service. We have a case like Miguel Sano [who signed with the Texas Rangers]. His papers were no good when they offered him $5 million, but he was good [two years later] when he signed with those same papers at $3 million."[20]

Somehow this economic practice or policy has singled out Dominicans because, as Jacobo points out, "The Cuban can come to the DR, and be 30 years old, and they'll [MLB] give him all the money in the world. And our kid? Once he's past 18 they don't wanna give him a penny."[21] Joel Peralta, a Dominican pitching for the Tampa Bay Rays, echoed this. Signing as a sixteen-and-a-half-year-old, Peralta was actually twenty. He said, "I wish I had never done that, but if I didn't do that I wouldn't be here. We don't have a chance after we turn 18, 19 years old. Here in the U.S. players can be drafted when they're 22. . . . The only chance when you're 20, like I was, to sign was to lie about your age."[22]

Because these Dominican player developers continued to flourish in the face of MLB attempts to corral them, and because Dominican practices seemed to run afoul of MLB policies that sought to maintain U.S. hegemonic control of player development, former commissioner Bud Selig threatened to institute a draft in that country. Jacobo's comments (cited above) speak to the willingness to confront MLB. There followed a string of aggressive moves on the part of MLB to stymie the *buscónes* who had challenged the system. Dominican *buscónes* had gotten bigger and bigger bonuses for their young charges against the desire of MLB to reinstitute "signing on the cheap." Jacobo, in a public forum, rhetorically put it to the Dominicans assembled: "Which is worse: the major league team that knows a kid is worth $1 million, but pays $25,000 for him, or me, who knows the kid is worth $1 million, gets it, and the kid goes home with $650,000? Which is better for the kid, for me, and the game here in the Dominican Republic?"[23] Threatened with a draft, the nation's leading *buscónes* formed their own development league that would cultivate top-tier players and circumvent MLB efforts to keep their influence local. These Dominican-controlled prospect leagues would travel abroad to find outlets for their players. Jacobo had his players travel to Puerto Rico and compete and then negotiate with Mexican teams. In a desperate effort to short-circuit these *buscónes*, Alderson pressed the draft issue in 2012. Jacobo and others, in a move that is akin to George Washington crossing the Delaware to catch the British off guard, traveled to the spring-training facilities of every Major League team with a petition for Latin American players to sign that demanded MLB cease and desist from further pressing the draft. A remarkable 165 of 166 players signed it and expressed outrage to the MLB Players Association (MLBPA), which in quick order confronted the commissioner. The issue died for the time being, and it illustrates the change in political climate of baseball in the DR.[24]

Transnational Commodity Chain: Two Overlooked, Revealing Perspectives

One perspective looks at baseball players as another form of international labor migration, while the second examines their production as part of a global commodity chain. In host countries baseball labor migration, despite pertaining to highly skilled labor, is still thought of as different, foreign, and inferior. Space prevents me from taking up this issue. Assessing the production and movement of players to North America for the few countries that produce significant numbers of players (such as the Dominican Republic, Venezuela, Mexico, and Japan) reveals a system in which donor countries are being treated as subservient. While MLB likes to paint itself as a benefactor of international baseball—at times even in partnership with baseball-rich countries—it operates as a governorship. MLBPA executive director

Tony Clark gushed in 2015, "With so many of our members calling the Dominican Republic home, it is an honor to join with Major League Baseball and USAID [the United States Agency for International Development] to provide funding that will help improve the lives of children and their families throughout the country."[25]

Similarly, when MLB International introduces its programs into schools in countries around the world, it does so to bring the sport to areas where it hopes to grow the sport, but also where it will control the production of future players. Its model is the National Basketball Association's astounding success in China following the signing of the seven-foot-six Yao Ming.[26]

The flow of Dominicans into North America (primarily the United States) is seen as a case of a migratory labor force that is temporary, fills a void for a specific labor pool, is regulated by the State Department and MLB, and represents a series of problems within the industry but projected as Dominican problems. Like any other migratory labor force (for example, the seasonal Irish workers who people the resorts on Cape Cod or the Mexican laborers who farm all over the United States), Dominican ballplayers come here to work and remit millions of dollars to their families. The Tampa Bay Rays encountered this in an unexpected way when they were faced with Dominican players in their rookie leagues who were losing weight through the season. Probing the cause, the team discovered that the players were sending their per diems back home rather than spending it on food. They instituted a clubhouse buffet and let the players keep their per diems. Dominican players in the Northeast also get involved with large communities of their countrymen in cities such as Boston, New York, Providence, and Philadelphia. They form part of a seamless transnational community that moves between host cities in the United States and their homeland.

The "transnational commodity chain" model helps us to understand the process that identifies and develops Dominicans, first by local player developers and then by Major League academies. The model also examines the career trajectories of these players as they move from the DR to the U.S. Minor Leagues. Like their American counterparts, most of these players will end their careers never having played Major League Baseball, but unlike those same counterparts Dominican players have often learned cultural skills that help them in their return to the DR. Familiarity with the English language and American ways opens the possibility of these returning Dominicans to be hired in the burgeoning business of making Dominican baseball players. They might become agents or *buscónes*. They might open businesses that service academies. They might work for Major League teams operating in the country. Or, like Junior Noboa, they might become landlords to Major League teams, powerful developers of academies that are leased by Major League teams. Noboa played in the Major Leagues for seven seasons, and when he saw the end was near he began thinking of things that would upgrade the system that trains prospects. Noboa became the director of international scouting for the Arizona Diamondbacks, and that gave him the idea of building a state-of-the-art facility for his prospects. Noboa thought big. He built partnerships with wealthy Dominicans, and together they created Las Americas Baseball Academy, which leased complete operating facilities to three Major League teams. He would go on to build even more grand venues.

Noboa is part of a phalanx of Dominicans who have combined their American baseball experience with resourcefulness and drive to change the traditional colonial-like way that MLB has operated in the DR. The commodity-chain model allows us to grasp this changing relationship in political and economic terms. Rafael Pérez, who now heads the MLB office in the Dominican Republic, was a prospect recruited to play baseball at the University of Southern Alabama and went on to play in the Pittsburgh Pirates' Minor League system for several years. Whereas most Dominican players return home with some skills, Pérez returned with a college degree and used it to carve out an opportunity in the newly formed Dominican Office of MLB. This office oversees the way that academies operate in the country, a task that has grown to be very important since 2000. Pérez interrupted his tenure in that office to take a position as international director for the New York Mets in 2005, before returning to the Dominican Office five years later. His role is influential and puts him squarely at the center of all international player development. Those who know Pérez think that he has the ability to rise to the top of the MLB hierarchy. He possesses the ability to work through the prism of MLB goals and interests while not relinquishing his Dominican identity. He has repeatedly instructed American team owners, general managers (GMs), and others on what they need to do and how they need to think to succeed in the Dominican market but with a Dominican soul.

For a time in the 2000s Omar Minaya was the most influential Dominican in baseball. Another "failed" Major League ball-playing prospect, Minaya became a scout for the Texas Rangers, in time rising to become the first Dominican general manager when he took over the Montreal Expos in 2002. He took that small-market, failing franchise to playoff status, garnering the attention of the New York Mets' owners, who hired him in 2004. As the Mets' GM, Minaya made mistakes that many big-market teams are vulnerable to: signing too many expensive free agents rather than developing future players in their own system. But in other ways Minaya was visionary. He turned the Mets into the first transnational Major League franchise. He made a concerted effort to bring Dominican Major Leaguers to New York (such as Pedro Martínez and Carlos Beltrán). His efforts extended beyond Dominican players. As I have written elsewhere, "What Minaya did, however, was craft a social order *within* the Mets that moved from the DR to Queens, New York."[27] He hired top-level administrators who were Latinos or, if not, people who were bilingual with a lot of Latin American experience. The franchise was called "los Mets" by the New York media, in acknowledgment of the changes Minaya was making. The team built a lavish academy in the DR. Dominican president Leonel Fernández, who had grown up in New York as a Mets fan, attended its groundbreaking. The idea was that the smallest decisions in the DR would be easily followed in New York and that personnel in the

Big Apple could be at the facility within a few hours to take part in decisions. Seamlessness was the cultural and organizational mantra.

The DR and the WBC

The World Baseball Classic, begun in 2006, was modeled after soccer's World Cup. Further comparisons between the two events should not be undertaken, as the WBC is a very limited international event (sixteen countries, with only about half being of a high-enough caliber to seriously compete). Still, the event has had limited success, and for the countries that are baseball rich, it is a chance for national competition among the best. Dominicans won the 2013 edition (the third such event), going undefeated, and after the final out poured onto the field, dancing, singing, and wildly celebrating. Some players from other countries felt it was excessive, but Dominicans celebrate everything with such emotion—whether it is Christmas or political rallies. Upon their return home the team was treated to a parade through sections of Santo Domingo, in what all took as a day of national pride. That same pride was in evidence in 2015 when Pedro Martínez was enshrined in Cooperstown's Baseball Hall of Fame. He, too, received a parade when he got home. Such celebratory nationalism is important to Dominicans, because not too far below the surface they feel the sting of not having received the respect from Americans—and particularly from MLB—they think they deserve.

Conclusion

The Dominican Republic holds a special place in the international baseball world. While it has, for most of its history, been like other baseball-playing countries, content to supply players for MLB, in recent years the DR has been able to take a more equal role in the relationship. Segments of the Dominican baseball community have emerged that challenge the way business is conducted in the island nation. Dominican player developers (*buscónes*) have taken control of the base of the player commodity chain and now control the flow of all talent into the system. They represent agency outside the official MLB channels, and Major League Baseball has been quite threatened by it. But Dominicans have also begun to exert considerable influence within official channels. As general managers and managers (such as Felipe Alou), as builders of academies and MLB's Dominican landlords, and as key administrators in the commodity chain (as academy heads, international scouting directors, and, most important, as the head of the MLB's Dominican Office), Dominicans have moved up the ladder to assume positions of power and hold considerable influence over operations at the highest levels. This represents real political-economic influence, but it could not have occurred in the absence of the ability of the Dominican Republic to produce prodigious numbers of highly skilled, talented players.

So while the academy system may look like it represents complete North American domination of the baseball scene in this country, a closer examination shows that the opposite is true. The game is no longer so exclusively Dominican in its content as it was in the first half of the twentieth century, but it also is not as dominated by U.S. interests as it was back then. The "new Dominicans" represent a kind of transnational Dominican who can maneuver and alter the political landscape of baseball. They bring an older Dominican understanding of how the United States has operated in their country and wed it to a newer sense of pride in what Dominicans have done to ensure that baseball continues to thrive at the highest levels. The goal for these men is parity.

NOTES

1. Quoted in Deena Yellin, "North Jersey Youth Baseball Leagues Find Fewer Kids on Deck," March 9, 2014, http://www.northjersey.com/sports/north-jersey-youth-baseball-leagues-find-fewer-kids-on-deck-1.735797.

2. Rich Radford, "Child's Play: Informal Baseball Games a Rarity," *Norfolk Virginian-Pilot*, May 16, 2010, http://hamptonroads.com/2010/05/childs-play-informal-baseball-games-rarity.

3. MLB.com press release, http://m.mlb.com/news/article/70623418/2014-opening-day-rosters-feature-224-players-born-outside-the-us/.

4. John Thorn, "Pride and Passion: Baseball in the Dominican Republic," http://mlb.mlb.com/dr/pride_passion_dr.jsp.

5. Alan Klein, *Sugarball: The American Game, the Dominican Dream* (New Haven CT: Yale University Press, 1991); Alan Klein, *Growing the Game: Globalization and Major League Baseball* (New Haven CT: Yale University Press, 2006); Alan Klein, *Dominican Baseball: New Pride, Old Prejudice* (Philadelphia: Temple University Press, 2014).

6. Klein, *Sugarball*, 11.

7. Klein, *Sugarball*, 12.

8. Klein, *Sugarball*, 16; Rob Ruck, *The Tropic of Baseball: Baseball in the Dominican Republic*, 2nd ed. (1991; reprint, Lincoln: University of Nebraska Press, 1999).

9. Ruck, *Tropic of Baseball*, 45.

10. Klein, *Sugarball*, 23–26.

11. Ralph Avila, interview by the author, Miami, November 20, 2007.

12. Quoted in Klein, *Sugarball*, 82–83.

13. Ralph Avila, interview by the author, Santo Domingo, June 1, 2008; Klein, *Sugarball*, 63–67.

14. Klein, *Sugarball*, 30; Klein, *Dominican Baseball*, 55.

15. Juan Henderson, interview by the author, Santo Domingo, May 26, 2005.

16. Klein, *Dominican Baseball*, 56.

17. Klein, *Sugarball*, 19.

18. Klein, *Growing the Game*, 142–43.

19. Quoted in Klein, *Dominican Baseball*, 146.

20. Quoted in Klein, *Dominican Baseball*, 143.

21. Quoted in Klein, *Dominican Baseball*, 124.

22. Quoted in Roger Mooney, "Dominican Players Willing to Lie to Achieve Their Dreams," *Tampa Bay Tribune*, February 21, 2013, D2.

23. Klein, *Dominican Baseball*, 163.

24. Klein, *Dominican Baseball*, 3.

25. Press release, MLBPlayers.com, February 2, 2015.

26. Sean Deveney, "Yao's Impact in Globalizing NBA Will Be Felt for Years to Come," July 20, 2011, http://www.sportingnews.com/nba/story/2011-07-20/yaos-impact-in-globalizing-nba-will-be-felt-for-years-to-come.

27. Quoted in Klein, *Dominican Baseball*, 109.

3

Puerto Rico

A Major League Stepping-Stone

Franklin Otto and Thomas E. Van Hyning

Our two families moved to Puerto Rico in the years after World War II, when our fathers accepted positions in international banking and government: Frank's father was a banker, and Tom's was an economist for Operation Bootstrap, the ambitious government program that paved the way for Puerto Rico's postwar industrialization. Frank was born in San Juan, and Tom was two years old when his family embarked on a four-day voyage from Baltimore to San Juan. The ship carried lumber to help rebuild the island, which had been devastated by a recent hurricane.

Growing up we were both avid followers of the Puerto Rico Winter League (PRWL), a professional league with a three-month season that began after the U.S. World Series and ended before spring training. We both attended games at Sixto Escobar and Hiram Bithorn Stadiums, home fields for the capital area's San Juan Senadores (Senators) and Santurce Cangrejeros (Crabbers), respectively. Radio broadcasts in Spanish and newspaper coverage provided our daily dose of box scores, league standings, and player statistics.

We idolized the Crabbers and many of its native players, some of whom made names for themselves in the Major Leagues, including future Hall of Famers Roberto Clemente and Orlando Cepeda. Rubén Gómez, who pitched for the New York Giants, was the father of a grammar school classmate of Tom's, whom he remembers joining them in pickup games after school, pitching for both sides.

Our fathers took us to our first games. In 1954 Frank watched Willie Mays get his first hit for Santurce. Throughout the game fans taunted the opposition with whistles, cowbells, and conga drums. They waved white handkerchiefs, chanting "Ese es tu papá!" (He's your father!) as Rubén Gómez shut down the opposing batters.

Tom remembers the open betting and money changing hands through a chain of fans between the losing bettor and the winner. Fans used hand signals—for example, five fingers up for five dollars that, say, Tony Pérez would get a hit. That was a lot of cash then, as the average worker on the island made about a dollar and a half an hour. The stakes were higher during a March 1965 spring-training game at Bithorn Stadium between the New York Yankees and the Washington Senators. Fans a few seats away from Tom bet ten dollars on whether Roger Maris would swing at the next pitch; twenty-five on whether Mickey Mantle would walk, strike out, or hit a home run; and fifteen on how far Frank Howard would hit the ball in pregame batting practice.

As adults our passion for the game transformed itself into research projects on Puerto Rican baseball, which resulted in articles and several books. We conducted interviews with many of our childhood heroes, a few quotes from which appear in this chapter. First, though, a brief history of how baseball came to Puerto Rico and evolved, then how the PRWL compares to professional baseball in the United States, and, finally, the status of professional baseball on the island today.

The Early Years

It is generally acknowledged that the Cubans introduced baseball to Puerto Rico shortly before the end of the Spanish-American War in 1898. A newspaper box score appearing in June 14, 1896, documented the first reported game as Borínquen, the Carib Indian name for the island, played Almendares, a team of Cuban expatriates. The newspaper deemed the game "dangerous for human beings and a silly form of entertainment."[1]

After the Spanish-American War, military and civilian personnel from the United States arrived on the island. Soon playing venues expanded, leagues formed around the island, and teams were established in the larger public high schools and universities. American military personnel were given time off from their duties to play pickup and club games. Differences in playing styles between the local players and their American counterparts began to be noted. For example, the natives were more demonstrative and vocal, using infield chatter and offering encouragement to their pitchers and hitters.

Initially, the game was played mostly by the educated middle class, but it later trickled down such that dockworkers, sugarcane hands, and farmers—of all skin tones—were also playing. By 1918 barnstorming teams from the Major Leagues and the Negro Leagues visited the island, as did Cuban all-star teams led by legendary players Cristóbal Torriente, Adolfo Luque, and Martín Dihigo, the latter being the only player in the world elected to the baseball halls of fame in three countries: the United States, Cuba, and Mexico.

The visiting teams exposed more Puerto Ricans to baseball and motivated Puerto Rican baseball aficionados and corporate sponsors to form Puerto Rican all-star teams of their own, who would play in the Dominican Republic and Venezuela. Some of the new Puerto Rican clubs took their names from North American companies (such as Wrigley) and North American products (Buick and Sherwin-Williams), illustrating the close economic ties between Puerto Rico and the United States. Two Puerto Rican barnstormers who relocated to the Dominican Republic and Venezuela each earned the title of father of Dominican and Venezuelan baseball.

The first Puerto Rican baseball stadium with a scoreboard was San Juan's Escambrón Stadium, completed in 1932, with a seating capacity of thirteen thousand and clubhouses with shower facilities. It was soon renamed after boxer Sixto Escobar, who won the world bantamweight

4. An early ballpark in Puerto Rico, ca. 1930. (Photo courtesy of the National Baseball Hall of Fame.)

title in 1934. The Cincinnati Reds held their 1936 spring training there and played against local Puerto Rican stars. Their presence added to the locals' knowledge of the game and appreciation of good baseball. Unlike in the United States, where the color ban was still in effect, Puerto Rico offered a convivial environment for fans and players of different racial and ethnic backgrounds. Black and white players mixed freely and often established lasting friendships.

The Middle Years

Baseball's popularity grew with the founding of the Semi-Professional League in 1938, and two years later the professional PRWL was established. The latter featured mostly Puerto Rican players with a few Cuban and Negro Leaguers. The early stars were Hiram Bithorn, who became Puerto Rico's first big leaguer (1942 Chicago Cubs); Pedro Cepeda, a shortstop and father of Hall of Famer Orlando Cepeda; Pancho Coímbre, outfielder with the Negro League New York Cubans in the 1940s; and Luis Rodríguez Olmo, who played for the 1943 Brooklyn

Dodgers. Whereas Bithorn's and Olmo's fair complexions made it possible for them to play in the pre–Jackie Robinson Major Leagues, the dark skin of Cepeda and Coímbre excluded them.

Puerto Rican fans still recall their own version of the Bobby Thomson "shot heard 'round the world"—the "Pepelucaso." In the seventh and deciding game of the 1950–51 island championship between perennial winner Caguas and Santurce, a record 16,700 fans packed into Sixto Escobar Stadium. The stakes were high, as the winner not only would be the island champion but would also earn the right to represent Puerto Rico at the Caribbean World Series in Venezuela. With the score tied at two in the bottom of the ninth and with two outs, light-hitting José "Pepe Lucas" St. Clair came to bat for Santurce. As he made contact with the ball, there was no doubt that it would clear the left-field fence. Pandemonium broke out in all corners of the ballpark. Caravans of fans in honking cars reveled throughout the capital city until the early-morning hours. Santurce had waited twelve years for its first championship.

Playing in the United States

Puerto Ricans playing pro baseball in the United States confronted the ugly face of racism, particularly in the American South, where "Whites Only" signs were evident and players of color could not stay in the same hotels as their white teammates. Víctor "Vic" Pellot Power related an incident at a restaurant where the waitress said to him, "We don't serve Negroes," to which Vic replied, "I don't eat Negroes, I eat rice and beans."[2] In 1953 Power was playing well in the Yankee farm system but had not gotten a call-up to the big club. "I had now been with the Yankee organization three years. They did not bring me up. There were problems at Yankee Stadium where black people from Harlem together with Puerto Ricans picketed the Stadium. This bothered the Yankees. Frequently the press would ask me why the Yankees didn't bring me up. I told them that the Yankees weren't ready for a colored player on their team."[3]

Similarly, Saturnino Escalera was with a Cincinnati Reds farm team heading north when they stopped in Atlanta for their last spring-training game. He was told blacks weren't allowed to play in Atlanta and to stay in his hotel room. When the National Association for the Advancement of Colored People asked him for a comment, he said, "I am not black, I am Puerto Rican."[4]

Nicknames

In Puerto Rico players often acquire colorful nicknames that may reveal the local culture and the intimate relationship island fans enjoy with the players. Josh Gibson's moniker was "Trucutú," based on an island cartoon hero. Bob "El Múcaro" (the Owl) Thurman was nicknamed for his hitting prowess during night games. Willard Brown was nicknamed "Ese Hombre" (That Man) for becoming the dominant player in the post–World War II period. Some native players used a childhood nickname in their baseball career, such as Luis Rodríguez "El Jíbaro" (Country Boy) Olmo; Orlando Cepeda was called "Peruchín," the diminutive for "Perucho," his dad's nickname; and Juan "Igor" González was known as Igor since age ten for his interest in "Mighty Igor," a pro wrestler. Second baseman Jim Gilliam earned the sobriquet "Black Sea," since nothing eluded him. Rubén Gómez—"El Divino Loco"—had permission to ride to away games in his sports car, instead of the team bus, and drove wildly. Nicknames of American players could be transformed in Puerto Rico. Willie Mays was the "Say Juey" (not "Say Hey") Kid, since *juey* is a land crab, and Mays played for the Santurce Crabbers.

Puerto Rican team names also tell stories. For example, the Guayama Brujos (Witches) referred to local residents who practiced a local form of voodoo; Aguadilla's Tiburones (Sharks) referred to the prevalence of sharks off this west coast town; the Caguas Criollos' name refers to the local landed gentry; Ponce Leones (Lions) came about when their team owner was photographed with a whip in his hand, appearing to be a lion tamer; Bayamón's constant traffic jams helped team officials

5. They were known as the "Escuadron del Panico," or the "Panic Squad," and were (*from left to right*) Willie Mays, Roberto Clemente, Buster Clarkson, Bob Thurman, and George Crowe. (Photo courtesy of the National Baseball Hall of Fame.)

and fans choose Vaqueros (Cowboys), named after the city's "cowboy drivers"; the Carolina Gigantes derive their name from a legendary seven-foot-eight native once dubbed El Gigante de Carolina; and the Manatí Atenienses (Athenians) were named after that municipality's rich cultural heritage.

Imported Players

PRWL teams have long been allowed to use "imports"—players not from Puerto Rico or the neighboring U.S. Virgin Islands. PRWL rules permitted three imports per team during the early years (1938–42) and up to ten per team from the mid-1950s to the mid-1980s when Major League clubs had working agreements with Puerto Rican teams. Each of Puerto Rico's teams is now permitted six imports on its active roster. During the first two decades, imports mostly came from the Negro Leagues. Satchel Paige (1948) and Bob Thurman (1955) made their Major League debuts after stellar winter performances in Puerto Rico. Some later imports came from elsewhere in the Caribbean and Latin America, such as Dennis Martínez (Nicaragua), Chili Davis (Jamaica), Tony Pérez (Cuba), Manny Sanguillén (Panama), and Manny Mota (Dominican Republic). An import used to be allowed to replace a Puerto Rican big leaguer if the latter opted not to play winter ball or got hurt.

The quality of the imports and their ability to produce for their respective clubs often determined whether a team had a winning or losing season. Reggie Jackson had already played three full MLB seasons when he arrived in Puerto Rico in 1970 to play on a team managed by Frank Robinson, who later became the first African American Major League manager. Cal Ripken Jr. was a twenty-year-old prospect when he first played in the PRWL. Ray Miller—Baltimore's pitching coach at the time—was his Puerto Rican manager, and Ripken wanted to impress him and the Orioles' management:

> We had a lot of big league players in Puerto Rico. A lot of the pitching was AAA, so the level was between AAA and the big leagues. So coming out of AA [1980] and AAA [1981] I had to compete at a higher level and learned quite a few things playing in the sixty-game season. . . . [I]t allowed me to reach the big leagues before I was twenty-one, and part of my goal in baseball was to reach the big leagues early and be able to play a long, long time. I don't think I'd have reached it without Puerto Rico.[5]

Many scouts and managers believed that if a prospect could succeed in Puerto Rico, he could play in the Majors. Hank Aaron went to Puerto Rico as a nineteen-year-old second baseman in October 1953. When Aaron did not hit well, there was pressure from the media and the fans to replace him with a better import. Mickey Owen, player-manager for Aaron's team, recalled, "I knew where I could get a better second baseman than Aaron. . . . [O]ne day I hit him a few fly balls and he went to them easy, and he threw good. I said, you're not an infielder, you're an outfielder. . . . I never told Aaron how to do anything except once. I told him to hit one to right field, and he hit a bullet there."[6]

Aaron saw Major League pitching almost every day, and after moving to the outfield he began hitting again. Aaron, who tied for the home run title and helped his club win the pennant, later said that Puerto Rico had been an important stepping-stone and a confidence builder in his getting to the Major Leagues.

Tony Gwynn played two winters in Puerto Rico (1982–84) to make himself a better player. He explained:

> In a sense, it's just like playing Major League baseball. . . . [T]here were so many guys down there that had so much experience, it enabled you to learn about what it was going to take to be successful at this level. . . . [A]nytime somebody asks me about winter ball, and they say they're going to Puerto Rico, I say "GO." You're going to learn a lot about the game. . . . [I]f you go down there and do your due diligence . . . there's no question that you'll come back a much better player.[7]

Salaries, Money, and Gifts

The top PRWL imports made about $1,500 a month from the mid-1950s to mid-1960s, which after inflation is even more than today's top monthly PRWL salaries of about $4,500. Jim Northrup, for example, recalled making $1,500 per month in 1964–65, more than his $1,330 monthly salary as a rookie with the 1965 Detroit Tigers. It was common for imports to make more money than native players, at least through the 1980s, when Rickey Henderson made $7,000 per month plus a Rolex watch from team management for setting the all-time PRWL single-season stolen-base record.

The players could also pick up a little extra cash from fans who gave money to players for game-winning hits and fine pitching during la Epoca Romántica (the Romantic Period) of 1938–49. After Roy Campanella's grand slam in the 1940–41 final series contest, for example, excited fans put dollar bills into Campy's hand as his teammates carried him on their shoulders. Ponce's mayor ran onto the field to shake the hand of a player after he hit a game-winning homer against the New York Yankees in a 1947 spring-training game, and the player enriched himself by $70 from fans passing the plate. Wilmer Fields received $125 from fans who passed money through the wire mesh at Escobar Stadium after Fields homered off Satchel Paige in 1948. When Arecibo's Claude Raymond won a tiebreaker game in 1962 to clinch a playoff spot, one fan thrust a $100 bill into his hand.

In the 1950s cash was given to the players by archrival San Juan or Santurce fans, depending on the outcome of the City Championship. Don Liddle, who pitched for the 1952–53 San Juan Senators, recalled the evening when he received cash from a fan under unusual circumstances. After besting Santurce and its ace, Rubén Gómez, Liddle received a police escort back to his apartment. As Liddle was leaving Escobar Stadium someone jerked his pants, and a policeman hit the fellow with his billy club. When Liddle got to his apartment, there was $300 stuffed into the back pocket of his uniform.

Conditioning and Training

Puerto Rican ballplayers were generally smaller and less muscular than their American counterparts, though this began to change in the 1970s when better diets, improved health care, and successful social and educational programs such as Head Start were introduced. No longer do the Puerto Rican players just play infield and outfield positions. In the 2003 Major League postseason, four of the starting eight catchers were from Puerto Rico—Ivan "Pudge" Rodriguez (Marlins), Jorge Posada (Yankees), Javy Lopez (Braves), and Benito Santiago (Giants).

Of the four, only "Pudge" was under six feet tall, and his weight of 210 pounds was all muscle.

Today youngsters benefit from the expertise and experience of native professional players, coaches, and scouts who provide clinics around the island in their free time. In a 1999 interview with Frank, Jorge L. De Posada talked about his approach to training his son, who was a New York Yankees catcher:

> I kept him [Jorge] out of little leagues until he was eleven years old because early on kids get hit with hard balls and then don't want to play anymore. Up until then, all he hit and played with was a plastic bat and rubber balls. We took it real easy until he gained confidence. When he started to play organized ball as a youngster, I never let him use an aluminum bat. Today, the "pop" he gets when he hits, and the way the ball jumps off his bat, comes from developing strong hands with the wooden bat. Later on, I also got him into cycling and bought him a rowing machine for conditioning and strong leg development.

Fans

Puerto Rican baseball fans are said to be very knowledgeable about the game, which they follow year-round. In the town plazas, *colmados* (mini grocery stores), workplaces, and homes, fans discuss the finer points of the game. They are passionate about the game as well, as the behavior of fans during one rain delay illustrates. John Strohmayer had pitched into the fourth inning of a 1970–71 game when a downpour halted play. It had rained all week, so fans did not look forward to another postponement. Strohmayer recalled, "Within 20 minutes the entire infield was covered with two inches of water . . . so everyone went into the clubhouse and started getting undressed. I put my arm in a bucket of ice. Somebody came into the clubhouse ten minutes later saying it had stopped raining. No way, anytime it rained like that in the States, the game was finished."[8] Fans from the neighborhood went home and got their wheelbarrows. A big pile of loam was under the stands and put to use. When the work was completed, play resumed. Strohmayer said, "That epitomizes the word 'fan'. . . . I felt a lot of satisfaction when I was able to perform well—so much appreciation on the part of the fans, more so than any other place I played."[9]

Ballparks

PRWL ballparks are similar in size and amenities to AAA ballparks in the United States (although we have not yet seen the new Roberto Clemente Walker Stadium in Carolina or Manatí's new Pedrín Zorrilla Stadium, named after the man who signed Roberto Clemente to his first professional contract).

Four of the stadiums have artificial surfaces. This is an adaptation to the tropical climate that produces torrential downpours, which pose serious drainage problems on natural grass fields that in turn require the rescheduling of games, a threat to revenues. When the city of Ponce won the bid to host the 1993 Central American and Caribbean Games, it installed the first artificial surface at Paquito Montaner Stadium.

Puerto Rico's baseball stadiums now present a more corporate and less intimate appearance than they used to. Bithorn Stadium's huge amount of foul territory, for example, makes the fans feel more removed from the players. And its location in a business district on a busy highway, across from the island's first major mall, has meant congestion and parking problems. The prevalence of company signs and sponsors on today's outfield fences reinforces the corporate environment. In contrast, the old Sixto Escobar Stadium was a stone's throw from the Atlantic Ocean and caressed by ocean breezes. With the trade winds blowing out toward left field, screwball-throwing Rubén Gómez mostly pitched right-handed batters low and away, whereas at Bithorn Stadium, when the wind came in from the outfield, Gómez threw up in the strike zone, conducive to hitting fly balls. Pine trees formed a backdrop in the outfield at Sixto Escobar, unlike the high-rise condominiums and office buildings fans now see behind the fences at Bithorn.

The clubhouse atmosphere in Puerto Rico tends to be more informal than in the U.S. Major Leagues, making it easier for journalists to converse with and interview players and managers. After a game Puerto Rican players typically go home to eat and sleep, whereas the imported foreign players stop at fast-food restaurants for a snack or meal prior to returning to their apartments.

Concession stands at today's ballparks feature a standard fare of American fast food—Pizza Hut, Taco Bell, Kentucky Fried Chicken—in addition to local products such as *platanutres* (plantain chips), *bacalaítos* (fried codfish), and rum and fruit drinks. One can still get oranges and *piraguas* (snow cones) outside the ballpark.

Recent Developments

Today Puerto Rico is less of a Major League stepping-stone because U.S. Major League clubs have the option to send their top prospects to winter leagues in the Dominican Republic, Venezuela, and Australia. And for younger prospects there is the Arizona Fall League. A greater number of native players now have the chance to play in the PRWL. However, several recent developments are making a significant impact on the quality of and support for baseball on the island.

The creation of the Puerto Rico Baseball Academy High School in 1999 was the brainchild of former Texas Rangers pitcher Edwin Correa. With the assistance of two grants of two hundred thousand dollars from MLB, the PRBAHS is the first specialized baseball high school in Puerto Rico or the United States. Its mission is to develop the students' academic, baseball, and social development in order to maximize their chances of making it in, and their adjustment to, American professional baseball. In the 2004 Major League draft, twelve of the academy's students were selected, the most players ever from one high school. Among its more than six hundred graduates is Carlos

Correa, the first pick in the 2012 Major League draft and the recipient of the 2015 American League Rookie of the Year Award.

The establishment of a Major League team in San Juan has been the dream of many Puerto Rican fans and some investors. MLB helped Puerto Rico experiment with the idea when in 2003 and 2004 it scheduled the Montreal Expos to play forty-three regular-season games in Bithorn Stadium. The Expos were greeted with great fanfare and high expectations. Thirteen million dollars was spent to upgrade the forty-two-year-old stadium, including a new artificial surface, an expanded home clubhouse, a new scoreboard and video board, and six thousand additional seats. While average attendance at the games for both years exceeded that of Montreal's home attendance, it was far less than many had hoped for. Attendance was hurt by higher than usual ticket prices (ten-dollar bleacher seats to eighty-five-dollar box seats behind home plate) and a lack of big-name Latino players on some visiting-team rosters.

Puerto Rico hosted rounds in each of the three World Baseball Classics (WBC), the only locale other than the United States and Japan to do so. The first round of the 2006 Classic was particularly significant for Puerto Ricans, with an opening game against Cuba, a rival not seen on Puerto Rican soil since its withdrawal from the Caribbean Series by Fidel Castro in 1961. "Let me put it to you this way," said Carlos Delgado of the New York Mets and leader of the Puerto Rican squad at the time. "There are no tickets left. It's sold out."[10] The Puerto Rican squad beat the Cubans 12–2 and advanced to the second round. In spite of home-crowd support, Puerto Rico fared less well in the second round, losing to Cuba and the Dominican Republic. But the Puerto Rican team's overall record of 4-2 placed them a respectable fifth in the final WBC standings.

In the 2009 WBC Puerto Rico again hosted six games in the first round and played to capacity crowds. The Puerto Rican team, led by Major League veterans Carlos Beltrán and Iván Rodríguez, allowed just one run in three games against the Dominican Republic, Netherlands, and Panama, advancing to the second round, where they again faltered, this time against Venezuela and the United States.

Expectations for the 2013 WBC were low, as Puerto Rico was to face Caribbean powerhouses the Dominican Republic and Venezuela in the first round. But with only a handful of Major Leaguers and a pitching staff of primarily globetrotters and unproven prospects, Puerto Rico sent Venezuela packing and, then in the second round eliminated the United States, which was favored to win. With hardly twenty-four hours rest, the Puerto Rican team flew to San Francisco and defeated Japan, the reigning champions.

Puerto Rico's unexpected run ended in a 3–0 loss in the championship game to the Dominican squad. Giancarlo Alvarado, Puerto Rico's starting pitcher in the championship game, said, "The entire island has been transfixed watching Puerto Rico's performance and now the world knows who we are. We felt like our fans were in the stands cheering us along like guardian angels."[11] "We put Puerto Rico back on the international map," said manager Edwin Rodriguez. He added, "[Our] extraordinary campaign will serve as inspiration for the rebirth of baseball that for some years has languished in popularity and stature on the island. The accomplishments in this Classic . . . should motivate the youth that are coming up and show them that developmentally they can play at the highest level of professional ball."[12]

Puerto Rico's success in the WBC appears to have increased the game's popularity at the youth and semipro levels. José Matos, an official with Little League of Puerto Rico, said without a doubt that all the promotion and fervor connected with the WBC gives baseball a boost. Kids idolize the local stars and want to emulate them, while parents steer their kids toward playing Little League. Noting that the Liga Superior AA (Amateur) had increased from thirty-three teams in 2006 to forty-five teams in 2015, the league's director, Carlos Maysonet Negrón, gave much of the credit to the WBC:

I believe the WBC had a lot to do with the increased interest and support of the Puerto Rican people. Most town mayors [now] have a genuine commitment to baseball not only with financial support of the AA league, Little League and the woman's league but also in the maintenance of our ballparks. . . . [F]an support has been so strong, attendance in 2015 which was our largest figures on record and we expect 2016 will surpass that. Despite what some say, baseball is still our national sport. It's the sport that binds Puerto Ricans as an entity. . . . We have more baseball franchises than those of volleyball and basketball franchises combined.[13]

What are the challenges facing the PRWL officials and club owners? Economic pressures forced the PRWL to contract from a long-standing five-team league to four. Paramount to its solvency is maintaining a dedicated fan base and being competitive with other local entertainment venues. Recognizing the viability of an off-island fan base, in 2015 the PRWL celebrated a first-ever three-game series in Florida. Ballparks must strive to offer reasonably priced seats, safe and accessible parking, and ancillary entertainment such as mascots and *pleneros* (popular musical groups). Giveaways, free transportation from low-income housing projects, clinics for youngsters, and more televised games all need to be pursued to increase the fan base and get more spectators in the seats. The midseason interleague all-star game between the Dominican Republic and Puerto Rico should be continued in order to capitalize on the interisland rivalry. All told, the storied history and passion for the game may not be enough to carry the PRWL without the sustenance of a stronger economic foundation.

We cherish our PRWL memories—the San Juan–Santurce City Championship, the open betting, the constant chants, discussing strategy with fans, and, perhaps most of all, how the PRWL launched the big-league careers of so many fine American and native ballplayers.

1. See Eduardo Valero's foreword to Thomas E. Van Hyning's *Puerto Rico's Winter League: A History of Major League Baseball's Launching Pad* (Jefferson NC: McFarland, 1995) regarding the claim that the first baseball game in Puerto Rico was in 1896. Other sources say the first game was in 1897. Regrettably, the source for the box score and the quotation cannot be located.

2. Quoted in Peter C. Bjarkman, *Baseball with a Latin Beat: A History of the Latin American Game* (Jefferson NC: McFarland, 1994), 93.

3. Quoted in Frank Otto, "Playing Baseball in America: Puerto Rican Memories," *NINE: A Journal of Baseball History and Social Policy Perspectives* 4, no. 2 (1996): 367.

4. Quoted in Otto, "Playing Baseball in America," 366.

5. Quoted in Van Hyning, *Puerto Rico's Winter League*, 27.

6. Quoted in Van Hyning, *Puerto Rico's Winter League*, 12.

7. Quoted in Thomas E. Van Hyning, *The Santurce Crabbers: Sixty Seasons of Puerto Rican Winter League Baseball* (Jefferson NC: McFarland, 2008), 195–96.

8. Quoted in Van Hyning, *Puerto Rico's Winter League*, 235.

9. Quoted in Van Hyning, *Puerto Rico's Winter League*, 235.

10. Quoted in Tom Singer, "Puerto Rico Can't Wait to Play WBC," February 1, 2006, http://mlb.mlb.com/news/print.jsp?ymd=20060201&content_id=1305070&vkey=wbc.

11. Quoted in Eric Núñez, "Puerto Rico vuelve a estar en el mapa del beísbol," March 20, 2013, http://news.yahoo.com/puerto-rico-vuelve-estar-en-el-mapa-del-045402838--spt.html.

12. Quoted in Núñez, "Puerto Rico vuelve a estar en el mapa del beísbol."

13. Frank Otto, interview with Carlos Maysonet Negrón, November 4, 2015.

4

Canada

Internationalizing America's National Pastime

Colin Howell

Although baseball in Canada today is flourishing at the youth, amateur, semiprofessional, and professional levels, most Canadians tend
to consider it an extension of American sporting life. Admittedly, the
country has a Major League franchise in Toronto and a number of
Canadians—including Joey Votto, Justin Morneau, Brett Lawrie, Russell Martin, Michael Saunders, Dalton Pompey, John Axford, James
Paxton, and Adam Loewen—play big-league baseball. It is fair to say,
however, that none of these ballplayers has achieved the national recognition and adulation of hockey players such as Sidney Crosby, Wayne
Gretzky, Mario Lemieux, or Bobby Orr. It is thus tempting to regard
the history of baseball in Canada, from the mid-nineteenth century
to the present, as part of the natural diffusion of America's national
pastime beyond the borders of the United States, just as Canadian
hockey enthusiasts frequently talk of the internationalization of what
they regard as "Canada's game."

Sport historians often apply a diffusion model to explain the globalization of twentieth-century sporting culture and games of all types.
According to historians Joseph Arbena, Allen Guttmann, Steven Riess,
and others, modern sporting forms originated in highly developed
metropolitan societies, spread outward into the hinterland or colonial territories where they were first introduced at the elite level, and
then percolated downward to the masses. The British game of soccer

provides a classic illustration of the process. Developing out of unruly and relatively unorganized "folk football" play, the game was regulated, codified, and modernized in the nineteenth century and exported to all corners of the British Empire and ultimately to the world, and it has assumed the status of the "people's game" from Football Association cup matches at Wembley Stadium to street football in the barrios of Rio de Janeiro.

In some ways the diffusion model obscures more than it reveals about the complicated history of the development of baseball above and along the forty-ninth parallel. In Canada the diffusion process is uncertain, given that games of town ball and variations of the British game of rounders were being played as early as the 1820s. In fact, baseball in Canada may have developed simultaneously with baseball south of the border. This is hardly surprising, given the porosity of the border and movement across it in both directions. Two Canadian historians, Robert Barney and Nancy Bouchier, have even suggested a Canadian origin of the game, based upon a set of rules and diagrams drawn up by Adam Ford for a game in Beachville, Ontario, in 1838, a year before the mythical "invention" of baseball by Abner Doubleday in Cooperstown, New York. Of course, as the late paleontologist and baseball writer Stephen Jay Gould pointed out, claims about the invention or origination of sports that evolved out of more traditional games are often dubious and suggest a "creationist" rather than evolutionary state of mind.[1]

Whatever the game's beginnings, baseball was widely played in Canada at midcentury, albeit with varying rules. During the 1850s and '60s baseball clubs in Ontario communities such as London and Woodstock followed the rules of the eleven-a-side Canadian game, while in the Maritimes the New England version held sway. Around 1860 teams in London, Hamilton, Toronto, Woodstock, and Guelph all adopted the New York Knickerbocker rules so that they could challenge baseball clubs south of the border. By the end of the decade the game's rules were standardized nationwide. Teams in New Brunswick and Nova Scotia had abandoned the New England game in favor of the New York rules as well. On the Pacific Coast baseball clubs were springing up in Victoria and Vancouver during the 1860s, largely as a result of the close connections between British Columbia and American states to the south.

In many cases it is hard to decide who was influencing whom. If the reliance on Americans to ensure a sophisticated level of play is any indication of a process of diffusion, there is little evidence to suggest that Canadian baseball was especially derivative of American influences. In the 1860s the *New York Clipper* warned readers that "the Canucks are not to be trifled with, and unless better teams are pitted against them in the future, the laurels may pass from the American boys to them."[2] In 1874 the Guelph Maple Leafs won the world semiprofessional baseball championship with a lineup of Canadian players. Less than a decade later young Canadian-born players from Ontario and the Maritimes—such as Mike Brannock, Bill Reid, Charles "Pop" Smith, and Bill Phillips—were playing in the National Association in the United States. Between 1870 and the end of the century, sixty-four Canadians played in the National and International Associations. Perhaps the best of all of them was James "Tip" O'Neill of Woodstock, Ontario, who captured the first Triple Crown in big-league history, playing for the St. Louis Browns in 1887.

Of course, some of these players had left Canada at a young age, as their parents sought work in the mill towns of New England or employment in big U.S. cities. For example, Toronto-born Art Irwin, who revolutionized fielding by padding a buckskin driving glove and sewing the third and fourth fingers together, moved to Boston with his family at the age of fifteen. John "Chewing Gum" O'Brien and Bill Phillips both moved with their families from New Brunswick to the United States as children. O'Brien moved to Lewiston, Maine, and Phillips to Chicago. By the first quarter of the twentieth century, moreover, many American-born players with family ties to Canada were in the big leagues.

Among the more notable were Franco-Americans such as Nap Lajoie, Del Bissonette, and "Frenchy" Bordagaray and recognizable stars such as Pie Traynor, Stuffy McInnis, "Doc" Gautreau, and Harry Hooper, who had family roots in the Maritimes. Known for diving catches, headlong slides, and confrontations with umpires, Bordagaray flaunted his French heritage, at one point taking up fencing and sporting a D'Artagnan-style beard in Three Musketeer fashion. Then there was big Larry McLean, whose birthplace is usually listed as Cambridge, Massachusetts, but who grew up in Fredericton, New Brunswick. A catcher with a rocket arm and proverbial bent elbow, McLean was known for biting off enormous chaws of Brown Mule tobacco and washing it down with a pint of corn whiskey. McLean was constantly in trouble with his managers. In 1906, for example, St. Louis manager Kid Nichols sent McLean to the Minors after a drunken escapade that included his jumping in the fountain court of the Buckingham Hotel. Said Nichols, "I can pitch to Larry real good, but I can't manage him worth a dime."[3] McLean later returned to the Majors with the Cincinnati Reds, but his drinking kept him in trouble and was responsible for his death at the age of forty in a bar fight in Boston.

Despite its rough edges and reputation for rowdiness, baseball had pushed other team sports in Canada aside in the last quarter of the nineteenth century. This was particularly true of British team sports such as cricket, soccer, and rugby, which the Anglo-Saxon bourgeoisie thought would encourage a respectable social order and a deeper allegiance to nation and empire. Despite the elites' hopes for respectable sport, British games were often resisted, especially in Quebec, and quickly gave way to North American sports such as lacrosse, hockey, and baseball. Even in parts of the country with strong imperial connections—in the Maritimes, for instance—baseball was the summer sport of choice for most people by the 1880s. By that time the game was rapidly spreading into newly settled regions in the West.

Baseball moved west from Ontario to Manitoba soon after the latter joined the Confederation in 1870. A Winnipeg baseball club was formed in March 1874, led by A. G. Bannatyne, a wealthy merchant and the city's first postmaster. A decade later there were three clubs operating in the city: the Hotels, the Metropolitans, and the Canadian Pacific Railway clubs. As Canadian baseball historian Bill Humber has noted, of the twelve thousand inhabitants in Manitoba in 1870 only seventy were Americans, suggesting that Manitoba's early baseball owed little to the influence of the United States.[4] The game prospered outside of Winnipeg, in places like Brandon and farther west in Battleford, and was well enough established that by 1880 teams from the province were seeking competition in Minneapolis and St. Paul. In Saskatchewan, Alberta, and British Columbia, settlers from the United States contributed more significantly to the growth of the game. Baseball thus came to the Canadian West from two directions: east from Ontario through Manitoba and along the rail line and north from the United States.

In the few decades leading up to the First World War, baseball in Canada was embroiled in commonplace Victorian discourses about respectable behavior and embellished with class, race, and nativist prejudices. For some snooty members of the Anglo-Saxon elite, baseball seemed a crass and disreputable sport, representing the worst characteristics of American culture. When the University of Toronto fielded a baseball team in 1885, a correspondent to the student newspaper warned readers, "The associations of the game . . . are of the very lowest and most repugnant character . . . degraded by Yankee professionalism."[5] Implicit in this, of course, was a critique and fear of the influence of American culture on Canadian life. The commentator's remarks were likely motivated just as much by concerns about baseball's popularity among the working class. Unlike curling, cricket, tennis, or golf—sports that appealed to the social elite—baseball attracted the support of all social classes and often encouraged vigorous class, ethnic, and community rivalries. Concerned about professionalism, gambling, alcohol consumption, and the frequently rowdy behavior of fans and players alike, proponents of "respectable" sport and of "gentlemanly amateurism" remained ambivalent about baseball's social value.

At the same time, some thought that baseball could teach recent immigrants "appropriate" North American social values. This was particularly the case in Saskatchewan and Alberta, which by the turn of the century were attracting hundreds of thousands of immigrants, many from eastern Europe, Scandinavia, and the Ukraine. According to historians Donald Wetherell and Irene Kmet, sports such as baseball were important in securing Anglo-Saxon hegemony in the West. For the most part, however, immigrants were involved in establishing farms and thus had little time for leisure pursuits. Rather, it was in the urban centers such as Calgary and Edmonton where baseball developed around the turn of the century.

Discourses about baseball's respectability were dissolving by the First World War in the face of the game's emergence as a marketable form of mass entertainment. In his study of the prewar Vancouver Beavers of the Northwest League, Robin John Anderson found the sport to be unencumbered by debates about respectability: "Professional baseball in Vancouver was all about money. . . . [O]wners, players, and fans eagerly sought monetary rewards from the game. Of course, none of this would have appeared out of character in the frantic acquisitory climate that coloured the boom years of pre-war Vancouver."[6] Vancouver was hardly unique, however, since these years generally witnessed the acceptance of professional sport as a legitimate form of mass entertainment.

After the war virtually every city, town, and village across the country sported a ball team, and baseball entered a new golden age. Amateur leagues, youth teams, semipro community baseball, and itinerant barnstorming teams flourished. A number of Canadian cities and towns also operated successfully in baseball's Minor Leagues. Most successful was the Toronto Maple Leaf club, which operated from the beginning of the century until 1912 in the Eastern League and then in the International League, where it continued to toil through the 1960s. Montreal had teams in a number of different leagues but, like Toronto, became a fixture in the International League in the 1920s. Professional Minor

League franchises also operated between the wars in Vancouver, Winnipeg, Hamilton, London, Ottawa, Quebec City, and Trois-Rivières. The Cape Breton Colliery League, which operated from 1937 through 1939 at the Class C level, had teams in Sydney, New Waterford, Glace Bay, and Dominion.

Baseball might have been a unifying community activity, but not all social divisions evaporated, as baseball games became highly desired marketable commodities. Invidious judgments about respectability still plagued African and Asian Canadians, recent immigrants, Native peoples, and women as they took up the sport. After the Great War some black players occasionally found spots on semiprofessional town teams, but for the most part they were confined to playing for all-black clubs like the Halifax Coloured Diamonds, the Saint John Royals (which won the New Brunswick Intermediate Championship in 1921), the Amber Valley team from Edmonton, and the Chatham, Ontario, All-Stars, whose roster included Ferguson Jenkins Sr. All of these clubs were capable of beating the best senior teams in their respective provinces. Of the ethnic-based teams, none was more successful than the Vancouver Asahi baseball club. Organized in 1922, the Asahis played in Vancouver's Terminal League at Oppenheimer Park in so-called Little Tokyo. Known for their slick fielding, their speed on the base paths, and their bunting prowess, the Asahis were prominent throughout the interwar period, winning five consecutive Pacific Northwest championships, beginning in 1937. The club disbanded as a result of the internment of Japanese Canadians in 1942. The Asahis were recently inducted into the Canadian Baseball Hall of Fame.

The interwar period was also the heyday of barnstorming black ball teams crossing the border to play exhibition games for a guaranteed portion of the gate. Chappie Johnson's Colored All-Stars, the Philadelphia Colored Giants, the New York Black Yankees, the Cuban Giants, the Boston Royal Giants, and other aggregations drawing upon players from the so-called Negro Leagues thrilled Canadian audiences with their skillful play. One of the finest of these touring clubs was a semipro team from Bismarck, North Dakota, with both white players and Negro League stars Satchel Paige, Ted "Double Duty" Radcliffe, Hilton Smith, Chet Brewer, and Quincy Troupe. The Bismarck club, which won the 1935 National Baseball Congress semipro championship in Wichita, Kansas, played a number of exhibition games in Canadian prairie communities. Occasionally, these clubs resorted to clowning and sometimes played upon racial stereotypes to attract an audience.[7] In the same year fifty-five thousand people in Montreal watched the Zulu Cannibal Giants play a trio of games in woolly headdresses, stripped to the waist, their faces and chests painted. When Benito Mussolini invaded Ethiopia, the club changed its name to the Ethiopian Giants.

Certain players were particularly well known for their clowning routines. Barnstorming provided a supplement to salaries in the Negro Leagues for many black players, and in a few cases Canadian semipro teams offered contracts to black stars. Independent leagues like the Quebec Provincial League (QPL), Ontario's Intercounty League, and, before 1937, the Cape Breton Colliery League offered employment to black players. In 1935, for example, the Granby, Quebec, club signed African American pitcher-outfielder Alfred Wilson, and Cape Breton's Dominion Hawks signed George "Whitey" Michaels of the Boston Royal Giants as playing coach. Both were dropped the following year as their leagues affiliated with organized baseball and accepted its unwritten prohibition against black ballplayers.

The interwar years also witnessed the steady development of women's baseball in Canada. Prior to the First World War, women were largely confined to the role of spectators, except for the traveling Bloomer Girls teams or variations of the same, which had been touring Canada since the 1890s. The few women who played had to endure moral and medical restrictions that suggested that those who entered male terrain were "unnatural" and that playing a man's game would subject their supposedly frail bodies and temperaments to unnecessary stress. Women's baseball developed rapidly, especially in Toronto and western Canada, during and after World War I. In 1914, for example, the Toronto Playgrounds Baseball Leagues introduced organized baseball for girls in two divisions. By 1920 more than fifty teams were registered. Women's baseball also flourished on the prairies and the Pacific Coast, and the Saskatchewan Ladies League was probably the most competitive women's league in the country after the war. Although women in the Maritimes had fewer opportunities to compete, Edna Lockhart, a five-sport star from Avonport, Nova Scotia, was recruited to pitch and play third base for Margaret Nabel's New York Bloomer Girls during the 1930s.

In 1943 chewing gum magnate Philip K. Wrigley established the All-American Girls Professional Baseball League and in his search for talent drew heavily on the experience of young Canadian players. Since the AAGPBL initially used a ball whose dimensions were somewhere between a fastball and a softball, the fact that most Canadian girls had played softball was not a liability. Of all the players in the AAGPBL between 1943 and 1954, about 10 percent were Canadians, with the majority of these coming from Manitoba and Saskatchewan. Among the more notable were Helen Callaghan of Vancouver, whose son Casey Candaele went on to play Major League Baseball (MLB); Helen "Nicki" Fox of Ardley, Alberta; Gladys "Terry" Davis of Toronto; and Evelyn Wawryshyn of Tyndall, Manitoba. The Canadian women who played in the league were inducted into Canada's Baseball Hall of Fame at St. Mary's, Ontario, in the summer of 1998.

The start of World War II altered the baseball landscape, weakening the organized baseball system and diverting many talented players into the service, where they often suited up for military teams. According to Paul Thompson, then a scout for the Chicago Black Hawks of the National Hockey League, the strongest clubs in the country outside of the Toronto Maple Leafs and Montreal Royals in the International League were those in Vancouver and Halifax, where troops congregated before going overseas. In Halifax, for example, Major Leaguers Dick Fowler, Joe Krakauskas, and Phil Marchildon, as well as a number of players from Triple-A baseball such as NHL star Bob Dill, played for their respective service clubs in the Halifax Defense League. Marchildon had played three years for Connie Mack's Philadelphia A's, winning 17 games in 1942, before joining the Royal Canadian Air Force. Shot down on a bombing run, Marchildon finished out the war in a German prisoner-of-war camp, but made it back to the Majors and along with Dick Fowler became a mainstay of the A's pitching staff. Fowler remains the only Canadian pitcher to throw a no-hitter in the Major Leagues. Playing for the lowly A's, who finished last in the American League three times between 1945 and 1950, Marchildon and Fowler combined to win an impressive 104 games against 91 losses over that five-year stretch.

The years immediately following the war were a period of significant adjustment for baseball across North America. The pent-up demand for entertainment that accompanied the war stimulated baseball's development at all levels, ranging from community and youth baseball to the Minor League system and the Major Leagues. Finding themselves with a surfeit of players, big-league clubs were faced with the enormous challenge of evaluating players in their organizations who had been on their way up through the Minor Leagues before the war and comparing them with the younger players they had signed in the interim. The result was the expansion of the Minors from twenty-three leagues in 1946 to forty-two the following year and fifty-nine by 1949. New circuits such as the Border League, the Can-Am League, the Northwest League, the Western International League, and the Quebec Provincial League located franchises in midlevel Canadian cities such as Kingston, Sherbrooke, Trois-Rivières, Quebec City, and Victoria. Toronto and Montreal remained fixtures in the International League. After a stint in the Western International League, Vancouver joined the Pacific Coast League. The Quebec Provincial League operated between 1950 and 1957 as a Class C league. Earlier it was an independent league and reverted to independent status once again in 1958.

The oversupply of baseball talent after the war kept player salary levels low—even at the Major League level—and provided an incentive for independent leagues to challenge the organized baseball system. The most celebrated of the postwar "outlaw" leagues was Jorge Pasquel's Mexican League, which offered lucrative contracts and lured a number of frontline Major Leaguers south of the border. Among those who jumped their existing contracts were Sal Maglie, Adrián Zabala, Alex Carrasquel, Max Lanier, Freddie Martin, and Danny Gardella.[8] Curiously, the Mexican League experiment had a significant impact upon the postwar baseball scene in Canada, owing in part to the influence of Brooklyn Dodgers pitcher and Quebec native Jean-Pierre Roy. After winning 25 games for the Montreal Royals in 1945, and having been called up to the Dodgers late in the season, Roy was unhappy with the contract offered to him the following year. He thus joined a number of players from the Dodgers organization, among them catcher Mickey Owen, Roland Gladu from the Brooklyn squad, and pitcher "Bucky" Tanner and Canadians Roger and Stan Breard off the Montreal Royals roster, who decided to play in Mexico. All were banned from organized baseball as a result. After the collapse of Pasquel's Mexican League experiment, Sal Maglie, Freddie Martin, Danny Gardella, and the others made their way to independent leagues in Canada. Most played in Roy's Quebec Provincial League, which was now considered an outlaw circuit. Mickey Owen played in Ontario's Intercounty League, and Bucky Tanner made his way to the Maritimes to play in the Halifax and District League, where he caught the attention of fans by regularly wearing a Mexican sombrero to the ballpark.

The province of Quebec also played a crucial role in "baseball's great experiment," the dropping of the color barrier in organized baseball. In 1945 the Brooklyn Dodgers signed Jackie Robinson to a contract with the Montreal Royals of the International League. The following year the Dodgers signed four more African American ballplayers. The Dodgers considered Montreal an ideal location for Robinson to break in, assuming that in Canada he would escape the racial taunting that would likely take place elsewhere. Of the other Dodgers signees, pitchers Johnny Wright and Roy Partlow spent the 1946 season at

Trois-Rivières in the Class C Canadian-American League, while Roy Campanella and Don Newcombe played for Nashua in the New England League. That same year Fredericton, New Brunswick, infielder Vincent "Manny" McIntyre signed with Sherbrooke, Quebec, of the Class C Border League. Sometime later, McIntyre was asked to suit up as Orestes "Minnie" Miñoso's replacement with the Negro League Cuban Giants, but there is no firm evidence of his having done so.

Robinson took the city of Montreal and the International League by storm, leading the 1946 Royals to the pennant, batting .349, and stealing forty bases. Montrealers and Canadians elsewhere embraced Robinson as their hero. When the Royals defeated the Louisville Colonels of the American Association to win the Little World Series, Robinson was mobbed and chased by adoring Montreal fans. According to one newspaperman, this "may have been the first time in history that a white crowd chased a black man with loving, not lynching on its mind."[9] The following year Robinson became the first black ballplayer of the modern era to play in the Major Leagues. "Jackie has been one of the greatest ambassadors of goodwill," wrote African Canadian journalist Cal Best. "He has proven to all concerned that a member of the race can conduct himself with all the decorum and dignity that is necessary in the face of the greatest obstacles."[10]

During the 1950s and early 1960s Canadian baseball became more closely intertwined with the game in the United States than it had ever been. The lifting of the suspensions of Mexican League jumpers in 1950 not only meant the return of Maglie, Martin, Gardella, and others to the Major Leagues, but also paved the way for the eventual return of the Quebec Provincial League to the organized baseball fold. The QPL operated as a Class C League from 1950 until 1957 and after that as an independent league until 1971. At the same time independent leagues in the Maritimes, Ontario, and the West provided fans with high-level competition. The cross-border Man-Dak League of the 1940s and 1950s drew heavily on players from the old American Negro Leagues, while others relied largely on collegiate players and seasoned semipro players from the United States. These leagues also provided a context in which Canadian players such as Ted Bowsfield, Vern Handrahan, Ken Mackenzie, Claude Raymond, Reno Bertoia, Glen Gorbous, Frank Colman, and others prepped themselves for future big-league careers. The most accomplished Canadian player of that era was Ferguson Jenkins of Chatham, Ontario, who went on to win 284 games in the Majors from 1965 to 1983. A National League Cy Young Award winner in 1971, Jenkins was the first Canadian to be inducted into the National Baseball Hall of Fame in Cooperstown, New York.

The face of Canadian baseball changed dramatically at the end of the 1960s when a Major League franchise was awarded to Montreal. Playing in matchbox-size Jarry Park, the Expos were an instant hit, and players such as Quebec native Claude Raymond, red-haired Rusty Staub—*le grande orange*, as he was affectionately known—and infielder Ron Hunt became heroes overnight. A decade later the Expos moved from Jarry Park to Olympic Stadium. In this cavernous structure, with less than ideal sight lines for baseball, the Expos experienced a period of stability and success on the field, led by catcher Gary Carter, outfielder Andre "the Hawk" Dawson, and pitcher Steve Rogers. In the midst of the 1994 season, with the Expos sporting the best record in Major League Baseball, a work stoppage brought the season to a halt. Thereafter, the club began to sell off or otherwise let go of its young star players, including Canadian native Larry Walker, who in 1997 became the first Canadian to win a Major League Most Valuable Player Award, and fans began to stay away from the increasingly decrepit, domed Olympic Stadium.[11] At the end of the 2004 season, Major League Baseball owners approved the relocation of the Expos to Washington DC. But support for Major League Baseball in Montreal has endured and grown in recent years, largely in response to former Expo Warren Cromartie, who established the Montreal Baseball Project to facilitate its return to the city. Two spring-training exhibition games in 2014 between the Toronto Blue Jays and New York Mets attracted capacity crowds of more than fifty-five thousand spectators. These were followed in 2015 and 2016 with two-game series in Montreal involving the Cincinnati Reds and Boston Red Sox.

When the Expos franchise was awarded to Montreal in 1969, Canada was experiencing the flush of nationalism that surrounded the centennial celebrations and Expo 67. In addition, the Liberal government of Pierre Trudeau was committed to building a national sporting edifice that would encourage nationwide competition for athletes in various sports, including baseball. In 1964 the federal government incorporated the Canadian Federation of Amateur Baseball, now known as Baseball Canada, and under its auspices national competitions at all levels were established. Made up of ten provincial associations, Baseball Canada now represents more than five hundred thousand players, sixty thousand coaches, and eleven thousand umpires. The national team program, which includes both men's and women's divisions, has flourished under Baseball Canada's leadership. Since the inauguration of the IBAF Women's World Cup in 2004, Canada has won a silver and three bronze medals. On the men's side a number of regional baseball academies and coaching clinics help prepare young players and coaches for high-level international competition. In 1991 the Canadian eighteen-and-under youth team, led by future Major Leaguers Stubby Clapp and Jason Dickson, won the country's first baseball gold medal at the World Youth Championship, held in Brandon, Manitoba. Clapp also starred for the Canadian club in the 1999 Pan-American Games, where Canada won six of its seven games, including a 7–6 victory over the United States on the way to the bronze medal. Clapp's eleventh-inning single with the bases loaded led the Canadians past the Americans. Canada's success at the international level has continued over the past decade. At the U18 Baseball World Cup, Canada won silver in 2001 and bronze in 2006. In addition, the senior national team—made up of players not on Major League forty-man rosters—finished third in 2009 and 2011 at the World Cup and defeated the United States 2–1 on its way to the Pan-Am Games gold medal in 2011 behind the dominant pitching of Andrew Albers. At the 2015 Pan-Am Games the Canadian

6. Canadian fans cheer as Canada plays Italy at the 2009 World Baseball Classic in Toronto. (Photo courtesy of Wikimedia Commons.)

squad repeated as gold-medal winners, once again knocking off the Americans in the final game.

For most Canadians the World Baseball Classic provides the most important measure of the country's ability to compete on the international diamond. Led by national team manager Ernie Whitt, Canada has participated in all three WBC competitions, compiling an overall record of three wins and five losses. In the inaugural event in 2006, the Canadians won two of three games, including an impressive 8–6 victory over a star-studded U.S. team led by Derek Jeter, Chase Utley, and Jason Varitek. Outfielder Adam Stern led the Canadian attack in that game, going three-for-four with an inside-the-park home run, while starting pitcher Adam Loewen silenced American bats over five solid innings. Canada, the United States, and Mexico all finished the first round with 2-1 records, but the Canadians were eliminated on a run-differential calculation and failed to advance to the next round of competition.

After its ninth-place finish in 2006, the Canadian team dropped to thirteenth place in 2009, losing its only two games, a 6–5 squeaker to the United States and a 6–2 loss to Italy. In 2013 Canada fared a little better. Following a loss to nemesis Italy in its opening match, Canada scored a lopsided 10–3 win over Mexico in a game marred by a bench-clearing brawl. This set up a crucial game against the United States to determine which team would advance to the next round. Over the first seven innings it was anybody's game, but the United States scored five runs late in the contest on the way to a 9–4 victory. By finishing in twelfth place overall, the Canadians qualified for the upcoming 2017 tournament.

The final chapter in the story of Canadian baseball in the modern era involves the Toronto Blue Jays. Toronto was awarded its Major League franchise in 1976 and, under the effective management and player-development tandem of Paul Beeston and Pat Gillick, gradually built a contending team. As they entered the 1990s the Jays had assembled a talented squad led by Joe Carter, Robbie Alomar, Dave Winfield, Dave Stieb, Jimmy Key, Pat Borders, and Tony Fernández. In 1992 and 1993, field manager Cito Gaston led the club to back-to-back World Series championships. Over the next decade, however, escalating costs and a weak Canadian dollar contributed to changes in ownership and made it difficult for the Jays to compete against wealthier organizations in the free-agent market. In September 2000 Rogers Communications took ownership of the club, subsequently purchasing the "Skydome" and renaming it "Rogers Centre" in 2005. Although the Jays have had a number of front-rank players since then, among them Roy Halladay, José Bautista, and Edwin Encarnación, they have struggled on the field and failed to qualify for postseason play—until 2015. Toronto's youthful general manager Alex Anthopoulos threw caution to the wind, however, acquiring Josh Donaldson, Russell Martin, Troy Tulowitzki, and David Price, who led them to a spot in the American League Championship Series against the Kansas

City Royals. Price and Anthopoulos have since left the Jays, but the 2016 team is in a tight battle with Boston and Baltimore for a playoff spot.

The future of baseball in Canada seems bright, regardless of what happens to the Jays. Major League teams are drafting more and more Canadian players, and a solid nucleus of Canadians playing in the Minor Leagues suggests that the numbers of Canadians in the big leagues will continue to grow. At the intercollegiate level more than eight hundred Canadians are on the rosters of college and university teams in the United States. This is almost twice the number of those playing hockey south of the border. Canadian university baseball programs are becoming more sophisticated as well. The University of British Columbia Thunderbirds, for example, has had a dozen players selected in MLB drafts in recent years. Both Adam Loewen and Jeff Francis of the Thunderbirds were first-round picks and went on to play in the Major Leagues. Two Canadians were chosen in the first round in the 2015 draft: Josh Naylor was selected twelfth overall by the Miami Marlins and Mike Soroka twenty-eighth overall by the Atlanta Braves. In 2016 Cal Quantrill, son of former Blue Jay Paul Quantrill from Port Hope, Ontario, was selected eighth overall by the San Diego Padres.

Canadians have passionately embraced baseball as a primary summer sporting activity over the years, and its players are as competitive today as they have ever been. In part this reflects the ever-present influence of the United States on the development of Canadian sporting culture. But this is by no means the whole story. Canadian baseball was also a product of local circumstances and conditions, growing side by side with the American game over the years, although never separate from it. There is no doubt that this will be the case in the future as the game continues to grow.

NOTES

1. See Nancy B. Bouchier and Robert K. Barney, "A Critical Examination of a Source on Early Ontario Baseball: The Reminiscences of Adam E. Ford,"

Journal of Sport History 15 (Spring 1998): 75–90; Stephen Jay Gould, *Triumph and Tragedy in Mudville: A Lifelong Passion for Baseball* (New York: W. W. Norton, 2003).

2. *New York Clipper*, June 1864, quoted in William Humber, *Cheering for the Home Team: The Story of Baseball in Canada* (Erin, Ontario: Boston Mills Press, 1983), 29. See also Colin Howell, *Northern Sandlots: A Social History of Maritime Baseball* (Toronto: University of Toronto Press, 1995).

3. Quoted in Stephen J. Gamester, "You Can't Tell the Canadian Big-League Heroes without a Program," *MacLean's*, August 22, 1964, 19–22.

4. William Humber, *Diamonds of the North: A Concise History of Baseball in Canada* (Toronto: Oxford University Press, 1995), 83.

5. *Varsity* (University of Toronto), November 14, 1885, 44–45.

6. Robin John Anderson, "'On the Edge of the Baseball Map' with the 1908 Vancouver Beavers," *Canadian Historical Review* 77 (December 1996): 573–74.

7. Tom Dunkel, *Color Blind: The Forgotten Team That Broke Baseball's Color Line* (New York: Atlantic Monthly Press, 2013).

8. John Virtue, *South of the Color Barrier: How Jorge Pasquel and the Mexican League Pushed Baseball toward Racial Integration* (Jefferson NC: McFarland, 2008).

9. Sam Maltin, *Pittsburgh Courier*, October 12, 1946.

10. Cal Best, *Clarion*, November 1, 1947.

11. Walker signed with the Colorado Rockies in 1995 and won the National League's Most Valuable Player Award in 1997. He was the first of three Canadians to win MVP honors, followed by Justin Morneau of the Minnesota Twins in 2006 and Joey Votto of the Cincinnati Reds in 2010.

5

Mexico

Baseball's Humble Beginnings to Budding Competitor

Jorge Iber

Since the creation of the World Baseball Classic, Major League Baseball (MLB) has worked to establish the event as the sport's version of soccer's World Cup and to spread the game more effectively worldwide. While the WBC has a long way to go before coming close to soccer's global fete, it has achieved a modicum of success with more than 2.3 million paid attendees. The slate of the tournament's finalists and semifinalists reads like a list of the "usual suspects" of baseball powerhouses, with Japan, Cuba, South Korea, the Dominican Republic, Puerto Rico, and the United States being the most prominent teams. One nation that has not performed well but has nonetheless made its mark in recent international competitions is Mexico. Although it has a long and impressive baseball pedigree, the tricolor's best WBC showing so far was a disappointing sixth-place finish in 2006.[1]

In the latest versions of the Caribbean Series, Mexico has shined, with Mexican Pacific League teams Yaquis de Obregón and the Naranjeros de Hermosillo claiming titles in 2013 and 2014. These teams join Culiacan, Mexicali, and Mazatlán as squads that have triumphed over competitors from the Dominican Republic, Venezuela, and Puerto Rico. Overall, Mexican sides have now earned eight Caribbean Series championships. Although baseball is certainly not Mexico's national game—soccer is—its recent success has renewed hope (and interest) that Mexican nines will be competitive in future WBCs. After the Naranjeros' 7–1 victory over Mayaguez, analyst Enrique Rojas noted, "Mexico deserves and should be considered one of the most powerful countries in Latin baseball." Jesse Sanchez of MLB.com echoed these sentiments, noting that the turnaround in the quality is legitimate and that the WBC will have to reckon with revitalized teams in the future. As Hermosillo manager Matais Carrillo noted, "Soccer is the favorite sport in Mexico, but baseball is making progress. There's a movement going on. We are demonstrating that we are no longer the ugly ducklings of the Caribbean Series anymore."[2] Since 1999 the Mexicans have had a winning record in the Caribbean Series (18-17, after struggling with a 61-114 record dating back to 1971). The transition from also-ran to competitor on the world baseball scene can be understood only by examining the game's turbulent past and current issues in Mexico.

It is challenging to document baseball's origins in Mexico. Historian Peter C. Bjarkman writes, "It is difficult, if not almost impossible to pin down . . . the dates and places of the earliest games played on Mexican soil."[3] Bjarkman's research and that of Gilbert Joseph, Pedro Treto Cisneros, and William Beezley provide records of competition on the diamond in the late nineteenth century in several locales, including Guaymas, Oaxaca, Nuevo León, and the Yucatán. The sport's earliest proponents came from the United States (military personnel and individuals associated with corporations) and exiled Cubans.[4] In addition, as agriculture and industry along the border region of the United States developed in the late nineteenth and early twentieth centuries, Mexican and Mexican American laborers north and south of the Rio Grande were exposed to the game. In his seminal work *Baseball on the Border: A Tale of Two Laredos* (1997), anthropologist Alan Klein argues, "If baseball was practiced in the Laredo area in the early 1880s, it is reasonable to assume that it was played in Nuevo Laredo as well."[5]

Two significant players of this early era were Mexico natives Vincent Nava and Leonardo "Najo" Alanis. Nava was raised in San Francisco and reached the pinnacle of his baseball career by the early 1880s with the National League's Providence Grays. Alanis was raised in Mission, Texas, and played on both sides of the border from the late 1910s through the 1930s and continued to have a significant role as a manager and promoter in transnational baseball until the 1950s.[6] Recent studies by Richard Santillan, José Alamillo, and Jorge Iber have documented the significance of baseball to the denizens of U.S. barrios in California and throughout the Midwest. Quite often, the barrio squads played teams from south of the border. In sum, there is evidence that baseball was an important aspect of daily life to individuals of Mexican descent on both sides of the Rio Grande by the early decades of the 1900s.[7]

While the sport's origins in the "old country" are uncertain, baseball's influence on the development of Mexican nationalism is much clearer. The late historian Joseph Arbena noted that once Mexico embraced Western sports as a sign of modernity during the *Porfiriato* era, success in international competition became an important component of social and governmental efforts. This applied to various athletic endeavors for postrevolutionary administrations and embraced the notion that "sport, with its implicit competitive nature," was "valuable to the mental and physical well-being of the individual in modern society." If Mexico was to "prove itself" worthy among the family of nations, it had to be competitive in such endeavors. What better way to demonstrate this than by playing, and hopefully beating, the Americans at their own "national pastime"? It is evident that part of businessman and baseball *empresario* Jorge Pasquel's efforts in the 1940s was rooted in challenging the notion that Mexico could not have a "major league" such as existed in the United States. Pasquel's plans did not succeed, yet they had many ripple effects.[8]

The game endured in fits and starts through the early twentieth century, especially during the Mexican Revolution (1910–20). By the mid-1920s there was serious interest in establishing a professional league in Mexico. The men responsible for this effort were sportswriter Alejandro Aguilar Reyes, known by the pseudonym of "Fray Nano," and promoter Ernesto Carmona. The initial game was played in the capital city on the last Sunday of June 1925. The league had five teams: Agraria, El Nacional de Bixler, a team simply called "Mexico," Guanajuato, and the 74th Regiment.

Major issues were evident by the end of the initial season. First, there were financial losses, causing some clubs to relocate and some to go bankrupt. Second, there was a substantial influx of talent from outside of Mexico, especially from Cuba.[9] Otherwise, relatively little is known about this earliest period of the league. As Treto Cisneros argues, the "Mexico of 1925, stained with the blood of the Revolution, was a long way from the present day. . . . Even the most exhaustive research produces almost nothing in the way of results."[10]

By 1936 the league was more stable and records more reliable, but the main problem continued to be the development of national talent. The paucity of Mexican stars meant that Cubans (such as Martín Dihigo) and Negro Leaguers (such as Satchel Paige, James "Cool Papa" Bell, and Josh Gibson) played important roles in the Mexican profession-al game.[11] During the 1940s, however, a new personage, millionaire aficionado Jorge Pasquel, attempted to elevate Mexican professional baseball to a new level and hoped that it would no longer be considered a "minor" league. Pasquel's endeavors generated mixed results, inside and outside Mexico.

Pasquel played an important role in the development of Mexican professional baseball (that is, the Mexican League) during the 1940s and early 1950s. In 1940 the entrepreneur sought to join the league by placing a team in his hometown of Veracruz. Disagreements among the league owners led to a schism, resulting in Mexico having two profes-sional leagues, the Mexican League and the newly founded Mexican National League (which lasted just a brief time in 1946).[12] Ultimately, through the sheer force of his personality and deep pockets, Pasquel be-came the leader of Mexican professional baseball. To improve not only his Veracruz Azules but the entire league, he aggressively pursued Cu-ban and Negro League players and thereby helped forge what has been called one of "the most important racially integrated leagues in baseball" before 1950.[13] Having accomplished this goal, his next target would be to use his vast fortune to bring Major League talent to his homeland.

Pasquel wanted to lure players to Mexico for two reasons. First, there was the nationalistic notion that Mexico was capable of supporting the highest level of professional baseball, just like the *Americanos*. Mexican newspapers gleefully noted that the 1946 raids on MLB teams came at the one hundredth anniversary of the start of the Mexican-American War.[14] Unfortunately, the assumption of widespread financial support was not realistic, and by 1951 Pasquel, tired of losing money, was out of baseball. Second, it was his way of tweaking the noses of MLB owners, who lorded over their players and paid them much less than what they could have earned in a truly free market. Suddenly, MLB owners, who often derided baseball in Mexico as "ramshackle," "ragtag," and "outlaw," had to deal with someone who had deeper pockets than most MLB owners. While Pasquel's raid on Major League players did not break the infamous reserve clause or overcome the *yanqui* owners, his endeavors set in motion trends that would eventually help open the door to African Americans and Latinos and to free agency in the United States.

Professional baseball's reign as the "national sport" of Mexico was brief, for as television expanded its reach, soccer soon surpassed in popularity the slower-paced game on the diamond. And since *fútbol* "did not require the expensive equipment needed by baseball," writes John Virtue in *South of the Color Barrier*, it "became the game of the masses."[15] Although Pasquel was no longer directly involved with the league, his death in 1955 and the leadership gap created in his absence led to a decline in the Mexican League's fortunes. Its problems were so acute that the association nearly died.[16] Baseball was not completely moribund, however, as several winter circuits commenced during the 1940s. First, the Liga Costa del Pacífico operated between 1945 and 1957. It was renamed the Liga Invernal de Sonora, until 1970, at which point the association took its current name, the Liga Mexicana del Pacífico. The league's champion competes in the Caribbean Series.

Just as circumstances looked their bleakest for the senior circuit, a revival took place during the late 1950s due to the success of the 1957 Monterrey team that won the Little League World Series behind the pitching of Angel Macias. According to Jesse Sanchez, Macias and some of his teammates not only provided a boost to national pride, but a decade later, as adults, also assumed leadership positions in the Mexican League and promoted the development of the Mexican League Baseball Academy, which recruited and honed the skills of Mexican-born players on the diamond and in the classroom. Another member of the Monterrey Little League champs, José "Pepe" Maiz, became owner of the Monterrey Sultanes and is now enshrined in the Mexican Baseball Hall of Fame. The infusion of new ownership into the Mexican League, plus revived interest due to the success of the "Little Giants," led to a period of stability and growth. By 1979 the association fielded twenty teams. During this era several Mexicanos made it to the Major Leagues, including Aurelio Rodríguez, Jorge Orta, and Francisco Barrios.[17]

Another significant booster of Mexican baseball pride materialized during the 1960s with the flourishing career of slugger Héctor Espino. Called the "Babe Ruth of Mexico," Espino clubbed somewhere between 755 and 796 round-trippers during his professional career (1960–84). (A legacy of the league's earlier years, record keeping was inconsistent; thus, it is not possible to know with certainty the number of home runs he hit.) Espino was under contract with the St. Louis Cardinals in 1964 and played thirty-two games for its AAA team in Jacksonville before returning to Mexico. It is unclear why he never made it to the Major Leagues. Some argued that Espino was not comfortable playing and living in the United States, while others believed that he simply could make more money in Mexico as well as basking in the adulation of his countrymen. Journalist Eric Nusbaum writes that Espino found "nothing unfortunate at all about staying in Mexico. He embraced the baseball of his nation, and in doing so rejected the notion that Mexico was some kind of little brother. . . . His reward . . . was a kind of heroism, a unique status of immeasurable respect and deep reverence that eludes all but a very few."[18]

Through the 1960s and 1970s the Mexican League did fairly well, though circumstances for players were never particularly good. Historian David G. LaFrance contends, "Owners viewed players more as expendable entertainers than workers. They felt little obligation to treat players according to labor codes and had no intention to allow them to organize."[19] The players had sought representation as early as the 1940s and had demanded better travel and hotel conditions on the road, a retirement fund, and a percentage of their selling price when they were traded or when their contracts were sold.[20] By 1980 the hard feelings generated over management's failure to address these issues came to a head in Veracruz in an incident where several Puebla players were arrested and beaten by police on the instigation of Veracruz team officials as a result of an on-field dispute with an umpire.

As a result of these matters, and led by Puebla athlete Alfonso "Houston" Jimenez, the players sought legal assistance to start a labor organization, called the Asociacion Nacional de Beisbolistas (ANABE). The owners reacted by threatening to dismiss or trade "troublemakers." This prompted a work stoppage. Ultimately, the government of President José López Portillo backed the owners. The players and the ANABE, in due course, refused to play in the 1981 Caribbean Series and then established their own league, the Nacional. The new circuit lasted five years. It folded in 1986 over resistance from the Mexican League team owners, the devaluation of the peso, and dramatically lower oil prices, all of which made the league unsustainable. Although unsuccessful, the ANABE has a lasting legacy. In 1989 Mexican League team owners finally established a pension plan for their players and decided to limit the number of foreign-born players.[21]

The Mexican League and the Liga Mexicana del Pacífico have been fairly stable since the late 1980s. The older association now has sixteen teams, and the winter league has eight. Further, all Mexican League teams contribute to fund the academy previously noted in order to teach the sport, as well as provide continuing education for a new generation of baseball-playing Mexican youths.[22] Hopefully, with time, the new academy system will develop more such athletes. Although baseball is still not Mexico's "national sport," it has become more competitive in international competition and more popular. It has a promising future as a homegrown game.[23]

NOTES

1. Peter C. Bjarkman, "Mexico: Traditions of Outlaw Baseball," in *Diamonds around the Globe: The Encyclopedia of International Baseball* (Westport CT: Greenwood Press, 2005), 266.

2. Enrique Rojas, "Confirmed: Mexico's Baseball Power," http://espn deportes.espn.g.o.com/blogs/index?entryid=2018681&name=enrique _rojas&cc=3888; Carrillo quoted in Jesse Sanchez, "Mexico's Caribbean Turnaround No Joking Matter," http://mlb.mlb.com/news/print.jsp?ymd =20140205&content_id=67487002&key=news_mlb&c_id=mlb.

3. Bjarkman, "Mexico," 267.

4. Bjarkman, "Mexico," 267–68. See also William Beezley, "The Rise of Baseball in Mexico and the First Valenzuela," *Studies in Latin American Popular Culture* 4 (1985): 3–23; Gilbert Joseph, "Documenting a Regional Pastime: Baseball in the Yucatán," in *Windows on Latin America: Understanding Society through Photographs,* edited by Robert M. Levine (Miami: University of Miami Press, 1987), 77–89; and Pedro Treto Cisneros, *The Mexican League: Comprehensive Player Statistics, 1937–2001* (Jefferson NC: McFarland, 2002), 9.

5. Quoted in Jorge Iber et al., *Latinos in U.S. Sport: A History of Isolation, Cultural Identity, and Acceptance* (Champaign IL: Human Kinetics, 2011), 84–85.

6. Iber et al., *Latinos in U.S. Sport,* 84–85. See also Noe Torres, *Baseball's First Mexican American Star: The Amazing Story of Leo Najo* (Coral Springs FL: Llumina Press, 2006).

7. Francisco E. Balderrama et al., *Mexican American Baseball in Los Angeles* (Charleston SC: Arcadia, 2011); José M. Alamillo, *Making Lemonade Out of Lemons: Mexican American Labor and Leisure in a California Town, 1880–1960* (Urbana: University of Illinois Press, 2006); Jorge Iber, "The Early

Life and Career of Topeka's Mike Torrez, 1946–1978: Sport as a Means for Studying Latino/a Life in Kansas," *Kansas History: A Journal of the Central Plains* 3 (Autumn 2014): 164–79.

8. Joseph L. Arbena, "Sport, Development, and Mexican Nationalism, 1920–1970," *Journal of Sport History* 18 (Winter 1991): 358. For a further discussion of Pasquel, baseball, and Mexican nationalism, see John Virtue, *South of the Color Barrier: How Jorge Pasquel and the Mexican League Pushed Baseball toward Racial Integration* (Jefferson NC: McFarland, 2008).

9. Many Mexicans were more than happy to support teams with Cubans and African Americans. The issue of the movement of teams deals more with the economic and socially disruptive aftermath of the revolution.

10. Treto Cisneros, *Mexican League*, 9.

11. Treto Cisneros, *Mexican League*, 9–12.

12. Virtue, *South of the Color Barrier*, 133.

13. Virtue, *South of the Color Barrier*, 74. The chapter titled "Pasquel Forms Team, Wins Title" in Virtue's book is an excellent overview of the schism in Mexican professional baseball and the move toward attracting Major Leaguers south of the Rio Grande. Also see Conor Nichols, "Pasquel Was a Force for Integration," http://mlb.mlb.com/news/article.jsp?ymd=20071114&content_id=2300489&c_id=mlb.

14. See also Marty Appel, "The Mexican League Raids," http://www.thenationalpastimemuseum.com/article/Mexican-league-raids-2.

15. Virtue, *South of the Color Barrier*, 199.

16. Treto Cisneros, *Mexican League*, 3.

17. Jesse Sanchez, "History of Baseball in Mexico," January 7, 2004, http://mlb.mlb.com/news/article.jsp?ymd=20040107&content_id=626058&vkey=news_mlb&fext=.jsp&c_id=null. See also Treto Cisneros, *Mexican League*, 3.

18. Eric Nusbaum, "The Unknown Slugger," May 21, 2013, http://www.sbnation.com/longform/2013/5/21/4348250/hector-espino-mexico-baseball-home-run-king-profile#3965459.

19. David G. LaFrance, "Labor, the State, and Professional Baseball in Mexico in the 1980s," *Journal of Sport History* 22 (Summer 1995): 113.

20. LaFrance, "Labor, the State, and Professional Baseball," 113–14.

21. LaFrance, "Labor, the State, and Professional Baseball," 113–14.

22. Jesse Sanchez, "Academy Schools Future Stars," January 7, 2004, http://mlb
    .mlb.com/news/article.jsp?ymd=20040107&content_id=626007&vkey
    =news_mlb&fext+.jsp&c_id+null.
23. Mark Saxon, "Adrian Gonzalez Helps L.A. Reconnect," March 6, 2013,
    http://espn.go.com/espn/print?id=9024724&type=story.

6

Nicaragua

In Search of Diamonds

Dan Gordon

As goes *el Presidente*, so goes *el Deporte Rey* ("the King of Sports"). I realized this in 2003, early into my second trip to Nicaragua. Riding into Managua behind a silent cabdriver who tailgated with inches to spare, I was shocked by the sheer number of children and families in tattered clothes along Carretera Norte selling cell phone covers, car mats, and other paraphernalia and by the increased congestion in a city that scarcely had cars in 1988, when I was first here. The driver was taking me to Barrio Jonathan González, where, as a Thomas J. Watson Fellow, I had hung out with the barrio baseball team and become friends with pitcher and manager Efraín Rosales.

As the cab neared the barrio, I recognized nothing. The road was lined with new strip malls and convenience store gas stations and a soon-to-open warehouse supermarket. The barrio itself seemed disheveled and forlorn. Although Nicaragua had slipped below Haiti to become the poorest country in the Western Hemisphere—reeling from hurricanes, famine in the countryside, and rampant political corruption—I had naïvely hoped that the absence of war would have improved things.[1]

But for all its harsh conditions, the barrio that I'd known then had been graced with *malinche* trees that bloomed reddish orange and provided shade. Farmland and open fields once bordered it, and many residents owned chickens and pigs. Now the *malinche* trees and livestock were gone, and the neighborhood was hemmed in by development—a forgotten ghetto. In poll numbers cited that week in *La Prensa* and *El Nuevo Diario*, I discovered the extent of the poverty: 46 percent of Nicaraguans (known colloquially as *Pinoleros*) were underemployed or unemployed; 46 percent lived in a state of poverty, surviving on less than a dollar per day; 40 percent resided in homes without plumbing; and 30 percent were without electricity.[2]

Unable to find the address I had given him, the driver doubled back on a parallel dirt street and passed young men who were playing soccer. This struck me as odd, because during nearly three months in 1988 I had never seen soccer being played in the barrio or elsewhere in the country. Instead, the streets had teemed with stickball played with a doll's head, rolled-up masking tape, socks, or small plastic jugs for balls.

I exited the cab at the barrio entrance and approached a young woman seated at the edge of the road, who dispatched her daughter to find Efraín. From the distance I saw the girl walking back with a man. I approached him slowly, still not convinced it was him. "Efraín Rosales?" I said. He nodded, looking me over unsurely. "Do you remember me? I'm Dan Gordon." Recognition dawned on Efraín's face. He shook my hand enthusiastically and embraced me, then invited me into his hut.

The only frills in Efraín's cramped abode were a toaster, tiny black-and-white television, and transistor radio, all sitting together on a workbench. I'd come bearing presents—a Red Sox yearbook, baseball cards, a ball signed by Luis Tiant—figuring we would pick up where we had left off in our discussions on baseball, which we'd talked about continually on my previous visit. Efraín received the gifts politely. He then said that Nicaraguan baseball had fallen in popularity in recent years and that he had lost interest. Efraín had remained captain of the neighborhood team for six years, but in 1994 the team had folded when the barrio's rustic diamond was paved over with highway. Ironically, city officials christened the road Pista Dennis Martínez, after one of the first *Pinoleros* to reach the Major Leagues and the Latin American pitcher with the most career wins. After that Efraín no longer played or watched baseball. "I followed our national team for a while, and they always lost," he said. "So I said, 'Enough with that!' It didn't make me happy, so I left it."

King of Sports

Efraín's disavowal of a sport he had once loved—one that had pre-occupied and sustained him through poverty and war—reflected a larger trend in Nicaragua. Although Nicaragua's national pastime was as popular as ever in some regions, and young ballplayers from those areas were signing with Major League organizations, in Managua and many other parts of the country baseball seemed to have lost its meaning. Baseball's decline coincided with the demise of publicly funded amateur baseball in the 1980s.

After the leftist Sandinista National Liberation Front overthrew Anastasio Somoza Debayle in 1979, organized baseball was remolded using the Cuban model. The FSLN eliminated scholastic sports and set up tiers of leagues ranging from children's leagues to top amateur winter ball. "It was the most successful, most structured baseball that there has ever been in Nicaragua," said Tito Rondón, a former Nicaraguan winter-league broadcaster and retired managing editor of *La Prensa*. "The quality of play was terrible, but the crowds came anyway. Attendance has not matched those levels since."[3]

In 1991 *Pinoleros*, worn out by war with the unrelenting U.S.-funded Contras, a U.S. trade blockade, skyrocketing inflation, and political censorship, voted President Daniel Ortega and the FSLN out of power, ushering in a return to capitalism. Private investment poured into the cities, creating a vast array of entertainment possibilities, such as refurbished movie theaters, nightclubs, shopping malls, and all kinds of sports. Over the next two decades, funding for baseball diminished, ballplayers' salaries dropped, and baseball languished. Attendance reached all-time lows, and increasing numbers of young people were turning to soccer, basketball, and other sports.

More than a decade later baseball attendance has rebounded due to investment by President Ortega, who returned to power in 2007. Rural teams are receiving financial help to travel to tournaments. The government is investing in stadium infrastructure. And leagues at all levels are better organized and better funded.

Nicaraguans refer to baseball as *el Deporte Rey*. "Baseball here is as big as apple pie back in the States," explained Aníbal Vega, a veteran outfielder and manager for the Nicaraguan national team, who was raised in California. "People here are more passionate with their baseball, and they take it more seriously."[4]

As I revisited Nicaraguan ballparks, Vega's description resonated with me. At Yamil Rios Ugarte Stadium in Rivas, the mascot for Gigantes of Rivas, a giant mango in uniform, swings its hips sensually with female cheerleaders, who wear green tights. Fans in the *barra* (coordinated cheering section) wave sugarcane and at any given moment break out in dance. In the Chinandega *barra* at Efraín Tijerino Stadium, trumpets, saxophones, and tubas play *bakanos* and *chinendeganan cumbia*. Fans blow shrill whistles and seem in perpetual motion. San Fernando fans, dressed in ornate Nicaraguan folkloric costumes, lead the crowd at Masaya's Roberto Clemente Stadium in indigenous dancing to marimba music. In the early years San Fernando fans had a tradition of releasing iguanas adorned with *cientas de papel* to bring bad luck to visiting teams. More recently, when Managua's Indios of Bóer visited Roberto Clemente Stadium, San Fernando fans hurled oranges in unison at the opposing team's players—unpeeled when they wished to make a statement.[5] The pelting grew so frequent in 1993 that league officials shut down the stadium for two weeks as punishment. Stone-throwing incidents have also occurred outside the stadium, where large groups of youths from one team target fans of the other. "Fans here love you, but they hate you," said Vega, who in 1992 helped lead San Fernando to its first national championship in fifty years.

"They'll throw stuff on the fields—bottles, mango seeds, big mangos, all kinds of stuff. Sometimes you have to stop the game."[6]

At crumbling Dennis Martínez National Stadium in Managua, a sea of red and white Indios of Bóer fans (*Bóeristas*)—some sporting Native American headdresses, war paint, bows and arrows, and spears with fake blood on the tips—do the tomahawk chop, substituting "Bóer, óer, óer óer, óer," for the soccer chant "Olé, Olé, Olé," closing it out with, "Long live fuckin' Bóer!" Between the chants are war whoops, drumming, the deafening sound of vuvuzelas, and fans abuzz with excitement.

Efraín and I had experienced a more serene atmosphere at a national team exhibition game at the same stadium in 1988. Enticing aromas filled the air at what was then called Rigoberto López Pérez Stadium in honor of the assassin of Anastasio Somoza García, the first of the Somoza dictators. On the ramp leading to the ticket gate, fans leisurely stopped to buy *vigorón*, which is fried pork skin, fermented cabbage relish, and boiled yucca wrapped in washed banana leaves. In the stands vendors, some with baskets on their heads, sold enchiladas, churros, *pastelitos*, fried plantains, mangos, coconuts, chewing gum, chocolate coins, and small plastic bags of Victoria beer (consumed by puncturing a small corner with one's teeth and sucking). The only events that seemed to get a rise out of the crowd were the occasional updates over the sound system of Dennis Martínez's outing that evening with the Montreal Expos and the zany dancing of Keith Taylor, the national team batboy. Taylor sprinted to home plate between innings carrying a miniature wooden coffin. He removed a voodoo doll and threw it on the ground, dancing around it to the delight of fans. Efraín told me that Taylor pretended to hex other teams. He would blow powder at them, spooking opposing players. Taylor was originally a batboy on the Atlantic Coast before he was hired by legendary coach Omar Cisneros to carry bats for the Sandinista Army team Dantos. Minister of defense General Humberto Ortega sent a private airplane to the Atlantic Coast to carry Taylor to Managua.[7]

Because travel between the two coasts is expensive for Nicaragua's professional teams, the Atlantic Coast region rarely fields teams in the winter league. Instead, since 1952 the Atlantic Series, an annual tournament between second-division teams from jungle-enclosed fishing villages along the coast, has been an outlet for baseball-loving *Costeños*. Rather than canceling seasons during the bloody civil war of the 1980s, teams armed themselves with rifles and white flags when they traveled through the war zone to away games.

As part of an evolving fusion of the cultural pastimes of their ancestors—former slaves from the Caribbean, African Americans who resettled in the region, and European and Asian tradesmen—baseball fans in the Atlantic Series have their own unique style. Boisterous, overflowing crowds dance to Caribbean music that mixes Spanish, English, Creole, and Miskito Indian lyrics—shouting "*¡winamba!,*" a Miskito rally cry, to the team they support. The refrain is often heard in music played at the tournament and is emblazoned on shirts of dancing troupes that perform before games.

The Evolution of a Game

In 1888 an American named Albert Adlesberg introduced Atlantic Coast cricket players to baseball. At the time the Miskito Coast was a British protectorate with a strong cricket tradition. Adlesberg, a lumber trader who routinely visited Bluefields, assumed correctly that locals would adapt well to a sport that called on similar throwing and batting abilities. Initially, the locals played barehanded, using balls made from the sap of rubber trees and tree limbs as bats. Then Adlesberg returned from a trip to New Orleans with balls, bats, and gloves. By 1889 the first two clubs, White Rose and Southern, were formed, representing the northern and southern barrios of Bluefields. A league developed, and baseball immediately upstaged cricket as the region's favorite pastime.

Three years after baseball took root along the Caribbean coast, a few dozen Nicaraguan youths from the Pacific Coast cities of Granada and Managua, who were studying in universities in the United States,

7. The Atlantic Coast celebrates its first Germán Pomares
League national championship in 2013. For financial,
logistical, and political reasons, the baseball-loving region had
rarely fielded teams in national tournaments until 2009. Since
then the small jungle-enclosed fishing towns have embraced
their local team with boisterous, overflowing crowds dancing
to Caribbean music that mixes Spanish, English, Creole,
and Miskito Indian lyrics—shouting "*¡winamba!*," a Miskito
rally cry, for the home team. (Photo courtesy of *La Prensa*/
Managua/S. León.)

brought home baseball equipment and formed clubs. Few details are
known of Pacific Coast baseball during this era. The local newspapers
did not regularly carry sports pages until the 1920s, and the teams did
not have scorekeepers. One of the earliest recorded traces of baseball
was a prolonged, fierce campaign in the Managuan newspaper *El Du-
ende* in 1893 to ban baseball. Newspaper editor Juan de Dios Matus
argued that the game was too common in the streets and posed a
threat to pedestrians. Soon after, city officials in Managua and Granada
prohibited street baseball. But when José Santos Zelaya took over the

country in a coup in 1893, one of his first moves to win over the public was to lift the ban.

Around the turn of the century baseball teams sprang up throughout the Pacific Coast region. The vast majority derived their names from international geographical locations or countries at war during the era: Bóer, Japan, Russia, America, Manchester, Waterloo, Chile, Argentina, Paris, New York, and Chicago. In response to the high demand for baseball equipment, a Managua harness maker unstitched a glove one of the ballplayers had imported from the United States, studied its design, and began producing waterproof gloves made from the rubberized seats in horse carriages.

The U.S. occupation of Nicaragua from 1912 to 1933 accelerated the spread of baseball. Twenty-seven hundred U.S. Marines landed in the country to protect U.S. fruit, mining, and transportation interests from a popular uprising and preserve the ruling Conservative government. Taking advantage of the curiosity and enthusiasm of *Pinolero* youth when the troops played baseball among themselves, military leaders set up children's leagues and tournaments in Managua's barrios. Among the Pacific Coast stars of the era were pitcher Julián Amador (nicknamed the "White Ape"), who won twenty-four consecutive games for the famous club San Fernando of Masaya. Far and away the biggest stars from the Atlantic Coast region were the brothers Jorge and Stanley Cayasso. Their barnstorming tour of the Pacific Coast in the early 1930s was part of what Nicaraguan baseball historians identify as the catalyst for modern baseball in Nicaragua. As I sat with ninety-four-year-old Jorge Cayasso, both of us in rocking chairs in his tidy cement home, behind a boxing gym his family had set up, he described the arrival in the West of his team, Navy, from the Atlantic Coast to play the first-ever series of games between the Caribbean Coast and Pacific Coast players. "We are a poor people," noted Jorge, with the widest of grins. "No resources. But I'm going to tell you something. I played catcher, pitcher, third baseman, and whatever position. I just wanted to play."

Navy had set out for the Pacific Coast intending just to see the world. As a gimmick they named themselves after a branch of the military and sported sailor caps. Many of the Navy ballplayers were also jazz musicians—including Jorge, who played banjo and guitar. They played ball during the day against the Pacific Coast teams and jazz at night on the bandstand at the municipal parks. Their music caused a sensation, and Pacific Coast residents took to dancing in the park. Few had experienced their fluid and happy style of music or heard the strumming of a banjo. The Pacific Coast people saw the player-musicians of Navy as exotic. When they walked in the streets with their sailor uniforms and black skin, people followed them. On the playing field they became known for their elegance, athleticism, and speed. When the country formed its first national team for the 1935 Central American Games in El Salvador, many of the former Navy players were selected. Although Nicaragua finished the tournament tied for second place with Panama, Jorge Cayasso tied for first in hitting and finished second in home runs. But the team that became etched in the consciousness of *Pinoleros* was the national squad in 1938—not so much for its performance at the Central American Games in Panama, but for the adventurous four-day journey that brought the team there. The team traveled by train and then continued by ferry. But the ferry caught fire and sank off the north coast of Costa Rica. As a result the squad had to travel by horse through the jungle to San José and finally by train to Panama. Bayardo Cuadra, a noted Nicaraguan baseball historian, felt the journey created a sense of national pride and mythic identification with *Pinolero* ballplayers that still exists. "That was the primitivism of baseball—the efforts of athletes with very little travel money," said Cuadra. "The country identified with their sacrifice to persevere and represent their country."[8]

Pipeline to the Pros

Outside the impoverished sprawl of Managua, in the smaller towns and villages of Nicaragua, where there is more open space for baseball, soccer is just a game and baseball is still the center of the universe.

Whole towns and villages converge on local diamonds, sitting on the outfield wall under tropical leaves or colorful umbrellas, on the roofs of neighboring houses, or casually reclining in the branches of trees. To the north, along Carretera Norte, is a world that, to the naked eye, capitalism seems to have left untouched. One passes majestic volcanoes, jagged hills, mahogany tree farms, sugarcane fields, farms that produce thatch for roofs, people lingering in the yards of their shanty huts in the shade of *malinche* trees that line the road, and villages with hammock shops and roadside stands that sell tortillas with *queso de mantequilla*. In the smaller towns the ballpark fills nightly during summer league, *pelota de calcetín* (stickball with a grapefruit or tightly wound sock) is common, and the locals strongly believe that because most males work with a machete, they have forearm strength, which makes them far better ballplayers.

Dennis Martínez set up an academy to develop this raw talent in May 2004. The academy was born out of an article *el Presidente* read that the majority of *Pinolero* males between the ages of fourteen and twenty-five had dropped out of school. During the tryout session Martínez asked prospects if they attended school. Many told him that they had left school to help their parents survive.[9] He decided at this point that the academy would assist ballplayers in attending school and university and require all enrollees to attend school.[10]

Since then academies have sprung up across the country. Bird dogs have realized that there is more money to be made by signing several players and hedging their bets that Major League Baseball scouts will discover at least one.[11] In 2015 MLB entered the mix with initiatives such as an amateur prospects league, consisting of fifty of the best fifteen- to eighteen-year-old prospects in the country, as determined by scouts. The two-team league plays one game per week, showcasing the players for MLB scouts. To date only one Major League team in Nicaragua has established an academy. In 2000 Calixto Vargas, a national hero, helped set up one for the Houston Astros, under the direction of legendary Latin American scout Andrés Reiner. The club backed out two years later as part of cutbacks in its Latin American scouting operations.[12] Vargas continued on with the Astros as an associate scout and then switched caps and established his own academy, where he groomed players and, when he thought they were ready, invited a scout to watch them play. If they signed, Vargas took 15 percent of the bonus. I had a chance to visit Vargas's academy on the sleepy grounds of Jackie Robinson Stadium. Although I'd never heard of Vargas prior to my first visit to Nicaragua, his name had been brought up so often in baseball history conversations by *Pinoleros* that I felt honored fifteen years later to have the opportunity to interview him. Vargas had starred on the much-celebrated national team that defeated Team Cuba in the 1972 Amateur World Series.

I watched him working with youngsters at all positions, showing shortstops how to field the ball, critiquing the pitchers' pickoff moves, refining the jumps ballplayers take for stolen bases. While youths were running laps under the intense midafternoon sun, Vargas sat down in the stands to talk with me. Beads of sweat ran down his forehead. Butterflies were gliding over the field, cicadas were humming, and a bulldozer on adjacent land was leveling trees for a new soccer field. To date, eleven of his students had signed on with Major League teams. Vargas pointed to a lanky youth who was long-tossing in the outfield. "This one, Lester Hernández Espinoza, is about to sign with the Padres. I converted him from first baseman to pitcher, because he's tall and has the body for a pitcher."

Vargas whistled over Espinoza, who told me he was from Barrio 14 de Septiembre and played Little League for his neighborhood team. He dropped out of baseball for a while because he couldn't afford a pair of shoes and needed to help his father, who owns a tailor shop. At age fifteen his coach invited him to come back. The coach called Vargas and told him they had a tall youth with the body of a ballplayer. Two years later Espinoza signed a contract. "My goal is not just to sign," said Espinoza. "I want to arrive at the dream of all Nicaraguans, which is to play professional baseball—to have money to help my family."

I thanked him for his time, and then Vargas walked over to eighteen-year-old pitcher Ron Montierro, who told me that in his hometown, Diriamba, a small town about twenty miles south of the capital, many talented players don't know there is a baseball school. "Now I have the opportunity to improve," he said. "But there are many who don't have the opportunity and are very good ballplayers, too."

Vargas traveled all over to find his players. He hosted a national radio sports talk program, and people often called in to invite him to check out a youth. He was known for stopping his car whenever he saw a teenager who was six feet or taller to ask if he played baseball. Whatever the boy's response, he said, "Come to my camp, and I'll teach you how to pitch so you will have a chance to play professional baseball in the States." Very rarely did a ballplayer refuse the offer. The typical signing bonus with a Major League club was more than they might make in a lifetime in Nicaragua.[13]

A player who signs with a Major League organization receives national press attention. Reaching the upper levels of the Minor Leagues makes him a national celebrity. Players who have the proverbial cup of coffee in the Major Leagues are anointed as folk heroes. One can imagine Vicente Padilla's flight to stardom when he soared to the Majors less than four months after his debut in the Minors, never mind his breakout season three years later with the Philadelphia Phillies. Newspapers ran daily coverage: game highlights, reports on his condition the next day, quotes on his abilities, and speculation about his next pitching matchup.

Enrique Armas, vice mayor of Managua and one of the country's most popular radio sports broadcasters, clearly demonstrated the grip that Padilla had on the country. As we were driving through the hilly southwestern outskirts of Managua toward the studios of Radio Nicaragua, past jarring squalor, which seemed to stretch onward indefinitely, he turned on the radio and then switched from one FM station to the next. All stops on the dial were broadcasting that evening's Philadelphia Phillies–Atlanta Braves matchup, in which Padilla was starting. Armas explained that every station had its own team of broadcasters, who were watching the game on ESPN from their studios and rendering it in Spanish for their listeners. He added that on nights when ESPN did not broadcast games, the broadcasters re-created the game from telephone descriptions of the action by colleagues in the States.

In 2015 the government-run television station Canal 6 purchased the rights to air MLB games, and for the first time *Pinoleros* got to watch live a full season of starts of one of their countrymen, right-hander Erasmo Ramírez of the Tampa Bay Rays. Rising to the occasion, Ramírez had a breakout year with the Rays. Following the completion of a one-hit shutout in September 2015, he thanked President Ortega and First Lady Rosa Murillo for permitting the game to be transmitted on Nicaraguan television. "When my mom told me, she and I were speechless," he told reporters, adding, "Now the most important thing is to continue on, move forward, and continue to demonstrate that in Nicaragua we have talent."[14]

Bringing Home Talent

One hope in *Pinolero* baseball circles is that the youth who are playing in the United States, as well as borrowed imports, will raise the quality of play at home. In the 1930s barnstorming Cuban and Dominican players shared their knowledge of the game. *Pinoleros* suddenly found that they could hold their own in international play. During World War II, Albrook Field, a ball club consisting of U.S. soldiers stationed in Panama, came to Nicaragua to play a series of games against the local teams and the national team. Terry Moore, four-time All-Star center fielder for the St. Louis Cardinals, was the main attraction, and Nicaraguans were thrilled to have a Major Leaguer on their soil. Hundreds flocked to the airport to greet the Americans as they landed.

After the country's poor performance in the 1948 Amateur World Series, Nicaragua's baseball authorities decided to take the sport to the next level by hiring an American to coach the national team. Florida native Andrés Espolita, a former player and coach in Tampa's immigrant semipro intersocial leagues, held a modern vision of baseball. He strongly believed in scouting new talent and setting up training camps around the country to hone the baseball skills of youngsters. The arrival of a second wave of talent from the Atlantic Coast was due in large part to the work of Espolita.[15]

Many of his players were adopted by Cinco Estrellas (Five Stars), the National Guard's ball club, whose name was derived from Anastasio Somoza García's status as a five-star general. The National Guard hoarded some of the country's best talent, hiring and paying them as privates and promoting them to a higher rank if they played well. While Somoza divorced himself from the team's day-to-day operations, he was an ardent fan of the team and of the game in general. Years before entering politics he had organized his own youth league team. In 1948 he named himself manager of the Nicaragua national team to put a fire in the belly of the players, although he let his staff take care of the baseball. Noted for its tremendous discipline, Cinco Estrellas dominated the baseball scene from the 1940s through the 1970s.

The 1950s and 1960s ushered in a new era with the emergence of professional baseball in Nicaragua. The Liga Professional en Nicaragua was founded in 1956 under the premise that foreigners needed to be brought in as a gate attraction. Nicaraguan ball clubs made working arrangements with Major League teams and imported prospects that needed seasoning before making the leap to the big leagues. Before it folded in 1967, the league hosted scores of ballplayers who had played or would go on to play in the Major Leagues. Among the notables were Ferguson Jenkins, Luis Tiant, Cookie Rojas, Bert Campaneris, Marv Throneberry, Lou Pinella, Phil Regan, Jim Kaat, George Scott, Zoilo Versalles, and Ron Hansen. "One would see lines of children in the hotels and at the practices watching the players," said baseball historian Julio Miranda. "It was a magical period for us and unforgettable."[16]

As the boundaries between amateur and professional baseball on the world stage blurred in the early 1990s, the newly elected neoliberal government and baseball officials softened their restrictions on allowing foreigners and professionals to play in Nicaragua. Winter-league teams started importing players, particularly Cubans. The Cuban government, which was short on funds during the "Special Period" after the collapse of the Soviet Union, hired out "retired" players to foreign countries, particularly Nicaragua. This included several who were in their early thirties and in some instances still in the prime of their careers.[17] "Nicaraguan baseball quality improved tremendously, because of the Cuban players," Tito Rondón explained. "They became one of the strongest generations of ballplayers Nicaragua has ever known."[18]

Since the Sandinistas return to power, there has been a slight increase in the number of players signing with Major League organizations. From 2010 to 2014 MLB teams signed forty-six Nicaraguans. Five Nicaraguan-born players have reached the Majors in the past six years.[19] A greater percentage of those players are making it further up the Minor League ladder than they were a few years ago, and many of those players are returning home to play in the Germán Pomares Ordoñez League, a summer national championship that the Sandinistas expanded in 2009 and in which they invested approximately one million córdobas per year.[20] After signed *Pinoleros* are released from Major League organizations through attrition and return to play alongside seventeen- to nineteen-year-olds in the league, the quality of play has been elevated, which in turn has ignited regional passion for the game.

Reason for Hope

Under a *malinche* tree on the disheveled sidewalk of a posh Managua side street, Efraín shared with me more of his thoughts on the state of Nicaraguan baseball. Efraín was on duty as a night watchman for the private residence behind us. Bats were circling above and periodically knocked small fruit off the *trees* overhanging the street, and lightning was eerily flashing in the southwest night sky. "The sport is almost dead!" said Efraín. "The state of baseball right now is like a house where the front is kept clean, but the inside is dirty."

Efraín prefers to follow soccer, which has grown increasingly popular among the poor and the younger urban population. Interest in the game that usually peaked and dipped according to the World Cup tournaments now holds steady. Sports bars broadcast European soccer games, and it is more common to see people in the street wearing Lionel Messi and Cristiano Ronaldo jerseys than donning baseball gear. The pickup game of preference has also been soccer because in congested barrios it is less complicated and less expensive to play.

Efraín and I were grateful for the opportunity to catch up. He picked a beautiful blossom from the tree and told me he recently planted a *malinche* tree in his yard. He said the fruit in his yard would eventually grow large, and he would have to trim the tree with a machete.

Efraín said he understood why I follow baseball—because it's my writing subject. I told him that I also follow baseball because it's a beautiful sport. The field is mesmerizing, the action is always unique, and there are so many stories and things to talk about. My first memory of baseball was of my late father taking me to Fenway Park and pointing out Rico Petrocelli's footwork at third base between pitches. Efraín smiled and nodded. "I understand that," he said. "In reality, it's not that I don't have interest. The truth is that it's just hard these days to follow."

It felt deeply meaningful to be seated again with Efraín. We spoke of our futures. He suggested I write a book about the poverty in Nicaragua—about fatherless children selling food in the streets that was plucked out of the trash, about how some kids end up addicted to sniffing glue and fumes from the gasoline pumps. He said that one twelve-year-old girl from the barrio walks around naked to advertise herself as a prostitute. "It's the story of how we're living in Nicaragua," he said.

Fifteen years earlier Efraín had been almost as grim about poverty under the Sandinistas. The government supplied him with rice, but inflation had made other goods, such as a bar of soap, unaffordable. On countless occasions Efraín had waxed ecstatic about his childhood as a batboy in the Mayor A League on remote Ometepe Island, where the community gathered around the diamond on Sundays and picnicked afterward with food brought over in carts by the visiting team. Many islanders had told me that the peak year for Mayor A baseball on the island was 1972, the same year that the national team upset Cuba, the Nicaraguan equivalent of the U.S. Olympic hockey team's victory over the Soviets in 1980. Any Managuan who was around during that era would remember the hail of bullets fired in the air all over the city after the final out. For days after the game, *Pinoleros* dragged tin cans through the streets.

The celebration was short-lived, however, as a few days later the city was devastated by a powerful earthquake that killed as many as ten thousand Managuans. Partially collapsed high-rise buildings littered the landscape of downtown Managua for decades before the ruins were finally leveled in 2011. Eight days after the quake, Hall of Famer Roberto Clemente died when his plane, which was carrying relief supplies to the Nicaraguan people, crashed off the coast of his native Puerto Rico.[21]

How could a country so in love with baseball grow weary of it? I posed the question in 2003 to Carlos García, then president of the Nicaraguan Federation of Amateur Baseball (Feniba), a private nonprofit that oversees all levels of Nicaraguan baseball. Called strong-willed and stubborn, charismatic and shrewd, innovative and old school, and a slew of other flavorful adjectives by fellow Nicaraguan *béisbolistas*, García was one of the most accomplished and controversial figures in the history of modern *Pinolero* baseball. In 1959 he spearheaded an eventually successful movement to make baseball an Olympic sport. Three years after the demise of the 1967 professional league, García breathed new life into the game by inaugurating an amateur league with Bob Feller throwing out the first pitch and Joe DiMaggio at the plate. When the Sandinistas took power, García was accused of treason and thrown in jail. Like so much of Nicaraguan political history, the truth behind his arrest was complicated. García explains that the Sandinistas may have felt threatened by his ties to North American professional baseball and his stature in the international baseball community. Historians point out that his public criticisms of Sandinista policies and his former ties with Somoza may have sealed the deal. After four and a half years in jail, García was released from prison and moved to the United States, where he organized the Nica League, which García refers to as "the Nicaraguan National League in Exile." The league consisted of municipal leagues of Nicaraguan Americans in Los Angeles, Houston, New York City, San Francisco, and Miami as well as an annual national championship in front of a packed house at Bobby Maduro Stadium in Miami.[22] Following the change of government, García returned to his homeland in 1990 and founded Feniba.

"Our main purpose is to develop ballplayers, but there's a cultural fence that impedes us from doing this," García told me. We were seated in his windowless office in National Stadium, where photos of Dennis Martínez and former president Ronald Reagan hung on the wall behind him. Occasionally, his attractive secretary walked into the office with a memo, and as she leaned over his desk each time he asked for a peck on the cheek. "Young people no longer want to play Little League—which not only teaches baseball, but how to think and learn better," he said.

Critics contended that responsibility for the disappearance of Little Leagues fell squarely on poor relationships between Feniba and the government. And the lack of public and private investment was extinguishing baseball at all levels. The national team had its most desperate budget shortfalls, and the country's best players declined to play on the team because the salaries were well beneath their standard of living.

As for the scarcity of children's baseball, part of the blame also rested on the Sandinistas—or perhaps on the decade-long war that prevented the Sandinistas from achieving their most ambitious social policies. The system of leagues the Sandinistas aspired to build after abolishing school baseball could not flourish because tens of thousands of youth were sent off to the front lines, fled the country, or went into hiding out of fear of being scooped up and thrown unprepared into the war zones, facing rebels with advanced training and weaponry from the United States. Likewise, Cuban-style sports academies that were in the planning stages couldn't be launched due to lack of funds. Attempts at stabilizing a weak córdoba sent inflation soaring, which suddenly made baseball an exorbitantly expensive game to play. In 1988 I witnessed firsthand the cost of a baseball skyrocket to six hundred córdobas, which at the time was about one month's salary for the average Nicaraguan. Efraín's barrio team owned only a few pieces of equipment and had no league to support it. Its plan to buy more equipment relied on placing wagers with opposing teams on the games they played.

The Sandinistas did, however, support national and local teams and sponsored winter- and summer-league teams (even an Atlantic Coast team for a gallant two-year stretch), ensuring that a significant number would stay afloat from one season to the next. Players on winter-league teams received free housing and money for food and rides. The government hired retiring athletes as physical education instructors, invested in Little Leagues as they could, kept homegrown talent at home, and ensured health care for all, including athletes. If a player performed well in an international tournament, he would be given a house, and a new car might show up on his doorstep as well. Attendance was also higher, as fans appreciated the stability. "In the 1980s, the stadiums were full because baseball followed only one course," said Gerald Hernández of *La Prensa*. "Nobody exited the league because it was prohibited. So there was more enthusiasm in the league and more interest."[23]

Organized ball during President Daniel Ortega's second presidency reflects the rightward evolution of the Sandinistas. Winter-league ball is now professional. Ownership pays for most operating costs, including player salaries. Player uniforms brandish advertisements similar to winter-ball leagues throughout Latin America, and in recent years professional teams (even two of the nation's oldest, Granada and León) under financial duress have folded without the government stepping in to help.

8. Teammates from Rivas run off the field after winning the 2011 Infantil A (nine-
and ten-year-olds) National Championship in Municipal Stadium in Sébaco,
Managua. Nicaraguan youth leagues flourished after President Daniel Ortega
returned to power in 2007. The Sandinistas poured money and resources into
the children's leagues, attempting to rebuild long-neglected organized baseball
from the bottom up. (Photo courtesy of *La Prensa*/Managua/G. Flores.)

Still the Sandinistas have received high marks for their adminis-
tering of the developmental leagues. Baseball officials have set out
to eliminate the technical deficiencies of *Pinolero* ballplayers, which
were widely thought to be a result of insufficient coaching in the youth
leagues. Specialized coaches work with youth all-stars and set individual
goals for each player. Gerald Hernández says this is already leading to
better-quality players signing with MLB teams. "Before the boys were
not trained by anyone, and they were signed by pure talent," he says.
"Now players who sign have talent and also have skills, because they
have been training since age fourteen and fifteen."[24]

"In the last four years we have seen significant change," adds Jorge
Luis Avellán, director of the children's leagues for Feniba. However, he

thinks that more needs to be done so that "in five years Nicaragua will be at another level."[25] Avellán advocates improving baseball facilities, including "purchasing pitching machines like one finds in the States."

The largest upgrade will be a new national ballpark. Ground was broken in Managua in 2015 for a state-of-the-art thirty-five-million-dollar stadium, paid for almost entirely by the government of Taiwan. Cuban sportswriter Yasiel Cancio Vilar says the building of a new ballpark complements the government's efforts to build up baseball. "Every great work needs symbols that endure over time," he wrote in 2015. "The new Dennis Martínez Stadium will be the crown jewel of this project, a facility capable of projecting to the world Nicaragua's eliteness as a baseball country."[26]

An infrastructure project outside of baseball could be a more monumental game changer. In July 2015 a Hong Kong business magnate broke ground on a 273-mile transoceanic canal intended to compete with the Panama Canal. Depending on whom you ask, the project is either a godsend that will revolutionize the economy and lift Nicaragua out of poverty or a ruse that will line the pockets of billionaires and politicians, compete poorly against the Panama Canal and other transoceanic ventures in Central America, harm ecosystems, expropriate farmland, and compromise national sovereignty. In at least one instance, protests against the canal turned into deadly clashes with police.

Nicaragua maintains official diplomatic relations with Taiwan, which China considers a renegade Chinese territory. It is possible that Taiwan's investment in the stadium may be part of the decades-long international chess game between the two countries, which would be par for the course in Nicaragua. The tentacles of *Pinolero* politics and sports are wrapped so tightly around one another that it's challenging at times to distinguish one from the other. Politicians serve prominent roles in sports administration, and beloved athletes and sports journalists serve key roles in government. On online sports pages comments on baseball often evolve (or devolve) into political discussions. Baseball has been embroiled in political controversies, but it has also united people from across the political spectrum.

According to former national soccer team goalkeeper Dr. Sergio Chamorro, baseball will continue to be the sport of the people, as "it is difficult to change the culture of a country. It is part of the idiosyncrasy of Nicaraguans, that which we all know of baseball, and we all enjoy about baseball."[27]

In the stands of Jackie Robinson Stadium for the National Little League Tournament, his point was well illustrated. "Williamsport," as the locals call this tournament, is a four-team competition. The winner moves on to play in the Latin American championship—the winner there earns a spot at the Little League National Tournament in Williamsport, Pennsylvania.

About fifty people were in attendance, and it seemed that almost everyone was coaching the players, who were indeed listening to the crowd's instructions. Many were also advising the umpire: "He didn't touch home!" "Umpire, he's pitching without his foot on the rubber!" "Change umpires!" A man with an ice cream cart rang his bell from time to time. Another vendor sold plastic bags of water.

When the game ended most of the people in attendance filed out, crossing two planks of wood that took them over a dried-up stream. Some stayed in the stands, watching many of the kids from both teams, who had decided that they would play another game just for fun. The pitcher for the losing team, 14 de Septiembre, was kneeing the ball like a soccer ball as they hashed out the rules. Several of the players were wrestling with a boy to keep him from running the bases.

"It's beautiful to watch the field," I said. A gentleman sitting next to me nodded and smiled. He was the proud parent of a second baseman from Nindirí.

As the pickup game started, the kids argued about and discussed each play. We chuckled at one point when it seemed like all the kids on the field were talking at the same time. The gentleman sitting next to me nodded approvingly and said, "That's how they learn."

1. An estimated 30,000 people lost their lives during the war.
2. In recent years conditions have improved only marginally. According to a World Bank study, in 2010 48 percent of Nicaraguans lived below the poverty line. An April 2015 survey by M&R Conductores Associates found that 38.7 percent of Nicaraguans said that their household income was not enough to make ends meet, yet 74.1 percent said they were hopeful that their economic situation would improve. See http://www.worldbank.org/en/country/nicaragua; and Ricardo Guerrero, "Desempleo vuelve a ser el principal problema del país," *El Nuevo Diario*, April 15, 2015.
3. Tito Rondón, phone interview with the author, December 16, 2015.
4. Aníbal Vega, phone interview with the author, April 14, 2003.
5. The rivalry between San Fernando and Bóer stretches back more than one hundred years. When San Fernando defeated its eternal rival in 1991 to win its first national championship in fifty years, jubilant fans removed patron saint San Jerónimo from his altar and carried him through the streets in a procession normally reserved for the famous festival in his honor.
6. Vega, phone interview.
7. Batboys in Nicaragua have been popular celebrities since the 1980s, when teams hired dwarfs to carry bats. Although Taylor retired in the 2000s, several *compañeros* serve as batboys to this day. Eduardo Cruz, "Keith Taylor, los Dantos y el General," *La Prensa*, July 10, 2016.
8. Bayardo Cuadra, interview with the author, 2003.
9. A 2003 poll by M&R and Associates found that 823,000 Nicaraguan children didn't even have access to a school system, 32 percent of the schools that did exist didn't have electricity, and 29 percent of schools didn't have running water.
10. Dennis Martínez, interview with the author, Phoenix, March 4, 2005. Martínez started a larger camp in 2010 in Rivas. In addition to baseball facilities, the academy has a fully equipped gymnasium and a dormitory with the capacity to sleep 40 prospects. Youngsters practice from 8:00 a.m. to 12:00 p.m. daily and spend a mandatory three and a half hours in the classroom.
11. Signing bonuses have climbed dramatically in recent years. To date the highest signing was Kansas City Royals third baseman Cheslor Cuthbert,

who was signed out of the Wilfredo Blanco Academy in 2009 for a $1.35 million signing bonus, a record amount for a *Pinolero* prospect.

12. For excellent background on the Astros' academy, see Jamail, *Venezuelan Bust, Baseball Boom*.

13. Calixto Vargas, interview with the author, Managua, June 18, 2003.

14. "Erasmo Ramírez agradece a Daniel y Rosario por la transmisión de sus partidos," *La Voz del Sandismo*, September 17, 2015.

15. Espolita also helped develop several future Major Leaguers in Tampa's intersocial leagues, including future Hall of Fame manager Tony LaRussa.

16. Julio Miranda, interview with the author, Managua, June 16, 2003.

17. The flow of talent from Cuba to Nicaragua continues to this day. Most notably, Omar Linares, considered the best amateur third baseman in modern baseball history, has been serving as batting coach since 2012.

18. Tito Rondón, phone interview with the author, December 16, 2014.

19. Compared to Venezuela and the Dominican Republic, the numbers are modest. MLB teams signed 247 players from Venezuela in 2014. On 2015 opening-day rosters, there were only 2 Nicaraguans compared to 83 Dominicans and 65 Venezuelans. Brian Costa and Ezequiel Minaya, "Why MLB Teams Are Fleeing Venezuela," *Wall Street Journal*, May 4, 2015, http://www.wsj.com/articles/why-mlb-teams-are-fleeing-venezuela-1430751423.

20. The league was named for a martyred Sandinista guerrilla fighter who played baseball in his free time. Teams are allowed to have a maximum of 9 players over age twenty-seven, a minimum of eight players between ages twenty-three and twenty-six, and a minimum of eight players between ages seventeen and twenty-two. Gerald Hernández, "Cuanto se ha producido?," *La Prensa*, July 2, 2012.

21. Clemente's altruism is memorialized in Nicaragua with eleven schools and two ballparks named in his honor and his uniform number retired. Following Roberto Clemente's death, Nicaraguan winter ball split into two leagues. One was named the Clemente League. The league lasted until the Sandinista Revolution.

22. The league continues to thrive, particularly in Miami, as it has since its inception in 1987. In 2004 the official name was changed to the Miami-Dade Baseball League, but the league still has a large percentage of Nicaraguan American players and is still popularly known as Liga Nica. Team names such as Rivas, Matanzas, León, and Bóer are borrowed from Nicaraguan

teams. And it is not uncommon to find Dennis Martínez, a veteran of the league, tossing the first pitch on opening day.

23. Gerald Hernández, interview with the author, Managua, June 14, 2003.
24. Gerald Hernández, phone interview with the author, October 9, 2015.
25. "En cinco años tendremos otro nivel."
26. Yasiel Canciel Vilar, *Prensa Latina*, August 28, 2015.
27. Quoted in "¿El béisbol en peligro?," *El Nuevo Diario*, March 26, 2014, http://www.elnuevodiario.com.ni/deportes/315444-beisbol-peligro/.

BIBLIOGRAPHY

Arrellano, Jorge E. *El doctor David Arellano*. Managua: privately printed, 1993.
"En cinco años tendremos otro nivel." *Revista Beisbolera* 3, no. 71 (2015).
García, Carlos J. *Resena de cien años de béisbol en Nicaragua*. Managua: Feniba, 1991.
Jamail, Milton H. *Venezuelan Bust, Baseball Boom: Andrés Reiner and Scouting on the New Frontier*. Lincoln: University of Nebraska Press, 2008.
Ruíz Borge, Martin. *Records Victoria del béisbol Nicaragüense de Primera Division*. Managua: privately printed, 1993.
Tijerno Mantilla, Edgar. *El mundial Nica*. Managua: privately printed, 1993.
World Bank. http://www.worldbank.org/en/country/nicaragua.

7

Venezuela

The Passion and Politics of Baseball

Arturo J. Marcano and David P. Fidler

Venezuelans are passionate about baseball. But describing baseball in Venezuela as a "passion" is superficial at best and a caricature at worst. Baseball's evolution in Venezuela is a more complicated story. What began with an embrace of an American sport became an independent cultural phenomenon. However, in the past two decades, Venezuelan baseball has become dependent on Major League Baseball and been transformed by Venezuela's "Bolívarian Revolution." Subordination to MLB involves the number of Venezuelans playing for MLB teams and their Minor League affiliates, the manner in which MLB brings Venezuelan talent into its orbit, how Venezuelan winter ball functions, and MLB's domination of the World Baseball Classic (WBC).

Venezuela's dependence is not, however, merely the consequence of MLB's strategies to globalize its influence, sources of talent, and markets for its products. The country's political and economic trajectory over the past fifteen-plus years contributed to this dependence. Venezuela's political and economic stability deteriorated, leaving many despairing about its future. These worsening conditions have deepened Venezuelan baseball's dependence on MLB, especially as more Venezuelans perceive MLB as an escape from a country becoming a shadow of its former self. In addition, political and economic crises pierced baseball's special place in Venezuela and politicized it in harmful ways.

The politics of the globalization of baseball and of Venezuela in crisis are as important as, or more, important than passion in pondering Venezuela's future relationship with baseball.

Sinking Roots: Origins and Development of Venezuela's National Pastime

As with many other countries, baseball was imported into Venezuela, sank roots, and influenced the country's culture. Like baseball's origins in the United States, the mythical mists of time have shrouded how baseball came to Venezuela. According to legend, its importation transpired through students returning from U.S. universities in the first half of the 1890s. At that time wealthy families often sent their sons to the United States to advance their education. Baseball was popular in the United States and was played on makeshift diamonds in rural communities, city streets, and the playing fields of academic institutions. Venezuelan students returned home with strange gloves, balls, and bats and infected with a "special illness" not seen before in that country.

According to Venezuelan baseball historian Javier González, Amenodoro Franklin and his brothers Emilio, Gustavo, and Augusto founded the first baseball club, the Caracas Base Ball Club (BBC), in 1895. The club played games on Sundays, with a blue team taking on a red team. The "special illness" proved communicable, and the game spread through Caracas. In 1902 the Caracas BBC defeated a team fielded by the U.S. Marines, which President Theodore Roosevelt deployed to Venezuela to deter intervention by European powers after Venezuela defaulted on debts owed to European investors.

The discovery of oil in the 1920s catalyzed baseball's spread across Venezuela. American companies were involved in extracting oil in Venezuela, and they promoted baseball as a pastime for their employees. Political scientist Robert Elias argues that company sponsorship of baseball was designed to "keep exploited local workers diverted," but the practice helped baseball grow in popularity, especially in areas

9. Sabios de Vargas, the first champion of the Venezuelan Professional Baseball League, in 1946. (Photo courtesy of the National Baseball Hall of Fame.)

distant from Caracas.[1] Baseball's spread across Venezuela helped produce internationally competitive players and incentives to organize professional baseball. By 1940 Venezuelan squads were playing teams from other countries, such as the Dominican Republic. In 1941 Venezuela won the Amateur World Series. From 1946 until 1950 Venezuela fielded teams for the Serie Interamericana, which was replaced by the Caribbean World Series.

In 1945 the Venezuelan Professional Baseball League, or Liga Venezolana de Béisbol Profesional, was established with four teams: Cerveceria, Magallanes, Vargas, and Venezuela. With baseball's growth in popularity and importance, the LVBP became one of the nation's most stable and respected institutions. The LVBP expanded to the current eight teams spread around Venezuela: Aguilas del Zulia, Cardenales de Lara, Navengantes del Magallanes, Tigres de Aragua, Leones del Caracas, Tiburones de la Guaira, Caribes de Anzoátegui, and Bravos de Margarita.[2]

Today LVBP teams play a sixty-three-game season—nine games against each of the other seven clubs—from the beginning of October to the end of December. The six teams with the best regular-season records compete in playoffs with two stages. The best four teams from the first round of the playoffs face off in best-of-seven semifinals. The winners then play a final best-of-seven series to decide the champion, which represents Venezuela in the Caribbean World Series. The Caribbean World Series includes the top clubs from the Dominican Republic, Puerto Rico, Mexico, and—starting in 2013—Cuba. The Venezuelan champion has won the Caribbean World Series seven times.

Although imported from the United States and spurred in growth by American economic activities, baseball in Venezuela took on a life of its own, largely independent from professional baseball in the United States. This independence allowed Venezuelans for decades to shape the roles baseball played in their society. As the next sections argue, this independence diminished as connections to and relations with MLB grew and changed baseball in Venezuela.

Becoming Interdependent: Venezuelan Baseball and the Globalization of Major League Baseball

Experiencing a baseball game in Caracas often feels like a trip back in time. Apart from better food and scoreboards, the facilities where LVBP teams play have changed little in the past forty years, a situation distant from what MLB teams invest in stadiums and the fan experience. Fans in Venezuela do not appear to care about the amenities commonplace in contemporary MLB stadiums. This difference suggests the two baseball contexts are worlds apart, but nothing could be further from the truth. In reality, baseball in Venezuela has become ever more intertwined with MLB, especially in the past twenty years.

Graph 1. Venezuelan players on MLB Major League teams. Source: Major League Baseball.

The process of Venezuelan baseball becoming interdependent with MLB can be captured with statistics. In 1945, when the LVBP began, no Venezuelans played in MLB. In 2014 98 Venezuelans were on MLB teams. In 1945 MLB teams signed no Venezuelans to play Minor League ball. In 2014 alone MLB clubs signed 225 Venezuelans to Minor League contracts, which are known as "July 2nd signings."

These numbers highlight the development of an intensive relationship between MLB and baseball in Venezuela that occurred during MLB's globalization, a phenomenon that accelerated in the 1990s and continues to this day. The statistics on Venezuelans playing MLB or Minor League ball reveal the deep interest MLB clubs have in Venezuelan players and prospects. Indeed, Venezuela is the second most important source of foreign talent for MLB after the Dominican Republic.

Looking at the number of Venezuelans who played, or currently play, on MLB teams, the data reveal interesting features of the growth of the Venezuelan presence on MLB clubs. Graph 1 plots the number of Venezuelans playing for Major League teams from 1940 through 2014. Between 1940 and 1950 the number did not increase. The largest number in this decade was 2 in 1944. Between 1950 and 1960 the number increased from 1 to 3 players, hardly an explosion of Venezuelan talent in the Show.

The first significant growth occurred between 1960 and 1970, when the number grew from 3 to 10 players, which, at that time, was an all-time high. However, between 1970 and 1980 there was no growth: this decade started with 10 Venezuelans, never exceeded that number, and ended in 1980 with 9. This trend means that Venezuelan talent was not a major feature of MLB in these decades, and the small numbers involved could not, and did not, cause MLB and Venezuelan baseball to interlink in systemic ways.

Real change started in the following decades. From 1980 to 1990 Venezuelan participation in the Major Leagues more than doubled (from 9 to 23 players). This growth is associated with free agency's impact on MLB, which started in the mid-1970s. With free-agency costs increasing, MLB teams sought cheaper labor. MLB teams began searching more seriously for players in, among other places, the Dominican Republic and Venezuela, which, in turn, required stronger scouting capabilities in these countries.

Another indicator of growing MLB interest in Dominican and Venezuelan talent was the opening of the first MLB academies, with the Los Angeles Dodgers starting an academy in the Dominican Republic in 1987 and the Houston Astros doing the same in Venezuela in 1989. This move into training facilities started a deeper MLB involvement in the Dominican Republic and Venezuela that would, in time, grow significantly and controversially. Thus, the decade between 1980 and 1990 witnessed still greater connections between MLB and Venezuelan baseball.

But the 1980s were merely a prelude to changes over the next twenty-five years. By the end of the twentieth century Venezuelan Major Leaguers numbered 44. By 2010 this number reached 82, with a peak of 88 in 2009, amounting to a third straight decade of approximately twofold increases. The scale of MLB efforts to secure Venezuelan talent in the Minor Leagues is equally important. By the early 2000s MLB clubs were signing each year around 200 Venezuelans to Minor

Venezuelans signed to MLB Minor League contracts

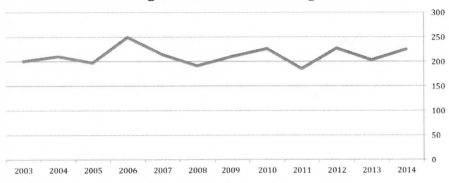

Graph 2. Venezuelans signed to MLB Minor League contracts. Source: Major League Baseball.

League contracts, with the total number signed between 2003 and 2014 equaling 2,521 (see graph 2).

These numbers indicate the growing interdependence between MLB and Venezuelan baseball. For MLB teams Venezuela grew into a rich talent source for the Major and Minor Leagues. Tapping this supply, MLB clubs expanded their scouting networks with both team scouts and Venezuelan *buscónes*—individuals who trained prospects in order to get them signed to pro contracts. MLB began the Venezuelan Summer League for Venezuelan Minor League players in 1997, and, by 2001, nineteen MLB teams participated in the league. By 2002 twenty-one of the thirty MLB clubs operated baseball academies in Venezuela to identify, sign, and train prospects.

This level of activity meant baseball in Venezuela—both the passion and the business—no longer operated independently from professional baseball in the United States. MLB created opportunities the LVBP could not, despite its respected place in Venezuela. The MLB relationship with Venezuela fed the Venezuelan passion for baseball, adding a prominent component to the country's love affair with the sport. From the perspective of the business of baseball, Venezuela was integrated into MLB's increasingly globalized business model, which involved securing cheap foreign talent and expanding consumer interest in MLB's products (for example, broadcast games and team merchandise).

Interdependence between Venezuelan baseball and MLB came with costs for Venezuela. The manner in which MLB recruited, trained, signed, and treated Latin Minor League players was exploitative and discriminatory and involved MLB teams violating the human rights of children. In 2000 Angel Vargas, president of the Venezuelan Baseball Players Association, argued:

> Virtually everything about the globalization of baseball that comes out of the MLB Commissioner's Office in New York is . . . one-sided propaganda. . . . The most serious problem today is the lack of MLB interest in, and respect for, what people in Latin America perceive as the problem with the way MLB teams behave in Latin America. . . . My arguments do not depend on academic theories about globalization, or . . . nostalgic myths about baseball as a national pastime, but arise out of MLB mistreatment of Latino children and their parents that unfortunately I and my Latin American colleagues see almost every day.[3]

Such criticisms did not slow Venezuela's relationship with MLB (see graphs 1 and 2). Explaining how this increase happened amid controversies about MLB treatment of Latin players requires more than believing a passion for baseball blinded Venezuelans to MLB's exploitation and discrimination against Latin Americans.

A theme in the Dominican Republic's relationship with MLB has been how the poverty many Dominicans experience makes baseball an escape from a grim socioeconomic future. Historically, Venezuela has been a more developed country than the Dominican Republic, in part because of Venezuela's oil wealth. However, when Venezuela became integrated into the MLB system, Venezuela endured difficult economic times. From 1960 to 1980 the gross domestic product per capita increased from US$6,000 to approximately US$7,000. After 1980 Venezuela experienced sustained economic problems, and GDP per capita declined to under US$4,500 by 2004.[4] In 1996 the Venezuelan poverty rate reached 70 percent.[5] These economic travails played a role in the election of Hugo Chávez as president in 1998.[6]

Thus, deteriorating socioeconomic conditions from the 1980s through the beginning of the twenty-first century occurred while MLB's globalization created opportunities for a baseball-crazy country that produced skilled players. In other words, strong supply and demand catalyzed the interdependence between Venezuelan baseball and MLB that emerged in the 1990s and early 2000s.

Emerging Dependent: Venezuelan Baseball's Subordination to Major League Baseball

The linkages between Venezuelan baseball and MLB led to greater MLB efforts to regulate the participation of Major and Minor League players in the Winter Leagues and changed how MLB teams deal with Latin Minor League players. In different ways these efforts demonstrated that MLB had become hegemonic in interactions with Latin American countries. We illustrate MLB's hegemony by analyzing the Winter League Agreement (WLA) between MLB and the Caribbean Confederation, the Collective Bargaining Agreement (CBA) between MLB and the Major League Baseball Players Association (MLBPA), and creation of the World Baseball Classic.

Winter League Agreement

Before free agency transformed MLB's economics, the Winter Leagues offered Major and Minor League players opportunities to earn additional income and gain experience. The Winter Leagues welcomed African American players before MLB teams would hire them and gave the small number of Latin players with MLB clubs the chance to play professional baseball back home. Prior to free agency the relationship between MLB and the Winter Leagues was rather laissez-faire, and MLB did not attempt to control or limit players heading south for winter ball.

Two developments changed the relationship between MLB and the Winter Leagues. First, free agency increased the cost of Major League talent, and, with more money at stake in Major League players, MLB clubs wanted to protect these investments by regulating their players' participation in winter ball. Second, the increasing number of Latin players in MLB reinforced MLB's desire to protect its interests by controlling the Winter Leagues. By contrast, representatives of the Winter Leagues did not want MLB to interfere with the quality of winter ball or undermine the viability of Latin American professional leagues.

Generally, the Winter League Agreement regulates the participation of players under MLB contracts in the Winter Leagues. Among other things, the WLA determines what MLB players can participate, imposes requirements on the quality of baseball facilities, and contains mandates related to insurance coverage for winter-ball players. Although the WLA forms part of the globalization of baseball, the WLA increasingly appears to those involved in the Winter Leagues as globalization on MLB's terms. To many with a stake in winter ball in Venezuela and other members of the Caribbean Confederation, the Winter Leagues have long contributed to a more balanced form of globalization because the Winter Leagues provided fans with quality baseball and sparked fan interest in not only winter ball but also the MLB season. From this perspective, the liberal flow of players between the leagues enhanced the globalization of baseball without intrusive regulation.

However, in the eyes of many involved in the Winter Leagues, the increasingly one-sided provisions of the WLA suggest MLB executives perceive winter ball as a risk they must manage in their vision for the sport's globalization. These views converge with arguments of critics who believe MLB dictates the terms of the MLB–Winter League relationship. MLB disagrees with this characterization and believes the WLA strikes an appropriate balance between the interests of MLB clubs and Winter League teams.[7]

One of the more controversial WLA provisions—the Extreme Fatigue Clause (EFC)—provides a window into the WLA's dynamics. This clause permits MLB clubs to prevent their Latin players from participating in the Winter Leagues under certain conditions. This power affects the ability of Winter League teams to field native superstars on their rosters, potentially hurting team quality, performance, fan support, and ticket revenue.

Before the 1998–2005 version of the WLA, the agreement contained no EFC and prohibited MLB teams from preventing native players from participating in the Winter Leagues. Recall from graph 1 that MLB experienced its first dramatic spike in the number of Latin players on MLB rosters from 1992 to 1998. The WLA negotiated for the 1998–2005 period (and extended through 2009) was the first to contain an EFC, which permitted MLB teams to prevent native players from playing winter ball in cases of illness, injury, or extreme fatigue—defined as players with more than 180 innings pitched, more than 60 games played in the Major or Minor Leagues combined by relief pitchers in the season immediately prior to the Winter League season, or 520 or more at bats in the Major or Minor Leagues combined taken in the season immediately prior to the Winter League season.

In the next two versions of the WLA, the EFC became more detailed and limiting, with the version applicable from 2013 through 2018 containing a less transparent, more complicated, and more restrictive EFC. Table 1 lists the clause's thresholds for various categories:

Table 1. Extreme-fatigue limits

PLAYER CATEGORY	WLA (2009–12)	WLA (2013–18)
Pitchers (Major Leagues)	170 innings	160 innings
Pitchers (AAA)	165 innings	160 innings
Pitchers (AA)	165 innings	155 innings
Pitchers (A)	165 innings	130 innings

Pitchers (A-short)	80 innings	75 innings
Pitchers (Rookie League)	70 innings	70 innings
Games (Major Leagues)	60 games	60 games
Games (AAA, AA, A)	55 games	55 games
Games (A-short and Rookie)	35 games	35 games
Hitters (Major Leagues)	500 at bats*	503 plate appearances*
Hitters (AAA, AA, A)	500 at bats	550 plate appearances
Hitters (A-short and Rookie)	325 at bats	370 plate appearances
Catchers (Major Leagues)	No provision	600 innings**
Catchers (AAA, AA, A)	No provision	700 innings
Catchers (A-short and Rookie)	No provision	550 innings

* "At bats" did not include sacrifice hits, walks, and when a pitch hit a batter, while "plate appearances" includes all of these, thus making this change more restrictive.

** The equivalent of approximately 66 games.

Source: Winter League Agreements between MLB and the Caribbean Leagues, 2009–12 agreement and 2013–18 agreement.

Increased complexity arises from making the Major League Baseball Players Association a party to the WLA because the Collective Bargaining Agreement between MLB and the MLBPA for 2012–16 mandates cooperation on globalizing the game. Winter ball falls within this mandate. With MLBPA a party, the WLA is divided into two parts: the part for players on the forty-man Major League rosters, whom the MLBPA represents in collective bargaining, and the part for players not on the forty-man Major League rosters, whom the MLBPA does not represent. From the perspective of winter-ball teams, the involvement of the MLBPA, which has nothing to do with the Winter Leagues, represents another encroachment of the MLB system on baseball in Latin American countries.

More restrictions appear in new provisions that increase the number of players MLB teams can prevent from playing in the Winter Leagues. The EFC kicks in for pitchers playing in Class AA at 140 innings pitched (rather than 155 innings in the previous WLA) and 45 game appearances (rather than 55). Minor and Major League pitchers aged twenty-four years or younger can be placed on the Extreme Fatigue List if their innings pitched or game appearances increase by a certain percentage from the previous season, provided that the pitcher's previous season amounted to 60 percent or more of the applicable EFC threshold. In addition, MLB clubs can designate up to three additional players as exempt from winter ball, even players who have not reached the EFC's thresholds.

The complexities and restrictiveness of the latest WLA place stress on Winter League teams, including those in the LVBP. These teams do not know what players will be available until late in the year. In fact, Oscar Prieto Parraga, the president of the LVBP, opposed the latest version of the WLA because he believed MLB was dictating terms rather than engaging in negotiations between partners. Despite this view, he and the other heads of Winter Leagues signed the WLA because they concluded they had no choice. Once independent from MLB, the LVBP is now subject to WLA regulations imposed to protect MLB interests in Major and Minor League players.

The Collective Bargaining Agreement and Latin Minor League Players

A similar tale of subordination appears in how MLB has behaved in bringing young Latin players into its Minor League operations. MLB's globalization has included scouting, signing, and training increasing numbers of Latin youth, a process we (and others) have criticized since the latter half of the 1990s. Our book *Stealing Lives: The Globalization of Baseball and the Tragic Story of Alexis Quiroz* (2002) told the harrowing tale of MLB's mistreatment of a Venezuelan teenager during this period. Expanding MLB team interest in Latin talent meant large numbers of Venezuelan children and young men came into contact with an exploitative and discriminatory "free agency" system—something never previously part of Venezuelan baseball.

Piecemeal MLB reforms undertaken in the face of criticism failed to achieve needed systemic change—a need MLB accepted only in 2009 after the findings of a committee led by MLB executive Sandy Alderson. These findings were followed by MLB and the MLBPA, including in the Collective Bargaining Agreement for 2012–16 provisions that transformed how MLB brings Latin prospects into its Minor League system. The CBA created a draft-like mechanism that regulates the order in which MLB clubs sign foreign prospects and limits signing bonuses. This approach ended the old free-agency system but stopped short of being an international draft.

For our purposes, the CBA's new mechanism reflects MLB's ability to impose rules on Venezuela and other countries without the involvement of, and input from, the societies and people affected. Under free agency Venezuelan prospects could bargain for higher bonuses among competing MLB teams. The CBA mechanism eliminates this opportunity in order to secure MLB's objective of decreasing bonuses for foreign prospects. Even though the CBA's provisions affected Venezuelans and people in other countries, neither MLB nor the MLBPA engaged in any serious attempt to involve these communities in the decision-making process. Instead, the CBA imposed a new system, which underscores the subordination of Venezuelan baseball to MLB and its hegemonic power in baseball's globalization.

The World Baseball Classic

Another example of MLB's control over the globalization of baseball is the World Baseball Classic. MLB spearheaded the WBC's creation as a showcase for globalizing the sport. The WBC is a tournament involving teams from professional leagues around the world, and the WBC has been held in 2006, 2009, and 2013, with the next tournament scheduled for 2017. Venezuela has participated in the WBC, with its best result being third place in 2009.

Ostensibly a global effort, the WBC is dominated by the MLB, with support from the MLBPA. Anthropologist Thomas F. Carter describes the WBC as "a business venture designed to expand the reach of MLB beyond North America" and argues that, through it, MLB has created a "New Economic Order" for baseball as a global sport that "does not account for domestic or national baseball industries or grassroots development unless they submit to MLB's own configuration and control."[8] MLB outmaneuvered concerns and alternative ideas about the WBC from other national baseball leagues, such as the Japanese professional league, making MLB, in Carter's words, the agent "determining what is good for baseball."[9] Given this reality, the biggest threat to the WBC in 2017 might be difficult negotiations between MLB and MLBPA on a CBA to replace the one that expires in 2016.

Venezuelan baseball fans and media welcomed the WBC when MLB first announced it. The WBC gave Venezuela—its tradition, talent, and passion for the game—the chance to win a global sports competition, something unlikely in the country's second most popular sport, soccer. For this reason, promoters sold the WBC as the Baseball World Cup to mimic the International Federation of Association Football's famous World Cup. However, unlike FIFA, which requires leagues and teams to permit superstars to play for their countries, MLB did not impose a similar requirement on its teams, which restricted many of their best players from playing in the WBC. As Efraín Ruiz Pantin argues, when Venezuelans saw that the WBC was not really a Baseball World Cup, they began to see it as an MLB-MLBPA marketing tool to globalize their vision of baseball without regard for what Venezuelans wanted.[10]

Baseball, Venezuela, and Hugo Chávez

Venezuelan baseball's subordination to MLB involves factors unrelated to the exercise of MLB's power. As noted above, the economic crisis that began in the 1980s and continued in the 1990s led to dramatic changes in Venezuela. Leading this transformation was Hugo Chávez, first elected president in 1998 and in power until his death in 2013.

Not since Simón Bolívar in the nineteenth century had Venezuela experienced a political leader like Chávez, whose charisma was captivating and disconcerting in equal measures. Like many Venezuelans, Chávez loved baseball, but his "Bolívarian Revolution" destroyed the unique place baseball enjoyed in Venezuelan culture by politicizing the sport and dragging it into the vortex of the country's political and economic crises.

Before Chávez baseball largely stood apart from Venezuelan politics. It provided a space for people to congregate and escape from economic and political realities. At the stadium fans would equally vilify players, managers, and politicians, but only rarely—and at substantial risk of backlash—did the political world seek to enter this space to use baseball for its ends. The changes Chávez made, especially how he fomented antagonism between the rich and the poor, transformed baseball into a political arena. Anti-Chávez chants became frequent at games. Endy Chávez is a well-known Venezuelan player, and one popular chant was "Endy sí, Chávez no!" During the crisis that nearly toppled Chávez in 2002, the LVBP's president stopped the Winter League season, which many saw as a political move—a view reinforced when this individual became executive director of a group of opposition parties called la Mesa de la Unidad. Venezuelan professionals and Major Leaguers, such as Magglio Ordoñez and Carlos Guillen, publicly supported Chávez, despite the risks that fans would respond negatively to such political actions.

During Chávez's time in office, the dependence of Venezuelan baseball on MLB deepened, even though Chávez challenged MLB. This outcome flowed from two causes. First, Chávez's animosity toward the United States (he once called President George W. Bush "the devil" in a speech at the United Nations) and his attempts to regulate MLB operations in Venezuela led MLB teams to change their approach. Chávez's government, reports sportswriter Dave Zirin, "told MLB that they would have to institute employee and player benefits and job protections. He wanted education and job training, subsidized by

MLB, to be a part of the academies. He also insisted that teams pay out 10 percent of players' signing bonuses to the government. Chávez effectively wanted to tax MLB for the human capital they blithely take from the country."[11]

In 2002 twenty-one MLB clubs had baseball academies in Venezuela. By 2015 only four did. MLB also scaled back the Venezuelan Summer League for Minor League players. Closing their academies and limiting the Summer League did not mean, however, MLB teams stopped scouting, signing, and training Venezuelan prospects. As graph 2 shows, the number of Venezuelans signed to Minor League contracts remained high during the time most MLB clubs shut down their Venezuelan academies. MLB teams simply sent Venezuelan prospects to academies in the Dominican Republic.

Second, Chávez's policies changed Venezuela for the worse. Although repeatedly elected president, Chávez aggregated power to himself, producing an increasingly authoritarian government that threatened civil rights and liberties associated with Venezuelan democracy. Economically, Chávez exploited rising oil prices by nationalizing oil companies and using higher oil revenues to redistribute wealth among the poor, which bolstered his popularity. His successor, Nicolás Maduro, continued "Chávezonomics."

However, these policies weakened the economy, leaving Venezuela dependent on high oil prices. Economists Carmen Reinhart and Kenneth Rogoff argue that Venezuela has been "so badly mismanaged that real (inflation-adjusted) per capita GDP today is 2% lower than it was in 1970, despite a ten-fold increase in oil prices."[12] Plummeting oil prices are, according to reporter Keith Johnson, "tearing at the sinews of an economy . . . already reeling from rampant inflation, consumer shortages, and widespread . . . unemployment."[13] The drop in oil prices reveals how much trouble the Venezuelan economy confronts and the unwillingness or inability of Venezuela's leaders to address the problems effectively.

A key aspect of the Chávez-Maduro economic strategy has been using restrictive foreign-exchange controls for political reasons. Government opponents are unlikely to gain access to U.S. dollars under such controls, leaving the black market as the only option, where the exchange rate was, in August 2016, 1,000 bolivars per dollar compared to the official rate of 12 bolivars per dollar. LVBP teams need access to dollars to pay players and buy equipment not made in Venezuela. Support for Maduro's government from two LVBP team owners, Magglio Ordoñez (Caribes de Anzoátegui) and Carlos Guillen (Tigres de Aragua), is believed to explain why the LVBP got access to more than US$12 million at the official exchange rate for the 2014–15 season.

However, the government did not provide access to sufficient foreign currency to fund the purchase of essential drugs for cancer, HIV/AIDS, or other health problems. People in Venezuela, including baseball fans, did not react well to these decisions, questioning how the government could prioritize baseball over many more important areas of the economy and society. This example underscores how Chávez and Maduro brought baseball within the government's control, making it no longer independent from domestic politics, as it had earlier been. How baseball's politicization will affect its future in Venezuela is unclear. Venezuelan playwright and novelist Ibsen Martinez is not optimistic: "In cruelly polarized Venezuela, mired in a disastrous economy . . . baseball culture has been a haven of joyful civility, togetherness and tolerance. Now even that bridge over the sectarian abyss seems to be collapsing."[14]

As economic and political problems mounted, crime and violence exploded, and personal safety and security of property became nightmares, as Venezuelans endured some of the world's highest homicide rates and levels of violence.[15] The kidnapping of Venezuelan Major Leaguer Wilson Ramos in 2011 demonstrated that Venezuelan baseball was not immune to the growing crime and violence. These problems factored into MLB teams' decisions to shut down Venezuelan baseball academies and limit the Summer League. A March 2015 memorandum from the commissioner's office advised MLB teams to heed "U.S. State

Department warnings regarding the prevalence of kidnappings and other violent crime in Venezuela."[16] More dramatically, the crisis led to the emigration of more than a million Venezuelans over the past fifteen years. Once upon a time, emigrants were mainly baseball players— the Alejandro Carrasquels, Luis Aparicios, and Cesar Tovars—who returned to play winter ball. Now, emigration is an exodus of people from many walks of life leaving Venezuela for a better future elsewhere.

The political, economic, and security crises adversely affect Venezuelan baseball by eroding the finances, economic prospects, and hopes of fans, sponsors, players, and prospects. With the Venezuelan economy falling apart, the government increasingly repressive, and individual insecurity pervasive, the chance to overcome these problems through baseball makes MLB look like a more attractive option for players and prospects. This desperation sounds disturbingly similar to what has long been a source of problems with MLB's activities in the Dominican Republic, a similarity that the MLB practice of shipping Venezuelan prospects to Dominican academies underscores. Venezuela's travails weaken its baseball institutions, economy, and culture vis-à-vis MLB's power in the ongoing globalization of baseball. In Venezuela baseball is becoming more than a way to escape poverty; it has become a way to get out of the country entirely.

The situation has deteriorated so much that President Maduro even accused MLB of pressuring Venezuelan players to join conspiracies to remove him from power. Maduro made this claim after some Venezuelan Major Leaguers posed for pictures next to an "SOS Venezuela" sign and posted them on Twitter. At the same time, and in a sign that the government's attitude toward MLB was seemingly schizophrenic, the minister of sport was encouraging MLB teams to invest more money in Venezuela.

More recently, the problems besetting Venezuela have spawned a proliferation of *buscónes*, agents, and operators of private baseball academies, many of whom have links to organized crime, schemes to launder drug-cartel money, and corrupt government officials. This emerging, corrupt, and criminal system seeks to access and control the millions of dollars MLB still spends on Venezuelan prospects each July 2. Without any effective responses from the Venezuelan government, MLB, and the MLBPA, this aspect of baseball in Venezuela is nearly out of control and threatens to damage baseball's place in Venezuelan society in alarming ways.

Conclusion

Baseball lore holds that the game came to Venezuela through young men returning from the United States enthralled with a new sport. Their efforts grew into an all-encompassing embrace and decades of the sport developing deep roots in Venezuelan society. Today young men in Venezuela increasingly see baseball as a way to escape a nation in political and economic turmoil. Between the distant past and the dismal present, baseball in Venezuela has become so interconnected with MLB's globalization and so politicized by Chávez's Bolívarian Revolution that the sport no longer functions independently in the country. These sobering observations raise questions about what the Venezuelan passion for baseball means now and in the uncertain times ahead.

NOTES

1. Elias, *Empire Strikes Out*, 109.
2. Liga Venezolana de Béisbol, "Historia."
3. Vargas, "Globalization of Baseball," 21–22.
4. "Venezuela GDP per Capita, 1960–2015."
5. Weisbrot, Ray, and Sandoval, *Chávez Administration at 10 Years*, 10.
6. Trinkunas and McCoy, *Observation of the 1998 Venezuelan Elections*.
7. Marcano, "El heredero al trono?"
8. Carter, "World Baseball Classic," 166, 171.
9. Carter, "World Baseball Classic," 172.
10. Pantin, "Llegó la hora de decirle no al Clásico Mundial."
11. Zirin, "Why Major League Baseball Owners Will Cheer."
12. Reinhart and Rogoff, "Venezuela's Spectacular Underperformance."
13. Johnson, "Venezuela, into the Abyss."

14. Ibsen Martinez, "Leaving Venezuela's Field of Dreams," *New York Times*, April 17, 2015, http://www.nytimes.com/2015/04/08/opinion/leaving -venezuelas-fields-of-dreams.html?_r=0.

15. Kiki King, "24,000 Murders Last Year Confirm Venezuela as One of the World's Most Dangerous Countries," *Guardian*, January 11, 2014, http://www .theguardian.com/world/2014/jan/12/violent-crime-makes-venezuela -dangerous.

16. Memorandum dated March 6, 2015, from Kim Ng, "Re: Travel to Venezuela" (on file with authors).

BIBLIOGRAPHY

Carter, Thomas F. "The World Baseball Classic: The Production and Politics of a New Global Sports Spectacle." In *Power, Politics and International Events: Socio-cultural Analyses of Festivals and Spectacles*, edited by Udo Merkel, 158–73. Abingdon: Routledge, 2014.

Elias, Robert. *The Empire Strikes Out: How Baseball Sold U.S. Foreign Policy and Promoted the American Way Abroad*. New York: New Press, 2010.

Johnson, Keith. "Venezuela, into the Abyss." *Foreign Policy*, December 8, 2014. http://foreignpolicy.com/2014/12/08/venezuela-into-the-abyss-maduro -oil-prices-pdvsa/.

Liga Venezolana de Béisbol. "Historia." http://www.lvbp.com/historia.php.

Marcano, Arturo. "El heredero al trono? Hablamos con Rob Manfred, el segunda al mando en Grandes Ligas." November 6, 2013. http://espndeportes.espn.go .com/news/story?id=1949578&s=bei&type=column.

Marcano, Arturo J., and David P. Fidler. "'Clean Up the Abuses': Building a Rule-of-Law Culture for Major League Baseball's Operations in Latin America." In *Sport and the Law: Historical and Cultural Intersections*, edited by Samuel O. Regalado and Sarah K. Fields, 115–33. Fayetteville: University of Arkansas Press, 2014.

———. *Stealing Lives: The Globalization of Baseball and the Tragic Story of Alexis Quiroz*. Bloomington: Indiana University Press, 2002.

Pantin, Efraín Ruiz. "Llegó la hora de decirle no al Clásico Mundial." *Béisbol13* (blog), February 18, 2013. http://beisbol13.blogspot.ca/2013/02/llego-la -hora-de-decirle-no-al-clasico_18.html.

Reinhart, Carmen, and Kenneth Rogoff. "Venezuela's Spectacular Underperfor- mance." *Project Syndicate*, October 13, 2014. http://www.project-syndicate

.org/commentary/venezuela-economic-underperformance-by-carmen
-reinhart-and-kenneth-rogoff-2014-10#Bl7wtPm0cpzk7cul.99.

Trinkunas, Harold, and Jennifer McCoy. *Observation of the 1998 Venezuelan Elections*. Atlanta: Carter Center, February 1998.

Vargas, Angel. "The Globalization of Baseball: A Latin American Perspective." *Indiana Journal of Global Legal Studies* 8, no. 1 (2000): 21–36.

"Venezuela GDP per Capita, 1960–2015." http://www.tradingeconomics.com /venezuela/gdp-per-capita.

Weisbrot, Mark, Rebecca Ray, and Luis Sandoval. *The Chávez Administration at 10 Years: The Economy and Social Indicators*. Washington DC: Center for Economic and Policy Research, February 2009.

Zirin, Dave. "Why Major League Baseball Owners Will Cheer the Death of Hugo Chávez." *Nation*, March 6, 2013. http://m.thenation.com/blog/173233 -why-major-league-baseball-owners-will-cheer-death-hugo-chavez.

8

Brazil

Baseball Is Popular, and the Players Are (Mainly) Japanese!

Carlos Azzoni, Tales Azzoni, and Wayne Patterson

For the better part of its first century, Major League Baseball (MLB) players were predominantly from the United States, with only a handful having learned their skills in a few neighboring countries such as Canada, Mexico, and Cuba. Since the 1970s, however, one country after another has made its presence felt in MLB: Venezuela, Colombia, Nicaragua, Panama, the Dominican Republic, Curaçao, and, farther afield, Australia, the Netherlands, Japan, South Korea, and Taiwan. Indeed, today's Major Leaguers come from eighteen different countries.

This chapter documents the emergence of a new country—Brazil—into professional baseball, one that is surprising in many ways. What is unique about Brazil's emergence in professional baseball can be expressed in three observations:

1. Baseball (*beisebol*) has developed in a country that is the leader in the world's most popular sport—soccer.

2. Baseball has developed into a major sport with almost no input from the United States for almost its first century in Brazil.

3. The majority of Brazilian players are of Japanese heritage; in effect, the game has been imported from Japan.

Although baseball is a long way from becoming as popular as soccer in Brazil (or in most of the world), baseball's expansion in Brazil is an interesting cultural phenomenon. As one looks at the development of baseball around the world, the game's introduction is often traced to the presence of players from the United States. But we also see some evidence of baseball being exported to neighboring countries without the direct influence of the United States. As Michael Oleksak and May Oleksak note in *Béisbol: Latin Americans and the Grand Old Game* (1996), "It was the Cubans' fight for independence from Spain during the last two decades of the 1800s that spurred the game's migration during this violent period. . . . Some [Cubans] went east to the Dominican Republic, while more headed west to the Yucatán Peninsula of Mexico."[1] In both cases, though introduced by immigrant Cubans, the game soon took root among citizens of the receiving country.[2]

In Asia the emergence of baseball is largely attributed to the popularity of the game in Japan, going back more than a century ago. Originally introduced by Americans, baseball spread from Japan to Korea and Taiwan.

In Brazil baseball's development is tied to Japanese immigrants. In fact, the game exists in Brazil primarily because of its popularity in the Japanese community; indeed, in the early days of Japanese immigration, the community was held together in part through its love for baseball.

Brazil the Country

It has frequently been noted that people in the United States have a limited understanding of other societies. U.S. president George W. Bush once astonishingly said to the president of Brazil, "Do you have blacks, too?"[3] Certainly, knowledge of Brazil is limited in the United States. Few Americans, for example, know that Brazil is larger in land area than the forty-eight contiguous U.S. states or that Brazil dominates South America in the same fashion that the United States dominates North America. Or that Brazil has a population of more than two hundred million people, the fifth largest in the world, or that São Paulo (population twenty-one million) is among the ten largest cities in the world, even larger than New York City. Nor do many Americans know that southern Brazil is the economic engine of the country, while the North is poorer and less industrialized. It is in the more affluent South that baseball has flourished.

Baseball's Appearance in Brazil

The first record of baseball being played in Brazil was in the early twentieth century, about the same time that it appeared in Mexico and the Dominican Republic. It was originally played by employees of U.S. companies who were in the country for short-term projects. Despite the enthusiasm of the U.S. visitors, the game did not take hold among Brazilians, who were already hooked on soccer. As Célia Abe Oi, director of the Museum of the Japanese Immigration History in São Paulo, notes, employees of American companies, particularly an electric company, introduced baseball to Brazil. The first recorded game was played in São Paulo. In the 1913–14 season, the Mackenzie team of São Paulo was able to attract a number of soccer players to turn to baseball. There was still a baseball league with American players, led by the telephone company, into the 1920s.[4]

In the 1930s baseball's development in Brazil took a turn unlike that in any other country. Rather than taking root in this soccer-mad country, baseball survived in Brazil because of the influx of immigrants from Japan, where baseball was enormously popular.

The first wave of Japanese immigration to Brazil began in 1908 with a formal agreement between the Japanese and Brazilian governments. Brazil needed workers for its coffee farms, and Japanese farmers were eager to move to Brazil, believing they could escape poverty in Japan. Immigration swelled in the period between the two world wars, and the immigrants brought baseball with them. The most popular destinations for Japanese immigrants were São Paulo and Paraná. São Paulo, now the second-largest "Japanese" city in the world after Tokyo, and Paraná have remained the centers for baseball's growth.

By 1929 a cultural and sporting association was formed in the Japanese community. Called Associações Japonesas Unidas de Presidente Prudente in Portuguese and Rengo Nihonjin Kai in Japanese, the association developed land in a community called President Prudente. This allowed for the construction of a sports complex with facilities for soccer, tennis, volleyball, basketball, and softball, as well as the first baseball diamond in the country. At the time there were more than thirty-five hundred Japanese immigrant families in the country, working primarily in coffee and cotton farming.

With the approach of World War II, fears about the allegiance of Japanese immigrants led to restrictive measures to weaken the links between the immigrant community and Japan. Unlike the measures taken in the United States (such as internment camps), the restrictions in Brazil focused on the reduction of cultural links with the home country. The Japanese language was prohibited, as were meetings of Japanese groups. Materials written in Japanese were destroyed. Thus, a permitted leisure activity such as baseball became a rallying point for the Japanese community. After World War II restrictions on the Japanese community were eased, but as in the United States there was little return migration to Japan. The Japanese community gradually became more integrated into Brazilian life and culture. Today the ethnic Japanese population in Brazil is around one million, with about half of the population employed in agriculture, 35 percent in commerce, and 15 percent in industry. There is also a growing presence of the ethnic Japanese in positions of leadership, including in the cabinet of the Brazilian government.

Post–World War II Baseball Development

With the arrival of peace, Brazil was again able to promote leisure activities. By 1946 the Japanese community, though still disillusioned with its wartime treatment in Brazil and with world affairs, was determined to develop culturally and socially. The first efforts in this direction were leisure and sporting diversions, including baseball. In 1946 the

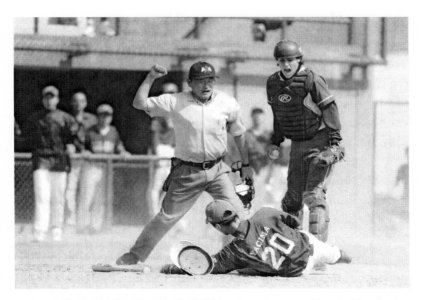

10. Junior Interclub Brazilian Baseball Championship, 2005: Nippon Blue Jays (base runner) versus Coopercotia (catcher). Ibiúna–São Paulo. (Photo by Flávio Torres/Fotomídia.)

São Paulo Federation of Baseball and Softball was formed under the leadership of a reporter from the *Gazette Esportiva*, Olímpio de Sá Silva, who served as president for seventeen years. Twenty-eight teams and their representatives were at the first meeting of the new federation in February 1947. Seventy percent of the representatives had ethnically Japanese names.[5] That year marked the first organized baseball competition in Brazil, with a league in São Paulo. The first champions were the EC Mailhense, who defeated Suzano in the championship game, 6–3. It is difficult in retrospect to judge the quality of the play, although two narratives offer some clues.

First, in 1951 the Columbia University baseball team came to play the Brazilian national team. It was the first international baseball presence in Brazil. The legendary Lou Gehrig notwithstanding, Columbia University had not been a powerhouse in U.S. college baseball. In a batting demonstration Anthony Mitcher, Columbia's left-handed first baseman, hit all of the available balls into a heath beyond the left-field wall. Second, seven years later, in 1958, a new stadium was dedicated in São Paulo, the Estádio do Bom Retiro. The inauguration was celebrated with a series between a São Paulo all-star team and the team from Waseda University of Tokyo. The cumulative score in the series was Waseda 372–São Paulo 5, with the Japanese university team hitting fifty-three home runs. Clearly, Brazilian baseball still had a long way to go.

In the mid-1980s the Confederaçao Brasileira de Beisebol e Softbol (Brazilian Confederation of Baseball and Softball, or CBBS) was formed as a governing body for both sports. As with many national sports bodies, it has focused on player and national team development and youth baseball and softball. Under the leadership of Jorge Otsuka, the confederation now has an estimated forty thousand players in Brazil and more than one hundred clubs participating in various levels of national championships.

Entrance of Brazilians into Professional Baseball

The first Brazilian to be signed to a professional contract in the United States was José Pett, who in 1992 signed for seven hundred thousand dollars as a sixteen-year-old free agent with the Toronto Blue Jays. A six-foot-six right-handed starting pitcher, Pett made the Pittsburgh Pirates' forty-man roster in 1998, but he never appeared in the Major Leagues. After a few years in AAA he was released by the Cleveland Indians in 2000. Pett appeared in 101 Minor League games, almost exclusively as a starting pitcher.[6]

Rafael Motooka of São Paulo was the second Brazilian to play professionally in the United States. He was playing for the Potomac Cannons, the Class A Carolina League affiliate of the Cincinnati Reds, when we interviewed him in 2005. When he arrived in the United States, Motooka knew no English, though he did know what the McDonald's sign represented. When we stepped up to the counter at a restaurant, Motooka detected that our server was Spanish speaking. He quickly slipped into

11. Junior Interclub Brazilian Baseball Championship, 2005: São Paulo versus Gecebs (batting). Ibiúna–São Paulo. (Photo by Flávio Torres/Fotomídia.)

fluent Spanish, which he had learned from his Hispanic teammates. Asked about differences in how baseball is played in the United States and Brazil, Motooka mentioned that in Brazil, if a team is ahead 10–0, they might still bunt. "Here in the United States," he said, "anyone who did that would be flat on his back at their next at bat." Motooka played for four years in the Reds organization before being released.

Jorge Otsuka

A seminal figure in Brazilian baseball development, and the longtime president of the Brazilian Baseball and Softball Confederation, Jorge Otsuka is optimistic about baseball's future in Brazil, noting that Brazil is a country where sports in general are extremely popular. Brazil has won numerous World Cup championships in soccer and is a growing world presence in basketball, volleyball, tennis, and auto racing. Otsuka also cited the recent adoption of a national baseball confederation and training program with international coaches. This latter approach has aided the development of baseball in other countries. He credits the work of the confederation, with the help of the Brazilian Olympic Committee, in lifting the level of play in Brazil. "Now we are able to face traditional countries such as Cuba, Mexico, Panama, and the Dominican Republic. In the last World Cup [played in Cuba], we finished proudly in seventh place. In the Pan American Games we finished fourth, and in the Olympic qualifying tournament we were eliminated in the quarterfinals by Cuba. Our biggest problem is that we need more people playing the game. Today, the majority of the players are concentrated in the most southern part of the country, and we need to change that."[7]

We asked Otsuka whether baseball being concentrated in the Japanese Brazilian community would limit its growth. He answered: "Baseball began in an organized form in Brazil only fifty years ago, and now finally we are being able to break the [Japanese] barrier and include non-Japanese in the game. With this change, we have been able to bring baseball to schools and colleges, and from here we will be able to become a top contender internationally. . . . To keep improving, we feel the Brazilians need to play more among top-level teams. That's why we endorse the policy to send more and more players to foreign leagues."[8]

We also asked Otsuka if Brazilians use the same training methods at the new training facility in Ibiuna as in Japan, knowing that, compared to the United States, the Japanese do more physical conditioning, have longer practices, and have very long repetitions of drills.[9] "The training methods," said Otsuka, "are a mix between the Japanese and Cuban schools. The Brazilian coaches tend to follow the Japanese methods, but three Cuban coaches [all Olympic medalists] were recently brought by the Brazilian Confederation to teach new methods."[10]

The Face of Brazilian Baseball

Clearly, Brazilian baseball has a different face from that found in the United States and in Japan. Although the Brazilian fan base is small, it is devoted. The players and their teams look much like their counterparts in other countries in terms of uniforms and equipment. However, the style of play is quite different. In the United States there is a greater attention to the unwritten rules or codes of the game, understandings about what behaviors and strategies are acceptable in game conditions. For example, in MLB there was great debate surrounding the successful bunt attempt by San Diego catcher Ben Davis in the eighth inning of a 1–0 game (in May 2001) when he broke up a no-hitter being pitched by Curt Schilling of the Arizona Diamondbacks. The unwritten rule in the United States is that one never breaks up a no-hitter in the late innings by bunting. This debate would have been incomprehensible in Brazil. In the Brazilian game a base runner whose team is ahead 10–0 may even steal second base. As Motooka mentioned above, the results in the United States would be quite different.

Nevertheless, with its enormous athletic talent and vast numbers of people, it seems that Brazil is poised to make a mark on baseball's world stage. However, organized professional baseball is a curious enterprise. In one respect it is the ultimate form of meritocracy: given the multitude of performance measures in the game, it is relatively easy to make personnel decisions, say, cutting a .200 hitter or promoting a .300 hitter. But in other ways the merit model breaks down. For almost seventy years many of the greatest performers in the sport were not eligible to participate in the American game. And while Jackie Robinson broke the MLB color barrier in 1947, baseball's racial bigotry toward African Americans and prejudicial judgments about other groups have not disappeared. Research has shown how prejudice has affected the advance of Caribbean players, Canadians, Asians, short right-handed pitchers, and African American players today who are not center fielders.[11] A similar phenomenon existed for Japanese players, as the first ten in the Majors were pitchers, including Masanori Murakami (1964–65) and then Hideo Nomo thirty years later. The first nonpitcher was Ichirō Suzuki in 2001. Through 2015 of the fifty-four Japanese-born players, 40 (74 percent) have been pitchers (despite the success of the outstanding Ichirō Suzuki). We wonder if ethnically Japanese Brazilian players are similarly "stacked," that is, relegated to certain positions based on racial stereotypes.[12]

In the first decade of the twenty-first century, Brazilian players were attracted more to Japan than to the United States. Japan offered fewer steps in the Minor League system, a more familiar style of play, possibly more recognition by Japanese scouts, and ethnic similarities. The United States offered potentially higher salaries and greater recognition. Language did not appear to be a factor, since few Brazilians of Japanese heritage of this generation speak Japanese or English.

Baseball has been growing steadily in Brazil in recent years, both in popularity and in the level of play. The national team made history by playing in the World Baseball Classic (WBC) for the first time, and several Brazilian players have made it into the Major Leagues (Yan Gomes, André Rienzo, and Paulo Orlando as of 2015), helping the sport attract some much-needed attention in a soccer-loving country. The growth in the baseball's popularity came despite many challenges, especially after government funding that was crucial to help develop the sport was cut when baseball was dropped from the Olympic Games starting in 2012. If it wasn't for MLB seeing the potential of the sport in Brazil, the gains made in the recent past would likely have been lost. In the words of Jorge Otsuka, "After the Brazilian Olympic Committee cut the funding to our sport, only Major League Baseball was able to help us. We went calling for help, and they helped; they saw the potential of the sport here. After ninety years of development with virtually no connection to the U.S. or MLB, the support of Major League Baseball was [now] fundamental for baseball in Brazil."[13]

The confederation used to receive about 250,000 reals a year (about US $100,000 at the time) from the Brazilian Olympic Committee to help develop the sport. But the CBBS faced financial jeopardy after the money stopped coming, shortly after Brazil hosted the 2007 Pan American Games in Rio de Janeiro. "No more Olympics, no more money," Otsuka said. "We had to start making significant cuts; everything really deteriorated. We became desperate. Conditions had been improving up until then."[14]

To make matters worse, Brazilian baseball players also lost their right to apply for the Bolsa Atleta, the government-run program that gives athletes a monthly income of about 1,000 reals ($400). The benefit could only be given to athletes from confederations that organize national championships with at least five state federations involved, and there were not enough states participating in baseball tournaments. "That was a huge setback for the athletes," Otsuka said. "That money was the only incentive that they had. It helped them with trips, training, and even with their education. It's natural that many lost interest in the sport and even gave up playing altogether."[15]

Looking to overcome the financial difficulties and continue developing the sport, the confederation went to the United States to seek help. Prior to this baseball's development in Brazil had virtually no influence from the Americans. As noted earlier, the sport's presence and growth in the country were always linked to the nation's huge Japanese community.

For years MLB's presence in Brazil was little more than visits by a few coaches who participated in clinics, but that changed after MLB learned of the Brazilian Confederation's financial problems and noticed the potential of the baseball market in the South American country.

In an interview in late 2014, Paul Archey, then MLB's vice president of international operations, told us: "We've gotten deeper into Brazil in the last five years. We started to get a little deeper with some of our programs, with coaching assistance, and with equipment. . . . Brazil is a large market and a growing economy, with a lot of athletes. We felt we could develop players as well as our business. We know it's long term, but we are already seeing some benefits."

"There were a few things that we saw that made Brazil a potential market," Archey added. "We saw a lot of good athletes playing. We saw a training facility that was really first class and a federation that was well organized and wanting to learn and grow."

Archey also said there was no reason to doubt Brazil's potential: "We are very optimistic about how baseball is going to grow in Brazil. We want to continue to grow our business, get more exposure for baseball on television, which is critical to grow the fan base."

In 2011 the Brazilian Confederation and MLB formed a partnership to host the league's Elite Camp for the first time in Brazil. The Elite Camp, which goes to several countries to develop the sport and find new talent, provided high-level training to some of the top players from Brazil and nearby countries such as Argentina, Ecuador, Panama, and Peru. Former MLB All-Star shortstop Barry Larkin was among the instructors helping train players and coaches from Central and South American baseball federations. "That's a critical program for us," Archey said. "We have about fourteen Brazilians playing professionally, and eight of them signed contracts out of the Elite Camp."

Barry Larkin and the 2013 World Baseball Classic

Another major step for the Brazilian baseball program was the agreement by Hall of Fame shortstop Barry Larkin to serve as the team manager for Brazil in the 2013 WBC. Brazil's performance in the WBC came in part because of the presence of Larkin as the national team's manager. The Hall of Famer led the Brazilians after MLB helped the confederation reach a deal with him. Larkin introduced "situational baseball" and "the ability to do small things" to the Brazilian team's game. These new skills developed by the Brazilian national team soon showed a payoff in the 2013 World Baseball Classic.

But what really helped the game develop was Brazil's surprising participation in the 2013 WBC.[16] The WBC was initiated in 2006, after baseball was voted out of the Olympics. The WBC was organized as a sixteen-nation tournament divided into four pools in four cities, then quarterfinals, semifinals, and finals. Brazil did not qualify for either the inaugural WBC or the second in 2009, as only sixteen teams were chosen by invitation.

For the 2013 WBC twelve teams qualified from their previous results, but four more spots were allocated to the winners of a qualifying four-team tournament. Brazil was invited to the "Qualifier 3" tournament in Panama City in November 2012 with Colombia, Nicaragua, and host country Panama. Brazil was a distant underdog, with all the other teams having fielded a number of prominent Major Leaguers.

The series opened with a surprising 3–2 Brazil win over favorite Panama, even though Panama had several veteran Major Leaguers. Two days later Brazil pounded out a 7–1 victory over Colombia. Later, Panama knocked out Colombia, setting up the final, leading to a dramatic 1–0 victory for Brazil.

In the next round Brazil faced a tough challenge after being placed in Pool A in Fukuoka, Japan, with China and Cuba. Brazil lost all three games, although it did lead former WBC champ Japan 3–2 in the eighth inning of the first game. Brazil also played well against Cuba and China, losing both games by identical 5–2 scores.

As result of this strong performance, Brazil's standing in international baseball rose, and in the November 2014 ratings by the International Baseball Federation Brazil was ranked fifteenth. "Inviting them to the World Baseball Classic was really the best thing we've done for them," said Paul Archey, then MLB vice president of international operations. "It really gave them a boost. They took full advantage of it. It gave them a lot of publicity, gave them some prize money."[17]

Because of Brazil's successful participation in the WBC, some of the country's main television stations aired specials about baseball, producing pieces on the Brazilian team and many of its players. There were tutorials about the sport's rules and traditions, and newspapers and some of the nation's top websites devoted space to the Brazilian team.

Jorge Otsuka said the WBC reignited the flagging interest of some Brazilian athletes in the game. "It made a lot of difference. Many players were already thinking about quitting. The exposure of the game was significant. Everyone was looking at Brazil. It gave a great motivational boost to the sport. Baseball was forgotten here until then, but today we can proudly say that we are the fourteenth-ranked team in the world, ahead of some more traditional teams."[18]

Yan Gomes: The First Brazilian Major Leaguer

In the first edition of this book we predicted there would soon be a Brazilian Major Leaguer. Our prediction was realized when the Toronto Blue Jays called up catcher Yan Gomes on May 17, 2012, who thus became the first Brazilian player in MLB history.

Gomes was first introduced to baseball in São Paulo after his father met a Cuban coach at a market, who invited the young Gomes to play for his club team in São Paulo. Subsequently, the Gomes family immigrated to Miami, where Yan played high school ball, earning a scholarship to the University of Tennessee, where he was a freshman All-American. In 2009 the Toronto Blue Jays drafted Gomes in the tenth round. He spent three seasons in the Minors before being called up to the Blue Jays. He appeared in 43 games before he was traded to the Cleveland Indians. The 2013 season was a breakout year for Gomes: he appeared in half the Indians' games, hitting eleven home runs and batting .294.

Prior to the 2014 season Gomes signed a twenty-three-million-dollar, six-year contract with the Indians. He has become a mainstay in the Indians' lineup, appearing in 135 games in 2014, batting .278 with twenty-one home runs and seventy-four runs batted in and taking over as the starting catcher. He also has a familial connection to baseball history, as his wife, Jenna, is the daughter of former Giants pitcher Atlee Hammaker.

André Rienzo: Second Brazilian Major Leaguer and First Developed Primarily in Brazil

André Rienzo joined the Chicago White Sox on July 30, 2013. He developed his skills through the CBBS. In a June 24, 2014, interview with the authors, conducted in Portuguese, Rienzo said, "I was four years old when I started playing. My two brothers played baseball and my mother played softball, so at first I was kind of forced to go because I was little. I began to like the game and began to play at age four."[19]

The right-handed pitcher was signed as an international free agent in

12. André Rienzo of the Chicago White Sox in the dugout at Oriole Park at Camden Yards. (Photo by Wayne Patterson.)

2006 at age eighteen. After six years in the Minors, he made his debut as a starter for the White Sox in July 2013. He made twenty-one starts over two seasons before being traded to the Miami Marlins, where he appeared primarily in relief in 2015.

Rienzo's six years in the Minors were challenging, as it has been for players from virtually all countries: "It was very difficult, and for Minor League players, we had to deal not only with one's mental challenges, but also the player's technical development as well. The player has to grow and improve. Then sometimes you are competing with other teams and with your own teammates as well to advance. So everyone wants to improve, improve. There are many players; the wages are too low; you live with five or six players in the same house. I spent seven difficult years and a few months. It was not easy to get here."[20]

The Future of Brazilian Baseball

Baseball in Brazil, in the view of MLB International's Paul Archey, has the potential to develop in the same way as it did in Australia: "Brazil is at a stage that can be compared to where Australia was back in the early 1990s, when they only had a couple of professional players and it was a niche sport in a country that had a lot of sports competing, a lot of good athletes. Weather is conductive to playing, and we've seen that, over the last twenty-five years, Australia has grown from having one professional to having eighty professionals and seeing their sport grow and having their own national competition."[21] The CBBS has been doing everything in its power to develop baseball. "We are trying to make sure the sport becomes more professional," said Jorge Otsuka. "We want to hire coaches, offer clinics, develop more programs."[22] Helping out, the Seattle Mariners and the Los Angeles Dodgers have sponsored a few youth tournaments in Brazil, distributing prize money and taking advantage of the opportunity to try to find new talent.

Beyond the success of Yan Gomes and André Rienzo, other Brazilian players are knocking at the door of the Major Leagues. Paulo Roberto Orlando joined the Kansas City Royals at the beginning of the 2015 season and had more than 200 at bats as a reserve outfielder for the defending American League champions. In addition, Orlando earned a World Series ring with the Royals in 2015, appearing in twelve postseason games, including every World Series game, batting .273, with three runs, an RBI, and a sacrifice fly. As such, he became the first Brazilian baseball player to achieve all of those milestones.

The success of the Brazilian national team in the WBC; the presence of Major Leaguers like Gomes, Rienzo, and Orlando; and the increase in the number of players in the country and the increased exposure bode well for the future of baseball in Brazil.

NOTES

The title of this chapter is the semifacetious response from the first person who responded to one of the authors (Patterson) when he first asked about baseball in Brazil.

1. Oleksak and Oleksak, *Béisbol*, 17.

2. Oleksak and Oleksak, *Béisbol*, 17. The first Mexican national to appear in the U.S. Major Leagues was Melo Almada in 1933. Dominican players were largely prohibited because of the color barrier. The first Dominican, Ozzie Virgil Sr., did not make his first MLB appearance until 1956.

3. "Bushs Allgemeinbildung: Gibt es Schwarze in Brasilien?," *Der Spiegel*, May 19, 2002, http://www.spiegel.de/panorama/0,1518,196865,00 .html.

4. Abe Oi, *Beisebol*, 4.

5. For example, Associação Esportiva Linense, Massayoshi Muto; Esport Clube Jundiaí, Taketaro Mita; Dragão Esporte Clube, Kango Kamijo; and Pereira Barreto Base-Ball Clube, Tomotsu Ishi.

6. With a win-loss record of 23-34 and a career earned run average of 4.70.

7. Jorge Otsuka, interview with the authors, São Paulo, October 12, 2007.

8. Otsuka, interview with the authors.

9. "Yakult's baseball training facility was built by Yakult Brazil, not Yakult Japan. Yakult Brazil's current president, Massahiko Sadakata, built the baseball complex because he wanted to give back to the nippon community after the profits made by his company in the country. Sadakata and Yakult Brazil gave the training facility to the Brazilian Baseball and Softball Confederation and still help finance its maintenance." Jorge Otsuka, private conversation with the authors.

10. Otsuka, interview with the authors.

11. Oleksak and Oleksak, *Béisbol*; Williams and Patterson, "*Trois balles, deux prises*"; Corbett and Patterson, "Social Significance of Sport." Other examples of scouting prejudice arise in the resegregation of African American players in the Major Leagues. Corbett and Patterson note that in 2002, 75 percent of Major League center fielders were African American, while there was no African American third baseman or first baseman, only one catcher, and only 3 out of 150 (2 percent) were starting pitchers.

12. Smith and Harrison, "Stacking in Major League Baseball."

13. Otsuka, interview with the authors.

14. Otsuka, interview with the authors.

15. Otsuka, interview with the authors.

16. Yan Gomes, André Rienzo, and Paulo Orlando (current Major Leaguers)

as well as Major League prospects Thyago Vieira and Leo Reginatto were all critical players on that team.

17. Paul Archey, phone interview with the authors, October 22, 2014.
18. Otsuka, interview with the authors.
19. André Rienzo, interview with the authors, Baltimore, June 24, 2014.
20. Rienzo, interview with the authors.
21. Archey, interview with the authors.
22. Otsuka, interview with the authors.

BIBLIOGRAPHY

There are unfortunately no writings on Brazilian baseball prior to Yan Gomes's ascent to the Major Leagues or the 2013 WBC available in English, other than the earlier version of this article. The citations below by Célia Abe Oi, director of the Museum of the Japanese Immigration History in São Paulo, written in Portuguese, are the only known publications on Brazilian baseball in any language. There is a fleeting reference to Brazilian baseball in Maarten Van Bottenburg, *Global Games*, translated by Beverley Jackson (Urbana: University of Illinois Press, 2001).

Abe Oi, Célia. *Beisebol: História de uma paixão*. São Paulo: Federaçao Paulista de Beisebol e Softbol, 1996.
———. *Guia de cultura Japonesa*. São Paulo: Fundaçao Japão, 2004.
Corbett, Doris, and Wayne Patterson. "The Social Significance of Sport." In *Proceedings of the Fourteenth Annual Cooperstown Symposium and Baseball and Society*. Jefferson NC: McFarland, 2003.
Lewis, Michael. *Moneyball*. New York: W. W. Norton, 2003.
Oleksak, Michael M., and May Adams Oleksak. *Béisbol: Latin Americans and the Grand Old Game*. 2nd ed. Indianapolis: Masters Press, 1996.
Reaves, Joseph A. *Taking in a Game: A History of Baseball in Asia*. Lincoln: University of Nebraska Press, 2002.
Smith, Earl, and C. Keith Harrison. "Stacking in Major League Baseball." *Journal of African American Men* 2 (December 1996): 113–29.
Wendel, Tim. *The New Face of Baseball*. New York: HarperCollins, 2003.
Williams, Savanah E., and Wayne Patterson. "*Trois balles, deux prises*: The Influence of Canada on Baseball, the Influence of Baseball on Canada." Paper presented at the Fifth Annual Symposium on Baseball and Society, 1993.

Part 2 Asia

9

Japan

"No Matter What Happens, Stand Up"

Dan Gordon

Minutes after the magnitude 9.1 earthquake on March 11, 2011, Ishino-maki Kōgyō High School Coach Yoshitsugu Matsumoto was directing traffic on a damaged bridge behind the school's baseball diamond when he noticed the canal underneath the bridge was flowing upstream and rapidly rising. He sprinted toward his ball field, hollering to his players, who were conducting fielding drills. From the third floor of the school, the team watched through steady light snow as black water spilled over the banks of the Jozan Canal and swept over the baseball diamond and school grounds. The surging water continued rising, and the first floor of the school was soon submerged. Cars were floating by with hazard lights flashing and pedestrians crying for help.

It took four days before the tsunami flooding receded and ballplayers were able to return to their neighborhoods and search for their families. Seventy percent discovered they had lost family members or their homes. Waves as high as thirty-plus feet had swept away industrial districts and residential neighborhoods, and thirty-seven hundred residents of Ishinomaki were missing or dead. One week later Coach Matsumoto held a meeting with his players, and they decided to resume practice, even though their equipment had been washed away and the ball field was buried under cars, household appliances, and debris.

Three years later I visit the high school. All of the players from the 2011 team have graduated, but I want to interview Coach Matsumoto, who took his team to the National High School Baseball Invitational Tournament (Spring Kōshien) the following year. Because the tsunami-damaged JR Senseki rail line is out of service, I travel by intercity bus, heading north from Sendai on the Sanriku Expressway, passing restored rice fields and rest areas that had served as triage centers and command posts. Portions of the elevated highway acted as a coastal levee, preventing the surging ocean from flowing farther inland. For some towns the highway became an evacuation route for children running from the tsunami surging toward their schools. The bus lets me off on Prefectural Road Route 16, a main thoroughfare in the northern section of Ishinomaki, and I head toward the school on foot. Although many of the stores and businesses along the road suffered major damage from the earthquake that preceded the tsunami, much of the road was spared the tsunami's full wrath. One mile farther toward the shore is the large swath of vacant land that had once been the vibrant center of the city.

As I descend the slope from the canal bridge, I see a few dozen players tending to the field, raking the frozen infield soil and covering the diamond with tarp strips. The team equipment manager leads me into a small two-story wooden building and up the stairs from the equipment storage room to Matsumoto's office. Lining the staircase wall are player handprints with handwritten captions such as, "You Can Shine the More You Get Dirty," "Be Like a Weed's Soul," and "No Matter What Happens, Stand Up." The office walls are covered with mementos from 2012 Spring Kōshien (Senbatsu)—a photo of the team bowing in front of sacred Kōshien Stadium, players collecting infield soil after their loss, and quotes from famous professional ballplayers offering the team encouragement. High on the wall is a small Shinto shrine for prayer, below that a banner on the wall with handwritten blue characters: "You have to focus and throw the ball to be in the right place." Hanging from the ceiling in the corner is a symbolic chain of origami paper cranes with well-wishings from students.

Coach Matsumoto comes up the stairs and warmly greets me. He sits down facing me on the tatami mat. He looks younger than many coaches and more introspective. He tells me in detail the story of the tsunami and how it was the father of one of his players who first suggested that they resume play. The parent said to the coach, "I lost my house, I lost my job, the one thing I look forward to now is seeing my son play baseball." Matsumoto realized at that point how important *kōkō yakyū* (high school baseball) was for the community. He tells me in detail the story of the tsunami and why his players started to play. He speaks about the team's philosophy. He shares that ever since the tsunami, he has been even stricter with his players. "I wanted to teach them that anything can happen in this life. I didn't want to see weakness such as complaining. I want players to be prepared because anything can happen."

"High school baseball is just for three years," he adds, "but we still have eighty years left to live. You have to prepare them for life."

High school baseball in Japan is not so much a sport as it is a philosophy and a tool of education—not in the sense of molding boys into gentlemen like one might see at an English boarding school but in the sense of building character and refining spirit. The spiritual underpinning of high school baseball is the same as in the martial arts. The philosophy plays out on the diamond in some of the most intense baseball I've ever had the privilege to watch.

In 1987 I traveled the globe on a Thomas J. Watson Fellowship, witnessing local versions of baseball. I spent about five months in Japan. And like most first-time spectators of Kōshien, I was enthralled by the unbridled pageantry and passion of players and fans.

The most watched high school sporting events in the world, the National High School Baseball Championship (Summer Kōshien)—and, in the past few decades, its spring counterpart—have been producing heroes since the inception of a schoolboy national tournament in 1915. Every August when the do-or-die summer tournament begins at the start of OBon, the whole Japanese archipelago grinds to a halt. On any given day millions of television viewers enjoy seesaw contests with sayonara home runs, squeeze-play bunts, players sliding headfirst into first base even on sure outs, and losing players crying and scooping the sacred infield soil into pouches to carry off as keepsakes.[1] Accompanied by a volunteer interpreter, Yoshihiko Sasai, who was taking time off from preparing for Japanese university entrance exams, I got a whirlwind look at Kōshien Stadium, which is considered a repository of Japanese spirit.[2]

The stadium has ivy-covered walls and a wailing siren, concessionaires speaking in earthy Osaka-ben selling noodles in broth, polite fans laughing tensely at their own team's defensive mistakes, marching bands playing "Popeye the Sailor Man" and "Mickey Mouse Club," female fans in the loge boxes fanning themselves with *uchiwa* (flat, nonfolding paper fans), elderly men in tank tops nursing beers and a scorecard, and fans of all ages propping *kachiwari* (packed crushed ice) on their heads to combat the intense August heat. Near the turnstiles vendors sell inflatable seat cushions. In the cafeteria near the pressroom one can buy spicy curry with coffee, popular fare at Kōshien. The pressroom looks like the newsroom of a major daily, with reporters from the six national sports tabloids and the large dailies scurrying in and out or tuned to the action on television.

A heroic performance at Kōshien earns a player instant stardom and typically ensures him a spot in the Japanese pros. An appearance at Kōshien inspires hordes of female students to sneak baked goods to a team's dormitory late at night. Yoshihiko, my interpreter, shared with me that at Shizuoka High School, where he went to school, female students would loan their handkerchiefs so players could wipe their brows, and then the girls would display them, unwashed, on the walls of their bedrooms. If the team wins the tournament, hometowns hold massive victory parades and shopkeepers create window displays in festive colors. After Kōnan High School won the summer tournament in 2010, becoming the first national champion from Okinawa, the team was greeted by an estimated four thousand screaming fans at the airport and three thousand more at the school. Thousands more jammed Naha's famous Heiwa Dori, clapping and throwing ticker tape skyward as some in the crowd performed *eisa* (Okinawan traditional dance) to *ōdaiko* and small hand drums.

I was first introduced to Japanese high school baseball at the semifinals of a tournament qualifier in 1987 in Osaka's Nissei Stadium. The nearly sellout crowd seemed blue collar, and the vast majority were over forty. The rain started to pour seconds after Yoshihiko and I arrived at our seats, and we hurried with fans into the furnace-like indoor corridors.

I had liked Yoshihiko from the moment I met him at a youth hostel in Osaka, and I quickly developed an immense trust in him as a cultural interpreter, undoubtedly biased by our mutual fascination with baseball. Although his English was shaky—like my Japanese—he was recently out of high school, which worked to my favor because he seemed to know in detail the inner workings of the Japanese high school baseball scene.

From the top of the ramp we watched several hundred players, all with close-cropped hair, hoarsely singing and chanting, marching in place, and thrusting fists in unison in the downpour. A handful of boys in the front rows wore buzz cuts like the players. Yoshihiko said they were freshmen. Demonstrating enthusiasm was a prerequisite for obtaining a spot on next year's squad. The buzz cuts represented purity, the most popular attribute of high school players. "Professional baseball is amusement," he said, "but the high school baseball player thinks of nothing but baseball. He has no interest in money. He thinks only of the team. When a person looks into the eyes of the Japanese high school player, he sees his earnest nature, fighting spirit, and Japanese purity."

After the final out the teams lined up at home plate, bowed to each other, and sprinted to their respective cheering sections, where they bowed to the fans, and then the winning team lined up again at home plate to hear their school song. As Yoshihiko and I left the stadium, winning players strutted out from an exit door carrying colorful origami chains. Yoshihiko explained that this was a good luck charm called *senbazuru*, made from one thousand paper cranes constructed by female students. Teams hung the chains in their dugouts and lockers. In ancient Japan paper was believed to contain a spirit. Losing players filed out with tears streaking down their faces. Hundreds of sobbing schoolgirls swarmed around them.

I looked inquisitively at Yoshihiko. He said, "In Japan tears are considered beautiful."

Purity

Shedding tears in Japan has traditionally represented shedding impurities. "Pureness is the symbol of Kōshien," says Mitsuyoshi Okazaki, senior editor at *Bungei Shunjū*. "At Kōshien all the uniforms are white, the ball is white, the caps are white, and the infield soil is pure; it's a special blend of sand trucked in from western Honshu. Purity is fundamental in Japan. It's the Japanese way of thinking."[3]

Robert Whiting, a well-regarded author on Japanese baseball, defines purity as moral rightness and total sincerity toward your chosen sport—clarity of thought so one can concentrate:

> It's not just in baseball, but in the martial arts. Judo athletes also wear white. Part of the whole package of learning judo and kendo was to learn how to be a better human being, to learn character and morality. In that sense, I think they talk of purity of heart: In any kind of judo and kendo, you don't violate the rules. You're not supposed to go around beating people up. When you come to practice, you bow as a sign of respect to the dojo. High school ballplayers do it. Even some pros do it.[4]

The purity ethic traces all the way back to Miyamoto Musashi, a seventeenth-century swordsman, who wrote about proper spirit, education, hard work, and state of mind—the idea that you can exceed your

13. Chiben-Wakayama High School players bow as their well-choreographed section looks on at 2010 Senbatsu. From an early age coaches instill in schoolboy players that proper attitude and respect for the game are as important as winning. (Photo by Deanna Rubin.)

physical limitations and overcome physical pain and injury through sheer force of will.

During the Meiji period (1868–1912), a wave of Western culture washed over Japan. Meiji rulers brought in American and European teachers, scientists, engineers, and professors as Japanese society changed from a system of feudalism to industrialization. A handful of American schoolteachers brought baseball equipment and an enthusiasm for sharing the game with Japanese youth. In a country emerging from three hundred years of self-imposed isolation, baseball was readily embraced because it pitted pitchers against batters in both physical and mental standoffs similar to traditional Japanese sports like sumo and the martial arts. The desire to return to traditional Japanese values such as purity was soon expressed through baseball and emerging martial arts such as judo and kendo.

The introduction of *koto gakkō* (elite preparatory schools) in Japan was a countermeasure against the Western influence in Japanese society. These schools were crafted by Meiji educators to teach Confucian philosophy (Bun) and martial arts (Bu) to the prospective elite. Students at *koto gakkō* embraced machismo, punishing physical training, and hazing rituals as a means of perfecting moral faculties. Ichiko (First Higher School of Tokyo), the most prestigious of the preparatory schools, approached baseball with the same rigid discipline as judo. Coaches started talking about "bloody urine." If you didn't urinate blood, you hadn't practiced hard enough. When Ichiko lost to bitter rival Meiji Gakuin, a school run by American Protestant missionaries, which symbolized to Japanese traditionalists the Western cultural invasion, Ichiko stepped up excruciating training methods. Players were forbidden to use the word *ouch* in practice, although if they were in severe pain they were allowed to use the word *kayui* ("it itches"). And players whose elbows were deformed from excessive throwing of curve balls would hang from trees to straighten out their arms. Ichiko went on to defeat a squad of American part-time ballplayers three games in a row, an accomplishment that drew national media attention and put baseball on the map in Japan.

Joseph A. Reaves, in his fine history of baseball in Asia, *Taking in a Game* (2004), writes about the larger significance of these victories: "Baseball, from that moment, assumed a new sociopolitical role in Japan. No longer was baseball an instrument of cultural oppression—a symbol of the perceived social and military superiority of the United States. Baseball, it turned out, could be a great equalizer. It opened doors to new levels of self-worth and international respect. Schools across Japan began forming baseball teams. From that moment, baseball was on its way to becoming the Great Japanese Game in Asia."[5]

A country already well attuned to amateur baseball showed phenomenal interest in the premiere of the national high school baseball tournament in 1915. The *Asahi Shimbun* sponsored the tournament with the aim of "rearing youths with a healthy body and mind." By 1923 the capacity crowds at Naruo Stadium in Nishinomiya prompted construction of the fifty-five-thousand-seat Kōshien Stadium, the largest stadium at that time in Asia.

Cultivating the Mind

In front of a teary-eyed Kōshien Stadium crowd and millions of television viewers, Ishinomaki Kōgyō High School team captain Shoto Abe stepped up to the microphone in March 2012 and declared in a player oath of fair play, "If we can overcome our hardship, we believe that great happiness will come. We will send our passion, courage, and smiles all over Japan." Playing in Kōshien is the dream of every schoolboy player in Japan, but for Ishinomaki Kōgyō players it was the culmination of one year of training under tremendous adversity. It had taken one month of working from dawn to dusk for the team to clear four hundred tons of debris from their field. Then they resumed baseball practice without equipment, which had been washed away. Players resorted to shadow swings and shadow pitches under the supervision of Coach Matsumoto. Starting pitcher Takumi Miura, determined to make up for the physical gap between him and other high school aces, began eating extra helpings of rice and gained twenty-two pounds. He had written in his elementary school graduation book years earlier that he would someday take his mother to see him pitch at Kōshien and after the tsunami was so relieved to find her alive that he doubled down on his efforts. In their opening game of Senbatsu (Spring Kōshien), Miura pitched using a new glove with the words *Strength of Ishinomaki* stitched on it. He developed a blood blister on his pitching hand in the fourth inning, and Ishinomaki Kōgyō ended up losing 10–5, but the team still left the field feeling satisfied. As Matsumoto puts it, the aim of their hard work was not baseball perfection, but self-perfection. "Kōshien was our goal," he says, "but it was not our purpose. Our purpose is to achieve complete spiritual and physical maturation as a human being.

We must have purpose inside and be the best person in Japan. Number one in taking care of our cleats, number one in cleaning the grounds, number one in being good students, number one in politeness."

One goal of training is learning to overcome adversity and to reach a higher state of being. Results are achieved only through process. Suishu Tobita (1886–1965), the "Ring Lardner" of Japan, embodied the samurai spirit of Japanese baseball as manager of Waseda University and in his extensive writings on baseball. He famously wrote, "The purpose of [baseball] training is not health but the forging of the soul, and a strong soul is only born from strong training." Students should train "until they were half dead, motionless, and froth was coming out of their mouths."[6] Minus the froth, his philosophy lives on. A typical practice in Japan is not shagging fly balls, taking ground balls, or leaning on a batting cage watching teammates hit. It is sprints, calisthenics, long-distance running, pitchers throwing two or three hundred pitches on the sidelines between starts, and infielders diving over and over (a grueling drill sometimes called one thousand fungo). Players train for long hours and with few days off. In a 2013 survey the Japan High School Baseball Federation put out to 4,032 teams in Japan, 95 percent said they practiced at least six days per week year-round. Twenty-seven percent said they practiced every day. On school days practices generally run three to five hours, although at least one hundred schools practice longer.[7] On Sundays and holidays 76 percent practice more than five hours per day, 59 percent more than six hours, and 33 percent more than seven.[8]

Teams practice longer hours during Japan's brutally hot summers. In 2013 nineteen high school managers reported having coached players during their career who died from heat stroke.[9] And even in the coldest regions of northern Japan, they practice outdoors in winter. Batting practices often occur on snow with orange baseballs and sprinkled-soil base paths. Hokkaido Memanbetsu High School, which made the 2012 Senbatsu, famously trained outdoors in below-zero (Fahrenheit) temperatures. "The training is really a spiritual practice," says Hitoshi Takashima, who coaches three-time national champion Chiben Academy. "The more they suffer now, the happier they will be when they win."[10]

Or lose, says Gen Sueyoshi, founder of YakyuDB.com, an insightful, well-followed blog that provides extensive daily updates on Japanese baseball.[11] As a youngster his first-generation Japanese American parents enrolled him in kendo to teach him traditional Japanese values. In kendo, as in other martial arts, training focused on kata, the series of movements in the martial arts that one cannot separate from the end results. As he grew older he understood that process was as important in other areas of life in Japan: for instance, *kodawari* (an uncompromising and almost stubborn relentlessness to pursuing something) in Japanese cuisine—a chef obsessing about having the exact ingredients from a specific source. Sueyoshi observes the same degree of focus on process in Japanese high school baseball. It's not just about competing; there are other aspects of baseball that a player has to think about. When players lose at Kōshien, he says, they are not kicking over the water cooler or watching with glazed eyes as the winning team celebrates.[12] "They always bow in front of their cheering crowd and collect dirt off the playing field. Winning is important to them, but I think at the end of the day, even if they lose, players feel a sense of accomplishment because of how they trained up until that point."[13]

Sueyoshi clarifies that an important idea in Zen Buddhism is that after you die, you are reborn according to how you lived your life. Coaches who believe in rebirth view the purpose of life as strengthening your spirit and becoming a better person: if a ballplayer becomes strong in spirit through excruciating physical training, daily brutal practice sessions are justified. "It's utopian in some ways," Sueyoshi says. "But people still feel that is the way things should be. I don't know if players think that way, but older coaches are thinking that to some degree."[14]

Selfless Play

Leading off opening day of the 1987 Kōshien tourney, players marched lockstep around the diamond and then took an oath to play ball "as

14. Nichidai San team captain Sho Agezami warming up at 2011 Summer Kōshien. The team's mantra was "Practice Makes Perfect," and their coach Masayoshi Ogura teaches his players self-restraint and caring for others. (Photo by Deanna Rubin.)

purely as the ball is white and the sky is blue." After securing press passes, Yoshihiko and I entered the right-field grandstand and sat in front of the Ika High School cheering section, which was made up of several hundred students wearing blue cardboard rice-paddy hats chanting "Ika, Ika, let's go!" in unison through plastic megaphones. With four games per day and only minutes separating each game, the corner grandstands would often dramatically change colors, composition, and movement. A section brimming with fans snapping red handkerchiefs might give way to hundreds of fans rhythmically thrusting blue pom-poms.

Ika's band played school songs, and a handful of the students, upbeat and enthusiastic although their team was losing 5–1 to Chuo High School, waved Japanese flags with prayers on them. A quieter larger contingent of fans surrounded the student section. Many wore whites

15. Noda Niko High School players doff their caps in respect to the dojo at the 2009 Summer Kōshien. From an early age coaches instill in schoolboy players that proper attitude is as important as winning. (Photo by Deanna Rubin.)

and straw hats to protect them from the sun. Even with all their protection, fans throughout the stadium often complained about the heat. Numerous fans had hand radios with headphones and were leaning forward in their seats, some softly predicting *sanshin* (strikeout) on two-strike counts. Standing on the staircase flanking the left side of the student formation, a man with a hand towel resting on the back of his neck held at shoulder height a framed photo of someone batting.

"Why is he doing that?" I asked Yoshihiko.

"Tradition. When a boy dies and does not play in Kōshien, a parent brings a picture to Kōshien for the son to see the game he might have played."

A man in the middle of the crowd stood up and shouted in a voice of desperation, and almost everyone in the section laughed. I turned quickly to Yoshihiko, "What did he say?"

"He says, 'Ganbatte. [Give your best.] Please listen to me! Ganbatte.' Everyone laughed because they think he is foolish."

Chuo increased their lead with a series of singles in the eighth inning. Fans surrounding us squirmed. Some young women sobbed with palms on their faces. With his hands on his knees, Ika's right fielder yelled, "It all depends on me!" The crowd didn't react. Yoshihiko said, "He said that to the pitcher to make him relax."

Ballplayers at Kōshien are famous for their selflessness. Stories abound of pitchers performing with injury, illness, or exhaustion. The most legendary in recent years was Masahiro Tanaka throwing 742 pitches in five games of the 2006 Kōshien tournament while battling intestinal inflammation, which kept him on intravenous fluids between starts and at times even during games. His opposing pitcher in the finals, Yūki Saitō, famously threw a modern record 948 pitches during the two-week tournament.[15] Tanaka would go on to dominate Nippon Professional Baseball League and eventually rise to stardom with the New York Yankees, while Saitō, beset with injuries, has floundered in the NPB minors.

At the 1998 summer tournament, Daisuke Matsuzaka hurled all eighteen innings of a scoreless tie in a quarterfinal match, pitched all nine innings of a replay game the following day, played the outfield in the semifinal and pitched the ninth inning, and tossed a no-hitter in the finals. Over the final four days of the tournament, he had thrown 535 pitches. He threw 250 pitches in the quarterfinal game only a day after hurling 148. Matsuzaka's performance similarly catapulted him to superstardom.

A more recent example in 2013 sparked international outcry. Over nine days in the summer tournament, sixteen-year-old Tomohiro Anraku threw 772 pitches, including 232 in a thirteen-inning game in which he threw every pitch. His arm went limp in the championship, and his team lost 17–1.[16] His performance was analyzed and dissected in American sports pages, and many in American baseball circles wondered if over pitching was ruining players' future professional careers. Sports agent Don Nomura compared it to child abuse.[17]

Medical science has only recently been introduced in *kōkō yakyū*. Pitching arms are now evaluated before the start of Kōshien, and days off are scheduled in the final three rounds. Extra-inning tiebreakers were introduced in 2015 in regional high school tournaments with no links to the spring or summer Kōshien tournaments. Once in a blue moon a pitcher comes along who will ask for more rest. Yu Darvish's father insisted that the coach at Tohoku High School limit his son's pitch counts during less meaningful games. Darvish was let loose at Kōshien and fired 505 pitches at the 2003 summer tournament. Former Yomiuri Giants star pitcher Masumi Kuwata, who in the 1980s led his PL Gakuen team to five Kōshien appearances and two championships, used to nap on a golf course rather than throw 300 daily pitches he was expected to toss between starts. "High school students are still growing," he explains. "If you overuse your shoulder or elbow you get injured, so I was being careful not to throw so much."[18] Like Darvish, Kuwata also threw caution to the wind in the big tournaments, pitching in almost every game, landing second all-time in the Kōshien record books with twenty wins. Down the stretch *kōkō yakyū* pitchers are expected to sacrifice themselves for the benefit of the team. Says Robert Whiting: "Kōshien is all about purity of heart and fighting spirit and fighting for your teammates and your school and your hometown. And [for a pitcher] to say, 'I can't do that because I have a future as a Major Leaguer—I'm gonna be making millions of dollars elsewhere,' would probably be the grossest thing you can say in light of that tournament. Nobody would be insane enough."[19]

Most Japanese work extremely hard and for long hours with dedication to their jobs, so they identify with a pitcher *going all out* in the moment and not worrying about tomorrow. Former Major Leaguer Masato Yoshii told *ESPN the Magazine*, "If Kōshien changes, I think we would lose what is beautiful about baseball."[20]

Coaches and ballplayers view *nagekomi* (repetition of the pitching arm beyond the point of exhaustion) as an indispensable training tool. Pitching coaches believe it stretches out the arm and leads to elasticity and arm strength. For this reason NPB teams actually covet these players, says Marty Kuehnert, former general manager of the Tohoku Rakuten Golden Eagles and now a senior adviser. "Some of the damn scouts think the more they throw, the stronger the guy is, which is diametrically opposite what we believe in the States."[21]

High school coaches also believe that marathon throwing sessions perfect mechanics, so there is less stress on the arm.[22] Japanese pitchers use their lower body to propel and power the pitch through the upper body and the arm, whereas in the United States most pitchers rely more on the upper body. Pitchers also learn to center their bodies on *kikai tanden*, which in martial arts is the body's center of gravity and source of energy (ki), located in the abdomen. Using this technique players are instructed to channel all their energy from the tips of their toes to the top of their head.[23]

Mind and Body

Among the wisdom Ishinomaki Kōgyō's Coach Matsumoto shares with players is to face difficulty with courage. Player handprints on the walls of the equipment room impart that "you can grab things that are dirty and smelly. The hands are stronger than the eyes, so when players see something bad, they don't run away."

"High school is a player's last step before entering society," says Matsumoto. "So part of my responsibility is to prepare them for life. I have seen lots of students get in trouble after high school. So that's why I want to build a better person."

In addition to teaching the game, high school coaches in Japan are also training player minds. One veteran coach instructs his players, "Be able to do the right things the obvious ways." Carry out your responsibility without people telling you to do it. As the coach explains, "Because when a student graduates and goes out into the real world they need that ability."[24] The coach of Kisarazu Sogo High School teaches his players self-esteem through improvisation. Players are required to wake up a teacher in the middle of the night, then perform a skit or tell a joke. According to the coach, the goal is to encourage players to emerge from their shyness even if no one responds favorably. Pitcher Yosuke Shimabukuro, who led Kōnan High School to the 2010 spring and summer Kōshien titles, says that during required daily morning strolls, players were instructed to smell the air, listen to nature, and touch roadside flowers in order to "use all five senses and create a sixth" that could raise alertness during games.[25] Many coaches teach Bun Bu Ryōdō (pursuing both Bun and Bu), descended from Bushido, the code and way of life of the samurai. When interpreted literally and applied to baseball, Bun Bu Ryōdō calls for players to study hard while they are training hard. But Bun Bu Ryōdō is often interpreted more broadly as a code of ethics. A typical example would be Eimei High School in Kagawa, which forbids players from any show of emotion on the playing field (no high fives, fist pumps, postgame celebration, and so on), in order to show respect at all times for one's opponent.[26]

Japanese high school players never argue with an umpire. If it's a called strike, the players won't question it. "They assume that's true. There's nothing else," says Gen Sueyoshi. "There's nothing there except player versus player."[27] High school players are also expected to give back to the local community. Following winter storms, in addition to shoveling their diamond, they shovel neighboring streets and sidewalks. "Even when I don't say it, they do it," says Ishinomaki Kōgyō's Coach Matsumoto. "They feel indebted, and people rely on them." When Ishinomaki Kōgyō players saw elderly pedestrians struggling in the tsunami's rapidly rising water, they rushed into the powerful, icy currents and piggybacked them to the school's upper floors. In a similar spirit Tohoku High School players spent weeks after the tsunami distributing food and water at a refugee center and then hauling away debris in Ishinomaki to clear roads.[28] The team was adhering to its motto, which appears prominently on a sign above center field of the school diamond: "Without principle, nothing can be accomplished."

Taibatsu

In his autobiography, *Sadaharu Oh: A Zen Way of Baseball* (1984), Japan's most prolific home run hitter explains the collective punishment when one of his freshman teammates hit out of turn or spoke out of line. His teammates were forced to line up in facing rows and punch each other. If the upperclassmen watching the lesson deemed your punch soft, then you were forced to punch again. Oh looked back on the ritual with nostalgia: "It is not easy to acquire a sense of shared responsibility. People by nature look out for themselves first and for others second. But it is higher consciousness to learn to care for others, to acquire a sense of genuine responsibility for the actions— good or ill—of the team or group to which you belong. On a baseball team, there is simply no avoiding this demand. The lesson is painfully learned—but it is learned."[29]

Taibatsu (corporal punishment) has long been considered a teaching tool in Japan. A recent survey found that 70 percent of Japanese high school students had experienced some sort of physical punishment in school.[30] A similar survey revealed that more than 10,000 high school students received *taibatsu* during the 2012–13 school year.[31] A survey of 270 active NPB players found that 46 percent had been beaten in high school by their managers.[32]

In a four-year period from 2011 to 2014, the Japanese High School Baseball Federation handed down punishments for 245 separate reported incidents of team violence. Of those incidents, 97 involved upperclassmen beating underclassmen and 148 involved managers physically abusing players.[33] Bludgeoning with bats, punching, kicking, and slapping were the most documented forms of *taibatsu*, resulting in broken bones, gashes requiring stitches, hospitalizations, and in one incident cardiac arrest. Managers and upperclassmen also resorted to firing fastballs at players at close range, striking players with helmets or metal chairs, forcing players to choose between drinking kerosene or swallowing a stink bug, and pouring boiling water on players.

Assaulting underclassmen is one of the methods used to teach obedience and respect towards elders. Players are expected to speak politely to upperclassmen and to greet them and bow properly.[34] "To a senior player, you don't talk back," says Takahiro Horikawa, a baseball writer with the *Asahi Shimbun*. "You listen to them when they tell you to take out the garbage. Senior players come around, you move over to the side, so they can go first in line."[35] Upperclassmen reinforce this "*senpai/kohai* [upperclassmen/underclassmen] system" through mental or physical torture. In a newspaper interview future Hall of Famer Ichirō Suzuki described the hazing he endured as a high school underclassman. Not only was he required to cook and do laundry for upperclassmen, but he was forced to kneel on the rim of a lidless garbage can for a half hour for infractions ranging from talking out of turn to upperclassmen to overcooking rice.

In his book *Discourses of Discipline* (2013), Aaron L. Miller suggests that Japanese ballplayers accept *senpai/kohai taibatsu* because of "a common desire that many Japanese athletes—indeed, many Japanese people—have to be part of an orderly, harmonious team (group) in which one's role is clearly defined. . . . So long as an individual feels that their presence within the group has purpose, they will be content or at least willing to obey the orders of their seniors."[36] *Taibatsu* is seen as a way to hammer down the nail that sticks out, such as a player who refuses to move a base runner over, works less hard than his teammates, or disrupts the team's harmony. *Taibatsu* maintains the traditional Japanese system of strict hierarchy and cohesiveness.

Recently, players have been physically punished for errors committed during practice and games, breaking curfew, smoking cigarettes, cooking *yakiniku* in the dorm rooms, not being vocal enough during practice, playing pickup soccer, riding two to a bicycle, forgetting to ask permission to use the bathroom, showing relief that a practice was scaled back due to rain, eating outside of permitted times, and looking down at the ground while laughing.

A dramatic shift in perception occurred in 2013 after fifteen judoka from the National Women's Judo Team filed a complaint with the Japan Olympic Committee detailing how coaches beat them with bamboo swords, pushed their breasts, kicked them, and pressured them to compete injured in the run-up to the Summer Olympics in London.[37] The following month a high school basketball player in Osaka hung himself after being slapped forty-one times by his coach the day before. Although it was neither the first team to protest abuse nor the first Japanese athlete to resort to suicide in response to physical punishment, the judo and basketball stories attracted widespread media scrutiny. "There was a societal change at that time," says Marty Kuehnert. "Athletes talked, and that gave others the motivation that they could talk about this subject. And it opened the floodgates."[38]

All of a sudden the national morning and evening news shows reported hundreds of incidents of recent physical abuse. Prominent politicians expressed concern that the coverage might torpedo Tokyo's bid for the 2020 Summer Olympics. "The incident is the gravest crisis in Japan's sporting history," Education Minister Hakubun Shimomura told reporters at a press conference. "This is the time that Japan can show both to those inside and outside the country that it has abandoned all violence in sports."[39]

Between 2012 and 2013, as the government called for reform, the number of coaches and teams suspended for corporal punishment in high school baseball doubled.[40] The typical severity of a punishment also increased from a warning or one-month suspension to six months or one year.[41]

Whether the crackdown was an anomaly or the beginning of a long-term decline in corporal punishment is yet to be determined. One veteran *kōkō yakyū* coach shares, "When I was a player physical punishment from coaches was very common, but nowadays it's not acceptable so I don't do it. I don't do it because times have changed."[42] Kazuhiro Tanabe, former executive director of the High School Baseball Federation and now a senior adviser, adds that there is a changing of the guard. He says that as younger coaches take over, more of whom have teaching degrees and are teaching other subjects, they tend to have a "less Spartan" approach and "emphasize the fun of baseball."[43]

In the High School Baseball Federation survey published four months after the scandals, 10 percent of coaches responded that they still practiced *taibatsu*.[44] Sankei sports journalist Yūsuke Abe says that those coaches resort to *taibatsu* with the player's growth in mind, and coaches do not know how to mold players without having the option of beating character into them. He disagrees on a personal level with corporal punishment, but adds, "Corporal punishment is wrong and I obviously think that coaches should not do it. But there is no clear difference between corporal punishment and educational guidance. There is no clear answer about how to teach the students."[45]

Distinction is in the eye of the beholder. At the wake for the Osaka basketball player, his mother told his coach to look at her deceased son's bruised face. "You can tell there's been physical punishment, can't you?" she asked. "Do you call that 'instruction' or do you call that 'physical punishment'?"[46]

"Teachers should use words and attitude to train players," says Masumi Kuwata, who has spoken openly about the corporal abuse he endured during his childhood, particularly as an elementary school player.[47] "There were no days when you weren't hit," he told NHK Television shortly after the news of the scandals broke.[48]

At a seminar he gave to Osaka high school coaches after the basketball player's suicide, Kuwata shared that he had visited a school in the United States while playing in the Pittsburgh Pirates organization. "There was no angry shouting or beating at all. They played baseball freely and leisurely. Seeing that major leaguers come from such an environment is proof that we can train people to become wonderful players without corporal punishment."[49]

The Future of Japanese High School Baseball

As I head downstairs from Coach Matsumoto's office, a player in the equipment room politely bows. He tells me he is a second baseman, although he is assigned to the cheering squad because he is a freshman. He practices with the team for one hour in the morning before school and for four hours after school. He explains that from training he learns group harmony as well as mental and physical strength. Coach Matsumoto comes down the staircase, and the student abruptly turns, doffs his cap, and bows deeply—the standard greeting all high school players throughout Japan have for their manager. Coach Matsumoto offers to show me to the bus stop. As we walk along icy sidewalks, he describes in more detail local damage from the tsunami and shares how two days after the tsunami, Japanese self-defense forces boat-lifted him from the high school and he assisted them in rescuing elderly residents stranded in their homes. Then he was brought to an evacuation center, where he served as the director.

That Matsumoto would be enlisted to serve on rescue missions and head a shelter did not surprise me, because of the respect afforded high school baseball coaches in their local communities. Both on and off the field, coaches are larger-than-life, and their authority and judgment are almost never second-guessed. However, the perception of baseball as authoritarian also contributes to some young people drifting away to other sports. In 2013 baseball dropped to ninth place as a sport Japanese children between ages ten and nineteen often play.[50] In a recent survey more than 40 percent of high school baseball coaches said it is possible that other sports such as soccer and basketball will be more popular than baseball in the future or that they in fact already are.[51] Soccer in particular has captured the Japanese imagination, partially because of its emphasis on individuality and freedom.

"Soccer is more about self in space," says Mitsuyoshi Okazaki. "But baseball is more instructive. Youths want to move away from that. Instead of hearing, 'Do this, do that, do this,' they don't want anything to do with that torture." "Soccer arose in Japan only recently and is based on the professional game elsewhere," says Masayuki Tamaki, an independent sports journalist. "Therefore it is not stalled in the rigidity of the past. Baseball models itself after tradition, while soccer took shape from the game in Europe."[52]

Japanese schoolboy baseball players are also turning West. The Major League Baseball success of Ichirō Suzuki, Hideki Matsui, Yu Darvish, and Masahiro Tanaka, who were established superstars in Japan, has inspired a whole new generation of ballplayers. Over the past five years three high school seniors have made headlines for contemplating a move to the States. Most prominent among them was six-foot-four high schooler Shōhei Ōtani, who after throwing 99–100 mph at Summer Kōshien shocked the baseball establishment by announcing his dream was to play baseball in the Major Leagues. Ōtani told *Sportiva Shueisha*, "I want to become a player that can give kids a dream to shoot for, like Ichirō and Daisuke Matsuzaka did for me when I was a kid."[53] The largest obstacle for Major League teams is that Japanese high school players who sign overseas are ineligible to play in the NPB for three years after their return. The so-called Tazawa rule came into effect after Industrial League pitcher Jūnichi Tazawa opted to skip the NPB draft to sign with the Boston Red Sox. Major League teams also have a league-enforced $2.2 million limit on how much they can spend on player bonuses and salaries for nonprofessional international free agents. So in many instances, scouts would rather target players in Latin America, who will sign for less money. "Most of the scouts are saying they can sign five to ten Latin American players for less than a million dollars," says Ira Stevens of ScoutDragon, which provides video of Japanese players to Major League scouts. "They don't want to blow it all on one player from Japan."[54]

Baseball analysts say that Japanese professional baseball has lost some appeal, but among the Japanese populace *kōkō yakyū* is as hard-core as ever.[55] Says veteran Kyodo News sportswriter Jim Allen, "High school baseball has a very strong and different following than pro baseball. In one sense they are kids and kids can identify with them. On the other hand, people appreciate that it's old-fashioned. It's the ultimate Japanese sport in the sense that it is one-shot, do-or-die, no saving it for tomorrow. I think that's so Japanese."[56]

"Kōshien is as huge and passionate as it has always been," says Gen Sueyoshi. "There's no money involved. It's just kids out there playing the sport and working hard because they love it. That really appeals to the masses."[57]

One father's adoration for the high school game is what inspired Ishinomaki Kōgyō's Coach Matsumoto to resume practice amid disaster and heartbreak. His team's determination to play inspired a nation. Coach Matsumoto thinks there will always be an essential role for kōkō yakyū in Japanese society. "The amount of people playing baseball goes up and down," he says, "but Japanese people don't pay notice to fluctuations in popularity, because high school baseball is always inside Japanese hearts."[58]

And in the collective memory of nine young men and a coach from Ishinomaki.

NOTES

1. The tradition started in the late 1940s when Kazuo Fukushima, the ace pitcher for Kokura Middle School, pocketed soil after losing at Kōshien for the second year in a row. Fukushima would go on to win two consecutive Kōshien championships and in 2011 was inducted into the Japanese Baseball Hall of Fame.

2. In 2013 the Asahi Shimbun newspaper reported that it used the phrase "step(ped) on Kōshien soil" more than one thousand times in the previous ten years. "VOX POPULI: Hallowed 'Kōshien Soil' Transcends Baseball as Symbol of Hope and Inspiration," Asahi Shimbun, August 17, 2013.

3. Mitsuyoshi Okazaki, telephone interview with the author, October 10, 2002.

4. Robert Whiting, telephone interview with the author, December 21, 2002.
5. Reaves, *Taking in a Game*, 51–52.
6. Quoted in Whiting, *You've Gotta Have Wa*, 38.
7. In Japan Saturday is a school day.
8. For reasons explained later, the amount of time teams spend practicing has been decreasing. Compared to 1993 approximately 35 percent fewer teams practice six or more days per week.
9. Up until recently high school coaches prohibited athletes from drinking water during practices. It was thought that clenching thirst was a sign of weakness. Enduring dehydration was considered a means of building mental toughness.
10. Source of quote is Kenneth Eng's outstanding documentary *Kokoyakyu* (2006).
11. Gen Sueyoshi, Skype interview with the author, January 26, 2015.
12. In 2014, after a loss in the Kōshien qualifying tournament, a high school team from Akita Prefecture famously stood outside the ballpark in the rain for an hour bowing in thanks to passing fans.
13. Sueyoshi, Skype interview.
14. Sueyoshi, Skype interview.
15. Saitō started all six of his team's games during the tournament, including four complete games in a row from August 18–22 for a total of sixty-nine innings. By comparison, many states in the United States limit the number of innings pitched in a three-day period to ten. Maryland and Utah limit the number per week to fourteen innings. Noted American orthopedics surgeon Dr. James Andrews recommends that high school pitchers should throw no more than ninety pitches per game and should have at least five days' rest between starts.
16. In the early 1990s Robert Whiting conducted a survey of Major League Baseball and Nippon Professional Baseball players and found that 40 percent of Major League pitchers were over age thirty, compared to 26 percent in Nippon Professional Baseball. Whiting feels the gap may be closing, since many NPB clubs have now adopted a six-man rotation and starting pitchers throw fewer pitches between starts.
17. Yahoo.com, April 4, 2013.
18. Masumi Kuwata, email interview with the author, August 10, 2015. Kuwata praises the efficient manner in which PL Gakuen practices were run, which

he says well prepared players for games and for a future career in the pros. "For fielding practice, we were not allowed to throw the ball higher than the face," he says. "And for hitting practice, in order to meet balls in the middle of the bat, we only used bamboo bats except on the day before practice."

19. Whiting, telephone interview, March 9, 2015.

20. Jones, "When 772 Pitches Isn't Enough."

21. Marty Kuehnert, telephone interview with the author, February 28, 2015.

22. At first glance a comparison of the number of Tommy John surgeries seems to support this idea. As of April 2014, 204 MLB pitchers in the history of the league have had Tommy John surgery, compared with 61 NPB pitchers. However, the numbers are skewed by demographics and past medical practice. Major League Baseball has thirty teams, while NPB has twelve. And until recently, elbow injuries in Japan were often misdiagnosed.

23. Whiting, telephone interview, March 9, 2015; email survey author distributed to high school coaches in Kumamoto Prefecture. The channeling of ki is audible during high school games, where batters utter a short yell as they settle into their batting stance. This technique, known as *kiai*, is also used in the martial arts and taiko drumming.

24. Email survey.

25. Riko Miyadera, "Rookie of the Year in His First Spring League," *Hakumon Chuo* (Summer 2011), http://yomiuri.co.jp/adv/chuo/dy/people/20110804.html.

26. Refraining from emotion is common in traditional Japanese sports such as the martial arts and sumo wrestling, where even the faintest smile after a victory is considered improper.

27. Sueyoshi, Skype interview.

28. Tohoku High School made headlines as well for playing in the Spring Kōshien tournament only sixteen days after the Tohoku quake. Although the school had not been damaged by the earthquake or the tsunami, several players lost relatives or homes. Tohoku manager Yukihiko Igarashi told the *New York Times* that the decision to play in Kōshien was the hardest he had ever made as a manager. Students were still in shock, he added, but "there are no words to describe how it feels to have people cheer for you" at Kōshien. Ken Belson, "A Call to Play Ball in Japan Followed Much Fretting," *New York Times*, July 16, 2011, D1.

29. Oh and Faulkner, *Sadaharu Oh*, 37.

30. Toru Nakakoji and Atsushi Akutsu, "Survey: Nearly Two-Thirds of College Athletes Say Corporal Punishment Is Acceptable," *Asahi Shimbun*, May 12, 2013.

31. According to Education Ministry survey results published in the *Japan Times*, June 3, 2013.

32. Conducted by former Yomiuri Giants pitcher Masumi Kuwata, the survey is described in the second article ("Severe Sports Training Methods Became *Taibatsu* in Time," *Japan Times*, June 2, 2013) of Robert Whiting's two-part series on corporal punishment in Japanese sports training.

33. These are incidents reported to the federation. Many analysts have said that most incidents of corporal punishment in scholastic baseball go unreported.

34. A Japanese business executive told me that when hiring, companies look for former players "because they know how to conduct themselves and they know how to respect authority within an organization."

35. Takahiro Horikawa, telephone interview with the author, January 13, 2003.

36. Miller, *Discourses of Discipline*, 144.

37. Scholastic judo in Japan has a greater incidence of death and injury than baseball. From 1983 to 2012, 118 students died as a result of judo accidents (60 percent of them from brain injury) compared to zero deaths in judo clubs in Europe and the United States.

38. Kuehnert, telephone interview.

39. ABC News, September 20, 2013.

40. "840 Corporal Punishment Cases Reported in Schools," *Asahi Shimbun*, April 28, 2013.

41. This is based on my statistical data compiled from monthly reports issued by the Japan Student Baseball Association. The monthly reports were accessed on http://www.yakyubaka.com.

42. The email survey I distributed to high school coaches from Kumamoto Prefecture, who all wished to remain anonymous (same survey as listed above). A 2006 survey of more than twenty-five hundred high school baseball coaches by *Asahi Shimbun* found that 70 percent admitted to practicing *taibatsu* at one time; however, only 7 percent said they had used corporal punishment recently. See "Taibatsu wo kangaeru, taibatsu wo kataru" [Thinking about *taibatsu*, talking about *taibatsu*], special series, *Asahi Shimbun*, June 9–13, 2006.

43. Kazuhiro Tanabe, email message to Marty Kuehnert forwarded to the author, April 16, 2015.
44. Japan High School Baseball Federation survey, 2013.
45. Yūsuke Abe, email interview with the author, February 12, 2015. For a more in-depth discussion, see passages on *ai no muchi* (whip of love) in Miller, *Discourses of Discipline*, 105.
46. "Basketball Adviser Apologizes for 'Physical Punishment' of Suicide Victim at Wake," *Mainichi Japan*, January 9, 2013.
47. Kuwata, email interview. Kuwata is the first prominent Japanese athlete to call for an end to corporal punishment.
48. Ed Odeven, "Veteran Athletes, Coaches Adamant That Corporal Punishment Has No Place in Sports," *Japan Times*, January 20, 2013.
49. Shigemi Sato, "Violent Coaching Rooted in Militarism," *Japan Times*, February 11, 2013.
50. "The 2013 SSF National Sports-Life Survey of Young People," Sasakawa Sports Foundation, December 2013.
51. 2013 Japan High School Baseball Federation survey.
52. Okazaki, telephone interview; Masayuki Tamaki, telephone interview with the author, January 28, 2015.
53. *Sportiva Shueisha*, October 15, 2012. Ōtani ultimately decided to play in Japan after the Nippon Ham Fighters promised him the opportunity to be the team's designated hitter on days he did not pitch. In 2014 he tied the record for the fastest pitch ever thrown in the NPB.
54. Ira Stevens, email interview with the author, December 3, 2014.
55. Samurai Japan, the team representing Japan in the World Baseball Classic, also has a strong following. More than one-third of all TV sets in Japan tuned into a first-round 2013 WBC match between Japan and Brazil, topping all broadcasts that year, including the 2012 Summer Olympics. Japan Baseball Federation, September 3, 2013, http://www.baseballjapan.org.
56. Jim Allen, Skype interview with the author, January 8, 2015.
57. Sueyoshi, Skype interview.
58. Yoshitsugu Matsumoto, interview with the author, February 17, 2014.

BIBLIOGRAPHY

Eng, Kenneth. *Kokoyakyu: High School Baseball* (documentary). 2006.

Japan High School Baseball Federation. "95th National High School Baseball

Championship Survey of High School Baseball: Investigation of Actual Conditions." 2013.

Jones, Chris. "When 772 Pitches Isn't Enough." *ESPN the Magazine*, August 5, 2013. http://espn.go.com/mlb/story/_/id/9452014/pitcher- tomohiro -anraku-future-japanese-baseball-espn-magazine.

Kelly, William W. "The Spirit and Spectacle of School Baseball—Mass Media, Statemaking and 'Edu-tainment' in Japan, 1905–1935." In *Japanese Civilization in the Modern World XIV, Information and Communication*, edited by Umesao Tada, William W. Kelly, and Kubo Masatoshi. Special issue, *Ethnological Studies* (National Museum of Ethnology, Osaka, Japan) 52 (2000).

Miller, Aaron L. *Discourses of Discipline: An Anthropology of Corporal Punishment in Japan's Schools and Sports*. Berkeley: Institute for East Asian Studies, University of California Berkeley, 2013.

Mita, Norifusa. "Hanamaki East and Shōhei Ōtani: 'After Ten Years We Want to Be Active in the Major Leagues.'" *Sportiva Shueisha*, October 15, 2012.

Murray, Elizabeth. "Japan's Coaching Abuse Problem Surfaces through Viral Video." September 20, 2013. http://abcnews.go.com/abc_Univision /japans-coaching-abuse-problem-surfaces-viral-video/story?id=20311087.

Oh, Sadaharu, and David Falkner. *Sadaharu Oh: A Zen Way of Baseball*. Tokyo: Kodansha, 1984.

"One-Third of All TVs on in Japan Tuned to World Baseball Classic." Japan Baseball Federation, September 3, 2013. http://www.baseballjapan.org /system/prog/news.php?l=e&i=350.

Passan, Jeff. "The Pitch-Count Problem: How Cultural Convictions Are Ruining Japanese Pitchers." April 4, 2013. http://sports.yahoo.com/news /the-pitch-count-problem--how-cultural-convictions-are-ruining-japanese -pitchers-012016897.html.

Reaves, Joseph A. *Taking in a Game: A History of Baseball in Asia*. Lincoln: University of Nebraska Press, 2002.

Roden, Donald T. "Baseball and the Quest for National Dignity." *American Historical Review* 85, no. 3 (1980): 511–34.

——— . *Schooldays in Imperial Japan: A Study in the Culture of a Student Elite*. Berkeley: University of California Press, 1980.

Sasakawa Sports Foundation. "2012 Kodomo no Supootsu Raifu Deta [2012 Sports Life Survey of Young People]." 2012.

Sasaki, Tooru. *Akiramenai machi Ishinomaki sono chikara ni oretachi wa naru:*

Ishinomaki kōkō yakyūbō no kiseki [Don't give up Ishinomaki, we become the power: The baseball miracle of Ishinomaki High School]. Tokyo: Baseball Magazine Sha, 2012.

Shimizu, Satoshi. *Kōshien Baseball Archaeology.* Tokyo: Shinkolon, 2002.

Whiting, Robert. *You've Gotta Have Wa: When Two Cultures Collide on the Baseball Diamond.* 1989. Reprint, New York: Vintage, 2009.

10

Japan

Professional Baseball Enters the Twenty-First Century

William W. Kelly

As several articles in this volume document, baseball went global early on, spreading to the Caribbean in the 1860s and to Japan in the 1870s, even as it was still taking shape in the United States. Baseball may fashion itself as the national pastime in the United States and in Cuba, but it has been even more solidly the dominant sport in Japan since the 1890s and remains so, longer than any other country.

It became the most popular sport of Japan's elite boys' schools by the end of the nineteenth century and then moved up to the new national universities and downward through the national secondary school system early in the twentieth century. The 1920s witnessed a burgeoning mass culture in the metropolitan regions, in which schoolboy baseball was watched by enthusiastic crowds in new sports stadiums and reported prominently in the national press and through a nascent national radio network.

The professional game appeared in 1936, with an initial league of eight teams. It was shut down by the military government in 1944, but after the war, in late 1946, General Douglas MacArthur, then supreme Allied commander of the Allied occupation in Japan, authorized the restart of baseball, schoolboy and professional. At his insistence, in 1950, the professional level was reorganized into two leagues of six teams each, to mimic Major League Baseball's American and National

Leagues. MacArthur believed that a two-league structure would be more democratic for Japan than the previous single league. Thus was born the Central League and the Pacific League of Nippon Professional Baseball (NPB). Most of the teams were located in the two major metropolitan regions of Tokyo-Yokohama and Osaka-Kobe, with single teams in the cities of Nagoya, Hiroshima, and Fukuoka. Although there have been changes in team ownership and a few location changes in the sixty-five years since, there has been no team expansion, and the two leagues have remained remarkably stable in size and organization.

The game's rules and the sport's organization in Japan will be familiar to Americans. The rule books and equipment are nearly identical, and the universal demands of the game impose a broad commonality. Nonetheless, the formal organization and the day-to-day practices of the professional game do differ somewhat. In this chapter I offer an overview of some of the key features of Japanese professional baseball in the early twenty-first century. The timeliness of this portrait is important because the NPB is facing some powerful challenges at the moment—a rapidly aging and shrinking national population, a digital media revolution, the rising popularity of soccer, the threat of asset stripping from MLB, and the demands of the World Baseball Classic (WBC). It remains to be seen whether NPB has the organizational resolve and imagination to overcome these threats, and I will turn to this issue in the concluding section.

Club Organization

One of the first things a visitor to a professional baseball game in Japan will notice is the names of the teams, which are often not that of a city but of a corporation—for example, the Hanshin Tigers, not the Osaka Tigers (named for a railroad company); the Chūnichi Dragons, not the Nagoya Dragons (named for the parent newspaper company); and the Yomiuri Giants (named for the media conglomerate, not its Tokyo hometown). Professional baseball is big business in Japan as well as in the United States, but MLB teams have generally been owned and operated by wealthy individuals or partners. Only recently have corporations begun to own and operate MLB teams. In Japan, though, major companies have always owned and run the teams as subsidiaries. Public information about club balance sheets is as scarce in Japan as in the United States, but it is widely believed that only two or three NPB clubs operate profitably; the rest run chronic operating deficits. Rather than being run as profitable ventures, they serve as publicity vehicles for the owning company, which is why they so often prominently showcase the names of their corporate owners.

Also, distinctively, the baseball clubs themselves are large organizations. The NPB has never developed a tiered minor league system as in the United States, and the twelve clubs maintain large rosters. Presently each can have seventy players under contract, and most are close to or at that maximum. To take the case of the Hanshin Tigers, which I know best from extended field research, its roster in 2014 had sixty-six contract players plus four trainee players. The roster is divided into two squads, a first team and a second team. The first team is the actual major league team, which is limited to twenty-eight players. The remainder are registered to the "farm" team, which plays a short season against the farm teams of the other clubs. Injuries and performances result in much up-and-down movement between first and second teams during a season.

Large team sizes have several consequences, one of which is the need for an extensive coaching staff. Hanshin's first and second squads each have a manager, ten coaches, three trainers, and several batting practice pitchers and catchers. The Tigers' second team practices and plays at a facility named Tiger Den, several miles from the main stadium, Kōshien. Tiger Den has been laid out in the exact dimensions of the parent park. Like many other clubs, it has a modern dormitory for bachelor players, which used to be mandatory but is now optional—and not particularly popular.

Because the seventy players range from the most talented stars to raw rookies, the coaching staff must devote a lot more time to teaching fundamentals than on an MLB club, which depends on its large farm system to prepare and winnow young players. For all NPB teams there are daily structured practices, requiring detailed scheduling to coordinate the drills of a hundred players and staff. In this regard NPB less resembles MLB than the National Football League (NFL), with its large staffs, highly orchestrated practices, and all-powerful head coaches.

Above the players and coaches on the field is the "front office," the club's management and support staff. Not surprisingly, the large team size requires a large front office; Hanshin's 65 employees range in positions from administration to accounting, marketing, player development, and press relations. Like other clubs, the Hanshin front office is organized in a corporate hierarchy of divisions, departments, and small sections that would be familiar to any Japanese office worker. In effect, then, to get nine players on the field to start each major league game, the Tigers baseball club has become a large organization of more than 160 employees!

And above that, each of the twelve baseball clubs is embedded in an even larger corporate nexus. In Japanese business shorthand, a club is a "child company," or wholly owned subsidiary of a "parent company." In the case of the Hanshin Tigers, for instance, until recently it was a subsidiary within the Hanshin Electric Railroad Corporation. The parent name recalls its urban transport origins, but it is now a family of businesses, including department store retailing, travel agencies, air transport, land development, taxi companies, and leisure park operations in addition to the railroad. Even baseball-related operations are distributed among a set of subsidiaries—the Tigers ball team, of course, but also a stadium management company, a horticulture and grounds-keeping company, a security company, and a goods and concessions company—all under the control of the parent corporation. Each club has a designated "owner," who is usually the chief executive officer or chairman of the board of the parent company. It is the owner who represents the club in all executive dealings with the league by sitting on the all-important Owners' Committee.

Thus, the business ethos of Japanese baseball is decidedly more corporate than the entrepreneurial image of MLB ownership (although actual MLB clubs have become quite corporate operations). Nonetheless, this intricate organization does not ensure harmony despite common perceptions that Japanese prefer supportive collectivism. I discovered the Hanshin organization to be rife with friction and infighting—between the parent headquarters and the child club, within the front office (especially between those who are dispatched by the main company and the others who are permanent employees of the club), and between the "suits" of the front office (claiming educational credentials and corporate seniority) and the "uniforms," the field manager and coaches who claim baseball expertise and public recognition.

The Baseball Season

The rhythms of the professional baseball season in Japan would be generally familiar to any fan of U.S. baseball, albeit with several distinctive features. Spring training is in the "South"—Okinawa and the southern island of Kyushu are current favored locations—and all of the monthlong camps open on February 1. Preseason exhibition games are played from late February through March. The 144-game regular season begins around April 1 and continues into mid-October. In recent years there has been interleague play in the middle of the season, during which time each team plays a two-game series with each of the six teams in the other league. The regular season concludes with a two-stage playoff in both leagues (dubbed the Climax Series). The two league champions then meet in a best-of-seven game Japan Series, which usually overlaps with the MLB World Series. Most clubs have a postseason camp and rookie leagues in October and November. The November through January off-season is busy with personnel issues: the player draft, free-agent signings and team trades, and player salary negotiations.

The shorter distances, the country's single time zone, and the high-speed train network in Japan make travel less of a determinant than in

MLB. For several decades almost all regular-season games have been evening games (starting time varies from 6:00 p.m. to 6:30 p.m.), and there are no doubleheaders. Teams typically play a three-game series twice a week (Tuesday, Wednesday, Thursday and Friday, Saturday, Sunday), with Monday dedicated as a travel day. Given the six-team leagues, each team faces its five opponents more than twenty times a year, which gives an intensity and frequency to the team rivalries that is greater than that of MLB.

It is often said that Japanese players put in many more hours of practice than MLB players, not just in the off-season but throughout the regular season as well. This is generally so, although as with other aspects of the global game we should not exaggerate the differences and we should be clear about the reasons. In both countries through the 1960s at least, the "off-season" was just that, and many players needed other jobs to augment their modest baseball earnings. (Alternatively, the Caribbean and Central American winter leagues provided income and playing exposure for local players and North Americans.) Only more recently have rising salaries permitted and competition demanded a full-year commitment by players to practice and training. In America, though, most of the off-season effort is beyond public notice because MLB vies for media exposure with two other powerful professional leagues, the National Basketball Association (NBA) and the NFL.

In Japan—as in most places—the situation is fundamentally different. The U.S. sports world is quite unusual in having three dominant spectator sports. In most countries there is a single "center sport" and other secondary sports. As with baseball in Cuba and the Dominican Republic, with ice hockey in Canada, and with soccer in many European and South American countries, baseball in Japan is the center sport. At least until quite recently, soccer, sumo, golf, horse racing, and other sports have had to fit around and within the baseball calendar.

This means that the NPB keeps itself in front of the public eye as much as possible—and it must do this to retain its media preeminence. The clubs' owners want maximum exposure for their corporate names.

The broadcast and print media, which have invested considerable resources in baseball reporting, need to generate nonstop news, and the players themselves, even those at the lowest rungs of the second squad, are playing for the club. The pressures—and the profits—of keeping the operations of baseball before the public even in the off-season (and even during breaks in the regular season) are enormous, and this goes a long way in explaining the distinctiveness of the pro-ball work year.

The Game

Sports are by definition rather tight sets of formal rules, basic equipment, and set strategies, and their modern history has been one of local games becoming standardized across wider regions, then being nationalized and eventually "transnationalized" across societies. The earliest Japanese baseball organized itself around American rules, and the regulation and patterns of game play have changed in tandem with the American game. The NPB rule book remains largely identical to the MLB rule book; the Pacific League in Japan copied the innovation of a designated hitter by the American League. Equipment is also much the same: for instance, like in the United States, metal bats are used in scholastic and amateur associations, while wood bats are used in the pros, and in both countries the transition to hitting with wood bats is difficult for players.

The Tigers' Kōshien Stadium (and several of the other older stadiums) could easily find a place among America's green cathedrals with its dimensions, grand ivy-covered exterior, and interior layout of covered stands and bleachers. Nonetheless, any visitor to a Hanshin Tigers game will notice small differences, some with important implications. Like most fields in Japan, the Kōshien infield is all dirt, and this makes for slightly slower ground-ball play. And while the MLB commissioner's office designates a single manufacturer's baseball to be used by all teams, in Japan each team can choose among three manufacturers' balls to use during the season. Managers select slightly livelier or deader baseballs according to their teams' strengths during the season.

NPB games have a reputation for taking a long time and for ending in ties. Games do tend to run longer because many pitchers prefer to work the count, batters take more elaborate setup time, and Japanese umpires are more indulgent of coaches and managers who want meetings on the mound. However, you will rarely see a tie game at Kōshien or elsewhere; they are possible within the rules, which limit the number of extra-inning games, but they are statistically insignificant (about 3 percent of all NPB games in the past six decades). It is the time limit, of course, that offends the sensibilities of MLB purists for whom the sport is limitless: the foul lines continue into infinity, and the game continues as long as required to produce a winner.

But the NPB has constraints. As with most stadiums, Kōshien is in the city, and almost all fans come by public transportation—largely by the trains, buses, and taxis of the parent Hanshin company! Almost all games are evening games, urban transit shuts down late at night, and the clubs will not risk inconveniencing tens of thousands of spectators of extra-inning games that extend into the early morning.

The Players

The life of a professional athlete is not Hobbesian—nasty, brutish, and short—but it is often ruthlessly competitive, unpredictable, and short. This is certainly true for baseball players in Japan, despite our preconceived images that Japanese sports professionals working for Japanese organizations must be securely enmeshed in a familiar nexus of long-term loyalty and mutual commitment. Not so. As with aspects of rules and game conditions, the contractual status of players and the course of their careers have broad similarities to MLB players, in part because the NPB has tended to borrow such features on the U.S. model.

For instance, like MLB, Japanese players (and coaches) are independent contractors. This is a legal status in Japan; it means that players are not legally members of their club in December and January, and every year they must negotiate salaries with the club (multiyear contracts are rare). And as independent contractors, they have no pension or other company benefits. Loyalty and commitment must be revalidated each year in November and December.

However, player vulnerability is not matched by club exposure. Through a reserve clause similar to but longer than MLB's, Japanese clubs have exclusive rights to all players on their roster for nine years, which is an effective hold over most players for their entire professional careers. There is less player movement among Japanese teams than in the American Major Leagues, but there is more than one might think. For instance, by opening day of the 2014 Hanshin Tiger season, fifteen players had retired or been released over the winter, and ten new players were drafted or signed. Twenty percent turnover in the rosters each year is fairly common.

In general, salaries are lower at the high end and higher at the low end of the player spectrum. Star players earn far less than those at the top of the MLB pyramid. Several NPB players have broken through the 70-million yen threshold (about $7 million), although the highest Hanshin salary in 2014 was the $2.7 million to an eleven-year veteran infielder, Toritani. At the other end of the scale, though, players are drafted to the clubs with higher average salaries than MLB draftees. There is a much smaller pool of professional-level players in Japan, and each club signs only four to eight rookies each year out of high school, college, and industrial leagues (compare this to the average U.S. professional club, which drafts thirty-five to fifty players a year!). Fierce competition has led to a salary structure that pays exorbitant signing bonuses of $1–$1.5 million to untried teenagers. What pro baseball shares everywhere, though, is a relatively short career path. Few players ever last beyond their early thirties. The average age of most rosters hovers around twenty-six or -seven years old. Fully 50 percent of the seventy players on the Tigers' 2014 opening-day roster had five years or less professional experience.

Even salaries controvert the standard Japanese corporate model of steady upward increments. Automatic steps in pay have no relevance in the baseball world, whose dense statistical indicators exactingly measure player performance as the basis for annual adjustments of salaries. In tracking the reported salaries of Hanshin players over the past ten years, I have calculated that less than half of the annual re-signings have been for salary increases (from 5 percent to 250 percent), about one-third of the players were forced to accept salary reductions (of 5 percent to 40 percent), and another quarter of the players were renewed at the same salary as the previous year.

The salaries themselves range widely across the roster. In 2014 more than a quarter of the players, those starting out or permanently stuck on the farm team, made from $50,000 to $100,000, most made between $100,000 and $500,000, and only ten of the sixty-six players exceeded the $500,000 mark, which is the minimum salary in MLB. About 40 percent of the club's total payroll of about $30 million went to the top five salaries.

The second-highest salary in 2014 went to an American outfielder, Mack Murton, who made just over $2 million. Murton played for three MLB organizations over five years, mostly in the Minor Leagues, before coming to Hanshin in 2009 and thriving.

This draws attention to the pivotal but controversial place of foreign nationals in the NPB. Professional baseball is multiethnic almost everywhere (except in Cuba), but everywhere the deployment and treatment of foreign players vary. In the early years of Japanese baseball, little was made of Japanese Americans, White Russians, Taiwanese, or Korean Japanese who were often prominent on the rosters, but by the early 1970s the rush to hire aging stars from MLB and other pressures created the foreign players as a category apart, "hired bats" brought over with large salaries, special perks, and separate treatment. At present about seventy-five of the eight hundred players in the NPB are foreign nationals. In 2014 the Hanshin roster had four (from the United States, the Dominican Republic, and South Korea), which is about average. Only three non-Japanese ballplayers may be registered on the major team roster at any one time; the others keep in shape, sometimes impatiently, on the farm. Those from South Korea and

Taiwan are generally treated the same as regular players; those from North America, Australia, and the Caribbean are often provided with luxurious condominium housing, interpreters, separate hotels on road trips, and the freedom to follow their own training routines. Mercenaries are well compensated, but patience is short, adjustment is difficult, and their time is brief. A few find what it takes to succeed (like Murton), but most are rarely re-signed for a second year, and their experiences often end in mutual bafflement and bitterness.

The Media

If you arrive at Kōshien early on a game day to watch batting practice and warm-ups, you will immediately notice a huge media contingent lounging in the dugouts, staked out along the sidelines, and standing behind the batting cages. Baseball clubs in major U.S. markets face intense media coverage, but not even the Yankees are scrutinized as intensely as the Hanshin Tigers. On any day in the season all three national newspapers, the five major sports dailies, two local dailies, the two major news agencies, three radio networks, and three television networks will all send reporters, photographers, announcers, and commentators to the ballpark. Such media attention is welcome but also problematic for the club. The Yomiuri Corporation that runs the rival Giants owns its own television network (Japan's first and largest private system), the largest-circulation daily newspaper in the world, and one of the major daily sports newspapers. Not surprisingly, the Giants are relentlessly featured in Yomiuri publications, which are favored by the club. Other media are often a step behind and sometimes heavy-handedly sanctioned for being too critical. The Hanshin Group by contrast owns no media, and it finds itself at the center of (and often at the mercy of) an intensely competitive Kansai regional media whose dominant yearlong subject is the fortunes of the Tigers. It needs the media, but it fears them at the same time. It is an anxious and uneasy balance of courting and controlling.

Walking the several hundred yards from the Hanshin train station to the stadium and passing the Babe Ruth plaque to the right of the main ticket office, one comes upon the one entrance that is not open to ordinary visitors. This is the "official entrance" for players, team officials, and the media, all of whom are funneled into a guarded door that leads directly under the infield bleachers. Straight ahead lies the runway to the field dugout and officials' rooms behind home plate. A stairway to the left leads to the second-floor team rooms and to the press box.

Throughout the year the media pack the pressroom of the club offices and hang out in a low-hanging, crowded room of old desks and chairs that is euphemistically called the press club room; they fill the field sidelines and dugouts during practices and game warm-ups. During the game itself they are packed into a center section behind the backstop—literally a press "box" with folding chairs and rickety wood boards for tables, open to the surrounding spectators and stadium noise, unchanged for seventy-five years. However, as with all stadiums in Japan, they are banned from the team locker room and the manager's office, and thus they keep watch in the runway to the field and in the hallways outside the team dressing rooms to catch players and coaches for a comment.

Professional baseball rose with the national newspaper and radio and became the national sport through television in the 1960s and 1970s, but of all the media those that have come to drive the gathering and reporting of Tiger news are the daily sports newspapers. These are also key sports media in other countries like Italy, France, Brazil, and Mexico, although not the United States. There are five national sports dailies, four of which date from the late 1940s; their big jump in circulation and notoriety happened in the 1960s. Their circulations remain in the millions, and they depend almost entirely on spot sales at street and station news kiosks and in convenience stores, not through subscriptions. Thus, to catch the eye of the passerby, they borrow from Japanese comic art and graphic design so that every front page is a garish, full-page multicolor spread about a single story. And almost invariably, it is professional baseball that dominates the papers' daily front pages, total coverage, and staff assignments. For the Kansai editions of the sports papers, this means the Tigers; the other teams are relegated to a few stories on the inside pages. The previous day's game if in season, front-office conflicts, draft plans, contract signings, spring camp—whatever the moment in the baseball year, the sports dailies will find a Hanshin topic to foreground, and Osaka commuters, whether they buy the papers or not, will glimpse the florid front-page spreads as they pass newspaper kiosks throughout the region.

The Fans

Equally conspicuous to anyone arriving early for a Kōshien game are the people who begin to fill the right-field bleachers, dressed in yellow-and-black jackets (the Tiger team colors), busily at work attaching banners to the railings of the walkways, assembling large flags, testing trumpets and drums. These are the officers of the many fan clubs, who are based in the right-field stands but spill over into adjacent outfield and infield sections and give a distinctive flavor and sound to Kōshien games. Indeed, no doubt the most striking difference that a fan from another baseball culture will notice at Kōshien is the level and form of cheering—it is loud, constant, and coordinated. From start to finish the stadium pulsates with the frenzied chanting of the fans, driven by the percussive beat of drums and thumping clackers, accompanied by blaring trumpets and huge flags.

Significantly, though, the official cheerleaders and the stadium announcer do not coordinate them. Rather, the energies of the crowd are directed by an elaborate organization of private fan clubs, several hundred in all, organized into several broad associations and all centered in the right-field bleachers. From there whistles and hand signals communicate downward from a single association field chief, who sits in the lower far-right corner of the bleachers, to a hierarchy of subordinates stationed throughout adjacent sections. There are anthems and marches and chants for individual players (when first announced and when coming to bat) and for moments in the game (at the start, at pitching changes, for home runs, at the end of each victory, and so on), all of which are composed and copyrighted by the lead association, not by Hanshin.

In this, too, the chanting and cheering parallel the support given the school teams in the spring and summer tournaments, and there is a historical connection that leads back to the early days of U.S. college football. When the first Japanese college baseball teams toured the United States in the opening decade of the twentieth century, they studied the baseball they encountered, but they were even more impressed with the cheerleader squads of the college football teams and the enthusiasm with which they could engage the student spectators. They took careful notes, which they used on their return to train student cheerleading squads that were immediately popular. It was this tradition of organized cheering that baseball fans later brought to the professional game.

And certainly Kōshien rocks in ways alien to any U.S. baseball game and at a level far surpassing even the exuberant fans at Caribbean and Mexican stadiums. Visiting American baseball fans sometimes complain that the cheering disrupts the concentration and decorum necessary to properly appreciate the game, but this has always seemed to be a hypocritical ethnocentrism. Spectator participation at Japanese baseball games is perhaps most similar to that seen in soccer stadiums in Europe, Africa, and South America, where there are also highly organized fan clubs to motivate and orchestrate the crowds. In both cases spectatorship is active—in fact, proactive—trying to create with collective voices and frenetic movement an emotional charge and a sensory atmosphere that will motivate their team. It is the fan as the "tenth player," trying to intervene energetically.

Yet the discerning visitor will note one further aspect of Kōshien cheering: it is done for only half the game, that is, for the half of each inning when one's team is at bat. For the defensive half of an inning, the fans relax—and schmooze. The key to appreciating the Kōshien fan-club organizations is that they serve not only to orchestrate a colorful outpouring of emotional support for the Tigers, but also to provide spaces and times for socializing among friends, fellow workers, business associates, and others who are drawn together by this network. It is where Osakans go to cheer on their Tigers but also to cheer up one another through the spring, summer, and fall evenings after long days in factories, offices, and homes.

Japanese Professional Baseball under Challenge

These, then, are some of the key features of the professional game in Japan, a mixture of the familiar and the unfamiliar to readers more attuned to baseball MLB style. What is common throughout the baseball world, however, is the following. We are all tempted to see baseball, even at the professional level, as the game played between the lines by eighteen fit and talented athletes. Indeed it is. However, "Hanshin Tiger baseball" or that of the Yomiuri Giants or of the Boston Red Sox must also be appreciated as the coordinated product of players, coaches, the front-office staff, the corporate owners, the numerous members of the media, and the spectators, readers, and fans who not only watch and listen but also talk and live through the rich histories and suspenseful games, day after day, season after season. Through their efforts and energies, they transform a sport into a sports world.

But the sports world of the Hanshin Tigers and the larger horizons of Japanese professional baseball are facing some fundamental challenges in this second decade of the twenty-first century. Japan is the most rapidly aging of the advanced industrial societies, baseball's own fan base is aging, and the clubs and the NPB itself have not been adept in attracting younger audiences. Mainstream media have also been under assault; broadcast television and the daily sports newspapers remain dependent on baseball, but cable, satellite television, and digital social media have cut heavily into their subscriber base and viewer audiences. The sports dailies have been particularly hard hit. In the 1990s when I would get on a local train or subway in Osaka, I would look around and usually see at least half the passengers reading one of the five daily sports papers that were purchased at the platform kiosks. Riding the same lines in 2014, it was unusual to see more than one passenger in a car reading the dailies. Smart phones and social media have replaced earlier print platforms, but the sports media have not kept up.

Part of the competition is coming from a new national interest in soccer. School soccer teams are attracting boys away from baseball; the professional J League has established itself in markets and media beyond baseball's stadiums and income sources with a new model of regional identity and community involvement. Top Japanese soccer players are now recruited to the European leagues, and Japanese digital media companies are now broadcasting European league play in Japan. Both the men's national team and the women's national team are gaining international prominence; the men's team has become quite strong within International Federation of Association Football's (FIFA) Asia Federation, while the women's team has been even more successful at the world championship level. Perhaps even more threatening to baseball in Japan is the greater potential of soccer as a platform for sporting rivalries among the East Asian nations of China, the two Koreas, and Japan.

Yet another threat looms on the other side of the Pacific: MLB itself. For twenty years now, a small but steady outflow of NPB's top stars has been drawn to the American Major Leagues, both within and outside the leaky "posting" system MLB and the NPB cobbled together. From the initial move by pitcher Hideo Nomo in 1994 to the present, MLB rosters have carried eight to twelve Japanese players per year. While this is a small percentage of Major Leaguers in the United States, the loss of their top draws has had much more serious consequences for the Japanese teams they have left. And what is less widely recognized is that for every star player who jumps to MLB, there are three or four young unknown Japanese players who choose not to enter the domestic draft at all, preferring to take their chances at the lowest levels of the American Minor League system. Few of them advance to the MLB level, but they shrink an already small pool of potential talent in Japan for the NPB.

In broader terms what is now going on between MLB and the NPB follows a historical pattern of "asset stripping" by American professional sports businesses. Earlier player recruitment devastated the Negro Leagues, Dominican Republic baseball, Venezuelan baseball, and perhaps soon Cuban baseball. National Hockey League recruitment proved seriously detrimental to ex–Soviet bloc hockey leagues, and the NBA has internationalized at the expense of European and South American leagues. To be sure European soccer leagues have devastated the quality of leagues in Brazil and Argentina, and even the Japanese NPB has regularly raided Taiwan and Korean professional leagues for their best players, but U.S. professional sports remain the master of this.

Can the World Baseball Classic Help Save Japanese Professional Baseball?

One of the most significant recent changes in international baseball has been the introduction of the World Baseball Classic, whose fourth rendition will come in 2017. The explosive popularity of the FIFA World Cup and the shock in 2005 of having baseball dropped from the Olympics prompted MLB to push the International Baseball Federation to sponsor a high-profile tournament like the FIFA World Cup. Over the first three WBC tournaments in 2006, 2009, and 2013, Japan was the dominant team, taking the gold medal in the first two Classics and the bronze medal in 2013. Its national team, dubbed the Blue Samurai, has gained a high media profile and lucrative corporate sponsorship, and NPB has ensured that top players and Hall of Fame managers are made available.

Nevertheless, it is not yet clear that the WBC will succeed on the global field of play or that it will significantly help the flagging popularity of the NPB. The FIFA World Cup is successful in part because the sport has a very deep history of simultaneous club and national team representation and an interweaving of club league play and national team play during the year. This is proving much more difficult with professional baseball. With the longest season of all professional sports, playing a near-daily game schedule in the United States and in Japan, it is turning out to be very difficult to schedule qualifying rounds and the tournament itself. Even the brief off-season is critical for recovery and for training before the next preseason, especially for pitchers' arms, so it is understandable that the players' union in Japan as well as in the United States has raised serious objections to the scheduling and to the pressures to participate.

When the Japanese pro baseball players' union threatened to boycott the 2013 WBC, it had another complaint beyond the dangers of physical injury and the disruption to the carefully calibrated season. The 2009 WBC had generated eighteen million dollars in revenue, of which the Japanese league and its players received 13 percent and MLB and its players' association took 66 percent. The Japanese players eventually capitulated, but it underscored an uncomfortable fact about the WBC. Although it is formally operated by what is now called the World Baseball Softball Confederation, it is still controlled by MLB, and it underscores the dependency that the NPB feels about its relation to U.S. baseball. MLB may not field the winning teams in the WBC (the Americans have yet to win even a bronze medal), but it wields the power and yields the profits. This rankles the Japanese baseball world, and it is a point of serious negotiation in the lead-up to the 2017 Classic.

Baseball has yet to be displaced as the center sport in contemporary Japan, but the domestic professional leagues are under serious assault by baseball elsewhere, by soccer and other sports, and by the inexorable dynamics of an aging and shrinking society and troubled economy. It is too soon to declare the game over, but it will require decisive leadership in the Japanese baseball world to sustain the joys and pride that the game has brought to the Japanese for more than a century.

Note on Sources
Much of the data for this chapter is drawn from observations and interviews by the author and club records provided to the author during extended field research with the Hanshin Tigers and other Japanese

professional clubs from 1996 to the present. Salaries, attendance, and other player data are drawn from the annual professional baseball yearbooks from several publishers (in Japanese), particularly the *Puro yakyuu paafectodeeta senshu meikan*, edited by the Bessatsu Takarajima Editorial Division and published annually by Takarajima-sha.

BIBLIOGRAPHY

Cromartie, Warren (with Robert Whiting). *Slugging It Out in Japan: An American Major Leaguer in the Tokyo Outfield*. Tokyo and New York: Kodansha International, 1991.

Guthrie-Shimizu, Sayuri. *Transpacific Field of Dreams: Baseball and Consumer Modernity in U.S.-Japanese Relations, 1872–1952*. Chapel Hill: University of North Carolina Press, 2012.

Guttmann, Allen, and Lee Thompson. *Japanese Sport: A History*. Honolulu: University of Hawaii Press, 2001.

Kelly, William W. "Kōshien Stadium: Performing National Virtues and Regional Rivalries in a 'Theatre of Sport.'" *Sport in Society* 14, no. 4 (2011): 481–93.

———. "Samurai Baseball: The Vicissitudes of a National Sporting Style." *International Journal of the History of Sport* 26, no. 3 (2009): 429–41.

Roden, Donald F. "Baseball and the Quest for National Dignity in Meiji Japan." *American Historical Review* 85, no. 3 (1980): 511–34.

Whiting, Robert. *The Meaning of Ichiro: The New Wave from Japan and the Transformation of Our National Pastime*. New York: Macmillan, 2004.

———. *You Gotta Have Wa: When Two Cultures Collide on the Baseball Diamond*. 2nd ed. New York: Vintage, 2009.

11

Korea

Straw Sandals and Strong Arms

Joseph A. Reaves

Everywhere it's played, baseball is a numbers game. Stats. Streaks. Sabermetrics. Numbers upon numbers accumulate continuously. Korean baseball is no exception. But in Korea numbers play an important role outside of the game as well, which the Los Angeles Dodgers used to their advantage in late 2012 when they made history by signing Hyun-Jin Ryu, arguably the greatest pitcher to come out of the Land of the Morning Calm.

Ryu was already a legend in Korea when he signed with the Dodgers. He had "Tommy John" surgery while still in high school in 2005, but returned a year later to throw twenty-two scoreless innings and lead Dongsan High to the Korean national championship. The Hanwha Eagles selected Ryu with the first pick in the second round of Korea's professional baseball draft in 2006. From his debut in 2006 through 2012, his last season in the Korea Baseball Organization (KBO), Ryu dominated the game. He was 18-6 with a 2.23 earned run average and 205 strikeouts in 201⅔ innings in his rookie season—leading the league in all three categories of the pitching Triple Crown. Ryu became the first player in league history to win both Rookie of the Year and Most Valuable Player in the same season.[1]

In his second season Ryu went 17-7 with a 2.94 ERA and a league-leading 178 strikeouts for Hanwha and also picked up a win for Korea in the 2007 Asian Championship.[2] A year later Ryu missed much of the professional season with elbow inflammation, but recovered in time to solidify his spot as a national hero by getting two wins—including one in the championship game against heavily favored Cuba—in leading Korea to its first baseball gold medal at the Beijing Olympics.

By 2012, with a career record of 98-52, Ryu had accomplished essentially all he could in Korea and wanted to pitch in the United States. He asked that his name be placed in the "posting system," which would allow his services to be auctioned to the highest Major League Baseball bidder. No Korean player had ever been "posted," though the KBO and MLB had a posting agreement in place since 2003. The agreement was similar to the one originally agreed upon in 1998 by MLB and Nippon Professional Baseball (NPB), the Japanese professional league. The Japanese posting agreement has since been revised, but at the time players who obtained permission from their teams were "posted," and any MLB team could bid for the rights to negotiate with them.[3]

On November 2, 2012, the day teams in the United States were formally notified the Hanwha Eagles had established a precedent and agreed to post Ryu, the original posting system was in place. Several MLB clubs scrambled to get their secret bids in as quickly as possible. Hanwha officials had set a tight deadline. They would decide in one week whether the highest bid was enough for them to agree to let Ryu go. The Dodgers had done their homework and won the right to negotiate with Ryu by offering Hanwha a curiously specific sum. As with most East Asian and Southeast Asian cultures, numbers often have special meanings for Koreans. Four, for example, is an unlucky number. In the Korean language the word for four is *sa*, which is almost identical to the Korean word for death. In many ways, it's similar to the superstitions about thirteen in U.S. culture. Major public buildings in Korea will skip the fourth floor, or, if there is a fourth floor, elevator buttons will simply use *F* instead of 4. On the other hand, some numbers are considered especially lucky in Korea. Three (*sam*) and seven (*chil*) are two of the luckiest, invoking sentiments of success and good fortune. The Dodgers' carefully crafted bid of $25,737,737.33 made an impression on Hanwha's executives. Dodgers general manager Ned Colletti and his staff knew how to play the numbers game.[4]

Dreams, Disciples, and Dictators

Ryu made history by becoming the first Korean to go directly from the KBO to the U.S. big leagues, but a dozen of his countrymen beat him to the Majors via free agency. The first, Korea's true baseball trailblazer, was pitcher Chan Ho Park (or more accurately, as Koreans prefer, Park Chan-ho), who signed with the Dodgers in 1993. He pitched for Los Angeles from 1994 to 2001 and returned to the Dodgers in 2008. Between and after his LA stints, Park was with the Texas Rangers, San Diego Padres, Houston Astros, New York Mets, Philadelphia Phillies, New York Yankees, Pittsburgh Pirates, Japan's Orix Buffaloes, and, finally, in 2012, alongside Ryu in Korea with the Hanwha Eagles. He finished with a 124-98 MLB record and then went 1-5 in Japan and 5-10 in Korea.[5]

In 2014 Ryu said he owed his career to Park: "When I was in third grade, Park Chan-ho was playing in the Major Leagues. He taught me that even a Korean can be successful in Major League Baseball. He helped me dream."[6] Dreams of playing for a Major League club long ago morphed from the exclusive fantasy of young men and boys across the United States into a burning ambition for ballplayers across the globe. And in Korea, perhaps surprisingly to some, baseball has been played as far back as the nineteenth century.

The games people play, and don't play, typically mirror their national priorities and customs. Baseball became popular in Korea not so much, originally, for the game itself but for what the game offered the Korean people. At times it offered a peaceful way to challenge oppressive rulers. Other times it was a convenient tool for politicians to sway public opinion. Eventually, it became an important part of the nation's economic growth. And, always, it offered an acceptable outlet for the barely bridled emotions of the Korean people.

Korean culture is rooted in Confucianism. Traditionally, within the

Confucian framework, emotions are discreetly controlled. Koreans strive to be stoic, but often fail. Passionate outbursts are common in the streets of Seoul, on the floor of the National Assembly, and in the stands at baseball stadiums. Violence is an integral part of Korean society. So, too, is politics. And the two are entwined in the history of Korean baseball.

Missionaries and military personnel from the United States brought baseball to Asia during the late nineteenth and early twentieth centuries. U.S. sailors and soldiers played the first games in China, Japan, and the Philippines. The same was true in Korea. A newspaper article discovered in 2014 by Patrick Bourgo dates the earliest games in Seoul to at least April 1896. The article Bourgo uncovered is from a newspaper called the *Independent*, which was published in English and Korean (*Tongnip Simmun*) and eventually became the first privately managed modern daily newspaper in Korea: "There will be a baseball match game [*sic*] between the U.S. marines and the American residents of Seoul this afternoon at 2:30. The lovers of the American sport are cordially invited to be present at the game. The party will meet at The Independent Building at 2 o'clock and go to the grounds outside of the W. gate Mo Ha Kwan. Ladies are specially requested to be present."[7] Sporadic similar notices of baseball games among U.S. military and American expats can be found during the late nineteenth century. But it wasn't until the first decade of the twentieth century that an American missionary named Philip Loring Gillett popularized the sport among Koreans.

Gillett was the son of a prominent surgeon from LaSalle, Illinois. Shortly after he was born in 1872, the family moved to Iowa City, where Gillett's father had accepted a position on the faculty at the University of Iowa Medical School. They stayed there until 1885, when the family moved to Colorado Springs, just before Gillett's father died.

During his teens and early twenties, Gillett worked as a janitor to put himself through Colorado College, where he played football and baseball and served as chairman of the school's missionary committee.

He graduated in 1897, moved back east, and attended Yale Divinity School for a year and a half before enrolling in the International Young Men's Christian Association Training School at Springfield, Massachusetts. Gillett graduated from the training school in 1901 and accepted an appointment as general secretary of the YMCA's International Committee for Korea.

In April 1901, more than two months before graduation, Gillett's superiors were already actively promoting him for the Korea position. A letter in the YMCA archives shows that one of Gillett's supervisors praised him for being "a strong, sturdy Christian man" with a penchant for "winning men to Christ." The letter also singled Gillett out as "a great organizer" who was "exceedingly active in athletic work."

Gillett's passion and penchant for sports figured prominently throughout his missionary career, but it was particularly evident during his first international assignment to Korea, where he introduced baseball and basketball to a culture that, like others in Asia, once considered physical exercise undignified. Several historical accounts, both in English and in Korean, credit Gillett with bringing basketball to Korea in 1903 or 1904—the dates are often contradictory—and organizing the first baseball team at the Hansong YMCA in Seoul in 1905.

The YMCA team held several scrimmages and played informal baseball games in 1905. However, historians widely consider the first formal organized baseball game in Korea to have taken place on February 11, 1906, between the YMCA team and a squad from the German Language Institute of Seoul. The game was played in an area known as Hullyonwon, then a training ground for military recruits near the current site of Seoul Stadium. Some of the players wore high leather boots and pristine white uniforms. Others took the field wearing straw sandals and traditional Korean clothing.

At the time of the first game, the YMCA was already famous for being "the center of the [Korean] basketball world" and for hosting weekly "football afternoons," which brought young players together for feisty soccer matches.[8] Basketball and soccer caught the fancy of Koreans quicker than baseball did. But a series of compelling factors—social, political, cultural, and martial—affected baseball's acceptance and development in Korea.

Most significant among these was the presence of baseball-loving Japanese soldiers and administrators as an army of occupation in the Korean Peninsula from 1905 to 1945. A U.S. missionary may have brought baseball to Korea, but it would be the passions and policies of Japanese soldiers, administrators, and educators that enabled the game to survive and prosper to the point where it would become an integral ingredient of local culture.

Learning to Sweat

Japan exerted strong influence over Korea for centuries, particularly during the last two decades of the nineteenth century. That dominion was consolidated in September 1905 with the signing of the Treaty of Portsmouth, which formally ended the Russo-Japanese War and recognized Japan's undisputed supremacy in Korea. Three months later the Korean emperor signed another treaty making Korea a Japanese protectorate.

A decade earlier, in July 1895, when Korea was ostensibly being protected by Japan during the Sino-Japanese War, a series of sweeping social and educational reforms had been announced in Korea. Among them was the introduction of a new approach to physical exercise— similar to the cultural reforms that took root in Japan during the Meiji Restoration and in China during the "self-strengthening movement," both of which opened doors for Western ideas and indirectly led to the introduction of baseball in those countries.

By late 1905, when Gillett introduced baseball to Korea, the new attitudes about physical education had begun to take hold, especially under the influence of Christian missionaries and Japan's military occupation forces. Colonial authorities used the school system and athletics to indoctrinate Korean youth with Japanese ways and at the same time undermine traditional Korean values. They eliminated such things as the study of Korean history and Korean language and active-ly promoted baseball. A Korean journalist summed up the Japanese influence neatly. Baseball, he wrote, started to be "deeply rooted" in Korea the moment the Japanese took control.[9]

It is not surprising, then, that it was a group of Korean students home on holiday from Tokyo in the summer of 1909 who provided what the Korea Baseball Organization later called "the turning point for Korean baseball."[10] A newspaper article decades later recalled the moment: "On July 21, 1909, twenty-five Korean students studying in Tokyo, led by Yun Ik-hyon, formed a baseball club and scored a large-margin victory over a selection of foreign missionaries in Korea. . . . The Korean students were excited over the victory and had a series of baseball matches while touring provincial areas. As a result, the students played a great role in the popularization of baseball across the nation."[11]

While baseball was clearly beginning to enjoy a strong measure of popularity by 1909, most accounts agree the game came into its own in 1910—the year Japan formally annexed Korea. In February that year Hansong High School and Hwangsong Christian School played a game Korean historians still refer to as "the foundation of Korean baseball."[12] The game was played in the dead of a typically bitter Korean winter with two umpires—one from the United States and one from Japan. A crowd of some two hundred fans watched, officially signaling baseball's transformation from a fringe pastime to a mainstream sport. "That baseball game is now regarded as important in the history of Korean baseball," a Korean reporter wrote. "Korean baseball was consolidated with increasing attention from the people in Korea."[13]

In his annual report for 1909–10, Gillett listed what he called "facts of encouragement" about the past year's work. He wrote briefly about the improved physical facilities of the Seoul YMCA and then launched into a glowing account of the association's athletic involvement. "The base ball team, pioneer team for Korea, reached its top notch of enthusiasm when they succeeded in both tying and defeating teams composed of Americans picked from among the missionaries and resident business

16. The Seoul YMCA team, coached by U.S. missionaries, surprised a team of visiting Americans by beating them 13–8 in December 1911. The original caption in the Kautz Family YMCA Archives at the University of Minnesota Libraries claimed the score "shamed" the visiting Americans. (Kautz Family YMCA Archives, University of Minnesota Libraries, St. Paul.)

men. The scores were 20–20 and 10–8. The significant thing about these athletics features is that the young men of the country are thereby being led to adopt a new ideal of energetic manhood."[14]

By 1912 teams from the Seoul YMCA were playing more than sixty games a year, and the association's top squad rarely lost. The popularity of the game, and athletics in general, was mind-boggling even to the missionaries who started it all. "It seems almost incredible to those of us who have seen the Korean young men five or more years ago trying to play ball or enter into athletics," wrote one of Gillett's colleagues. "The remark of a Korean gentleman seeing a foreigner covered with perspiration from a game of tennis, 'Why don't you have your coolie do that work' will not be heard from this generation. Like the Korean top-knot and American horse car, it is a thing of the past."[15]

A Japanese Game

Missionaries tended, reasonably enough, to see the popularity of sports as a validation of their efforts. As one official of the Seoul YMCA wrote, "The enthusiasm and zeal to learn more about Western customs is seen on the base-ball diamond, in basketball, in football."[16] But Korean attitudes about baseball seem to have been shaped by forces closer to home—culturally and geographically. Even as early as 1910 many Koreans perceived baseball to be a Japanese game or, if not strictly a Japanese game, then certainly a game the Japanese had embraced and mastered to a degree worth emulating.

As such baseball offered an intriguing outlet for young Koreans opposed to Japanese military rule. Just as it did in other countries at other times, sport provided a way to vent political, as well as physical, frustrations. It brought Koreans and Japanese together in "nonpolitical commonality," offering an opportunity for the downtrodden to peaceably challenge their political masters.

Korean and Japanese teams began routinely playing one another—at venues in both countries. Another group of Korean students on summer vacation from school in Tokyo defeated a Japanese squad in Korea and then returned to Japan in November 1912 to play six games against Waseda University, a powerhouse of collegiate baseball then and since. The *Korea Times* hailed the Waseda series as "the first time in Korean sports history that a Korean sports team had overseas matches."[17]

In his annual report of 1912–13, Gillett refers to a YMCA team that traveled to Tokyo to play a series of games against Japanese university squads. "This has been a great year for athletics in the Seoul Association. Our baseball team beat every Korean team in the country and went to Tokyo to play the championship teams there. They were badly walloped by the university teams but when playing boys of their own age [middle school students] they captured one game, tied another and lost one."[18]

Missionaries, especially those involved with the YMCA, remained active in promoting baseball. In 1917 the sports club of the Chongno Central YMCA sponsored what proved to be a memorable baseball tournament featuring six high school teams. Competition was especially keen, and tempers rose steadily until the final day of the Yonghap Baseball Tournament, when police had to be called to break up a riot that broke out over a dispute about the batting order. The *Korea Times* called it "the first violent game in Korean baseball," but it was hardly the last. In sports, as in politics and almost every other endeavor, the Korean penchant for resorting to fists over words is legendary. The phrase *fighting spirit* is invoked with monotonous regularity in Japanese baseball. In Korea the phrase has been taken literally with similar regularity since that turbulent tournament in 1917.

The Yanks Are Coming

Korean baseball got an important boost in 1922 when the Herb Hunter All-Americans, a team of U.S. Major Leaguers, stopped briefly in Seoul on a winter tour of Asia that included a series of games in Japan and brief exhibitions in Shanghai and Manila. In Seoul the Koreans assembled an all-star team of their own to play the Major Leaguers. Not surprisingly, they were overmatched, losing 21–3. But as the *Korea Times* later rationalized, "The score was not so important as learning the American players' superb baseball skills for the Korean team."[19]

Baseball was so popular by then that construction was begun on a major stadium in Seoul. The facility opened in 1925, a year before the University of Seoul was established, and regularly hosted high school and intercollegiate games.

Despite the new stadium and interest among high school and college players, baseball in Korea essentially faded for a decade from the mid-1930s through the mid-1940s. The outbreak of the Sino-Japanese War left little time for leisure. Some baseball still was played, of course, but the game essentially disappeared until the war ended in 1945.

Once peace came, the game was resurrected quickly. As the *Korea*

Times reported, "With the liberation of Korea from . . . Japanese rule in 1945, baseball also awoke from its . . . hibernation to become more active than before."[20] One of the first sports organizations founded after the war was the Taehan Baseball Association, which promised to be "vigorous in promoting baseball interest in the post-Liberation era as never before."[21]

Baseball's swift postwar resurgence was fueled by the presence of U.S. troops stationed in southern Korea. Many of the soldiers who waged war from 1950 to 1953 were diehard baseball fans. They spread the gospel of baseball so well that by 1954, a year after the fighting stopped, South Korea was accepted into the International Baseball Association.

Four years later, in 1958, the St. Louis Cardinals made a sixteen-city tour of the Pacific that began in Hawaii and ended in Tokyo. Hall of Famer Stan Musial, nearing his thirty-eighth birthday, and just finishing his seventeenth season in the Majors, pleaded exhaustion and was allowed to miss the first five games in Hawaii, Manila, and at Kadena Air Force Base in Okinawa. But Musial joined the team in time to play a game against a group of Korean all-stars—mostly military players—at Seoul Stadium on October 21. The game drew more than thirty thousand fans, including fifteen hundred U.S. military personnel and Korean president Syngman Rhee, who threw out the ceremonial first pitch. The Cardinals won 3–0, but the fans were delighted that their all-stars were able to hold their own against the Americans, and baseball took another giant leap forward in Korea.

A series of successes in international competition, beginning in the early 1960s and carrying through the 1970s, transformed baseball from a pastime into a passion in Korea. The South Koreans defeated Japan to win the fifth Asian Amateur Baseball Championship in 1963 and then hosted and won the Asian tournament again in 1971 and 1975. A third-place finish at the World Baseball Championships in 1978 reinforced the growing belief that Korea had the talent to compete with anyone. But when South Korea won silver at the World Baseball Championships in 1980, then followed that by upsetting the United

States to win gold at the World Youth Baseball tournament in 1981 and adding its first gold medal at the World Baseball Championships in 1982, the game officially became a national mania.

Political Hardball

The steady rise in baseball's popularity in the early 1980s came at a time when political and social conditions in Korea were unraveling. Antigovernment riots broke out in Pusan in October 1979 and had to be suppressed by the military. A month later President Park Chung Hee, who had come to power in a 1961 coup, was assassinated. The strong military crackdown that followed led to a bloody uprising in Kwangju in May 1980 and the subsequent closure of all universities and colleges across South Korea.

In August 1980 Chun Doo Hwan was elected president, and two months later a new constitution was approved, ushering in the Fifth Republic of Korea. The political situation had stabilized enough by January 1981 for martial law to be lifted, and the government actively began trying to put a kinder, gentler face on its authoritarian image. Baseball became an important part of those efforts.

From its birth in December 1981, there never was any doubt that one of the primary objectives of the Korea Baseball Organization was to provide an outlet for restless and increasingly rebellious elements of society, particularly young males. As the authors of one study on sports and politics in Korea wrote in 1993, "The start of pro baseball in the country did much towards diverting the public's interest from politics to sports."[22]

The government's role in orchestrating that diversion and the economic significance of baseball on the national economy became obvious at the first public meeting of the league's top officials. Each of the six charter teams was owned by a major conglomerate closely tied to the government. The first commissioner of the KBO, elected unanimously and waiting in the wings with a prepared text when the results were announced, was Suh Jyong-chul, a former defense minister and president of the Korea Anti-Communist League. In addition to his political connections, Suh brought solid baseball credentials to the job. He learned the game in Japan as a youngster, playing first base and batting cleanup for Tachi Commercial High School in Miyazaki Ken, where he studied. Later in life, while serving as chief of staff of the Korean Army in 1961—the year of the military coup that brought Park Chung Hee to power—Suh managed the Korean Army baseball team.

At the inaugural meeting of the KBO in December 1981, Suh and representatives of the six company-owned teams established elaborate ground rules that ensured professional baseball would mirror the autocratic ways of doing business—and running the government—in Korea. Play would begin in March 1982, and for five years no professional team could scout another's players. The six teams would share income equally. A salary cap was in effect, players were rated and paid according to their ratings, and contract fees for managers and coaches were carefully categorized.

In the first few months of 1982 the government made it clear that the introduction of professional Korean baseball was merely part of a comprehensive campaign to ease political tensions and win the hearts and minds of the younger generation. The first gesture came in January 1982, when President Chun lifted a midnight curfew that had been in effect in Seoul since 1945. Not long afterward, students in middle schools and high schools were freed unexpectedly from having to wear the uncomfortable military uniforms that had been imposed on successive generations of youngsters since the Japanese colonial era.

Support the National Economy and Train Like Spartans

Two weeks before the inaugural professional season, Korean newspapers began running a series of profiles on each of the teams. Like a number of other articles published in the run-up to opening day (and for weeks after), the team profiles were notable mainly for the heavy-handed way in which they promoted baseball and social values, linking both with the success of the country and nation building.

"Samsung Organizes Team to Expedite National Unity," read the headline on a profile of the new Samsung Lions, who represented the east coast region of Kyongsang-pukto and featured a team made up mostly of players from that area. The headline on the article was taken directly from a quote by team president Lee Kunhee, vice chairman of the Samsung Business Group. The "major objective of the Samsung Lions to participate in the professional baseball is to expedite national unity and building national strength through sports and to encourage actively the social environment," Lee said.[23]

A similar profile of the Haitai Tigers emphasized the "harsh Spartan training" the team had undergone in its first spring. "Manager Kim [Dong-yeb] set up the rules of five points that the players must adhere to in camp. They must have clean uniforms, drink no wine, avoid smoking, be thoroughly health oriented, and not play cards."[24] Part of the manager's "Spartan" training session was a daily drill called "American knocking," in which players were forced to field a series of line drives and grounders hit from a distance of just five to ten meters.

The manager of the Sammisa Superstars also stressed personal behavior in his preseason rundown. "Always act as a good baseball player. Get dressed properly and be punctual," Park Hyon-shik told a reporter when asked what he demanded of his players.[25] Unlike most of the other managers, Park set his sights low, saying his goal for the season was "staying out of the cellar position among the six clubs." And he was less of a disciplinarian. The Superstars were the only team that spring to tolerate even moderate drinking among its players—a somewhat surprising exception since manager Park proclaimed himself a teetotaler.

A Beginning That Blossomed

The long-awaited birth of Korean professional baseball in 1982 was a national showcase. The commissioners of the only other two major professional baseball leagues at the time—Bowie Kuhn of the United States and Takeso Shimoda of Japan—were in the stands. President Chun Doo Hwan, his ample belly bulging under a vest and tie, threw out the first pitch. And thirty thousand fans were jammed into bunting-draped Seoul Stadium.

Pregame ceremonies lasted for two and a half hours, with hundreds of high school cheerleaders, dance troupes, and rural bands parading around before players from all six teams in the new league were called onto the field to swear an "athlete's oath" of good behavior and fair play. The game was broadcast live in Japan and Korea and couldn't have been scripted better. The MBC Blue Dragons, owned by a broadcasting conglomerate, came back from a 5–0 deficit to defeat the Samsung Lions 11–7 on a grand slam in the bottom of the tenth inning.

After the game most newspapers and media were filled with predictable praise and euphoria about the "historic meaning" for Korean sports.[26] But it was interesting to note the focus of one newspaper columnist who looked at the game from a different perspective and saw in the sport things he felt were most noble in Korean society in general. "The umpires were firm and authoritative," wrote columnist Kim Young-won. "Their showy gestures added to the excitement and fun. But it was their firm attitude that pleased the fans most."[27]

As exciting as that first game had been, the attention of most baseball fans in Korea quickly shifted to their true passion—the annual high school tournament. In Korea, as in Japan, the country almost comes to a stop when the spring high school championships begin. *Time* summed up the fever with one sentence in a 1982 article: "Playoffs among [Korea's] 52 high school teams are so popular that they are televised during hours of low electrical demand so that games will not cause brownouts." But *Time* saw hope for the future of professional *yagoo*—the Korean word for baseball. "Some fans are dreaming even now that in ten years South Korea will be ready to challenge the U.S. in a real *yagoo* World Series."[28]

That never happened, of course. But in the generation and a half since that first professional game, the KBO has prospered, despite a series of setbacks and scandals. As the league prospered, the caliber of players improved dramatically. During the late 1990s and early

2000s, the level of competition in the KBO was generally considered well below that of Japan and probably on par with Double A ball—or, at best, Triple A—in the United States. But by 2015 sixteen Koreans—thirteen pitchers and three position players—were Major Leaguers. The three position players—Hee Seop Choi, Shin-Soo Choo, and Jung Ho Kang—combined for nearly two hundred home runs, seven hundred runs batted in, and 120 stolen bases for eight Major League clubs,[29] though the overwhelming majority of those offensive numbers were put up by Choo, who had been in the Majors a decade and signed a seven-year, $130 million contract with the Texas Rangers in 2014.[30]

From "Korean Spotting" to Korean Stars

Before the creation of the KBO, Korea's best baseball players had few outlets for their talents beyond Japan. In his superb *The Chrysanthemum and the Bat* (1977), Robert Whiting writes about the roles foreign players from the United States and Korea played in Japanese baseball. "The American is not the only 'outsider' in Japanese baseball, he's just the most visible," Whiting notes. "Koreans also fall into the same category. But while the American is merely resented, the Korean is often looked down upon."[31] Whiting claims many Koreans born and raised in Japan played baseball because the game offered a way up and through Japan's strict social hierarchy. Even so the escape route was open only to Koreans who suppressed their heritage by assuming Japanese names and trying to pass for natives. Most did it so well that even their Japanese fans were duped. A favorite activity in Japanese ballparks to this day is "Korean spotting"—trying to figure which players, if any, are second-generation Koreans. Whiting quotes another knowledgeable writer who calculated there were so many Korean players in Japan, "if you removed them all there wouldn't be any more Japanese baseball."[32] To underscore Whiting's point, few realize that Masaichi Kaneda, considered the greatest pitcher in Japanese baseball history and nicknamed the "God of Pitching," was a Japan-born Korean. Scores of other stars in Japan's two professional leagues were born in Korea and emigrated to play baseball.

Much has changed in the four decades since Whiting broke cultural and historical ground with *The Chrysanthemum and the Bat*. Korean stars now have a native outlet for their talents—a highly competitive professional league that sometimes hones the best of the best for a shot at Major League Baseball in the United States. The shift began in 1993 when the Los Angeles Dodgers paid $1.2 million to sign Park Chan Ho. His signing was a source of enormous pride for South Koreans, and they followed his every move as he went to the States and worked to prove himself against the best players on the planet.

To do that, though, Park was forced to radically change his pitching motion, which for years featured an excruciatingly long pause at the top of his windup. Japanese pitchers often use the same pause and compare it to *ma*, the dramatic pauses so essential to Kabuki dialogue. In *You Gotta Have Wa* (1989), Whiting quotes a fan of the famous Japanese relief pitcher Yutaka Enatsu, who claimed to know the secret of his hero's success: "He was good because he knew how to use the *ma*. He waited for just the right moment—a lapse of concentration by the batter—to deliver the pitch."[33] But umpires and fellow professional players in the United States took one look at Park's *ma* and cried foul over something they had never seen before. Park took it all in stride, quietly altered a lifelong habit, and was a pitching star in the Major Leagues within two years.

Imports

The globalization of Korean baseball officially became a two-way street in 1998, two years after Park Chan Ho emerged as a regular in the U.S. Major Leagues. That year the KBO reluctantly followed the lead of Japan's professional leagues and voted to allow foreign players on its rosters. Initially, each team was permitted to "import" two foreigners, though it wasn't uncommon for teams to bring in only one, and occasionally none.

Asia was in the midst of a devastating economic slump in 1998, and the eight teams in the KBO signed twelve "imports" that first season. Known despairingly as *yongbyeong*, or mercenaries, eight of the original imports were position players. Four were pitchers—one starter and three relievers. Most were from the United States and Latin America. The move to bring in foreign players provoked more than a little nationalistic resentment among fans, and a number of players groused about lost jobs. In an effort to ease those concerns, the KBO expanded rosters to provide two more spots for Koreans.

In 1996, two years before the league voted to allow foreign players, baseball historian Thomas St. John interviewed a number of KBO players and reported they were "equally divided" on the idea of allowing imports. Interestingly, the split was along generational lines, with older Korean players noting that "imports" could help improve the quality of play, while younger players complained that "imports" were taking jobs from locals. On the eve of the 1998 season, with the economy in dire straits, the generation gap had slammed shut. St. John was unable to find a single Korean player, young or old, who supported the use of foreign talent. "I definitely do not want them to come," said a player who asked to be identified only by his family name, Lee. "They will be my teammates and I will treat them the same as others. [But] now is just not the right time. A foreign player's salary used to be equal to that of about three [Korean] players. Now it equals about eight."[34]

Within a couple of years the Asian economy rebounded, and Korean players were drawing dramatic salary increases. Foreigners often still made considerably more money, but at the start of the 2000 season a record thirty-two Korean players were earning 100 million won or more. The 100-million mark was a psychological barrier, much like becoming a millionaire in the United States, although 100 million won was worth just about US$89,000 at the time.

In 1998, when the first foreign "mercenaries" signed with the KBO, their salaries were capped at $120,000. A year later the cap was raised to $200,000. By 2004, with the global economy on the rise and baseball firmly entrenched as the national pastime, KBO owners agreed to a top pay of $300,000 for foreign imports.[35]

At their annual meetings before the 2014 season, KBO owners made two important decisions. They voted to increase the number of imports each team could employ to three, with a special exemption for two incoming expansion teams—the NC Dinos and KT Wiz—which each could bring in four imports for their first two seasons. The owners also voted to abolish the $300,000 salary cap for foreign imports. That move was far less dramatic than it might first seem. Anyone following Korean baseball closely knew owners had been quietly ignoring the salary cap for years. As an official of one of the teams said, skirting the salary cap was "the worst kept secret in the KBO."[36] But foreign "mercenaries" weren't the only ones seeing their salaries explode. In 2014 the *average* salary of KBO players—excluding imports—reached the magic 100-million-won mark, which by then was US$93,800. In all 122 Korean players made 100 million won or more in 2014. The highest paid was thirty-two-year-old power-hitting first baseman Kim Tae-kyun of the Hanwha Eagles, who made 1.5 billion won ($1.41 million at the exchange rate at the start of the season).[37]

Polluting Purity Again

Just as has happened in the United States, soaring player salaries in Korea spawned some fan alienation. Korean fans, like their counterparts in Japan, have always been somewhat ambivalent about professional baseball. The baseball-loving Japanese took nearly six decades to organize a professional league—and even then they needed the emotional catalyst of a triumphant tour by U.S. Major Leaguers to make the move acceptable. Before the 1934 tour by Babe Ruth, Lou Gehrig, and their fellow All-Stars, few Japanese believed professional baseball could succeed in their country. "The sport was undeniably popular," Whiting writes. "But tradition-bound Japanese were expected to remain loyal to favorite college teams, leaving pros with no one to cheer them on. Furthermore, monetary considerations would, it was argued, so dilute the purity of the sport that right-thinking people would turn away in disgust."[38]

That same question of "purity" of sport was far less an issue in Asian cultures by the time the KBO took the field in 1982. Still, there were concerns that the advent of professionalism would diminish amateur baseball, which was beginning to bring so much international honor and prestige to Korea in the early 1980s. Mindful of these concerns, KBO organizers met with officials of the Korea Amateur Baseball Association and drew up a set of strict rules to prevent the professionals from draining the young talent that fed both the Korean national squad and various university teams. The regulations stipulated that high school or college students must graduate before turning pro. High school graduates who were playing on company teams had to spend at least three years with the team before turning pro. College graduates had to spend two years with their company teams. And members of the Korean national team had to seek permission from the commissioner of the KBO to turn pro.

More than three decades later, professional baseball in Korea has survived—just as it did in Japan—despite concerns about polluting the sport's purity. The amateur game continues to thrive. The South Koreans won the Little League World Championship in 1984, 1985, and 2014.[39] They won the eighteen-and-under World Baseball Cup in 1981, 1994, 2000, 2006, and 2008—defeating the United States in the gold-medal game each time.[40] In the Asia Baseball Championships, played semiannually, Korea won the gold or silver medal eight times in fifteen tournaments from 1983 to 2012.[41] Meanwhile, the annual high school tournaments remain a national fixation.

Still, the evolution of the professional game has underscored South Korean's prominence on the global stage. In 2000, the first year professional players were allowed to compete in the Summer Olympics, Korea finally won its first medal. Southpaw Koo Dae-Sung outlasted Japanese ace Daisuke Matsuzaka in a magnificent pitchers' duel that enthralled an overflow crowd of more than fourteen thousand and gave Korea the bronze medal. After being carried off the field by his players, Korean manager Kim Euong-Yong was near tears. "The win against Japan is more meaningful than a bronze medal," he said. "Since I was young, Korean players are taught we have to always beat Japan."[42]

Professionals dominated the Korean teams that competed in the first three World Baseball Classics in San Diego (2006), Los Angeles (2009), and San Francisco (2013). Korea won a bronze medal in 2006 and was a bust in 2013, getting eliminated in the first round.[43] In between, in Los Angeles in 2009, the Koreans came within an out of defeating Japan in the championship game, losing a heartbreaker in extra innings in front of fifty-four thousand frenzied fans at Dodger Stadium.[44]

Yet the greatest impact professionals had on Korean baseball, the moment no one in the peninsula gave a thought to polluting the purity of the game, came in August 2008 when Hyun-Jin Ryu held a powerful Cuban team to two runs in eight and a third innings to win the gold medal at the Beijing Olympics.

Quiet Riots

The Olympic victory was easily the most emotional in Korean baseball history. Even seemingly trivial midseason games in the KBO are passionate affairs. Just one example came during a July game in 1996 when the LG Twins were being trounced 6–0 by the lowly Ssangbangwool Raiders at Chamsil Stadium in Seoul. The Twins were playing poorly, and the umpires weren't helping much either. Late in the game three Twins fans finally became so irate at one call that they started angrily shouting and demanding a meeting with the offending umpire. When a policeman stepped in to try to calm matters, he was beaten. Next a door was smashed. Suddenly, more than 150 Twins fans joined in the mayhem. Two hundred riot police had to be called in, and it took fifty minutes to restore order. Only three people were arrested. Hardly anyone in Korea gave the incident a second thought. Korea is one of the few places in the world where a riot can be quiet—perhaps not literally, but of so little consequence that it is quickly forgotten the next day.

Violence is an integral, and accepted, part of Korean culture—not just on the baseball field but in all walks of life. A phrase heard often in Japanese baseball is *fighting spirit*. The Japanese even give out a "fighting spirit" award during the annual Japan Series. Koreans invoke "fighting spirit" as well. In Korea the phrase takes on a whole new meaning. In Japan the emphasis is on *spirit*. A player is revered for his hustle and heart. In Korea, however, the emphasis clearly is on *fighting*.

In *The Chrysanthemum and the Bat*, Robert Whiting discusses the role of violence among the Japanese, who played such a prominent role in preserving and promoting Korean baseball. "Violence just isn't supposed to happen in Japan," Whiting writes. He points out that violence does occur in Japan—both on the playing fields and elsewhere. But he rightly notes that violence is the extraordinary exception to acceptable behavior. "When this happens," he writes, "Japanese players will lash out with an intensity seldom seen in American ballparks."[45]

Violence in Korea, on the other hand, is a socially accepted way of expressing everything from political frustration to sporting failure. Student riots and union demonstrations are regular, accepted, and often choreographed exercises. During the early 1990s Korean students regularly doused themselves with gasoline and leaped from buildings to protest government repression. A Korean demonstrator once bit off the tip of his finger in front of a group of Western journalists and used his own blood to scribble the name of opposition leader Kim Dae-jung on a wall to vent his rage at the government.

Emotional venting—particularly violent emotional venting—is part of Korean culture. That is one reason beer sales are banned in Korean ballparks—even at games of the OB Bears, whose animal nickname is a clever allusion to the team's sponsor, the Oriental Brewery, makers of OB Beer. The absence of alcohol does little to diminish the fervor of the fans. Riots and near riots are relatively routine. That is not to say Korean baseball is Asia's answer to ice hockey, where occasionally a game interrupts the fight. Long stretches pass during the Korean season without chaos. Still, violence is an accepted part of the game in Korea.

Baseball in Korea is the product of a pair of sometimes parallel yet distinctly different influences: U.S. missionaries and Japanese imperialists. The missionaries weren't always religious, although Philip Gillett, the "father of Korean baseball," certainly was. A new generation of "baseball missionaries"—U.S. soldiers in Korea after World War II—rekindled the game at a time when it easily could have died. On the other hand, not every Japanese imperialist came in conquest. The owners of the Yomiuri Giants, Hanshin Tigers, and other Japanese teams that provided opportunities for Korean professional players for decades after World War II performed as important a role in the salvation and safekeeping of baseball in Korea as their colonial forefathers who decreed the game be used to indoctrinate Korean youth into Japanese ways.

No one who sets foot in a Korean ballpark can doubt the Japanese influence. A missionary from Illinois may have introduced the game to Korea, but the Japanese nurtured baseball and kept it alive for decades. Almost everything in the Korean game—strategy, scoreboards, managing styles, cheerleaders—more closely resembles baseball the way it is played in Japan than the way it is played in the United States.

What distinguishes Korean baseball is not the indisputable Japanese influence on the game or its long ties to the U.S. military and U.S. missionaries. It isn't even necessarily the relative propensity for violence among fans and athletes alike. The most distinguishing element of Korean baseball is the level of political involvement.

Baseball has always had strong political ties. It has been used as a tool of diplomacy by the United States, Japan, China, and almost every country where the game has held sway. The Japanese certainly turned to baseball as an instrument of cultural conciliation during their colonial rule of Korea. And the Japanese government hardly hesitated to impose political and ideological constraints on the game in their own country during World War II.

But the unabashed way the Korean government went about establishing professional baseball in the 1980s as a diversion and channel for political and social unrest is probably unparalleled. Baseball and politics have always gone hand in glove in Korea—with a little passion thrown in just to spice things up. It's all part of the game's globalization.

NOTES

1. See Hyun-Jin Ryu KBO statistics, http://www.baseball-reference.com /minors/player.cgi?id=ryu-000hye.

2. See Hyun-Jin Ryu Biographical Information, http://www.baseball-reference .com/bullpen/Hyun-Jin_Ryu.

3. The bidding was "blind," which encouraged MLB teams to gamble and go high with their bids—as high as the $51.7 million the Texas Rangers submitted for star Japanese pitcher Yu Darvish in 2011. The team with the highest blind bid was given thirty days to negotiate a separate contract with the player. If the MLB team and player reached agreement by the deadline, the original bid, known as the "posting fee," would be sent to the NPB or KBO team as, essentially, a transfer fee. MLB and the NPB negotiated a new agreement in December 2013 that changed the name of the "posting fee" to "release fee" and set a cap of $20 million. Japanese teams now set the release fee, and any MLB team willing to match that amount—whatever it is, up to $20 million—has thirty days to negotiate a deal. The new system allows players to better leverage themselves by negotiating with several teams, while still allowing the Japanese clubs a substantial return for granting the release.

4. Ned Colletti, interview with the author, May 25, 2013.

5. See Park's MLB records at http://www.baseball-reference.com/players /p/parkch01.shtml. For his international statistics, see http://www.base ball-reference.com/bullpen/Chan-Ho_Park and http://www.baseball -reference.com/japan/player.cgi?id=park-001cha.

6. "Ryu's Pitching Speaks Volumes at Dodgers," November 12, 2014, http:// www.reuters.com/article/us-baseball-dodgers-ryu-idUSKCN0IW0BU 20141112.

7. *Independent* (Seoul), April 25, 1996, 1.

8. Allen Guttmann, *Korea: Its Land, People and Culture of All Ages* (Seoul: Hakwon-sa, 1960), 689; Philip L. Gillett, YMCA Archives, University of Minnesota.

9. Su-Wan Lee, "U.S. Missionary Taught Koreans Baseball Skills," *Korea Times*, March 27, 1982, s2.

10. See a "History of Korean Baseball," a guide published in Korean by the Korea Baseball Organization, 22.

11. Lee, "U.S. Missionary Taught Koreans Baseball Skills," s2.

12. Lee, "U.S. Missionary Taught Koreans Baseball Skills," s2.

13. Lee, "U.S. Missionary Taught Koreans Baseball Skills," s2.

14. Report of P. L. Gillett, general secretary, Seoul, 1909–10, YMCA Archives, University of Minnesota, 370.

15. Robert of Lloyd H. Snyder, September 30, 1912, YMCA Archives, University of Minnesota, 625.

16. Snyder, undated (ca. 1910), YMCA Archives, University of Minnesota.

17. Lee, "U.S. Missionaries Taught Koreans Baseball Skills," s2.

18. Report of Gillett, 1912–13, YMCA Archives, University of Minnesota, 791–92.

19. Lee, "U.S. Missionaries Taught Koreans Baseball Skills," s2.

20. Lee, "U.S. Missionaries Taught Koreans Baseball Skills," s2.

21. Guttmann, *Korea*, 689.

22. James F. Larson and Heung-Soo Park. *Global Television and the Politics of the Seoul Olympics* (Boulder CO: Westview, 1993), 159.

23. "Samsung Organizes Team to Expedite National Unity," *Korea Times*, March 28, 1982, 1.

24. Kim Young-tae, "Haiti Tigers under Harsh Spartan Training," *Korea Herald*, March 6, 1982, 7.

25. Kim Young-tae, "Sammisa Players Young, Strong in Teamwork," *Korea Herald*, March 16, 1982, 7.

26. Kim Young-won, "Pro Baseball Era," *Korea Herald*, March 30, 1982, 4.

27. "Pro Baseball Era," *Korea Herald*, March 30, 1982, 4.

28. "Yahoo! *Yagoo!*" *Time*, March 29, 1982, 57.

29. See http://www.baseball-almanac.com/players/birthplace.php?loc=Korea.

30. Evan Grant, "Texas Rangers Agree to $130 Million Deal with Top Free Agent Shin-Soo Choo," *Dallas Morning News*, December 21, 2013, http://www.dallasnews.com/sports/texas-rangers/headlines/20131221-source-texas-rangers-agree-to-contract-with-shin-soo-choo.ece.

31. Robert Whiting, *The Chrysanthemum and the Bat: Baseball Samurai Style* (New York: Dodd, Mead, 1977), 203.

32. Quoted in Whiting, *Chrysanthemum and the Bat*, 203.

33. Quoted in Robert Whiting, *You Gotta Have Wa: When Two Cultures Collide on the Baseball Diamond* (New York: Vintage, 1989), 50.

34. Quoted in Thomas St. John, "Ten Foreign Players in Korea to Face Hardship This Season," *International Baseball Rundown* 7, no. 3 (1988): 9.

35. Yoo Jeeho, "Top Baseball League Abolishes Salary Cap on Foreign Players," January 14, 2014, http://english.yonhapnews.co.kr/full/2014/01/14/93/12 00000000aen20140114006100315f.html.

36. Yoo, "Top Baseball League Abolishes Salary Cap on Foreign Players."

37. "Average Salary of S. Korean Baseballs Tops 100 Mln Won Mark," February 26, 2014, http://english.yonhapnews.co.kr/culturesports/2014/02/26/55 /0702000000aen20140226003500315f.html.

38. Whiting, *Chrysanthemum and the Bat*, 3.

39. Jeré Longman, "South Korea Secures Title in Return to Little League World Series," *New York Times*, August 24, 2014, http://www.nytimes.com /2014/08/25/sports/baseball/south-korea-secures-title-in-return-to -series.html?_r=0.

40. See http://www.ibaf.org/en/tournament/u-18-baseball-world-cup/6c51 adc0-6ca5-49dd-84c0-2752c2d5cd21?view=halloffame.

41. See http://www.baseballasia.org/bfa/include/index.php?Page=1-1.

42. Quoted at a postgame news conference in Sydney at an event the author managed as senior media manager for the Olympic baseball competition. Also quoted by Agence France Press reporter Jim Slater in a dispatch from Sydney headlined "Koreans Beat Japan to Capture Baseball Bronze," September 27, 2000, available on LexisNexis.

43. See http://web.worldbaseballclassic.com/wbc/2013/results/index.jsp? season=2006, http://web.worldbaseballclassic.com/wbc/2013/schedule _and_tickets/, and http://www.sportingnews.com/mlb/story/2013-03-02 /world-baseball-classic-2013-results-scores-tv-schedule-pool-standings.

44. Kevin Baxter, "Japan Beats South Korea in a Classic Finale," *Los Angeles Times*, March 24, 2009, http://articles.latimes.com/2009/mar/24/sports /sp-wbc-championship24.

45. Whiting, *Chrysanthemum and the Bat*, 53.

12

China

A Century and a Half of Bat Ball

Joseph A. Reaves

The 2008 Beijing Olympics were supposed to be a coming-out party for baseball in China. The Chinese government, Major League Baseball (MLB), and Japan's professional baseball league, Nippon Professional Baseball (NPB), had worked hand in glove for more than seven years to promote the game by fielding a competitive team under the five-star red flag. For a while it seemed the exhaustive push would pay off. The baseball competition was played in a beautiful new venue, Wukesong Stadium, built on prime real estate in the heart of Beijing. The Chinese national team, competing in its first Olympics, stunned longtime political rival and baseball powerhouse Taiwan (Chinese Taipei) with a remarkable 8–7 come-from-behind, extra-inning win. And before the first pitch was thrown, five Chinese players had signed Minor League contracts with the New York Yankees and Seattle Mariners, each hoping to be the first player from the People's Republic to make it to the U.S. Major Leagues.

But as one die-hard yet realistic baseball fan in China later bemoaned, it was all a "fastball to nowhere."[1] Within months Wukesong Stadium was torn down to make room for a mall. The Chinese national team was outscored 43–6 in losing the final five games of the Olympics. And none of the five players signed to professional contracts ever made it past rookie ball.

Baseball has a long, mostly forgotten history in China, spanning all of one century and parts of two others. The sport was played at the Shanghai Base Ball Club as early as 1863—more than a decade before the first game in Japan. It was instrumental in bringing a premature end to one of the most ambitious educational exchanges of all time in the late nineteenth century. University baseball clubs served as cover to help Sun Yat-sen's revolutionaries overthrow the Chinese emperor. And generals of the People's Liberation Army claimed baseball helped their soldiers learn how to throw hand grenades. Baseball was played in prisoner-of-war (POW) camps across China during the ghastly Sino-Japanese War and was a passionate diversion for General Claire L. Chennault's Flying Tigers during breaks in their spectacular job providing air cover for the Burma Road and protecting the city of Chongqing when it was the capital of China. Chinese players fielded teams in secret in the countryside during the Cultural Revolution and, when the chaos finally ended, became regulars in international tournaments across Asia.

Time and again, from the late nineteenth century through the first decades of the third millennium, China has played an important role in the globalization of baseball. But time and again, efforts to transform significant headway into a solid foundation for the game's future in China have floundered.

Silk Gowns and Gold Gloves

The Imperial Court of the late Qing dynasty (1644–1911) realized things had gone too far when word got back to Beijing about the games of "bat ball." China's proudest students were smitten by the strange sport. One hundred twenty mandarins of the future had been shipped to the United States to learn the secrets of *Meiguo*, "the beautiful country," in the hopes that they could use the foreigners' scientific knowledge to make China strong again. Instead of absorbing the best of the West, the students seemed to be embracing the worst. Beijing's spies reported a litany of sins. The students had become undisciplined, had squandered precious funds on personal vacations, formed themselves into secret societies, and ignored their Chinese teachers. Many were attending church and Sunday school, and a few were even planning to convert to Christianity.[2]

Then there was the problem of sports. Physical exercise was considered beneath the dignity of a Confucian scholar. The concept of team games was virtually unknown in China. Yet these scholars—the very elite upon whom the dying Qing dynasty placed its greatest hope for the future—were spellbound by sports. "Within a few months, they were on the best of terms with their American schoolmates and were competing for honors both in their classes and on the baseball diamond."[3]

The students went to the United States in 1872 under an ambitious scheme devised by Rong Hong, an 1854 graduate of Yale who had become a naturalized U.S. citizen in 1852 and married an American woman, Mary Louise Kellogg of Avon, Connecticut, in 1875. Rong Hong returned to his homeland soon after graduating from Yale and spent the rest of his life professing his "undying love for China" the best way he knew how—by relentlessly advocating "reformation and regeneration" for it.[4] His efforts reaped amazing rewards for China. The students he fought so hard to send to the United States returned home and introduced, among other things, a modern navy and sophisticated shipbuilding techniques, the long-distance telegraph, specialized mining skills, and the Beijing-to-Mongolia railway, an engineering marvel that Western experts said was impossible to build without foreign help.

The students might well have contributed much more, had not their love of all things American—particularly baseball—given Rong Hong's imperial enemies the ammunition needed to scuttle the Chinese Educational Mission prematurely.

Under a petition approved by the emperor in the spring of 1871, the Chinese Educational Mission was to be composed of 120 handpicked students who would travel to the United States in groups of 30 per year for four years. The students, generally aged twelve to sixteen, would be accompanied by a retinue of Chinese teachers, translators, and attendants and were to be supervised by two government commissioners. They were to study in the United States for fifteen years, concentrating on scientific, engineering, and military fields, where the West was more advanced. At the end of fifteen years the students would be allowed to travel for two years to gain practical experience before returning to China to spend the rest of their lives in government service.

The first group of 30 students from the Chinese Educational Mission arrived in San Francisco on September 12, 1872. By 1875 all four "detachments" were in the United States and so thoroughly assimilated into their new culture that a conservative corps of Chinese officials began calling for an end to the daring experiment. The conservatives saw the educational mission as nothing more than "bowing down to the power of the hated foreigners."[5] They warned the Imperial Court that if the students remained in the United States, "they would soon lose their love of their own country" and "would be good for nothing or worse than nothing."[6] Two arguments the conservatives cited were intertwined: the students' newfound love of sports, particularly American baseball, and their disdain for traditional Chinese clothing, culture, and accoutrements.

The students arrived in the United States wearing magnificent ankle-length brocaded silk gowns, known as *chang pao*, which were emblematic of Confucian scholars. Their hair was braided into long queues that symbolized their loyalty to the Manchu regime. Neither fashion was particularly practical or welcome on the school grounds of nineteenth-century New England. "At first they were required to wear their long Chinese gowns and plaited cues [*sic*]," wrote one observer. "It made them look like girls and their fellow American students took great delight in teasing them and calling them Chinese girls. These taunts led to many blows and black eyes and a determination on the part of the Chinese lads to abandon their Chinese dress for American trousers and coats."[7]

During the first few years of the mission, any student cutting his queue was shipped home immediately. But by the spring of 1881, when the government abruptly canceled the program, most students had so embraced the American lifestyle that they had shorn their hair and wore Western clothing exclusively.

Photographs of the students taken during their stay in New England clearly show their cultural confusion and conversion. Early in the mission young members can be seen dressed in the traditional clothing their Qing sponsors supplied so they would "present a dignified appearance."[8] As the students matured and became increasingly comfortable in a new world, their attire changed dramatically. Many even qualified as "dandies," sporting spiffy golf attire, natty derbies, classy frock coats, and cravats. By 1878, three years after the last group arrived in the United States and three years before the program summarily ended, a photograph shows nine students looking considerably more like future Major Leaguers than mandarins.

The nine students in the 1878 photograph gained a measure of fame, both individually and as a team, in the United States as well as in China. Two of the nine died young, but the seven others played significant roles in China's future. Liang Dunyan, also known as Liang Tun Yen, was one of the last foreign ministers of the Qing dynasty and as minister of communication in the first Republican government after the revolution of 1911 helped negotiate a treaty with the United States that provided funds for a new university on the outskirts of Beijing (Tsing Hua College, now known as National Qinghua University) that specialized in preparing young men to study abroad, specifically in the United States. The school's curriculum reflected a strong U.S. influence. English was the medium of instruction, and physical education was emphasized, with baseball the most important and popular sport in the school program.[9]

Zhan Tianyou, also known as Tien Yow Jeme and Jeme Tien Yau, a star pitcher of the "Orientals" baseball club, was "honored by all Chinese as China's first railway builder."[10] Zhan graduated in engineering from Yale University's Sheffield Scientific School in 1881, just weeks before the Chinese Educational Mission was recalled. (Only two members of the ambitious mission were to return home with a degree from a U.S. university.)

Both Liang and Zhan played starring roles in what probably was the most important, and certainly the most memorable, Chinese baseball game of the nineteenth or twentieth century. The game took place in Oakland, California, as the Chinese Educational Mission was making its way back to Shanghai. Members of the mission were in San Francisco waiting for the steamer that would take them home when a baseball team from Oakland challenged the Orientals to a match. A rousing account of the game was left by Wen Bingzhong, a member of the second group of Chinese students to arrive in 1873, who later became one of China's foremost engineers.

> The Chinese nine had a twirler that played for Yale, and could do some wonderful curves with the ball, although in those days it was underhand pitching. Before the game began, the Oakland men imagined they were going to have a walk-over. . . . But the Oakland nine got the shock of their lives as soon as they attempted to connect with the deliveries of the Chinese pitcher; the fans were equally surprised at the strange phenomenon—Chinese playing their national ball game and showing the Yankees some of the thrills in the game. Unimaginable! All the same, the Chinese walloped them, to the great rejoicing of their comrades and fellow countrymen.[11]

As important as baseball appears to have been to some members of the Chinese Educational Mission, and as rousing as the unexpected victory in Oakland must have been on the eve of their departure, there is little to indicate the sport played a prominent role in the lives of the students once they returned to China. In truth baseball never gained widespread acceptance in China. But the game did have a small following. And, more important, baseball was played in China far earlier than heretofore widely believed—perhaps earlier than anywhere in Asia.

Shanghai Base Ball Club: A Decade before Japan

As in other Asian countries, missionaries are credited with introducing baseball to China. Foreign missionaries were known, though hardly plentiful, in the Middle Kingdom in the early years of the nineteenth century. However, they began moving into China in significant numbers after the Treaty of Nanjing ended the first Opium War in 1842. That was the year the Knickerbocker Base Ball Club of New York gathered for its first organized games in the United States. Clearly, it would have been some years, at least, before baseball made its way to China, even as a novelty. But by 1861, in the wake of another humiliating defeat for the Chinese in the Arrow War (1856–60), there was a growing willingness to accept Western ideas as part of a new "self-strengthening movement."[12]

The ideological champion of the self-strengthening movement was Feng Guifen, a scholar and official who came into frequent contact with Westerners in Shanghai and developed a grudging appreciation for their abilities. He urged his countrymen to adopt the "barbarians' superior techniques to control the barbarians," a philosophy that indirectly led to the Chinese Educational Mission of 1872–81, the influx of missionaries to China, the spread of Western-style schools, and the arrival of baseball.[13]

A book published by the American University Club of Shanghai in 1936 deals extensively with foreign influences on the modernization of China and reveals the early existence of baseball. Only 1,001 copies of the book were printed. The text was composed of thirteen essays by separate writers. In a chapter titled "The Missionary and Philanthropic Sphere," author Charles E. Patton, a Princeton graduate, deals with the life of Henry William Boone, a medical missionary, who was born in Java in 1839 and was one of only four foreign children in Shanghai when his parents brought him there in 1845. According to Patton, "As a charter member of the first rowing and baseball clubs in Shanghai and in the Masonic brotherhood, Master of the Ancient Landmark Chapter, [Boone] was prominent in the Shanghai of the 'sixties.'"[14]

There is more proof baseball existed in China as early as the 1860s. The activities of the Shanghai Base Ball Club and the Rowing Club of Shanghai were closely related. The rowing club was founded on May 1, 1863. Details about a loan the club took out that year make it clear the Shanghai Base Ball Club was in existence already—a full decade before the date generally accepted for the first baseball game in Japan.

Bat Ball and the White House

The Chinese word for baseball is *bangqiu*, which translates literally to "bat ball" or "stick ball." American missionaries were taught to call the game *P'ai-ch'iu* or *paiqiu*, which means "line ball"—*pai* being the term for a line, as in a file or a rank. Today *paiqiu* refers to volleyball.

Toward the end of the nineteenth century and through the years preceding World War II, baseball was often known as *yeqiu*, or "field ball," a term closely related to the Korean term *yagoo* and the Japanese term *yakyu*. The lexical connection is no coincidence. It mirrors the game's strong historical ties within Asia—distinct from its U.S. roots.

In 1895 Japan emerged as a major world power when it defeated China in the first Sino-Japanese War. Japan's swift victory humiliated China, exposed the weaknesses of the dying Qing dynasty, and bore testament to the merits of modernization. Although the climate in China remained distinctly anti-foreign—indeed, the Boxer Rebellion was only four years away—the lingering impact of the self-strengthening movement and the recent lessons learned from Japan "spawned an interest in physical training in a very small number of Western-oriented Chinese schools."[15] Three such schools—St. John's University of Shanghai, Tongzhou College of Beijing, and Huiwen College of Beijing—established baseball teams in 1895. That same year the first YMCA opened in China at Tianjin, and its staff promoted sports "as a useful front for its principal mission of Christian indoctrination."[16]

An early convert to the promise of athletics was Liang Pixu, also

17. Kan Yen, catcher for the Chinese team. Date unknown. (Photo courtesy of the National Baseball Hall of Fame.)

known as Liang Cheng, who was twelve years old when he arrived in the United States with the final detachment of the Chinese Educational Mission in 1875. Liang Cheng went on to play baseball for Andover Academy in Massachusetts and was the hitting star of a dramatic Andover win against bitter rival Exeter Academy just weeks before the Chinese Educational Mission was recalled.

Liang Cheng went into government service after his return to China and was knighted in 1897 while serving in London as secretary to the Special Chinese Embassy to Queen Victoria's Diamond Jubilee Celebrations. From then on he was known as Sir Chentung Liang Cheng and went by that title in 1903 when he was named China's minister to Washington.

Sir Chentung had always been proud of his baseball experience and believed it helped his diplomatic career in Washington. Once, shortly after taking his post, Sir Chentung met U.S. president Theodore Roosevelt, who said an old friend had recently told him he thought the new Chinese minister played baseball for Andover and helped win a championship with a key hit in the 1880s. Sir Chentung happily confirmed the story, and Roosevelt asked who had been the best player on that Andover team. The new minister temporarily abandoned his Chinese manners and diplomatic reserve and replied that he was the best. "From that moment the relations between President Roosevelt and myself became ten-fold stronger and closer," Liang Cheng said.[17]

Curve Balls and Hand Grenades

The Russo-Japanese War, which ended in 1905, gave Chinese baseball a boost. The Japanese had taken on and beaten the Russians—one of the "Great Western" powers. Chinese students flocked to Japan to learn how a once humble Asian land had grown so mighty. In 1905 the number of Chinese studying in Japan was estimated at twenty thousand. Within a few years that grew to thirty thousand. They studied at Japanese institutions, where, already, in 1905 "intercollegiate baseball was the country's major sport."[18] Some absorbed baseball as thoroughly as their other subjects, bringing the game back with them far more openly and extensively than the students of the Chinese Educational Mission had done a generation earlier. One student who learned baseball overseas and put the game to practical use in his political life was the famed revolutionary Sun Yat-sen.

Sun was born in southern Guangdong Province and traveled to Hawaii in 1879 at age twelve to join his brother, who had emigrated earlier as a laborer. By 1883 Sun Yat-sen was back in China, having learned to play baseball. Just how enamored Sun was with the game and how often he played is unknown. But years later, on the eve of the 1911 Republican Revolution in China, Sun saw baseball as a convenient revolutionary tool. His party, the Tongmenghui (United League), formed a baseball club in Changsha, the capital of Hunan Province, which was a hotbed of unrest for nearly a century. The Changsha Yeqiu Hui (Changsha Field Ball Society) "took in young students to learn baseball techniques to improve their physical qualities . . . and to unite everybody."[19] Essentially, the baseball team was a cover for Sun Yat-sen's anti-imperialist revolutionary activities in Changsha. "Part of the stated purpose of the association was that teaching baseball to young men also gave them practice in throwing hand grenades," explains Lawrence Lee of the Hong Kong Baseball Association.[20]

The idea of using baseball for military training, specifically to prepare soldiers and revolutionaries for throwing hand grenades, recurs frequently in Chinese history. It is difficult to say with certainty whether the notion is fact or folklore. The authors of *Zhongguo Bangqiu Yundong Shi* (1990) treat it with credence, as do numerous Western newspaper and magazine stories.

The most famous and most repeated tale about baseball and military training is about Marshal He Long, an illiterate peasant who rose to fame when he formed one of the early units of the People's Liberation Army, equipped only with vegetable knives. Every man in the unit was ordered to use his knife to kill a Nationalist soldier and steal a rifle. The daring tactics worked. Marshal He became one of China's most revered revolutionaries and was rewarded after the establishment of the People's Republic in 1949 by being named head of the Physical Culture and Sports Commission. While in that post through the 1950s, he actively promoted baseball—particularly among military units—and the old stories about hand grenades and baseball were resurrected. In a 1981 article in the *Asian Wall Street Journal*, reporter Adi Ignatius, later editor of *Time* in Asia, gave the clearest evidence that Marshal He, indeed, thought baseball had a role to play in training China's modern warriors. Ignatius appears skeptical at first, referring to the story as "legend," but goes on to give specifics. "Marshal He pushed baseball because the Chinese lacked any sport which involved throwing an object about the size of a grenade," Ignatius writes. "As the soldiers became skilled at throwing a baseball, the Marshal reasoned, their skills at throwing grenades would improve as well."[21]

Whether baseball was or ever could be an effective infantry training regimen remains questionable. But the game clearly served, on a small strategic level, the political interests of Chinese leaders as diverse as Sun Yat-sen and Marshal He Long. And in doing so, the "Great American Game" played at least trifling roles in both the revolution that brought down the Qing dynasty in China and the modernization of the People's Liberation Army.

Glory Days and War

In the early years after Sun Yat-sen's revolution, baseball began to show signs of catching on in China, certainly not with the speed or general acceptance it enjoyed in Japan and other Asian countries, but more widely than is generally acknowledged. In April 1912 *Leslie's Weekly*, a popular illustrated magazine in the United States, ran a feature hailing the amazing rise of baseball in China. "Out in China, a baseball race just finished, concerned more people than did the overturning of the monarch. This year there will be an eight-club league in Shanghai. Last year, when the league had only four clubs, the games played there were very successful. Baseball promises to sweep through the coast cities of China with the same force that carried the Philippines and Japan."[22]

The article was written by former Major Leaguer Arthur "Tillie" Shafer, whose personal passions and pride perhaps led him to embellish the popularity of baseball in China. But there can be little doubt the sport was steadily gaining acceptance, particularly in Shanghai, where foreign influence was strong. The famed Hunter All-Americans featuring future Hall of Famers Casey Stengel and Waite Hoyt toured Shanghai in 1922. More than a decade later, Babe Ruth and Lou Gehrig played an exhibition game in Shanghai after their final triumphant prewar tour of Japan.

Communist revolutionaries played baseball throughout the 1930s and 1940s. A photograph published in *Zhongguo Bangqiu Yundong Shi* shows peasants and workers in Yenan, the Communist stronghold, playing baseball sometime during the Sino-Japanese War (1937–45). Another photograph shows members of a baseball team formed by the "511 Unit" of the People's Liberation Army in 1949, the year of the Communist victory. A cutline with the second picture says, "Baseball is one of the most-loved sporting activities of the People's Liberation Army. In the past, baseball was known as 'Junqiu,' or army ball."[23]

Some historians have assumed that baseball was dormant in China from 1937 to 1949 when the Chinese were busy fighting the Japanese and each other. Broadly speaking, that is true. But military units on all sides kept the game alive and even fostered its development. Baseball was most popular in areas where U.S. troops were stationed during the later years of the war against Japan and the final years of the civil war between Chiang Kai-shek's Nationalists and Mao Zedong's Communists.

One U.S. veteran, Major Roger B. Doulens, came home in 1946 and wrote a glowing account of baseball's past and its promise in China for *The Sporting News*. He was cheered by a recent announcement that U.S. troops would remain in China at least another eighteen months to help rebuild the Chinese Army and felt it meant "the American national pastime will take on a definite Oriental flavor."[24]

Somewhat surprisingly, baseball prospered in China even after U.S. troops left and Mao's Communists won the civil war. For more than a decade after the founding of the People's Republic in October 1949, baseball was played across China. Both baseball and softball were included in the first postrevolution National Games held in 1956. The winning baseball team, from Shanghai, was coached by Liang Fuchu, the "grandfather of Chinese baseball," who had been recruited by Marshal He to teach the game to soldiers. Three years later baseball was popular enough to attract more than thirty provincial, military, and city teams to the first New China Baseball Tournament.

During Marshal He's reign as sports commissioner, tens of thousands of soldiers played baseball. The dominant team of the time was known as the Fighting Sports Brigade, and its star player was Staff Sergeant Du Kehe, who served as assistant coach of China's national baseball team. Du was a lifelong admirer of Marshal He, although Du admitted the man he called simply "my marshal" was "not much of a player himself." Du learned the game during the war and believed in its benefits long after. "My first coach was a Japanese POW," he told a reporter in 1991. "And my marshal used to say: 'Baseball and sports are the pillars of national defense and development.' [Baseball] made better soldiers, and our pitchers could toss a grenade faster and farther than anyone else . . . and with a curve on it."[25]

Both baseball and Marshal He fell from grace in the 1960s. From 1961 to 1974 baseball disappeared from regular national competition. Some say the game was banned, but Xie Chaoquan, deputy secretary of the Chinese Baseball and Softball Federation in the late 1970s and early 1980s, blamed baseball's disappearance from national sports competition in the early 1960s on economic problems caused by the disastrous Great Leap Forward. The game was still played in many large urban areas until the outbreak of the Cultural Revolution in 1966 and, rarely, during the Cultural Revolution. "Some of us still played in secret in the countryside," said Du Kehe. "We posted guards to whistle if someone came. Then we hid the bats and gloves and pretended to be doing exercises."[26]

Marshal He was denounced during the early days of the Cultural Revolution for criticizing Mao Zedong's economic errors. He was imprisoned in a remote country camp where he reportedly starved to death in 1968 after gnawing through the padding of his old military overcoat. Zealous Red Guards across China impeached sport in general, and baseball in particular, as an unwanted extravagance of Western decadence. Coaches were ridiculed and persecuted, sometimes by their own players. "My own coach was 'struggled' to death by the Guards," said Du Kehe, referring to a common practice of the Cultural Revolution where someone deemed to be an enemy of the people was beaten, spat upon, and harassed in public—often to the point of death.

The Cultural Revolution nominally ended in 1969, but baseball was not officially "rehabilitated" until 1975, when China built a Major League–size stadium on the outskirts of Beijing and organized a series of exhibition games between a newly formed national team and players from Japan. As with most other things after the upheaval of the Cultural Revolution, the history of baseball had to be rewritten to fit new realities. A particularly propagandized book put out by the official government printing house in 1978 waxed eloquently about the political correctness of baseball: "Opposing the counter-revolutionary revisionist line [of the Cultural Revolution], Chairman Mao Zedong's revolutionary sports line deeply penetrated the people's hearts. The baseball movement generally progressed. Through urban workers, peasants and students, baseball organizations were developed."[27]

What the post–Cultural Revolution Chinese leadership really wanted was to use baseball in much the same way they used other sports to promote friendship and gain credence and acceptance from other countries. The oft-touted policy of "Friendship First; Competition Second" was applied to baseball in the 1980s and 1990s as it had been earlier to Ping-Pong, soccer, basketball, and other sports. The fact that the breakaway province of Taiwan, still known then as the Republic of China, emerged in the late 1960s as the dominant power in world Little League baseball clearly had an impact on the Chinese rulers in Beijing.

In 1988, after years of slowly cultivating baseball, the People's Republic of China hosted its first official international baseball tournament, the Beijing International, for eleven- and twelve-year-old boys.

Big-League Help

In the early years of the twenty-first century, as Beijing prepared to host the XXIX Olympiad in 2008, Chinese sports authorities welcomed the assistance of MLB and the NPB. Both were eager to see baseball talent blossom in China. As host of the Games, China was guaranteed a spot in the baseball competition without having to qualify. The Chinese intended being competitive, at the very least and, ideally, winning a medal.

The road to respectability began in 2002 with the creation of China's first professional baseball league. One hundred and forty years after the Shanghai Base Ball Club was founded, the China Baseball League (CBL) began play with four teams—the Beijing Tigers, Tianjin Lions, Guangdong Leopards, and Shanghai Eagles. Each team was affiliated with an NPB club, which provided equipment, coaches, and moral support. Crowds were sparse, almost nonexistent, and play was ragged, but the league muddled through a forty-eight-game schedule and Chinese officials were pleased with the progress.

In the fall of 2003 the China Baseball Association showed just how serious it was about trying to field a topflight team in the 2008 Olympics. The CBA hired two former Major League stars to coach a Chinese national team that seemed to have potential, but pathetically little experience. Jim Lefebvre, a former National League Rookie of the Year with the Los Angeles Dodgers and manager of the Milwaukee Brewers, Seattle Mariners, and Chicago Cubs, was brought in to coach the national team. Hired to help him was Bruce Hurst, who pitched for four teams in a fifteen-year big-league career and was an All-Star in 1987. Lefebvre and Hurst did a masterful job, training in Arizona for three weeks before heading to the Asia Games in Sapporo, Japan, where the Chinese National Team won its three opening-round games against the Philippines, Indonesia, and Pakistan by a combined score of 41–1. In the finals, though, China was overmatched against perennial Asia powerhouses Japan, Korea, and Taiwan. The Chinese scored only three runs in three games, but did themselves credit with a tough 3–1 loss to Taiwan in the last game of the tournament.

Shortly after the 2003 Asia Games, MLB and the CBA announced an agreement to promote the game. The agreement called for top Chinese coaches to travel to the United States to work with Major League clubs, training sessions for Chinese umpires, the establishment of youth development programs in China, and permission for U.S. scouts to begin scouring China for talent.

Two years later the CBL expanded to six teams and increased its season to ninety games. Joining the original four clubs were the Sichuan Dragons and the China Hope Stars. The Hope Stars comprised top college and amateur prospects. To make up for their relative lack of experience, the Stars were allowed to bring in six professional players from outside China. All six were Korean. The other five teams were allowed up to three foreign professionals. Guangdong used its slots to bring in two Dominican players on loan from the Hiroshima Carp of Japan's Central League. The Sichuan Dragons had one Japanese player who came to China, asked the club for a tryout, and made the roster.

Arguably the biggest boost to baseball came in the spring of 2008, just before the Olympics, when the Los Angeles Dodgers and San Diego Padres opened the newly built—and soon to be scrapped—Wukesong Stadium with a pair of sold-out exhibition games. MLB commissioner Bud Selig was on hand for the historic games and gushed to a reporter that he had no doubt that "in a decade baseball will be big in China."[28]

That euphoric prediction seems ill founded in hindsight. Baseball in China took a hard hit four months later at the Olympics. The amazing 8–7 win over Chinese Taipei was epic and almost impossible to understate. But the subsequent drubbings in the final five games left a bitter taste, and the Chinese sporting authorities, who like to spend their money backing champions, began to lose interest in baseball.

There were a few minor highlights in the wake of the Olympics. In the preliminary rounds of the 2009 World Baseball Classic in Tokyo, China again upset Chinese Taipei 4–1, but lost its only two other games to Japan and South Korea by a combined score of 18–0.

In the 2013 WBC, China was seeded in a different bracket, apart from Chinese Taipei and Korea. Unfortunately for the Chinese, they were in a grouping with two tougher teams, Japan and Cuba. China lost to those two by a combined score of 17–2, but salvaged a measure of pride, and automatically qualified for the 2017 WBC, by defeating tournament newcomer Brazil 5–2 in the preliminary rounds at the Fukuoka Dome in Japan.

At the Asian Games in 2010 and 2014, China finished fourth behind the three traditional baseball powerhouses—Japan, South Korea, and Taipei—while dominating the lesser names in Asian baseball: Mongolia, Pakistan, Hong Kong, the Philippines, and Thailand.

The CBL continued to play through 2011 but canceled all of its games in 2012 and 2013, before scrambling to put together a makeshift fourteen-game schedule in 2014 and rebounding with a forty-five-game schedule in 2015 and 2016. Rawlings Sporting Goods gave the league hope for the future in the spring of 2014 by signing a six-year sponsorship deal to provide apparel and equipment. The deal also included China's national team and the national youth team.[29]

Long Live Bat Ball

The Boxer Rebellion, the collapse of the Qing dynasty, the Japanese invasion of Manchuria, World War II, the civil war between the Communists and Nationalists, and the upheavals of the Great Leap Forward and Cultural Revolution all hampered the development of sports, particularly foreign sports, in China during much of the twentieth century. But baseball somehow survived. It survived not because China's leaders sought to emulate the United States or its culture. Baseball survived because there was something practical to be gained by keeping it alive. In the early days of the People's Republic, Marshal He believed baseball made better soldiers—or, at least, better grenade throwers. In the late 1990s and early twenty-first century, China's leaders clearly saw new practical benefits to baseball. China was awakening. During the final two decades of the twentieth century, China's leaders did what Rong Hong and the Chinese Educational Mission set out to do more than a century ago: they reached outside the Middle Kingdom, seeking the knowledge of foreigners to make China strong again. No one would argue that baseball played a leading role in China's modernization. But baseball proved to be an important tool of diplomacy as China returned to its long-abandoned role as a global leader.

This essay was adapted from an article published in NINE: A Journal of Baseball History and Social Policy Perspectives 7 (Spring 1999) and from a chapter in Taking in a Game: A History of Baseball in Asia (Lincoln NE: University of Nebraska Press, 2002).

NOTES

1. Michael Donohue, "Fastball to Nowhere," National (Arab Emirates), December 19, 2008, http://www.thenational.ae/news/world/fastball-to -nowhere.

2. Yung Wing, My Life in China and America (New York: Henry Holt, 1909), 204–5.

3. Thomas E. LaFargue, China's First Hundred (Pullman: State College of Washington Press, 1942), 35.

4. Yung, My Life in China and America, iii–iv.

5. LaFargue, China's First Hundred, 14.

6. Yung, My Life in China and America, 204.

7. LaFargue, China's First Hundred, 38.

8. LaFargue, China's First Hundred, 37.

9. LaFargue, China's First Hundred, 124–32.

10. LaFargue, China's First Hundred, 111.

11. LaFargue, China's First Hundred, 53.

12. Feng Guifen, "Feng Guifen's Stance on the Self-Strengthening Movement,"

China Daily News: Self-Strengthening Movement, 1860, https://ntan2322 .wordpress.com/1860/01/01/post-1/.

13. Hugh Dyson Walker, *East Asia: A New History* (Bloomington IN: Author House, 2012), 405.

14. *American University Club of Shanghai: American University Men in China* (Shanghai: Comacrib Press, 1936), 49.

15. Jonathan Kolatch, *Is the Moon in China Just as Round? Sporting Life & Sundry Scenes* (Middle Village NY: Jonathan David, 1992), 165.

16. Kolatch, *Is the Moon in China Just as Round?*, 165.

17. Walter Muir Whitehill, *Portrait of a Chinese Diplomat: Sir Chentung Liang Cheng* (Boston: Atheneum, 1974), 14.

18. Robert Whiting, *You Gotta Have Wa: When Two Cultures Collide on the Baseball Diamond* (New York: Vintage Books, 1990), 34.

19. Chen Yi Ming, Liang Youde, and Du Kehe, *A History of Chinese Baseball* [Zhongguo Bangqiu Yundong Shi] (1978; reprint, Wuhan: n.p., 1990), 8.

20. Laurence Lee, interview by the author, Hong Kong, April 26, 1997.

21. Adi Ignatius, "Baseball in China Makes a Pitch to Be Re-established," *Asian Wall Street Journal*, February 8, 1981, op-ed page.

22. Arthur Shafer, "Baseball All around the World," *Leslie's Weekly*, April 4, 1912, 408.

23. Chen, Liang, and Kehe, *History of Chinese Baseball*, overleaf.

24. Major Roger B. Doulens, "Chinese Grabbing Chance to Learn Game," *The Sporting News*, March 14, 1946, 13.

25. Uli Schmetzer, "Chinese Baseball Hangs in There," *Chicago Tribune*, May 3, 1991, sec. 4, p. 6.

26. Schmetzer, "Chinese Baseball Hangs in There," 6.

27. *Bangqiu* [Baseball] (Beijing: People's Sports, 1978), 1.

28. Ken Gurnick, "Selig: Baseball Will Catch in China," March 16, 2008, http://web.yesnetwork.com/news/article.jsp?ymd=20080316&content _id=1439118&vkey=1.

29. Lisa Brown, "Rawlings Signs Chinese Baseball Sponsorship," *St. Louis Post-Dispatch*, March 14, 2014, http://www.stltoday.com/business/local /rawlings-signs-chinese-baseball-sponsorship/article_9c07301c-87f1-55 d1-88a4-5fe2a207e9e2.html.

13

Taiwan

Baseball, Colonialism, Nationalism, and Other Inconceivable Things

Andrew D. Morris

The year the first World Baseball Classic (WBC) was held, 2006, was also celebrated as marking "a century of baseball" in Taiwan. The Taiwanese government (that is, the Republic of China [ROC]) and media observed this anniversary with a series of public events, exhibits, television shows, and book publications on the topic. The observances were clearly designed to appeal to and to construct Taiwanese nationalism, but they also were meant to spotlight memories of Japan's "contributions" to Taiwan during its fifty-year occupation of the island. Baseball is a visible and still very popular colonial legacy that was planted and sank deep roots during the fifty-year Japanese occupation of the island from 1895 to 1945.[1]

Taiwan's complicated history vis-à-vis the People's Republic of China regime on the mainland has given rise to the common cultural practice of presenting and understanding Taiwan as part of the world community in its own right, *not* as part of the PRC. The fact that Taiwan's national game is Japanese in origin—and, the point being, *not Chinese*—is of inestimable propaganda value for supporters of Taiwan independence, cultural or political. This obsession is stifling and self-defeating, though. By the early 2000s it became far more important for the Taiwanese to beat China's baseball team in international competitions than to have a chance against powers South Korea or Japan.

Managers of Taiwan's national team thus always sent their best pitchers out against China's weak teams—baseball has never been a popular sport on the mainland—hurting their chances against other rivals but guaranteeing at the very least that they would not be the manager to suffer the shame of losing to the PRC. This tactic worked for many years, until the Beijing Olympics in 2008. Despite vowing in the media that "on Chinese soil, no matter what we cannot lose," and despite sending their finest pitcher, Pan Wei-lun, against the home underdogs, the ROC team gave up five runs in a breathtaking twelfth inning to lose to the PRC team for the first time ever, 8–7.[2]

Within hours Taiwan's media was calling this "the most humiliating day in Taiwan baseball history," "the most sorrowful and insulting defeat," and "the most embarrassing battle in history." Bloggers went further, calling for observation of a "Day of National Humiliation" every August 15 thereafter and asking their government to lower the national flag to half-mast. Another netizen screamed the players' way, "A deathly loss of face! Tell [American gold medalist Michael] Phelps to teach you how to swim home!"[3]

This anger and humiliation, tied so closely to one of the most crucial pillars of Taiwanese identity for almost a century, was not just harmful to the nation's collective psyche. One elderly woman from Taizhong, upon seeing PRC outfielder Sun Lingfeng score the winning run, suffered chest constrictions, was unable to breathe, and had to be hospitalized. A countryman of hers from Gaoxiong was not so lucky; he died of a heart attack at that same fateful moment. After these tragedies psychological and heart specialists were interviewed in the *United Daily News* for advice that they could share with an angered and exhausted nation. No wonder, then, that one blogger could only ask his countrymen to stay inside the rest of the day, since "only Heaven knows what other inconceivable things might happen."[4]

Before baseball's contemporary position as a clear stand-in for Taiwanese political and cultural identity, the first eight decades of the game's history in Taiwan were recorded during eras of colonial and authoritarian rule at the hands of the Japanese imperial and Chinese Nationalist regimes. While there was little space for expression of individual interest in or attachment to the game, baseball certainly brought great enjoyment to the many millions of Taiwanese people who played it during these many years under the twentieth-century modes of Japanese colonialism and Chinese nationalism.

Baseball in the Japanese Colonial Era

Baseball in Taiwan, introduced by the Japanese colonial regime, has never thoroughly shed its Japanese heritage. The sport, which was well developed in Japanese schools by the 1890s, was imported to the colony of Taiwan around 1897, just two years after its incorporation into the Japanese Empire. Initially played by colonial bureaucrats, bankers, and their sons in Taihoku (Taipei), by the mid-1910s there were teams all over Taiwan representing businesses, occupational and medical schools, military units, railroad and postal offices, bureaucratic and legal agencies, engineering firms, banks, newspapers, private clubs, and merchant associations. In 1915 Northern and Southern Baseball Associations were established in Taihoku and Tainan to further organize and routinize this colonial institution.[5]

It was not long before Taiwanese youth joined in as well. In the early 1910s Taiwan governor-general Sakuma Samata encouraged the development of baseball among Taiwanese youth. As he explained it, this was his humble way of repaying the local Taiwanese deity Mazu, who had appeared to his ailing wife in a dream and miraculously cured her. In 1921 Karenkō (Hualian) native Lin Guixing formed a team of boys of the Amis Aborigine tribe. They became known as the "Savage Team Nōkō" for their mountainous home region and achieved great fame when they traveled to Japan in the summer of 1925 and won four of their nine games, losing four and tying one, and winning wide praise for their "serious attitude and scientific strategies."[6]

The most famous of all Taiwanese baseball traditions was that born at the Tainan District Kagi Agriculture and Forestry Institute (abbreviated Kanō) in the late 1920s. Under the guidance of manager Kondō Hyōtarō, a former standout player who had toured the United States with his high school team, Kanō dominated Taiwan baseball in the decade before the Pacific war. What made the Kanō team special was its triethnic composition: in 1931 its starting nine was made up of two Han Taiwanese, four Taiwan Aborigines, and three ethnic Japanese players. Kanō won the Taiwan championship, earning the right to play in the hallowed Kōshien High School Baseball Tournament, held near Osaka, five times between 1931 and 1936. The best of these, the 1931 squad, was the first team ever to qualify for Kōshien with Taiwanese (Aborigine or Han) players on its roster. Kanō placed second in the twenty-three-team tournament that year, their skills and intensity winning the hearts of the Japanese public and remaining a popular nostalgic symbol even today in Japan. This team of Han, Aboriginal, and Japanese players confirmed to nationally minded Japanese the colonial myth of "assimilation" (*dōka*)—that both Han and Aborigine Taiwanese were willing and able to take part alongside Japanese in the cultural rituals of the Japanese state. Meanwhile, the six Taiwanese players on the starting roster probably also saw their victories as a statement of Taiwanese (Han or Aborigine) will and skill that could no longer be dismissed by the Japanese colonizing power.

The southern town of Kagi (Jiayi) cemented its reputation as the baseball capital of Taiwan when several of its sons went on to star in baseball in Japan. The greatest of these was Wu Bo, who starred on Kanō's 1935 and 1936 championship teams and signed with the proud Tokyo Giants in 1937. Wu, known in Japan as Go Ha (the Sino-Japanese reading of Wu Bo), played for the Giants for seven years, acquiring the esteemed nickname "the Human Locomotive" for his rare speed and power. In 1943 Wu took the more properly Japanese name Go Shōsei, keeping the same surname, pronounced "Go" in Japanese, and notably (despite the nationalistic pressures of wartime) resisting the native Japanese *kun* reading of Kure. Wu left the Giants outright the next year—some say refusing to travel to Manchuria with the Giants

18. Three members of the 1931 Kanō (Tainan District Jiayi Agriculture and Forest Institute) baseball team. Kanō placed second in the empire-wide Kōshien tournament and became famous for its triracial composition of Han, Aboriginal, and Japanese players. (Photo courtesy of Cai Wuzhang.)

to rouse Japanese troops stationed there—but went on to play for thirteen more years with the Hanshin Tigers and Mainichi Orions, and in 1995 he became the first Taiwanese player selected to the Japanese Baseball Hall of Fame.[7]

Taiwan did not just produce an elite class of standout baseball players. The sport became popular at all levels, making baseball as dominant a sport in the colony as it was in the home islands of Japan. Peng Ming-min would later trade his baseball mitt for the pen, enduring much sacrifice under house arrest and in exile as he led the struggle for Taiwanese self-determination and independence during the Chinese Nationalist era. But as a boy in Takao (Gaoxiong) in the 1930s, young Peng was a typical Taiwanese schoolboy obsessed with baseball. In a conversation with me in 1999, Peng fondly remembered huddling around the radio to listen to broadcasts of the Japanese high school championships at Kōshien every spring. In his memoir, *A Taste of Freedom* (1972), Peng recalls, "I was an ardent baseball fan. When Babe Ruth visited Japan I boldly wrote a letter to him and in return received his autograph, which became my treasure. . . . [I] reserved my greatest enthusiasm for baseball. Our school masters took baseball very seriously, treating it almost as if it were a military training program. Although I was a poor batter, I was an excellent fielder, and played on our team when it won a citywide championship. Needless to say, my Babe Ruth autograph gave me great prestige among my classmates."[8] The enthusiasm of millions of young people like Peng, who played and paid feverish attention to this Japanese institution, is what made baseball a "national game" (if Japan's) in Taiwan long before it was claimed as such by Chiang Kai-shek's Nationalist Chinese regime.

This Taiwanese excellence in baseball, the sport of the colonizing metropolis, reflects an important aspect of the experience of almost any colonized people. In Taiwan baseball was one way in which the colonized population sought to negotiate its relationship with the Japanese colonizing power on terms that the Japanese had to accept.

Japanese exclusion of Taiwanese baseball teams or players would have given the lie to Japan's entire colonial enterprise.

Participation in Japan's "national game" allowed Taiwanese people to prove and live their acculturation into the colonial order at the very moment that Taiwanese baseball successes worked to subvert it. Taiwanese subjects, both ethnic Chinese and Aborigine, could use baseball skills and customs taught by the Japanese to appeal for equal treatment within the national framework that baseball represented in so many ways. The Taiwanese baseball community, through its many triumphs, was able to use this arena to offer the final proof, in a "national" language that the Japanese had to understand, that the colonial enterprise was bound to fail.

Baseball in Guomindang Taiwan, 1945–1980s

When the Guomindang (Chinese Nationalist Party) took the reins of Taiwan's government in late 1945, it enforced policies of "de-Taiwanization," officially degrading distinctively Taiwanese cultures or customs in order to cut the colonial ties to Japan. At the same time, however, the GMD also realized what a valuable exception baseball could be to this rule of erasing any and all colonial remnants. The Nationalists had promoted physical culture in planning the construction of a strong and healthy Chinese populace and state on the mainland for more than twenty years. Official endorsement of baseball soon became one method of officially "Sinicizing" a cultural realm that still represented a Pandora's box of colonial thinking and customs. Baseball was included at the First Taiwan Provincial Games, held in October 1946 at Taiwan National University; twenty counties, cities, colleges, and government organizations sent baseball teams to this meet overseen by ROC National Government chairman Chiang Kai-shek.

A baseball tournament was held in Taiwan in August 1947, even as government "anti-Communist" forces continued their massacres, begun that March, of thousands of Taiwanese elites who were seen as a threat to Chiang's regime. It is telling that the baseball world was not able to escape this horror. Lin Guixing, coach of the great Hualian Nōkō teams of the 1920s, was killed on August 1, 1947, during the violent and sustained aftermath of what was called the "February 28 Incident."[9] Fudan University and Shanghai Pandas teams also came to play against teams from Taipei, Taizhong, Taiwan Power, Taiwan Sugar, and Taiwan Charcoal, as if all was well that bloody summer. In 1949 a Taiwan Province Baseball Committee was formed, organizing annual provincial baseball tournaments at all levels of play.[10]

What is interesting about the Guomindang efforts to promote baseball in Taiwan in the immediate postwar period is that the former Japanese colony of Taiwan was the only region of the ROC with any baseball tradition whatsoever; the Nationalists could hardly promote baseball as a "Chinese" custom. Thus, their work to hijack the game's unique popularity in Taiwan for official uses still had to be in explicitly Taiwanese terms. Baseball remained an arena where Taiwanese people could successfully challenge the Guomindang's policies of "de-Taiwanization" and claims to represent a true Chinese culture.

Baseball, then, is central to the story of Taiwan's rapid and traumatic transition from wartime to decolonization to a new oppression delivered in the rhetoric of "Retrocession" to Chinese rule. Original support for Chinese rule in Taiwan was dashed by the actions of tens of thousands of carpetbagging Guomindang troops, bureaucrats, and hangers-on. Relieved and enthusiastic searching among Taiwanese for a "Chinese" Taiwan thus quickly gave way to a yearning for cultural artifacts from the good old colonial days.

Yet the vagaries of decolonization and Retrocession do not provide the full extent of this history. The Taiwanese people now had to contend with the reality of an invigorated American Cold War imperialism in Taiwan and Asia as a whole. Taiwan's baseball history offers a look at this process as well. In 1951 the first All-Taiwan baseball team was organized for a series of games against Filipino teams in Manila. The Manila sporting public fell in love with the All-Taiwanese, especially the astounding home run hitting of Hong Taishan. But the young team from Taiwan made an even deeper impression when team members "volunteered" to give blood to American soldiers recuperating in Manila hospitals from casualties sustained in the Korean War.[11] This episode, though anecdotal, thus provided a profound metaphor to describe life in small Asian nations during the depths of the Cold War. In the end the greatest triumphs that could be won were in activities (like baseball) defined and approved by the United States, in locales dependent on and exposed to American beneficence and greed, and in ways that figuratively sucked life from these locales as they were integrated into America's new postwar empire.

This incredible tightrope walk between Japanese colonialist legacies and Guomindang-U.S. hegemony in Taiwan continued into, and was in many ways exemplified by, the international success of Taiwanese Little League baseball teams beginning in the late 1960s. In a tremendous run perhaps unmatched in the history of international sport, Taiwanese teams won ten Little League World Series titles between 1969 and 1981 and sixteen in the twenty-seven-year period from 1969 to 1995. This success brought desperately needed attention to Taiwan on the world stage and allowed the playing out of a complicated jumble of national and racial tensions in Taiwan.

Taiwan's Little League success began in August 1968 with two great victories by the Maple Leaf (Hongye) Elementary School team over a visiting team from Wakayama, Japan. The Hongye Village team, made up of Bunun Aborigine youth representing their tiny Taidong County school of just one hundred students, earned the right to play Wakayama after winning the island-wide Students' Cup tournament held in Taipei. They became superstars after their victories over Wakayama at Taipei Municipal Stadium. The twenty thousand fans who managed to get tickets for these historic games were joined by an island-wide television audience treated to more than thirteen hours of Taiwan Television broadcasts on the first game alone. The overall significance in Taiwan of the Maple Leaf boys' success is hard to measure. Virtually all of Taiwanese society was energized in a way that has few parallels in American history; perhaps the closest examples are the Olympic triumphs of Jesse Owens or the 1980 hockey team. To this day, the Maple Leaf 1968 victories against Wakayama are cited as a defining moment in the history of Taiwanese nationalism.[12]

The next year, 1969, was Taiwan's first foray into the Little League World Series in Williamsport, Pennsylvania. The youth of Taiwan spared no time in making this tournament an almost yearly blowout of any challengers. The Taizhong Golden Dragons, Taiwan's 1969 champions, swept opponents from Ontario, Ohio, and California to take the world title. Impressed, if politically incorrect, *The Sporting News* described the skill and infectious enthusiasm of "the Orientals": "Thousands of gong-clanging, cheering fans in the stands at Williamsport adopted the Chinese as their favorite team. [Chen Zhiyuan] captured the fans' imagination when, after every out, he'd turn around and shout to his fielders, raising the ball above his head. In return they yell in Chinese the American equivalent of, 'Go men!'"[13] The players' confidence was also boosted by the presence at their games of thousands of delirious Taiwanese and Chinese flag-waving fans who would make these yearly baseball pilgrimages to Williamsport for many years to come.

Fans at home in Taiwan were even more jubilant, glued to their radios into the wee hours of that humid summer night. One radio DJ remembered thirty years later how "the Taipei night nearly boiled over. When the game finished at 3 a.m., the streets of the city erupted with the constant banging of firecrackers, as ordinary citizens opened their windows and yelled out to the night sky, 'Long live the Republic of China!'"[14] At a time when Taiwan's standing in the international community was becoming less and less stable, this, like the Maple Leaf triumphs the year before, was a satisfying victory indeed.

Yet this championship, unfortunately, was also plagued by irregularities. It was common knowledge in Taiwan that the 1969 world champions, technically a school team from Taizhong in central Taiwan, had actually been recruited as a national all-star team, a fact that clearly violated the Williamsport charter. Only two of the team's fourteen players were from Taizhong, while nine of the starting players were from Jiayi and Tainan in the south of the island.[15]

These geographical technicalities mattered little to the Taiwanese public of the time. In 1971 when the Tainan Giants won the Williamsport championship, some ten million people in Taiwan—two-thirds of the island's population—watched the game on television, from 2:00 to 5:00 a.m. Baseball stardom became an almost universal aspiration among the boys and young men of Taiwan. Li Kunzhe, who starred professionally for the China Trust Whales in the late 1990s, remembers, "I grew up watching baseball. . . . I remember the days when everyone would wake up in the middle of the night to watch our national teams perform in the international competitions. They were national heroes. We all wanted to represent our country and be a hero."[16] These triumphs were especially thrilling for Taiwanese people, but the humbled Americans were reduced to booing these Taiwanese youngsters (when the Tainan Giants won again in 1973, on their third consecutive no-hitter) and eventually even banning all foreign teams for a year in 1975 in order to guarantee an American "winner."

Success in this Taiwanese (and not mainland Chinese) sport of baseball also invigorated dissidents and critics of the Chiang Kai-shek regime, who were thirsting for tangible measures of uniquely Taiwanese accomplishment. Williamsport soon became a "new battlefield" for Taiwanese dissidents and independence activists. In 1969 frenzied Taiwanese fans shouted upon the Golden Dragons' victory, "The players are all Taiwanese! Taiwan has stood up!" Taiwanese supporters soon raised the stakes in this implicit protest against the Guomindang government. In 1971 as the Tainan Giants swept to a world championship, Taiwanese independence activists at Williamsport hired an airplane to fly over the stadium towing a bilingual banner reading, "Long Live Taiwan Independence, Go Go Taiwan." The Taiwan teams' games attracted fans from all points of the political spectrum, so each Taiwan independence flag or banner was matched by pro-Nationalist fans waving national flags and cheering for the "Chinese" team. The pro-state fans had an advantage, however, in the dozens of New York Chinatown thugs hired by the Guomindang to identify and rough up Taiwan independence activists at the games. The 1971 championship game was interrupted when a dozen of these toughs ran across the field to rip down a banner reading in English and Chinese, "Team of Taiwan, Go Taiwan."[17]

In 1972 when the Taipei Braves challenged for the world title, the Guomindang was better prepared, renting every single commercial aircraft for miles around to keep the Taiwan independence crowd from repeating its coup. Some seventy to eighty ROC military cadets training in the United States were also recruited to Williamsport, as they shouted while beating Taiwanese male and female supporters with wooden clubs, "Kill the traitors!" One wonders what American fans at Williamsport thought of all this violence, but these concerns did not stop either side from carrying out their battles. In 1975 at the Senior Little League Championships in Gary, Indiana, Taiwanese activists floated a balloon bearing the message "Long Live Taiwan Independence." Thanks to the generous and curious ABC cameramen on the scene, this sky-high subversion flashed across millions of Taiwan's television screens for the first time in history. Thus, through the manipulation of satellite technology and the tweaking of the connection between sports and nationalism that the Guomindang itself had tried to disseminate in Taiwan, Little League baseball became one of the most effective and joyous ways of challenging Chinese Nationalist hegemony in Taiwan.

The many jumbled and precarious directions along which Taiwanese baseball developed under Guomindang rule did not resemble in the least the neat white lines of the baseball diamonds themselves. During these martial-law seasons, baseball was one realm where Taiwanese people could register their own contributions to Taiwan culture and society. In many ways baseball represented a table of negotiation, where Taiwanese baseball communities exchanged measures of integration for measures of independent expression, measures of "Chinese" identity for measures of pro-Japanese nostalgia, and measures of the martial-law autocratic Guomindang state for measures of an independent Taiwanese culture and society.

The Chinese Professional Baseball League: Beginnings, 1990–1994

Planning for a Taiwanese professional baseball league began in late 1987, the year that martial law was lifted in Taiwan. The events of this year marked the end of four decades of authoritarian rule by the Guomindang and signaled the beginning of a new era in Taiwan. The nation now faced two challenges: defining a unique identity for the Chinese-but-not-really-Chinese island nation and ensuring Taiwan's inclusion in a global world order. Both of these goals were realized with the creation of the Chinese Professional Baseball League, which began play in 1990.

The CPBL consisted of four corporate-owned teams: the Weichuan Dragons, Brother Elephants, President Lions, and Mercuries Tigers. Each team's uniforms clearly demonstrated the effort to present a product that was a pleasurable mix of the global and the Chinese; the teams' names and parent companies were represented on the jerseys and caps in various mixtures of English and Chinese script. The four corporate-owned teams did not represent cities, as teams do in most professional leagues; instead, the teams played weekly round-robin series together up and down the island's west coast. Each baseball city had fan clubs supporting each of the CPBL's four teams, which provided enthusiastic, flag-waving, drum-beating support, but also could at times turn violent. The sight of angry fans—Lions fans in the President Corporation's hometown of Tainan were notorious for this—hurling bottles, cans, eggs, and garbage at opposing players, or even surrounding the opposing team's bus in a mob, was not uncommon in the league's early years.

Another important element of the new CPBL was the presence of foreign players (*yangjiang*, literally "foreign generals") culled from the rosters of American AA-level Minor League teams. Sixteen American and Latin American players were selected to join the CPBL (with a league limit of four *yangjiang* per team).[18] The presence of these players was meant to add an international flavor to the league and to provide an external stimulus for the improvement of the quality of CPBL play. In a 1993 conversation pitcher Tony Metoyer of the new Jungo Bears described to me how these foreign players also served as "silent coaches" who could share their knowledge of American strategies and training methods with the Taiwanese players. Their many contributions allowed the Taiwanese game to become similar in strategy to the more open or risky style of baseball played in the Americas and less like the conservative game that suited Taiwan so well in its years of Little League dominance.

Steps were also taken to Sinicize the identities of the foreign players. Each player was given a "Chinese name," which usually sounded something (if only vaguely) like the player's original name and usually bestowed fine and admirable qualities on the foreigner. Freddy Tiburcio, the Elephants' star Dominican outfielder, was called "Dibo," or "Imperial Waves and Billows." Luis Iglesias, the Tigers' home run champion from Panama, was called "Yingxia," or "Chivalrous Eagle." These players were photographed for magazine covers dressed in "traditional" Chinese scholars' caps and robes, as Taiwan's baseball public was taught that even in the realm of baseball, the Chinese ability to assimilate outsiders was as powerful as ever.

Yet this "assimilation" could occur on the most crass of terms, as many of the foreign players' "Chinese" names were just merely advertisements for products sold by their team's parent corporation. The Mercuries Tigers inflicted names of noodle dishes from their chain restaurants onto pitchers Cesar Mejia and Rafael Valdez. The President Lions, whose parent company specialized in convenience stores and prepackaged foods, did the same with the names A-Q (instant noodles) and Baiwei (Budweiser) for pitchers José Canó (the father of MLB superstar Robinson Canó) and Ravelo Manzanillo. Later, the China

Times Eagles resourcefully used names from their minor corporate sponsors, dubbing pitcher Steve Stoole "Meile" (Miller Beer) and calling the African Dominican outfielder José González "Meilehei" (Miller Dark).[19]

Outsiders from the larger world of baseball came to Taiwan to endorse the CPBL, and the league won several valuable publicity coups in its early years. In 1993 the Los Angeles Dodgers visited, only to be beaten in two of three games by CPBL teams. The presence in Taiwan's ballparks of these representatives of the great American baseball tradition only boosted the status of the CPBL in the eyes of Taiwanese and foreign baseball communities.

Besides these efforts to connect Taiwanese baseball and culture to global trends, baseball officials emphasized the CPBL's local composition in marketing the league. The most direct connection was the presence of former Little League heroes who had won such great honors for Taiwan in the 1970s. During their prime years in the 1980s, before the CPBL was founded, these stars could play only in Japanese or Taiwanese semipro leagues. The CPBL was extremely fortunate to have begun play while this celebrated group could still perform well; after a few years it was obvious that some of their careers were coming to an end. But their presence in the CPBL's first years was crucial in making the league a viable and popular enterprise.

Other accoutrements of "traditional Chinese culture" helped cement the league's special Chinese characteristics as well. Fan favorites like Dragons pitcher Huang Pingyang and Lions captain Zeng Zhizhen (known as "the Ninja Catcher") were often featured in magazines that recounted their pursuits of self-consciously Chinese or Taiwanese customs such as drinking fine tea, taking in traditional Taiwanese puppet theater, or collecting teapots or Buddhist paintings. Popular television variety shows even featured noted numerologists and geomancers using these "traditional" Chinese sciences to predict the results of upcoming baseball seasons.

Thus, the roots of the CPBL's early success lay in this important effort to combine the local and global. International symbols of sporting culture were carefully balanced with aspects of the local—expressed through the involvement of particular individuals identified with past Taiwanese sporting successes or through linguistic or cultural particulars that remained a part of CPBL baseball.

Minor League Foreigners and Tensions in "Chinese" Baseball

The CPBL reached its peak popularity, measured by crowd attendance, in its third through fifth seasons (1992–94), when some six to seven thousand tickets were sold to each game. In 1993 two new teams joined the league—the Jungo Bears and the China Times Eagles—each loaded with seven young popular members of Taiwan's 1992 silver-medal Olympic baseball team. That same season the all-sports station TVIS paid NT$90 million (US$3.6 million) to broadcast CPBL games over the next three seasons—hardly American network money, but a great improvement over the NT$3,000 (US$120) per-game fee paid previously by Taiwan's major broadcast stations before that point.[20]

But somehow, despite all these signs of vigorous growth, the league's popularity began to wane seriously by 1995, as the game slowly lost the local Taiwan flavor it had worked so hard to cultivate. The CPBL mishandled the important balance between the local and the international that was so crucial in to sustaining public interest in the league. As owners developed a dependence on international networks, the league became simply less appealing.

Perhaps the most visible form of this dependence was the CPBL's reliance on foreign ballplayers invited to Taiwan to supplement the native rosters. Although most of these foreign players would never reach the American Major Leagues, several of them were able to excel in Taiwan. It became apparent in the league's first year that a team's success could depend heavily on the performance of its foreign "supplements." Teams began putting more emphasis on the foreign element of their rosters, seeing it as the quickest path to improvement—it was certainly easier to wave money at a foreigner with proven skills than to dedicate several years to developing a young Taiwanese player. The situation was exacerbated when, in 1994, the board of CPBL owners raised the foreign-player maximum to seven per team. In 1995 this ceiling was again raised to ten foreigners per team, and in March 1997 the league owners voted to eliminate all limits whatsoever on roster composition.

Public interest in the league fell consistently as the CPBL became less and less "Chinese" or Taiwanese and more and more reliant on American and Dominican players. By 1995 44 percent of the players on CPBL rosters came from outside Taiwan. Many of these *yangjiang* made the situation even worse. Some admitted far too candidly to being baseball mercenaries who played in Taiwan solely for the relatively high salaries they could earn there. Others alienated local society with their promiscuous and even sometimes brutish behavior; in fact, a book titled *Foreign Pro Baseball Players' Sex Scandals* (1997) was published on the topic.

In 1998, commenting on the dominance of foreign pitchers in the CPBL, a *Liberty Times* (Taipei) columnist summoned up ugly images from modern Chinese history in calling the league's pitching mound a "foreign concession" (*waiguo zujie*). Indeed, the predominance of foreign pitchers that season reached ridiculous heights. Of the one hundred CPBL pitchers who took the mound that year, only twenty-two were Taiwanese. The 1998 CPBL champion Weichuan Dragons carried twelve foreign pitchers on its roster (combined record 56-48-1), but only two Taiwanese pitchers (combined record 0-0-0).

In an editorial written in March 1997, a Taiwan sportswriter addressed the problem of the dominance of foreign players in Taiwan baseball differently. He credited the *yangjiang* with aiding the development of pro baseball in Taiwan. However, he reminded fans that the use of these foreigners truly came down to one question: Would these "AAA-level [Minor League] foreigners" ever be able to help Taiwan win an Olympic medal in baseball? In terms of national loyalty or the crucial international baseball stage, these foreign players could never truly contribute anything to Taiwan's future.

Fans' own wishes for a more Taiwan-centric CPBL were seen in the votes cast for the annual All-Star Game. In 1997, a season marked by foreign dominance more than any other, fans did not select a single foreigner to the All-Star teams.[21] They preferred marginal (at best) players like Whales outfielder He Xianfan (batting average .218) and pitcher Huang Qingjing (1 win and 9 losses, 5.65 ERA) over the dozens of foreign players who were more deserving by any statistical standard. The presence of these foreign players and managers achieved one of the original goals of the *yangjiang* strategy: the quality of CPBL play improved greatly over the league's first few years. However, it is telling that as the CPBL improved in technical terms, it simultaneously became a subject of such little interest to Taiwanese baseball fans.

The Taiwan Major League

In December 1995 a new chapter in the story of Taiwan baseball began. A group of investors, led by the Era Communications and Sampo Electronics dynasties, announced the formation of the Taiwan Major League, which would begin play in 1997. The new TML was designed to trump the CPBL, not with better-quality baseball but with a media-savvy and authentically "Taiwanese" approach that made the old league's "Chinese" identity look cheap and outdated. This explicitly politicized strategy fitted perfectly within the crucial dialectic between globalization and local Taiwanese identity: Pride in Taiwan's unique culture and in the contributions Taiwan can make justifies a place for Taiwan in the international community. Likewise, the pursuit of international (often specifically American or Japanese) trends and symbols can also be understood as solidifying a status for a Taiwan independent of the PRC and its threats of reunification. Mastering this dialectic between the uniquely Taiwanese and the international or universal is necessary for the success of any cultural, social, commercial, or political enterprise in contemporary Taiwan. The TML met these requirements when Taiwanese people felt the need to distinguish themselves from their mainland cousins.

Unlike the CPBL the TML did not allow its productive connections with Japanese and American baseball to overshadow the league's explicitly "Taiwanese" character. Where the CPBL clung to dry stereotypes of "traditional China," the TML's identity was squarely based in Taiwan's unique culture and history. The name of the Naluwan Corporation, which ran the TML, and the names of the four teams—Agan (Robots), Fala (Thunder Gods), Gida (Suns), and Luka (Braves)—were taken from languages of Taiwan's several Aborigine tribes. Team uniforms were designed to reflect "the special characteristics of the Aborigine peoples," but also only after "consideration of the colors and design of professional baseball uniforms of other nations."[22]

Another important choice made by the TML was to follow what it called a "territorial philosophy," where each team has a home city or region and its own home field, unlike the CPBL, whose teams never enjoyed a true home-team advantage. This "territorial" doctrine dictated that teams take these "home" connections seriously. Before the 1997 season teams took part in New Year's ceremonies in their home cities and took oaths before city officials to serve as loyal and morally upright urban exemplars. These hometown loyalties took on more significance with the tragic earthquake that struck central Taiwan in September 1999. The Robots quickly dubbed themselves "the Disaster Area Team" and set up their own Robots Van that delivered disinfectants, vitamins, and medicines to the residents of the quake's epicenter.

Participation in the international sport of baseball, as well as impressive connections to powerful baseball networks all over the world, created a cosmopolitan image for the TML. Yet the early success of the TML came from this bold celebration of the local, the authentic, the Taiwanese. Even though the new league offered an inferior quality of baseball than the old CPBL, the TML consistently outdrew its rival at the gates. One random but revealing example was a night in September 1998, when 14,385 Jiayi fans attended a TML Braves-Robots game, compared to crowds of 629 and 1,113 that showed up for CPBL games in Taipei and Gaoxiong, respectively.[23]

The TML's official theme song, "Naluwan—Chéng-keng é Eng-hióng" (Naluwan—true heroes), was perhaps the finest example of the fascinating mixture of historical and cultural legacies that makes Taiwan society so unique and dynamic and so difficult to fit within most standard models of historical, economic, cultural, social, or political development. The TML anthem, supposedly based on rhythms and patterns of several types of Aboriginal tribal songs, consists of lyrics in Mandarin, Taiwanese, English, Japanese, and Aboriginal languages:

> Take charge—the fervent spirit of the rainbow,
> Our hearts are filled—with great fire shining bright,
> Struggle on—with hopes that never die,
> Start anew—a space for us alone.
> Fight! Fight! Fight, fight! Speed just like the wind,
> K! K! K! Power stronger than all,
> *Homu-ran batta*—truly strong and brave,
> Aaa . . . Naluwan, the true heroes![24]

Each singing, each playing of this league anthem, became a neat and tidy re-creation of the last several centuries of Taiwan history and culture. To be sure, little room for critical analysis of, or retrospection on, this history was allowed in this rousing, commercialized theme song. But the tune was one more way in which the TML sought to portray itself as the true heir and "the true heroes" of the proud, complicated history of Taiwan.

The Fall of Taiwanese Pro Baseball, 1997–2001

In the winter of 1997 the future of Taiwan's pro baseball enterprise looked bright. The CPBL was beginning the first year of a rich new television contract with the China Trust conglomerate worth NT$1.5 billion (US$60 million) over three years. The TML stirred up controversy by stealing some of the CPBL's best players and promised to provide healthy competition for the old league.

Unfortunately, 1997 would bring only disgrace, both domestic and international, to the CPBL. In late January 1997 law enforcement uncovered a gambling scandal that revolved around the fixing of CPBL games by ballplayers in return for huge payoffs—often double a player's monthly salary. The nation was shocked by the front-page news that some of the game's greatest and most popular stars had accepted payoffs of NT$300,000–$500,000 (US$11,000–$18,000) per game that they threw for the local gangs handling the "gambling" on each team. The China Times Eagles, who were disbanded after the season ended, threw games most spectacularly; it was revealed that the entire team was bought off regularly for a single team fee of NT$7.5 million (US$270,000) per game.[25]

This scandal, which was later found to be linked to gambling interests in Hong Kong and Macao as well as southern Taiwan, led to the near unraveling of the league as the public learned the sordid details of this enterprise. This was a tricky business: Lions stars Jiang Taiquan and Guo Jinxing lost some NT$200 million (US$7.3 million) of one gambling outfit's money in a 1996 game by accidentally winning after assuring gamblers that the Lions would lose.[26]

No team or player was safe from these gangs and their members' frustrations when their favorite teams won. Loyal Elephants gamblers, furious at their team's winning ways, kidnapped five Elephant players, pistol-whipped one, and shoved a gun down the throat of another. Seven Tigers players (including two Americans and two Puerto Ricans) were abducted at the Gaoxiong Stardust Hotel by gun-packing thugs who used similarly violent ways of "encouraging" the players to throw games. And one day, while picking his daughter up at school, Dragons manager Xu Shengming was stabbed in the lower back by a representative of yet another gambling outfit.

Understandably, fewer and fewer fans paid much attention to a league whose games they feared were still being decided by sleazy mob kings. Attendance fell by 55 percent in 1997, a change also due to the easier availability of American and Japanese baseball games via Taiwan's bounding cable TV market. By the 1999 season fan attendance at most games was below 1,000. One day in October 1999 the two scheduled CPBL games, both crucial to the late-season pennant race, drew just 176 and 116 fans, respectively. During the winter after the 1999 season, the league lost two more teams, as the Mercuries Tigers and three-time defending champions champion Weichuan Dragons both cited financial pressures in folding their baseball operations.

The fall of the CPBL came at the exact moment when American and Japanese Major League teams were beginning to aggressively scout young Taiwanese baseball talent. In 1999–2000 seven young players who would have starred in Taiwan signed lucrative contracts with American and Japanese teams. The Los Angeles Dodgers, well connected in Taiwan, struck first by signing young outfielder Chin-Feng Chen. Chen was named League MVP in his first U.S. Minor League season (California League, Class A) in 1999 and made his Major League debut in September 2002, although he never developed into a productive Major Leaguer. The Colorado Rockies were next, bagging eighteen-year-old Chin-hui Tsao, toast of the 1999 World Junior Championships, with a US$2.2 million contract in 2000. Tsao, who had been scouted by Major League teams since junior high school, was called the "the Hope Diamond of the Rockies' Minor League system" and would later reach pitching speeds of 101 mph. (Despite a series of shoulder injuries, Tsao's talents were enticing enough that the Los Angeles Dodgers signed him in 2014 despite his involvement in yet another Brother Elephants game-throwing scandal in Taiwan in 2009.) The New York Yankees, Seattle Mariners, Seibu Lions, and Chūnichi Dragons also invested heavily in young Taiwanese players whose talent the Taiwanese professional game now had to live without.

Baseball in Twenty-First-Century Taiwan

On December 31, 2000, Taiwan's president, Chen Shui-bian, made his first New Year's address to the nation. His remarks were meant to sum up his first seven months in office and to "bridge the new century."

Chen had much to discuss, from the political revolution completed by his own victory and his once-illegal Democratic Progressive Party's climb to power to entry into the World Trade Organization and Taiwan's increasingly tense relations with China. The president summed up his remarks with comments on the unique "Taiwan spirit" forged during the twentieth century, and closed his address with an interesting symbol of the Taiwan experience:

> I recently had the opportunity to read some of Taiwan's historical records and was deeply inspired by one picture in particular: a portrait of the Maple Leaf Little League baseball team. In this black-and-white photograph, there was a barefoot aboriginal boy at bat. His face showed full concentration, as he focused all of his energy on his responsibility. Meanwhile, his teammates stood by on the sidelines anxiously watching and giving encouragement. Such a beautiful moment perfectly captures 20th century Taiwan and is a memory that I will never forget.
>
> My dear fellow countrymen, history has passed the bat to us, and it is now our turn to stand at the plate. The 21st century will undoubtedly throw us several good pitches, as well as one or two dusters (*huaiqiu*). Regardless of what is thrown to us, however, we must stand firm and concentrate all of our strength and willpower for our best swing.[27]

Chen may have understated the case by calling a possible People's Liberation Army invasion of Taiwan a mere "duster." But his metaphor still demonstrated the centrality of baseball in Taiwan. Taiwan successfully hosted the 2001 International Baseball Federation World Cup, a development that speaks to the weight that Taiwan carries in the world baseball community despite efforts by the PRC to shut down this type of international Taiwan presence.

Taiwan also hosted Pool B of the World Baseball Classic at the attractive new Taichung Intercontinental Baseball Stadium in March

19. China Trust Whales manager Xu Shengming, featured in a bookstore advertisement for the official Chinese Professional Baseball League 2004 video game. (Photo courtesy of Andrew D. Morris.)

2013. Taiwan's team, which included Major League pitchers Chien-Ming Wang and Hong-Chih Kuo, won the pool in front of large home-town crowds, sending island-wide television viewing figures "out of the park," according to the *Taipei Times*, and also sending Taiwanese fans "flocking to Japan" for the second round of the tournament. The Taiwan team ran out of luck at the Tokyo Dome, losing a ten-inning thriller to Japan, 4–3, and being destroyed by Cuba, 14–0, in less than twenty-four hours, to finish in eighth place. The first of these games set AC Nielsen Taiwan records and was also cause for an instant health epidemic: when Japan tied the game in the ninth inning on a single by

Hirokazu Ibata, hospitals in New Taipei City alone recorded thirty-two calls for emergency medical aid, including twenty-two cases of people fainting, three heart attacks, three strokes, and four asthma attacks.[28]

After everyone recovered from the shock of these losses in Tokyo, there still was much congratulation all around. President Ma Ying-jeou praised the team for making history and unifying the nation, and the national Sports Administration announced it would reward each national team player with a prize of NT$200,000 (US$6,730) for their "extraordinary performances" and for "lift[ing] the national mood."[29] Other critiques remained, however, namely, the international sports community's continued "belittling . . . demeaning" of Taiwan by forcing its national team to compete as "Chinese Taipei." That is to say, even at a tournament cohosted by Taiwan, the home team was bound by the "Olympic formula," designed in 1979 to keep both China and Taiwan in the Olympic movement, but also to limit the small island to regional status as "Chinese Taipei," instead of national status as "Taiwan" or the "Republic of China." This was only the latest of several international sporting events where Taiwan was humiliated like this in their own modern stadiums and arenas. The *Taipei Times* called this practice degrading and disrespectful, blaming the PRC for "openly and clandestinely . . . downgrad[ing] Taiwan's sovereignty through the use of language." And the baseball community was energized when Baltimore Orioles manager Buck Showalter, inspired by his close relationship with pitcher Wei-Yin Chen, spoke up again about this deceptive tradition: "Taiwanese are Taiwanese. . . . [The Chinese Taipei] baseball team jersey should show the word 'Taiwan.' Don't use 'Chinese Taipei' anymore. . . . I know this very clearly. China is China and Taiwan is Taiwan. They are different countries."[30]

The WBC was also an occasion for another diplomatic humiliation: Taiwan baseball officials had to apologize to the Korea Baseball Organization for sending advance scouts to impersonate umpires and spy on the Korean team's training sessions in the small town of Douliu.[31] Despite this embarrassment Taiwan's role as a competent international host has continued. Taiwan cohosted (with Japan) the first World Baseball Softball Confederation Premier 12 world championship, which replaced the International Baseball Federation Baseball World Cup, in November 2015.

More than a century ago Mark Twain wrote that baseball was the perfect expression of American society, declaring that the game had become "the outward and visible expression of the drive and push and rush and struggle of the raging, tearing, booming nineteenth century!"[32] The same can be said for Taiwan. Baseball has been repositioned at the center of a new Taiwanese nationalism and project of self-definition. In early 2003 President Chen won great face when he was able to achieve a long-awaited merger between Taiwan's two pro leagues, ending the bickering that had robbed baseball of its national unifying power.

The renewed national attachment to baseball was illustrated perfectly by the newly designed NT$500 bill issued in December 2000. As the sagely visage of Generalissimo Chiang Kai-shek was removed from Taiwan's currency for the new millennium, what better indigenous symbol to replace him than an image of the young Little Leaguers who won his regime so much fame in the 1970s? Since 2000, instead of facing the gaze of the Chinese military leader known for four decades as "Savior of the People," Taiwan consumers handing over NT$500 bills have been inspired by the smiles on the faces of the Puyuma Aborigine boys from Taidong County whose victory celebration is portrayed on the bill.

This national attachment has, in recent years, been routed through American and Japanese Major League Baseball as Taiwanese players like Chien-Ming Wang (New York Yankees), Hong-Chih Kuo (Los Angeles Dodgers), Wei-Yin Chen (Chūnichi Dragons, Baltimore Orioles, Miami Marlins), and Yang Dai-Kang (Hokkaido Nippon-Ham Fighters) have thrived in those elite leagues instead of toiling in their home island's scandal-ridden CPBL. Before his 2008 right foot injury, sustained running the bases in an interleague game against the Houston Astros, the Yankees' Wang had truly become a national obsession.

For several years every Yankees game was shown live on Taiwanese television, usually on two networks, and then replayed at least once later that day, leading many to joke that the Yankees were Taiwan's new "national team." *Money Weekly* even went so far in July 2007, in a cover story, to explain how Wang's first ten victories of the season had added NT$1.43 trillion (US$43.6 billion) in value to the nation's stock market.[33] The sight of the tall (six-foot-three) and handsome Wang becoming one of the finest pitchers in the American League was a joy for Taiwanese fans, although at times to an unhealthy extent. In September 2007 a man in Taoyuan was clubbed to death for trying to steal a four-page newspaper supplement celebrating Wang's nineteenth win of the season.[34] Wang's struggles in recent years have allowed Wei-Yin Chen to become a new focus of attention; Orioles hats and #16 jerseys were a common sight in Taiwan as he led his team to the 2014 American League Championship Series.

The larger trend illustrated by the standouts above does not bode well for the future of Taiwanese professional baseball: a professional career in Taiwan is now scarcely a consideration for most of the island's best players. Besides the three Taiwanese players on MLB rosters at the time of this writing (the Marlins' Chen, the Dodgers' Tsao, and the Kansas City Royals' Wang), there are fourteen more Taiwanese players on American Minor League rosters, in addition to five more players in Nippon Professional Baseball. Taiwan's silver-medal team at the 2014 Asian Games in Incheon included thirteen (of twenty-four total) who were playing professionally abroad. The persistent game-throwing scandals that seem endemic as long as player salaries are low, and the money to be made gambling on the games is plentiful, unfortunately make Taiwan's professional game hard for fans or players to take too seriously. In 2008 the dMedia T-Rex baseball team was expelled from the league after it was found that mafia members indirectly owned the team for the express purpose of controlling players and game results.[35] And even more depressing were the government and media accusations that same fall that Taiwan's "tragic" Olympic baseball game against

China (explained earlier) had also been purposely thrown for the players' illicit financial gain.[36] The high-profile signings of former Major League stars like Manny Ramirez and Freddy Garcia (both by the EDA Rhinos in 2013 and 2014, respectively) have not been nearly enough to return the league to any real prominence. The league was further embarrassed in July 2014 when, after merely three months, it lost its "historic six-year NT$2.04 billion [US$67.1 million] [television] deal with MP & Silva, a London-based international media rights company [that was] originally expected to be a huge boost to the league's four debt-ridden teams."[37]

The brightest realm of baseball in Taiwan, partly because of the recent troubles described here and partly because of larger cultural-political trends, relates to the game's history under Japanese colonialism. The Kanō teams known for their 1930s triumphs were the subject of a blockbuster film, titled *KANO* (2014), which is about these successes of Japanese colonial rule. Like *Cape No. 7* (2008), a film directed by *KANO* producer Wei Te-Sheng, this baseball film wallows in and celebrates the legacy of Japan's fifty-year rule of Taiwan—a provocative but also popular move in Taiwan, as many Taiwanese residents continue to value most of the things that set them apart from the intimidating PRC across the strait. A recent press release from the city government of Jiayi, home of the former Kanō school, refers to that idealized 1930s Japanese moment when "a group of people shared common goals, mutual respect and tolerance . . . . a simple town full of human touch."[38] The politics of colonialist nostalgia are so useful that the mayor of Jiayi, Huang Min-huei, traveled to Kanō's long-ago manager Kondō's hometown in Matsuyama, Japan, to unveil a large baseball-shaped memorial in his honor in 2014.

"Baseball is back," the Taiwanese media always trumpet in the wake of some important baseball-related event. It never went anywhere, though. For more than a century—if sometimes in unexpected ways—Taiwanese baseball has been an appropriate and crucial window for understanding the complicated histories and cultures of modern Taiwan. From the game's Japanese origins to the high-profile successes of Taiwanese Little League baseball from the 1960s to the 1980s, the professional era since 1990, and Taiwan's current role as an exporter of talent to Japan and the United States, the game has always been an important avenue by which Taiwanese people have navigated historical relationships with their Japanese, Chinese, and American rivals and allies.

Most of the ideas in this chapter can be found in expanded form in my book *Colonial Project, National Game: A History of Baseball in Taiwan* (Berkeley: University of California Press, 2010).

NOTES

1. For more on this legacy, see Andrew D. Morris, ed., *Japanese Taiwan: Colonial Rule and Its Contested Legacy* (London: Bloomsbury Academic, 2015).
2. "Liang'an zhan: Zhonghua gaohan bang" [Cross-strait war: ROC shouts superiority], *Shijie ribao* [World journal], August 8, 2008, F2.
3. "Xuduo youxing, wuxing de shiwu, zaocheng Zhonghua shu Zhongguo" [Many visible and invisible errors make ROC lose to China], NOWnews.com, August 15, 2008, http://uocn.bestroc.org/archiver/tid-15852.html; Hong Zhenyuan, "Yanchang 12 ju Zhonghua 7:8 zao Zhongguo nizhuan, tun xia zui beiru de yi bai" [ROC loses to China 7–8 in 12 innings, swallow the most sorrowful and insulting defeat], *Li Tai yundong bao* (*LT Sports*), August 15, 2008, https://goo.gl/1DoUPF; Xiao Baoyang, "Shi shang zui nankan yi zhan, Taiwan shou ci shu Zhongguo" [The most embarrassing battle in history, Taiwan's first loss to China], *Yam News*, August 15, 2008, https://goo.gl/h3p6Di; "815 guochiri, wangyou huyu Taiwan jiangbanqi zhi'ai" [August 15 a day of national humiliation, bloggers call for Taiwan to lower flag to half-mast to express grief], NOWnews.com, August 15, 2008, http://goo.gl/VMFiyE.
4. Hong Jinghong, "Aoyun zhenghou qun, qiusai nizhuan ta cu si" [An Olympic-sick people, one dies after tide turns in ball game], *Lianhebao*, August 20, 2008; "815 guochiri, wangyou huyu Taiwan jiangbanqi zhi'ai."
5. Yukawa Mitsuo, *Taiwan yakyū shi* [The history of baseball in Taiwan] (Tai-

hoku: Taiwan nichinichi shimpō sha, 1932), 1, 12–13, 1–2 of chronology at end of book.

6. Gao Zhengyuan, *Dong sheng de xuri: Zhonghua bangqiu fazhan shi* [Rising sun in the East: The history of the development of Chinese baseball] (Taibei: Minshengbao she, 1994), 41; Sakamoto Shigeru and Katsura Chōhei, "Nōkō yakyūdan to banjin gakusei no seikatsu" [The Nōkō Baseball Team and the life of the savage students], *Yakyūkai* 15, no. 12 (1925): 46; Suzuki Akira, *Takasago zoku ni sasageru* [Dedicated to the Takasago people] (Tokyo: Chūō Kōronsha, 1976), 188; Morris, *Colonial Project, National Game*, 17–22.

7. Gao, *Dong sheng de xuri*, 94–95; Morris, *Colonial Project, National Game*, 49. Go also pitched a no-hitter in 1946 and retired with a .272 batting average over twenty seasons and seventeen hundred games. One baseball expert has ranked Go the forty-fifth-best player ever to play professional baseball in Japan. Jim Albright, "Japan's Top Players," 2004, http://baseballguru .com/jalbright/analysisjalbright01.html#Shosei_Go.

8. Peng Ming-min, *A Taste of Freedom: Memoirs of a Formosan Independence Leader* (New York: Holt, Rinehart, and Winston, 1972), 16–17.

9. Gao, *Dong sheng de xuri*, 47–50.

10. Zhan Deji, "Woguo bangqiu yundong de fawei yu zhanwang" [The development of and perspectives on our nation's baseball movement], *Jiaoyu ziliao jikan* (Educational information quarterly) 10 (June 1985): 436.

11. Gao, *Dong sheng de xuri*, 13–16; Zeng Wencheng and and Yu Junwei, *Taiwan bangqiu wang* [Baseball king of Taiwan] (Taibei: Woshi chubanshe, 2004), 106.

12. Unfortunately, the jubilation over these victories was soon dampened by an unfortunate revelation. The Maple Leaf roster of eleven players included nine ineligible boys who were playing under false names. Months after these victories, the Maple Leaf Elementary School principal, coach, and head administrator were all sentenced to a year's imprisonment by the Taidong County Local Court for these gross violations.

13. Ray Keys, "Taiwan Team Sprints Upset . . . Tops Santa Clara in L.L. Final," *The Sporting News*, September 6, 1969, 32.

14. Laura Li, "Empowering the People: 50 Years of Struggle," translated by Brent Heinrich, *Sinorama* 24, no. 10 (1999): 101.

15. Star Yu Hongkai, from Taidong, had played illegally as a ringer for the 1968

Maple Leaf team and was recruited from across the island for the 1969 Golden Dragons. Guo Yuanzhi, who would go on to star for the Chūnichi Dragons in Japan, was also recruited from far Taidong.

16. Paul Li, "Baseball Tries to Make a Comeback," *Taipei Journal* 17, no. 45 (2000): 8.

17. *Taiwan duli jianguo lianmeng de gushi* [WUFI: A history of World United Formosans for Independence] (Taibei: Qianwei, 2000), 58; Taipingshan, "Wei-lian-si-bao guan qiu ji" [A record of watching the game at Williamsport], *Duli Taiwan* [Viva Formosa] 38 (October 1971): 54–55; Lance Van Auken and Robin Van Auken, *Play Ball! The Story of Little League® Baseball* (University Park: Pennsylvania State University Press, 2001), 167.

18. Of the nineteen foreigners who played during the CPBL's first season, only two had Major League experience: Tigers infielder José Moreno and Elephants pitcher José Román.

19. In 1997 the Sinon Bulls, owned by the Sinon Agrochemical Corporation, cleverly named several of its foreign players after the conglomerate's bestselling pesticides.

20. Jackie Chen, "Major League Controversies—Professional Baseball Enters a New Era," translated by Phil Newell, *Sinorama* 21, no. 3 (1996): 80.

21. In the CPBL's major statistical categories for 1997, there were the following numbers of foreign players in the top ten: batting average, eight; home runs, eight; runs batted in, seven; and victories, seven.

22. "Qiuyuan quan chong mote'er: zhanpao shanliang xianshen" [Ballplayers moonlighting as models—battle gear unveiled in its glory], *Naluwan zhoubao* (Naluwan Weekly) 7 (February 1, 1997): 3.

23. Lin Xinhui, "Yiwan siqian ren, dao Jiashi kanqiu" [14,000 to Jiayi to watch game], *Lianhebao*, September 23, 1998, 29; CPBL box scores, *Lianhebao*, September 23, 1998, 29.

24. Huang Jianming, "Naluwan—zhenggang de yingxiong (Naluwan zhibang lianmeng zhuti gequ)" [Naluwan—true heroes (Taiwan Major League theme song)], *Naluwan zhoubao* (Naluwan Weekly) 5 (January 4, 1997): 5.

25. Dubbed the "Black Eagles" (Heiying), the team was suspended from the league in late 1997 and formally disbanded in 1998.

26. After being banned from Taiwan professional baseball, Jiang got a second chance five years later in mainland China as coach of the Tianjin Lions of the new China Baseball League and manager of the PRC national team.

Tianjin also hired fallen Taiwan stars Guo Jiancheng and Zheng Baisheng, banned as well in 1997 for throwing CPBL games, as coaches.

27. Chen Shui-bian, "Zongtong fabiao kua shiji tanhua" [The president's century-bridging address] (Office of the President of the Republic of China, 2000), http://goo.gl/zbXUJ6; Chen Shui-bian, "Bridging the New Century: President Chen's New Year's Eve Address," December 31, 2000, *Taipei Update* 2, no. 2 (2001): 3.

28. Shelley Shan, "Baseball Fans Flocking to Japan," *Taipei Times*, March 7, 2013, 3; Yi Hui-tzu and Jake Chung, "Baseball Game Viewing Figures Out of the Park," *Taipei Times*, March 9, 2013, 3; Lin San-feng, Wu Jen-chieh and Jason Pan, "Taiwan-Japan Game Sets TV Ratings Record," *Taipei Times*, March 10, 2013, 1.

29. Mo Yan-chih, "Taiwan Baseball Team Get Praise from the President," *Taipei Times*, March 22, 2013, 4; Shelley Shan, "Sports Agency to Reward Baseball Team," *Taipei Times*, March 15, 2013, 5.

30. "'Chinese Taipei' Belittles Taiwan," *Taipei Times*, March 7, 2013, 8; Cheng Yu-chia, Jordan Huang, and Jason Pan, "Use 'Taiwan,' Not 'Chinese Taipei': Orioles Manager," *Taipei Times*, March 14, 2013, 3.

31. Evan Drellich, "Taiwan Scouts Pose as Umps to Scout Korea," February 22, 2013, http://m.mlb.com/news/article/41883462/taiwan-scouts-pose-as-umps-to-scout-korea/.

32. Quoted in Allen Guttmann, *Games and Empires: Modern Sports and Cultural Imperialism* (New York: Columbia University Press, 1994), 79.

33. Gao Yongmou, "Shengtou daidong zhang, 16 dang sizhong gu zui pengchang" [Victories driving (the market) up, 16 loyal firms boost the most], *Licai zhoukan* (Money Weekly) 360 (July 19, 2007): 46.

34. "Man Clubbed to Death for Stolen Baseball Supplement," *China Post*, October 1, 2007, http://www.chinapost.com.tw/taiwan/2007/10/01/124769/Man%2dclubbed.htm.

35. "Taiwan's Baseball Team dMedia Involved in Foul Play," *Taiwan News*, October 9, 2008, http://www.etaiwannews.com/etn/news_content.php?id=759107; He Ruiling et al., "Heibang hezi, zhibang Midiya laoban she da jiaqiu" [Joint venture with gangsters, pro baseball dMedia boss involved in game-fixing), *Ziyou shibao* (Liberty Times), October 9, 2008, http://www.libertytimes.com.tw/2008/new/oct/9/today-t1.htm#.

36. Zhang Yahui, "Beifuyin: 1/3 yuncai wanjia saiqian kanshuai Zhonghua

dui dalu" [Taipei's Fubon Bank: 1/3 of sports lottery participants picked the ROC to lose against the mainland before the ball game), *Zhongguang xinwenwang* (Sina.com), August 28, 2008, https://goo.gl/zKcgZn; "Aoyun da jiaqiu yiyun, Hong Yizhong fanwen meiti: Nimen bulei ma?" [Haze of doubts and suspicions about Olympic Game throwing, Hong Yizhong asks media: aren't you tired?], NOWnews.com, August 30, 2008, https://goo.gl/6OS4q5.

37. "No-Win Situation in CPBL Broadcasting Disputes," *China Post*, July 25, 2014, http://www.chinapost.com.tw/editorial/taiwan-issues/2014/07/25/413085/No-win-situation.htm.

38. "The Film 'KANO' Which Is Based on the Story of Jianong Baseball Team Is about to Start Shooting & Sankei News from Japan Interviews with Chiayi City Mayor Huang Ming-Hui," July 30, 2012, http://www.chiayi.gov.tw/2011web/en/index.aspx?mid=97&rid=1471.

Part 3 The Pacific

14

Australia

Baseball's Curious Journey

Rick Burton

The history of baseball in Australia is perhaps best discussed in three phases: the earliest attempts by Americans to introduce and cultivate their favorite game in another land, the influence of famous Americans to promote the sport in Australia, and, finally, investments by various global parties, including Major League Baseball (MLB), to grow Australian baseball despite the entrenched presence of well-developed and well-funded sports, such as cricket, soccer, rugby, swimming and, most significantly, Australian Rules football.

Certainly, for modern aficionados of baseball, the March 2014 National League games played between the Los Angeles Dodgers and Arizona Diamondbacks in Sydney (at the historic Sydney Cricket Ground) was a novel initiative: a contemporary MLB experiment with all of the glitz of American showmanship and pageantry. Strangely enough, this 2014 special event wasn't the first time the Americans had come to Sydney with an interest in establishing an overseas beachhead for their sport. That initiative had previously been attempted by "Yanks" more than 125 years earlier, in 1888–89.

To understand why the Americans would bring their biggest stars to Australia, we need to understand American ambition—sometimes called American Manifest Destiny—and its influence on the development of baseball in Australia.

Australian baseball historians think an early form of the game was first brought to Australia during the country's formative gold-rush era in the mid- to late nineteenth century. While erroneous or unsubstantiated reports have long suggested American gold miners first played the game in rough mining towns like Ballarat in the early 1850s, historian Joseph Clark contends in his excellent *A History of Australian Baseball: Time and Game* (2003) that baseball probably first came to Australia when it was played in the Australian state of Victoria circa 1853–57. These informal exhibitions or contests were staged by American merchant Samuel Perkins Lord and styled after the American form of "rounders," also known as the "New York Game." Lord repeatedly attempted to organize baseball in Melbourne, but it appears the absence of Australian enthusiasm for baseball kept the game from becoming a regular activity. When organized contests did occur, they were instigated by "newly arrived Americans [who] played an early form of baseball in Melbourne at the Exhibition Grounds on Saturday afternoons and on cricket grounds in the shadow of the great Exhibition Hall."[1]

Clark suggests the first recorded baseball event was a series of three games between Collingwood and Richmond, with Collingwood easily winning the second game, 350–230.[2] Given the score, the players, be they American expatriates or local Australians, were likely playing a combination of English rounders, the New York Game, and cricket.

At the same time in the United States, baseball was growing rapidly in popularity. As Americans spread westward across their continent (following the Civil War), they sought ways to express their economic and social influence internationally. Baseball was an easily exportable activity and an efficient way to feature or showcase "the American way."

In New South Wales, Sydney's first recorded game reportedly took place in Moore Park on July 9, 1878. Baseball historian Bruce Mitchell contends, "Americans living in Sydney in 1882 played in the Domain and had two teams which played on Saturday afternoons in Moore Park."[3] Still, baseball was "not played regularly by Australians" until a prominent tour arrived in Sydney in December 1888.[4] That outing took place two months after American entrepreneur Albert

20. Future National Baseball Hall of Fame inductee Albert G. Spalding served as one of baseball's earliest visionaries when he led two teams (his own Chicago White Stockings and a group of All-Stars) on a world tour that targeted Australia as its most important stop in 1888–89. (Photo courtesy of the National Baseball Hall of Fame.)

G. Spalding, a former player and part owner of the Chicago White Stockings, arranged for two American teams, one his own and the other composed of All-Stars, to participate in a round-the-world tour that targeted Australia as its most important destination. In fact, the entire undertaking was promoted by Spalding as "Spalding's Australian Baseball Tour," and it is clear the businessman's intention was to promote America's game in another English-speaking setting while simultaneously selling his Spalding sporting goods and rules guides to more baseball players.[5]

Spalding planned for games to be played in Sydney, Melbourne, Adelaide, and Ballarat in December 1888 and January 1889. So important was this lengthy expedition to the promoters of the American game that influential baseball writer Henry Chadwick called the tour "the great event in the modern history of athletic sports."[6] That might sound far-fetched today, but readers should remember that the modern Olympics would not begin until 1896 when French aristocrat Baron Pierre de Coubertin reestablished the Olympic Games in Athens. For many Americans during the 1880s, baseball was a cultural touchstone, and Spalding's baseball venture, by Chadwick's estimation, was worthy of the hyperbole.

Clark notes that Spalding's tour was intended to provide a "top-class professional sporting tour bringing the trappings of legendary Americana, which Australians had only read or heard about." Skeptics dared not shun the tour, nor could journalists avoid covering it. By its very hype and gravitas as a sporting spectacular, it was too newsworthy, rare, and unique. "One might criticize it, but no one could ignore it."[7]

Mark Lamster, in *Spalding's World Tour: The Epic Adventure That Took Baseball around the Globe—and Made It America's Game* (2007), notes that after Spalding departed, it was obvious "the Australian press had taken [a strong liking] to the [American] athletes, to their game, and to the indefatigable man who had brought them together."[8] If that wasn't enough, the *Melbourne Herald* went so far as to invoke rhyming verse with this couplet:

Let football find its votaries,
And cricket do the same,
In days sensational such as these
It's baseball is *the* game![9]

Spalding had come to Australia with two rosters filled with the biggest stars of the day, including four future Hall of Famers: Adrian "Cap" Anson, John Montgomery Ward, Ned Hanlon, and George Wright (a former great player who had joined the tour as a coach). The eighteen U.S. players on the tour were accompanied by an African American dancer and baton twirler and a daredevil stunt performer, who went by the name of Professor Bartholomew.

The professor's carnival act included using a hot-air balloon to ascend to heights between two and four thousand feet while hanging from a trapeze. At the conclusion of his act, he would parachute to safety. Unfortunately for Bartholomew, his descent in Ballarat produced an unplanned crash landing into the Buck's Head Hotel.[10] Viewed more than one hundred years later, it is likely the Americans were unconvinced their national game on its own was sufficient to win over Australians without some additional circus-style sideshows.

Despite the absence of the professor, who was seriously injured, the final game of Spalding's tour was played in Melbourne in front of a crowd of nearly twelve thousand people with an opening act featuring players from the All-Americans taking on the local Melbourne Baseball Club. Spalding recognized the need to create a spectacle, so the actual game between his two teams was terminated after five innings in order to stage a long-distance throwing contest. Here, New York Giants star pitcher Eddie "Cannonball" Crane set what was then believed to be an Australian distance record by throwing a baseball almost 129 yards (which was just short of the American record of 132 yards set by Johnny Hatfield in 1868).[11] Regardless of how anyone viewed the various American antics, and there was some "press antagonism and anti-American feeling," the "Spalding Tour was one of the most important events ever in Australian baseball" and hugely relevant to Americans living in Sydney and Melbourne. Permanent baseball clubs were soon established in capital cities, and some of these teams, such as Goodwood in South Australia and East Melbourne, are still operating.[12]

Today Spalding's visit to Australia might not seem any more memorable than the 2014 visit of the Dodgers and Diamondbacks, but in 1889 (when the tour finished in New York City) the immensity of the concept delighted many American expansionists. One American who was likely influenced was famed author Mark Twain, who used baseball in one of his last great novels. Twain had long loved baseball and began attending games in Hartford, Connecticut, in the 1870s, where he saw Spalding pitch for the Boston Red Stockings. At some point in the 1880s it appears that Twain began thinking about how to incorporate baseball into his writing.[13]

In December 1885 Twain had started work on *A Connecticut Yankee in King Arthur's Court*, which was published to great acclaim in the spring of 1889, just before a welcome-home banquet was held for Spalding and his players in New York. In Twain's time-traveling story, Hank Morgan is transported to the sixth century, where he stages a baseball contest played between knights, kings, and emperors and finishes with a line that seemed to reference Spalding's visit to Australia: "The first public game would certainly draw fifty thousand people; and for solid fun would be worth going around the world to see. Everything would be favorable."[14]

Twain was so taken by Spalding's Australian exploits that six years later, he booked a trip to Australia in September 1895 to give a number of paid presentations. During his time in Adelaide Twain appears to have wanted to see how baseball in Australia was developing. The *South Australian Register* reported on October 11, 1895, that Twain had promised to attend a doubleheader between North Adelaide and Goodwood followed by Norwood and South Adelaide, if his business schedule permitted.[15]

Twain's ambassadorial efforts were likely influenced by flagging development efforts that had been initiated by Harry Simpson, a baseball missionary Albert Spalding left behind in Australia after his tour departed from Port Adelaide in January 1889. Simpson immediately began organizing games and quickly became "Australian baseball's first Development Officer."[16] During the next three years (1889–91), Simpson arranged numerous contests and small leagues, including interstate games between South Australia and Victoria. Simpson even wrote to the American publication *The Sporting News* in 1890, expressing his belief that baseball in Australia was making good progress and that he intended to bring another American side to Australia in 1891 to play his rapidly improving Australian teams. An 1890 edition of the *Adelaide Observer* included an interview with Simpson, and excerpts detail the following:

> Yes, I am very well satisfied with the progress the game has made. . . . We did not expect the game to catch on all at once, but its popularity has increased marvelously. . . . The players field capitally and there is not the slightest doubt that in time they will equal the Americans in this department. The difficulty is to get good catchers and pitchers. The latter, like your bowlers, are really born pitchers and I have no doubt that some of the Australian players with assiduous practice will pitch as scientifically as anyone. As to catchers, practice will make them. Some of your cricket wicket keepers ought to make good catchers. But it is in batting that Australians excel. . . . American ball players do not practice batting so much perhaps as fielding which is their specialty.[17]

Tragically, Simpson died of typhoid fever in 1891, and in the only known tribute to him it was noted, "The deceased, who was only 27 years of age . . . came to these colonies as a baseballer with A. G. Spalding's teams in 1888, when it was decided to establish the game here."[18] Despite the efforts of Simpson's successor, much of Simpson's development work for Australian baseball did not endure, and Twain's visit in 1895 was clearly not enough to reinvigorate the game.

By 1897 Australian baseball players were ready to visit the United States. The *South Australian Chronicle* headlined a story "International Base-Ball: Australians in America" and detailed a three-month tour by an Australian team known as the "Kangaroos."[19] This small team, plagued by fiscal mismanagement, played its way across America in cities such as Denver, Omaha, Chicago, Pittsburgh, Boston, Providence, Atlantic City, and Philadelphia; on reaching New York they were welcomed by Cap Anson and an accommodating Spalding. The *Chronicle* lauded the achievements of Queenslander Joe Quinn, the only Australian to play Major League Baseball before 1986.

Despite Quinn's exploits in the United States, the Kangaroos' tour was so ill-fated or mismanaged that media coverage in Australia was overwhelmingly negative, and reports suggest that Australian baseball was "severely set back by the tour, at least in Victoria and South Australia." Further proof of the tour's residual impact is that formal baseball games were not held in South Australia between 1898 and 1908.[20]

The stagnation of baseball in Australia at the start of the twentieth century and for much of the next 125 years must ultimately be linked to Australia's political ties to England (it has been an independent commonwealth since 1901, although traditionally seen as a dominion of the British Empire), its Anglo-Australian support of cricket, and the growing importance of the famed Ashes five-day test cricket tournament regularly contested between England and Australia that first came to prominence in 1882–83.

That Australia's baseball pioneers (and diehard developers) were unable to compete with cricket as Australia's principal summer game or able to dent the juggernaut that Australian Rules football developed as Australia's most popular winter game is understandable. That is not to say baseball was invisible in Australia during the twentieth century. As Ken Gulliver, the captain of the Australian baseball team in 1946 and 1949 and a longtime member of the Mosman Baseball Club, notes in the foreword to Clark's book: "Though cricket was always the big summer game all over Australia, baseball had a strong following, especially as a winter game. There was room in my life for both games, just as there is room in Australia for both games. Australia has hundreds of baseball clubs around the nation, tens of thousands of tee ball and junior players, and hundreds of top-grade players in state and Australian Baseball League competitions."[21]

One major example of baseball prominence took place in December 1956 when baseball was played as a demonstration sport at the Melbourne Summer Olympics in the Main Stadium (the famed Melbourne Cricket Ground [MCG]). The U.S. team comprised amateur players from the Far East (Military) Command. Australia fielded an all-star team that included Victorian Football League player Peter Box. The Americans won a shortened exhibition game, 11–5. The game ended after six innings to make way for the main track-and-field events. The MCG had been relatively empty when the game began, but by the final inning the stadium was full to capacity (114,000) in anticipation of the finals for the Olympic 1,500 meters and the marathon. As noted in the Olympic program, "Five of the six States of the Australian Commonwealth are now affiliated with the Australian Baseball Council and take part in the Australian Baseball Championship series, which is played in several States in annual rotation."[22]

Those yearly gatherings appear to have been difficult to maintain, and there are several possible explanations. First, there was no viable professional national league. Like its Australian American cousin, the National Basketball League, the Australian Baseball League (1989–99) and International Baseball League of Australia (1999–2002) enjoyed great enthusiasm from devotees and developed pockets of regional success. But the absence of mass spectator interest, significant investors or team owners, proper league management, committed sponsors who could truly leverage the game's appeal, and baseball-only stadiums or fields to generate grassroots sustainability has limited the game's expansion.

As a case in point, it is not unusual to find baseball facilities in Australia that are no more than a simple prefabricated building adjacent to multipurpose playing fields.[23] Much worse, as anthropologist George

Gmelch notes in the next chapter, in the entire Australian state of Tasmania there is not a single field designated just for baseball. Not only must baseball share grounds with cricket or soccer, but often the netting behind the backstop must be erected and taken down for each game.

While baseball has never disappeared from the Land Down Under, it has produced a limited number of MLB players. A few notable exceptions have been Joe Quinn, who became a player-manager for the St. Louis Browns in 1895, and recent MLB All-Star catcher David Nilsson (1992–99) and pitcher Grant Balfour (2001–15).

Major League Baseball has long known of baseball's toehold in Australia, so perhaps it is unsurprising that it attempted to replicate Spalding's efforts in March 2014. MLB saw that the National Basketball Association was taking its preseason and regular-season games to places like London, Mexico City, Shanghai, Beijing, the Philippines, and Brazil. Similarly, the National Football League and National Hockey League also played early-season contests overseas. So it was not surprising when Dodgers president and chief executive officer Stan Kasten announced that the Dodgers "were committed to growing the game of baseball internationally" and eager to start the season in "one of the most exciting and rapidly developing baseball markets on earth in Sydney, one of the greatest cities in the world."[24] Sadly, little has been done since March 2014 in Sydney to suggest that the Dodgers and MLB are truly interested in building the game in Australia.

While it might not be fair to characterize baseball as a failed experiment in Australia, Bruce Mitchell's 1991 assessment is still valid: "The first 10 years of serious baseball in Australia (1888–1897) raised the problems which have dominated the sport ever since. For baseball to have attempted to rival or supplant cricket would have meant to attack not only what was accepted as the 'national game' but to challenge the special sense of identity expressed in cricket: an admiring emulation of Britain combined with an intense rivalry with the Mother Country. A challenge to cricket was, then, virtually impossible to contemplate; and was certainly quite out of the question from an American game."[25]

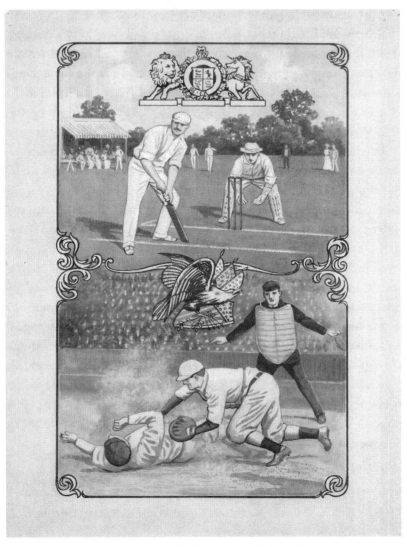

21. Cricket versus baseball. (From the New York Public Library.)

Australians are a sports-loving people. Indeed, Nike founder and chairman Phil Knight reportedly once said that if Nike were a country, it would be Australia. Knight could have meant that Australians are ferocious competitors and willing to try anything and even fail at things gloriously. To Australia's credit, the country's baseball development system has produced several dozen players capable of reaching the U.S. Major Leagues, with nine players on big-league rosters in 2011.

Further, Australia has been successful at select international competitions, winning a silver medal at the 2004 Athens Olympics and defeating Cuba in the 1999 IBAF Intercontinental Cup (a short-lived baseball tournament played by members of baseball's international federation and traditionally dominated by Cuba). In the World Baseball Classic (WBC), however, Australia has never finished better than twelfth place. This is not to suggest Australians are incapable of playing the game at an international level. Rather, it is just that Australia produces fewer world-class baseball players in part because the game has never taken root in the face of Australian passion for cricket, rugby, and Australian Rules football. Ultimately, baseball's "outsider" status (or legacy as an American invention) makes it challenging to establish Australian national teams capable of dominating a tournament like the WBC. However, were Australia to win or do well in the WBC, it is possible baseball's roots might once again gain a greater purchase in fan interest and youth participation.

NOTES

1. Joe Clark, *A History of Australian Baseball: Time and Game* (Lincoln: University of Nebraska Press, 2003), 4–5.
2. Clark, *History of Australian Baseball*, 5.
3. Clark, *History of Australian Baseball*, 5; Bruce Mitchell, "Baseball in Australia: Two Tours and the Beginnings of Baseball in Australia," *Sporting Traditions* 7 (November 1990): 2.
4. Mitchell, "Baseball in Australia," 2.
5. Rick Burton, "Australia, Baseball's Diamond in the Rough," *New York Times*,

March 10, 2014, http://www.nytimes.com/2014/03/10/sports/baseball
/australia-baseballs-diamond-in-rough.html?_r=0.

6. Quoted in Clark, *History of Australian Baseball*, 7.

7. Clark, *History of Australian Baseball*, 10.

8. Mark Lamster, *Spalding's World Tour: The Epic Adventure That Took Baseball around the Globe—and Made It America's Game* (New York: Public Affairs, 2006), 148.

9. Quoted in Lamster, *Spalding's World Tour*, 148.

10. Clark, *History of Australian Baseball*, 13–14.

11. William J. Ryczek, *Blackguards and Red Stockings: A History of Baseball's National Association, 1871–1875* (Wallingford CT: Colebrook Press, 1992), 32.

12. Clark, *History of Australian Baseball*, 16–17.

13. Darryl Brock, "Twain and Crane: The Old Ball Game," *New York Times*, March 14, 2010, SP2.

14. Mark Twain, *A Connecticut Yankee in King Arthur's Court*, edited by Bernard L. Stein (1889; reprint, Berkeley: University of California Press, 1979), 448–50.

15. Burton, "Australia, Baseball's Diamond in the Rough."

16. Clark, *History of Australian Baseball*, 18.

17. Quoted in Clark, *History of Australian Baseball*, 19.

18. Quoted in Clark, *History of Australian Baseball*, 21.

19. Mitchell, "Baseball in Australia," 17.

20. Clark, *History of Australian Baseball*, 35.

21. Clark, *History of Australian Baseball*, ix.

22. xvi Olympiad program.

23. Clark, *History of Australian Baseball*, 134.

24. Quoted in Burton, "Australia, Baseball's Diamond in the Rough."

25. Mitchell, "Baseball in Australia," 21.

15

Tasmania

Baseball Struggles to Survive

George Gmelch

Ever since I was a boy watching Caribbean winter-league games on Saturday-morning TV, I've had an interest in how baseball is played in other cultures. A few years ago, when my wife and I moved our anthropology field school from Barbados to Australia's island state of Tasmania, I wondered if there might be baseball there (in Barbados, like the rest of the former British Caribbean, cricket is the national passion, leaving no room for another bat-and-ball game). My online search came up with a website for the "Tasmanian Baseball Association," which fielded several teams in Kingston, a town just to the south of Hobart, the island's small and charming capital city. When I arrived in Tasmania, however, and drove down to Kingston to see its baseball facility, there was no ball field to be found. I soon learned that the baseball diamonds—the only two in all of Tasmania—had been replaced, one by a cricket pitch and the other with a soccer field.[1] The president of the Tasmanian Baseball Association was alleged to have run off with all of the organization's funds, about forty thousand dollars, causing the organization to collapse and with it baseball. I wondered if baseball could really be that fragile. That was 2004, and over the next three trips to Tasmania I never gave baseball another thought.

Then in the summer of 2010, one of my anthropology students, Alan Zulick, who was studying sport in Hobart, offhandedly mentioned hearing about a baseball league in the northern suburbs. He and I went to investigate. In this chapter I describe what we found, with an update from 2015.[2] But first some background on Tasmania and its involvement with America's national pastime.

Tasmania is an island about the size of Ireland or West Virginia, located about two hundred miles off the south coast of Australia. If mainland Australia is "down under," Tasmania is "down, down under." With just a half-million people, it is sparsely populated (scarcely twenty people per square mile); half of its population lives in the capital city of Hobart. Europeans first settled Tasmania in 1803, when it became Britain's newest penal colony. Then known as Van Diemen's Land, most of its residents were either convicts or former convicts and their military guards. Many Tasmanians are descendants of these early prisoners who were "transported," often for minor transgressions (for example, stealing a loaf of bread in London drew a seven-year sentence to Van Diemen's Land). For many decades Tasmania was a "convict society." The native Aborigines were mostly wiped out by the 1860s.

Tasmania has an image problem among mainland Australians, many of whom view the island as somewhat backward, a place that has failed to grow or develop as fast as the mainland—the little brother that never quite made it. Tasmanians are to "real Australians" as the Irish once were to the British or Newfoundlanders are to mainland Canadians, sort of country bumpkins. As Hobart journalist Peter Timms notes, the jokes mainlanders tell about Tasmanians "usually involve poverty and inbreeding—like one about a Tasmanian virgin being a girl who can run faster than her brother."[3] On the other hand, Tasmania gave birth to the world's first Green Party, and its well-educated, middle-class Hobartians rank among the greenest people in the world.

Tasmania today is a major tourist destination, attracting visitors to its old-growth forests, world-heritage wilderness, and exotic marsupials such as the Tasmanian devil of Warner Bros. cartoon fame. More recently, Tasmania's popularity has increased dramatically with the opening of the Museum of Old and New Art near Hobart and the international recognition of its high quality of food, wine and spirits, and more. The island's temperate climate has become a selling point to mainland vacationers for whom lazing on the beach in the hot sun has become less fashionable as concern over melanomas has risen. Although Tasmania draws a million visitors a year, it is not yet well known to many Americans. But that is likely to change with recent accolades from the *Lonely Planet* travel guide, which lists Tasmania as one of the top-ten places to visit and *Travel + Leisure* magazine naming it the fourth-best island destination in the world.

Baseball made a brief appearance in Tasmania well over a century ago, when in 1874 several visiting Americans taught the game to members of the South Tasmanian Cricket Association.[4] The cricketers formed themselves into two teams of nine and practiced for a few weeks, hoping to challenge the crew of a U.S. Navy ship (the USS *Swatara*) the next time the vessel was in port. That didn't happen, and enthusiasm soon waned. The game wasn't entirely forgotten, however, and was resurrected by cricketers several times over the next few decades. In 1890 some cricketers organized themselves into the Southern Tasmanian Baseball Club in order to play a visiting football club from the mainland that had a reputation for "fielding a strong baseball side."[5] For a while the Tasmanian club fielded two teams—the Reds and Blues—and later added the Browns. They played weekly games throughout the winter on a cricket ground and, like many Australian sports, competed for a championship trophy. The players were said to be keen, but there were not many spectators. After the 1898 season the cricketers' interest in baseball died again.[6]

A decade later, in 1907, several cricketers once again revived the game, organizing two teams—the Brown Legs and the Blue Legs. They played in sweaters, knickers, and stockings of the team colors. Occasionally, the teams played informal games against visitors from the mainland and even from the United States. But by the 1930s baseball had once again fallen out of favor, as soccer and hockey rose in popularity as men's premier winter sports.[7]

Baseball was not to be revived again until the 1950s when it became a popular winter sport on the mainland. A public meeting was called to organize a baseball team in the Tasmanian city of Launceston in April 1950, but only three people turned up. Soon thereafter, a local showing of a movie about Babe Ruth (most likely *The Babe Ruth Story* [1948]) had created enough interest that a local baseball association was reconstituted after a lapse of thirty-six years. Fifty players were registered and organized into four teams. The association limped along over the next few decades.

By the 1970s there were four clubs in Tasmania's North and five in the southern region, which included Hobart, and for a brief time there was a Tasmanian state team that competed in interstate championships on the mainland. In 1985, however, Tasmanian baseball's prospects brightened considerably when in Kingston the Kingsborough Council received a government grant of several million dollars to build two first-class baseball diamonds and a clubhouse. The facilities were completed, and six new teams formed a league that competed there for a decade (1986–97) until, as noted earlier, all of the baseball association's funds mysteriously disappeared. But Kingston also proved to be a poor location, as many of the players lived forty-five minutes away in the northern and eastern suburbs of Hobart. Transport difficulties took their toll, especially on the junior teams, whose players were dependent on public transportation or their parents to get them to ball games. Soon the local Kingsborough Council turned over the baseball diamond to the town's cricket club, and the diamonds were bulldozed. Most of the players abandoned baseball; a few took up softball (formerly just a women's game until 1980, when some softball teams began to invite men).[8]

In 2007 Tasmanian baseball once again rose from the ashes.[9] It began with two enthusiasts, Brett Leppard and Chester Wilcox, placing an advertisement in the Hobart *Mercury* newspaper, inviting anyone interested in playing the sport to come to an open day. Enough people showed up to form a new league of four teams: Red Sox, White

Sox, Green Bay, and Blue Jays. Over the next few seasons the Green Bay team would change its name to the Athletics, and, for a couple of seasons, attempts were made to field five teams. The league muddled along until there was a change in leadership prior to the 2013–14 season. The new leaders, President Nigel O'Brien and Vice President David Searle, were keen to see the league become more "professional" and to reintroduce baseball for juniors, initially through T-ball, then "coach toss," and ultimately junior baseball. "This was not an easy task," recalled Searle, "as society had changed over the years with more things to interest children, and with parents having less time to volunteer to help out with sporting events, especially given baseball's marginal status in Australia where cricket is king. Few people even knew there was a baseball competition in Hobart."

To increase the new league's visibility, the leadership allocated each team its own geographical region in the Hobart area, for recruiting purposes and to encourage locals to be able to identify with a team.[10] Funding for the new league came mainly from membership fees paid by players and from several generous anonymous donations. Posters were printed and put up in businesses, articles were run in the free suburban papers, and the league and individual teams promoted themselves on Facebook.

What follows are condensed and edited field notes from two games, between the Red Sox and the Athletics, supplemented by several follow-up interviews.

Baseball is played at only one site—the Prince of Wales Bay Recreation Ground—in a working-class suburb on the north side of Hobart. The field looks toward majestic Mount Wellington (elevation 4,170 feet), which rises behind Hobart and is a focal point for all its inhabitants. Apart from the batter's box, the field is all grass. The four teams in the league (the Red Sox, Athletics, White Sox, and Blue Jays) play a twenty-two-game schedule from November through March (the Australian summer), followed by playoffs, in which all four teams compete. The games are mostly played on weeknights, apparently so that the players can keep their weekends open for other things. The games are timed, lasting just ninety minutes, from 6:00 p.m. to 7:30 p.m., squeezed in between when the mostly working-class players get off work and are able to get to the ballpark and before the daylight fades. Although anyone over age fifteen can play in the league, most of the players are in their thirties and forties. This is a senior league; the only youth baseball leagues in Tasmania died in the late 1990s.

A wide range of skills are evident; the best players are of a good U.S. high school level, and one player, raised in the mainland city of Adelaide, was once signed to a Minor League contract with the Tokyo Giants. There are also a few Taiwanese and Japanese players who are skilled, having learned the game at home before coming to Tasmania to study at the local university. At the other end of the spectrum, there are players who are fairly new to the game: in the batter's box a few of them are nervous about standing too close to the plate, even though the pitchers do not throw very hard. There is some uncertainty about some of baseball's rules. One batter is confused, for example, when he strikes out but is able to run to first base when the pitch gets past the catcher and rolls to the backstop. The Asian players look to be in better shape than most of the locals, some of whom sport beer bellies, or what Aussies call "beer guts." Besides the Asians themselves, I learn that several other players also learned baseball in Japan. One is a pastry chef who worked in a Japanese island resort where he was invited to play in the local league. Another player, Sarye, is an African immigrant from Mali, who spent three years in Osaka watching the Hanshin Tigers play on television, but never had the opportunity to play the game until moving to Hobart with his Tasmanian wife.

The players wear their team colors, but no one has a complete uniform. Some have baseball pants; others have jerseys. With the pitching being quite hittable and the fielding uncertain (fly balls are often overrun or dropped), a fair amount of runs are scored. There is a mercy rule: a team is allowed to score only seven runs in an inning. There are also a number of unwritten "gentlemen's rules," such as no bunting

22. League play at the Prince of Wales Bay Recreation Ground, in a northern suburb of Hobart. Majestic Mount Wellington (elevation 4,170 feet) rises in the background. Apart from the batter's box, the field is all grass. (Photo by George Gmelch.)

(the older players don't have the speed to cover bunts) and no stealing when your team is up by six runs or more.

Each team has a half-dozen bats, a mixture of wood and aluminum; the league allows both. Although players understand the disadvantages of using wood, some want to get accustomed to wood to get ready to play in a "Masters" tournament at the end of the season. Masters baseball (over age forty-five) allows only wood bats. One manager has just bought four wood bats for his team at fifty dollars each and is upset when he breaks one in his first at bat. On the bench there is some speculation over whether the bat broke because the batter got jammed or because the wood was of inferior quality. The teams buy their bats from a mainland distributor and, not having the opportunity to personally select them, must accept whatever is shipped. The players must also buy their gloves online, as no sporting goods store in Tasmania carries baseball equipment. Some players bring them back on visits to the mainland.

In a country that has so many entrenched and widely popular sports, from cricket to soccer to Aussie Rules football, I am curious about what the attraction of baseball is to these men. Several answer my query by saying that baseball is more exciting than cricket because it has a lot more action. In the words of the Athletics shortstop, "Unless you're a bowler there's not much happening in cricket. . . . You do a lot of standing around waiting for a ball to come your way. And most balls are only handled by one fielder, whereas in baseball you're involved in a lot more fielding plays." Two others speak of how much quicker baseball is than cricket. One of the handful of spectators, the mother of a middle-aged player, tells me that most of the players on the field are disgruntled cricketers, impatient with cricket's slow pace and limited action. Two of the older players say they enjoy playing baseball because they had learned the game in their youth, when there was still a youth league in Hobart.

When I tell the manager of the Athletics, David Edwards, of my interest in Tasmanian baseball, he invites me to sit in the dugout. From this vantage, it's clear that the games are more social than competitive, that having fun rather than beating your opponent is what counts. No one appears to keep close track of the score. It is not acceptable to complain about an umpire's call or get perturbed when a teammate muffs a ground ball, not even when the Athletics' right fielder overruns an easy fly ball with the bases loaded. When a batter is hit by a pitch and throws down his bat and mutters under his breath, it's quickly made clear that this behavior is inappropriate. Comments are made, and the pitcher tells him to "fuck off," repeating it several times. In the two games I watch, this is the only untoward display of emotion.

As in all Australian sports, once the game is over the players from both teams get together behind the backstop to drink beer. Cold beer is stored, along with all of the league's equipment, in a freight container behind one of the dugouts. The players stand around talking for an hour or so, until the daylight is gone. I ask a group of players if they watch any American Major League Baseball (MLB) on cable television (four games a week are broadcast). They have all seen a game on TV, but no one says they watch often; it's mostly a game or two during the World Series. No one has a favorite MLB team. When I ask the players about the future of baseball in Tasmania, they talk about their hopes of a seeing a youth league get off the ground, but they are not optimistic about that happening. There are too many competing and entrenched sports, too many other things to do, and right now no one is willing to step in and undertake the considerable job of trying to sell baseball to a new generation of schoolkids.

The last point seems especially important to me because looking back over the history of baseball in Tasmania, each time the game faded away it took a determined individual or small group with a passion for the sport to bring it back. If I had to guess, I would say that the future baseball in Tasmania is likely to follow its historical pattern—short periods of enthusiasm among a small group of followers, followed by waning interest and decline. On mainland Australia enthusiasm for baseball has also waxed and waned, but not nearly to the degree in Tasmania. It may be that climate is the big difference. On the much warmer and drier mainland, baseball has always been an off-season winter sport, enjoyed by cricketers. In fact, Albert G. Spalding's group first promoted the game to Australians during its 1888–89 world tour. Today Tasmanian winters are regarded by many as too cool and wet and the daylight too short for baseball.

The players understand that if Tasmanians don't learn to play and enjoy baseball as youngsters, they are unlikely to have an interest in the sport as adults. Without any baseball being taught in Tasmanian schools and with few games broadcast on television, today's youth have little exposure to the sport. When I learned that the Red Sox's manager, Michael Scott, the fellow who had played professionally in Japan, was holding an open and free baseball clinic for Hobart youth, Alan and I went along. Despite having widely advertised the clinic, distributing more than a hundred flyers around town, not a single child showed up. Without young players coming along to replace the retiring old-timers, the Senior League is unlikely to have a future.

Update

In 2013 the league lost its only ballpark—the Prince of Wales Bay Recreation Ground—when the town council dug up the field to put in storm-water drains. Games had to be played on a school ground using a makeshift batter's box and with the backstop netting having to be erected and taken down for each game. Occasionally, even that field was unavailable, with the only alternative field an additional fifteen-minute drive from town, making getting to the 6:00 p.m. games on time problematic for players who finished work at 5:00 or 5:30 p.m. Adding to the league's challenges, a promise by a local supplier to provide uniforms for all the teams fell through. At the 2014 annual general meeting, Nigel O'Brien stepped down from the presidency to concentrate on developing interest in baseball among juniors. Things began to look up for the league in 2015 when play was resumed at the Prince of Wales Bay Recreation Ground and David Searle, who took over as president, launched a new website (http://www.baseballtasmania.com) and Facebook page to promote the league and to get out game announcements.[11] Several community newspapers came on board again with free advertisements and by publishing articles and photos on the teams. Uniforms from the mainland finally arrived.

All four teams now have full rosters, each game is assigned a scorer to compile stats, aluminum bats have been banned in the interest of safety for pitchers and third basemen, and, to avoid the fiasco of previous seasons when sometimes not enough players would turn out to field a team during the holiday season, rosters have been expanded to twenty players. The league has also received inquiries from women interested in playing. Though none has yet taken the next step and joined a team, the league is hoping that will change sometime soon. Finally, while the teams have returned to their original and only suitable ball field, they must share it

23. The reigning premiers of the 2014–15 season, the Northern White Sox. President of Baseball Tasmania David Searle is second from the right in the back. (Photo courtesy of Naomi Searle.)

with soccer teams and therefore are unable to put in a permanent pitching mound or a fixed outfield fence. The limited interest and fragility of baseball in Tasmania make me wonder about the MLB and World Baseball Classic's boast that baseball is becoming a global game.

I wish to thank Trey Strecker, Chris Berke, Adrian Franklin, Alan Zulick, and David Searle (the president of Baseball Tasmania) for their comments and members of the Athletics and Red Sox teams—notably David Edwards, Jordan Edwards, and Michael Scott—for their hospitality at the ball field.

NOTES

1. Although no longer used for baseball, there is still a diamond in Spreyton, outside of Devonport in northwestern Tasmania.

2. My fieldwork in 2010 was updated in 2015 through correspondence with the new Baseball Tasmania president, David Searle, whom I wish to thank.

3. Peter Timms, *In Search of Hobart* (Sydney: University of Australia Press, 2009), 43.

4. This account of the early history of baseball in Tasmania relies heavily upon David Young's *Sporting Island: A History of Sport and Recreation in Tasmania* (Hobart: Tasmanian Department of Sports and Recreation, 2005). For an excellent account of the history of mainland Australian baseball, see Joe Clark, *A History of Australian Baseball: Time and Game* (Lincoln: University of Nebraska Press, 2003).

5. Young, *Sporting Island*, 112.

6. Young, *Sporting Island*, 110.

7. Young, *Sporting Island*, 174.

8. Since then men's softball has died out, though Tasmanian women still play the game.

9. Information provided by David Searle.

10. The teams and the districts they represented were Eastern Athletics (representing the eastern shore of the Derwent River), Northern White Sox (representing the northern suburbs of Hobart), Southern Red Sox (representing those suburbs south of Hobart), and Blue Jays (representing the central suburbs of Hobart).

11. Searle came from a cricket background, but after attending a few baseball games in the United States during the 1980s, he said, "I was hooked and now follow the game religiously . . . even to the extent of subscribing to MLB At Bat so I can watch games on my cell phone and smart TV!"

16

New Zealand

Baseball between British Traditions

Greg Ryan

The timing of sustained British settlement of New Zealand, beginning in 1840, meant there was little opportunity for baseball to take hold during the nineteenth century. Unlike those British migrants who had departed for North America a century earlier, the new migrants to New Zealand were far more likely to carry with them a taste for the moral and social values of organized sport in the context of the emerging British "games revolution." Not only did the eighteenth-century colonists to North America come from a less developed sporting culture in Britain, but in the North American colonies especially there was a determined Puritan opposition to sports that retarded their growth and contributed to an enduring cleavage between English and American traditions.[1] Without such obstacles most settlers in New Zealand displayed a pronounced enthusiasm for sports such as cricket, horse racing, and various types of football (primarily rugby and soccer). Baseball made only sporadic appearances and was regarded as something of a novelty diversion.

Although Americans made up perhaps 5 to 10 percent of those on the New Zealand goldfields of the 1860s, there are no surviving accounts of baseball being played.[2] The first recorded game in New Zealand took place in Christchurch in late September 1881 between boys of the elite Christ's College and a team of former pupils and others captained by future prominent politician and scholar W. P. Reeves. How and why this game was initiated is not recorded. The only surviving report of the game observed, "Base-ball may perhaps be best defined as rounders reduced to a system. To be understood, it requires to be seen, and that more than once, for the rules are tolerably complicated; the movement of the game [is] rapid; and the changes continual. . . . Something has long been wanted here to fill up those slack times of the year which fall between the seasons of cricket and football, and for this purpose base-ball would seem to be well adapted."[3] This fixture did not prompt any imitation, as there appears to have been no further baseball played in New Zealand for the next seven years.

The true dawn of New Zealand baseball came in late 1888, following the formation of a Wellington club in mid-October, almost certainly under the influence of Americans residing in the city. The *Evening Post* predicted good prospects for the game: "Baseball, which is very popular in America, is something after the style of rounders, but more scientific and very favourable opinions respecting it were expressed by the spectators on Saturday."[4] A number of newspapers throughout New Zealand then published the rules and diagrams of the playing field.[5] A subsequent exhibition game between the Wellington Baseball Club and members of the touring African American Hicks-Sawyer Minstrel Troupe triggered the establishment of a Wellington Baseball League with at least five teams, including the Native Baseball Club composed of Waiwhetû Mâori. The league lasted two seasons but attracted little press comment beyond lists of fixtures and scores before all of the clubs disappeared.[6]

Yet the seriousness with which the games were played can be seen in a dispute by one club that was referred to an unnamed "American baseball representative" in Australia for arbitration.[7] Meanwhile, following the transfer in early 1889 of Cyrus Webb, the founding secretary of the Wellington Baseball Club, to the small town of Blenheim, a club flourished there for the next two years. But without a rival all of its games were intraclub affairs.[8] A third, and potentially more august, beachhead for baseball did not translate to much. On Monday, December 10, 1888, Albert G. Spalding's touring party of Major League players arrived in Auckland for an exhibition game. But as their arrival was a day later than scheduled and the weather was unfavorable, the event was anticlimactic, with poor attendance and minimal press interest. Although a few games were played between fledgling Auckland clubs, there was no enduring organization.[9]

A new avenue for baseball opened in April 1889, but less in its own right than as a winter adjunct for cricketers. In Christchurch, the acknowledged power base of New Zealand cricket, two clubs, Christchurch and Hagley Park, began playing intraclub fixtures such as married versus single players and A to L versus M to Z before finally meeting each other at Lancaster Park, Christchurch's premier cricket ground, in late May 1889. Among the many Canterbury provincial cricketers who dominated both clubs were Leonard Cuff, a fine all-around athlete and later a founding member of the International Olympic Committee, and Frederick Wilding, a multitalented sportsman and father of 1910–13 Wimbledon tennis champion Anthony Wilding. Despite the athletic credentials of these baseball enthusiasts, their play did not impress local critics. Of a Christchurch Club game, the *Press* complained that "although the players exhibited a better knowledge of the game than on the previous Saturday, the fielding was not so good, and the pitching and catching of a decided in and out character." The following week the club was condemned for its bad pitching and failure to provide a competent umpire. "It is much to be regretted that an umpire with some semblance to a reputation could not be induced to fill this very important post. On Saturday nearly all the players tried their hand, and the natural result was that a good many erroneous decisions were given." While the Hagley Park club was praised for the improvement in its fielding, "the rules still require a lot of reading up." Nevertheless, a challenge had apparently been issued to the baseballers of Wellington to meet in "friendly competition."[10] That it was considered unlikely that the Wellington players could secure work leave to come to Christchurch, but that the Christchurch players may have been able to travel to Wellington, is possibly an indication of the social class and means of the respective baseball communities.

At the beginning of the following season, an American visitor to Christchurch offered a trophy for competition between the two clubs, but beyond a few practice games both disappeared almost immediately.[11] Thereafter, the only sign of baseball anywhere in New Zealand for at least the next decade seems to have been a few practices and games played by a club in Wanganui during the winter of 1895.[12] A report that an American team bound for Australia in the same year would also visit Auckland amounted to nothing.[13]

By comparison with neighboring Australia, New Zealand and its more temperate climate severely curtailed the prospects for baseball as a winter alternative to cricket. Indeed, climate also had a relatively detrimental effect on New Zealand cricket compared to Australia. By the early twentieth century it was clear to most New Zealanders that opportunities for international sporting credibility resided not with the summer game, where national teams had suffered several heavy defeats to Australia, but with the winter code of rugby. The triumphant tour of the All Blacks to Britain in 1905 dramatically confirmed this status.[14] Consequently, other winter sports ran a distant second to rugby, and there was simply no interest in a "foreign" game without tradition among a population that regarded itself as the most quintessentially British of any in the British Empire.

Aside from brief efforts in Christchurch by Canadian visitors to the 1906–7 New Zealand International Exhibition, and by other visitors during 1909 and 1910, there appears to have been no more baseball in New Zealand until the eve of the First World War.[15] Exactly what prompted the next revival is not clear, although it possibly stemmed from greater consciousness of the United States following the All Blacks rugby tour of California in late 1913 and reports that the team enjoyed watching baseball. According to the *Poverty Bay Herald*, "The visiting New Zealand ruggers saw their first baseball game here yesterday, and liked it so well that many are keen to introduce it when they return home. They cheered San Francisco's big pitcher, Orval Overall, terming him a 'tip-top bowler.' Their war cries, copied from the native Maoris, attracted attention from the regular fans."[16]

Winter leagues were active in Auckland and Wellington from mid-1914 on, and in October 1914 A. R. Durrant, a Wellington businessman, presented a trophy for interprovincial competition. It was first to be held by Wellington, but challenges were confidently expected from Auckland, Canterbury, and Hawke's Bay.[17] Following the outbreak of war, the novelty of baseball was also turned to patriotic purposes, with a fund-raising fixture billed as "America v. New Zealand" in Wellington in September 1914. The Americans in question were expat residents of the city. As ever the reference point for the local press was rounders, "the familiar, good old game played at picnics along with kiss-in-the-ring, etc. But it is a decided cut above that. It is much more strenuous and requires skill, speed and many more essentials that do to make a really exciting game."[18] However, the curtailment of much competitive sport during the war ensured that this latest baseball foray did not last beyond early 1915, and none of the anticipated interprovincial games took place.

The emergence of new clubs in Wellington in 1920 and Auckland in 1922 reveals efforts to again establish baseball as a summer sport, but by the time Canterbury and Wellington played the first interprovincial fixtures in July and August 1924, it was again a winter activity regarded as an ideal opportunity for cricketers to "keep their eye in" during the off-season.[19] Canterbury's visit to Wellington was played as a curtain-raiser to a field-hockey match between the same provinces.[20] The following year enthusiasm for baseball was sustained by the visit of a U.S. naval fleet. Although a proposal from Canterbury that a New Zealand team be selected to play the visitors amounted to nothing, an exhibition game between teams drawn from the *uss Oklahoma* and *Pennsylvania* attracted about two thousand spectators in Wellington.[21]

Although there were sporadic signs of baseball clubs in Auckland in particular into the early 1930s, the game was no closer to capturing the

New Zealand sporting imagination. Indeed, so limited was understanding of it that when softball began to achieve popularity during the late 1930s, it was generally described as baseball and as "America's national game." Why softball took hold and endured when baseball could not is unclear. But from the time softball was introduced to Wellington in 1935 by Bill Wilson, a Canadian employee of the Ford Motor Company, the game flourished. A Wellington Baseball (Softball) Association established in 1937 had more than six hundred registered players in separate men's and women's leagues by 1939. The game spread rapidly throughout New Zealand, assisted in part by influence from American Mormon missionaries, although again it is unclear why they promoted softball rather than baseball. The first interprovincial contest, between Auckland and Wellington, took place in October 1938. By March 1939 softball was sufficiently strong for Wellington to host an interprovincial tournament that drew teams from Auckland, Canterbury, Otago, Wairarapa, and Wanganui. In January 1940, notwithstanding the outbreak of war, a national club championship was staged.[22]

With an influx of U.S. servicemen into New Zealand from early 1942, baseball was again revived and a clear distinction established with softball. New Zealanders soon adopted the correct terminology for their game. While some American service teams played in local softball competitions, most preferred their own baseball competitions. The games at Carlaw Park, Auckland, on October 22, 1943, were between the New York Yankees (U.S. Navy) and the Detroit Tigers (U.S. Navy) and the Cleveland Indians (U.S. Army) and the Washington Senators (U.S. Navy).[23] In January 1943 a crowd of twenty thousand watched a fund-raising match in Wellington between "National League" and "American League" teams drawn from the U.S. Marine Corps. But the fact that the United States was protecting New Zealand from a very real Japanese threat did not engender sympathy for or interest in its national game. Indeed, it would be several decades before most New Zealanders moved beyond their deeply held attachment to Britain to fully recognize the strategic significance of the United States and to comfortably engage with its culture. The *Evening Post* mused that although the spectators probably had an enjoyable afternoon in aid of a patriotic cause, "it was when people came to compare America's first sporting love with their own favourites (particularly cricket) that impressions became varied. To many the complete absence of cricket's ordered dignity was something of a shock. To see players entering into disputes with the umpires (and frequently adopting threatening attitudes) was just as novel to the cricket follower as the spectacle of a player who had been ruled out flinging his bat to the ground in disgust."[24] Nevertheless, late in the war Royal New Zealand Air Force personnel were trained in the rudiments of baseball and other American sports such as volleyball and basketball so that they could find some sporting common ground when serving with Americans who provided most of the Allied forces in the South Pacific.[25]

Notwithstanding New Zealand's strategic reliance on the United States during the postwar years and increasing cultural influences from American music and films, there were to be no more flirtations with baseball of the sort that had characterized the interwar years. Rugby for men and netball for women dominated the winter and cricket and horse racing the summer, with softball a minor but viable alternative among a range of other sports for men and women. Moreover, softball was a sport at which New Zealand began to achieve considerable international success. The men won five world titles and finished outside the top three only twice in fourteen events between 1966 and 2013. The women won the world title in 1982. There is no obvious explanation for this success other than to say, following the example of rugby in particular, that this was not the first time New Zealand had succeeded internationally by channeling some of its limited sporting resources to a game that was insignificant to most other countries.

By the 1980s globalization and diversifying sport and leisure patterns were making New Zealand more receptive to American and other non-British sports. Basketball in particular boomed from the middle of the decade and has continued to hold a strong following.

A New Zealand Baseball Association (now Baseball New Zealand) was formed in Auckland in 1989 through the efforts of enthusiastic expats and keen locals. Although the core of support remained in Auckland, New Zealand's largest city, the expansion of satellite television coverage of Major League Baseball from the early 1990s, albeit rather unsystematically, also exposed many more people to the game. In 1992, having affiliated with the International Baseball Federation, a national team, dubbed the Diamond Blacks, competed in the Merit Cup in Florida. Another combination, reinforced by sponsorship from a major brewery, attempted to qualify for the 1996 Atlanta Olympics but was easily defeated by Australia.[26] In the same year the game received a significant boost in profile when the Atlanta Braves signed nineteen-year-old Travis Wilson, a star of the world-champion Black Sox softball team. He played Triple A Minor League ball and nearly made the Braves' Major League roster in 2001 before returning to softball in 2004. Scott Campbell, who played in the Minor Leagues for the Toronto Blue Jays organization, followed Wilson. Canadian-born New Zealand citizen Scott Richmond pitched for the Toronto Blue Jays in 2008. American-born sometime–New Zealand resident Nick Maronde pitched for the Los Angeles Angels in 2012 and 2013. In 2014 John Holdzkom, American born of a New Zealand father who had pitched for the Diamond Blacks in 2012, found success as a reliever for the Pittsburgh Pirates.[27]

Under the influence of dynamic American chief executive officer Ryan Flynn, the number of registered players with Baseball New Zealand rose from eight hundred in 2010 to more than six thousand in 2014, with the game beginning to move beyond Auckland to Northland, Waikato, Wellington, and Canterbury. During the same period the Diamond Blacks' world ranking improved from 119 to 28th, and baseball secured its first funding, albeit only twenty thousand dollars, from the government funding and policy agency Sport New Zealand. National teams now compete in the Australian Provincial and under-twenty-three championships and in Asian Zone age-grade championships.[28]

In 2014 an under-twelve team competed in the Cal Ripken World Series in Maryland.[29]

That same year Ryan Flynn suggested that the future for baseball might rest in an administrative amalgamation with softball.[30] Perhaps, following the lead of basketball, rugby league, and soccer, prospects may also be enhanced by incorporation into the top Australian domestic baseball competition. But the chances of New Zealand baseball becoming anything more than a relatively minor sport with a passionate following seem remote. Rugby and cricket still dominate the sporting landscape with extensive professional and international programs, albeit their appeal has been diluted in recent decades by a plethora of new sport and leisure choices. Baseball can thrive in this more diverse environment, but it can never hope to dominate.

NOTES

1. Allen Guttmann, *A Whole New Ballgame: An Interpretation of American Sport* (Chapel Hill: University of North Carolina Press, 1988), 23–34.
2. Determined from a search of Papers Past, http://paperspast.natlib.govt.nz/cgi-bin/paperspast.
3. *Star* (Christchurch), September 27, 1881, 3.
4. *Evening Post* (Wellington), October 15, 1888, 2.
5. For example, *Otago Witness* (Dunedin), December 28, 1888, 27.
6. *Evening Post* (Wellington), November 17, 1888, 2; September 23, 1889, 2; *Star* (Christchurch), March 6, 1889, 4.
7. *Marlborough Express* (Blenheim), February 5, 1890, 2.
8. *Marlborough Express* (Blenheim), February 24, 1890, 2.
9. Mark Lamster, *Spalding's World Tour: The Epic Adventure That Took Baseball around the Globe—and Made It America's Game* (New York: Public Affairs, 2006), 119–24.
10. *Press* (Christchurch), May 6, 1889, 6; May 13, 1889, 3; *Star* (Christchurch), May 25, 1889, 4.
11. *Press* (Christchurch), April 2, 1890, 5.
12. For example, *Wanganui Herald*, April 23, 1895, 2; May 1, 1895, 3.
13. *Ashburton Guardian*, May 6, 1895, 2.

14. Greg Ryan, *The Making of New Zealand Cricket, 1832–1914* (London: Frank Cass, 2003), 153–74.

15. For example, *Press* (Christchurch), January 17, 1907, 8.

16. *Poverty Bay Herald*, November 15, 1913, 10.

17. *Poverty Bay Herald*, June 15, 1914, 5; *Auckland Star*, August 22, 1914, 2; *Ashburton Guardian*, October 20, 1914, 3.

18. *Free Lance* (Wellington), September 12, 1914, 18.

19. *Evening Post* (Wellington), October 9, 1920, 6; *New Zealand Herald* (Auckland), November 21, 1922, 5.

20. *Evening Post* (Wellington), August 26, 1924, 3; September 5, 1924, 2.

21. *Evening Post* (Wellington), July 1, 1925, 9; August 12, 1925, 5; August 18, 1925, 9.

22. *Auckland Star*, April 13, 1937, 14; January 22, 1938, 11; October 25, 1938, 7; *Evening Post* (Wellington), March 25, 1939, 11; January 26, 1940, 4.

23. *Evening Post* (Wellington), April 12, 1943, 3; *Auckland Star*, October 22, 1943, 5.

24. *Evening Post* (Wellington), February 1, 1943, 6.

25. *Auckland Star*, May 11, 1945, 2.

26. *New Zealand Sport Monthly*, October 1995, 57.

27. Derived from http://www.baseball-reference.com/play-index/.

28. Hayden Meikle, "Baseball: Hope Shines Like a Diamond," *Otago Daily Times*, April 26, 2014, http://www.odt.co.nz/sport/other-sport/300113/baseball-hopes-shine-diamond. See also http://www.baseballnewzealand.com/index.php/component/ohanah/cal-ripken-world-series?Itemid=379.

29. See http://www.baseballnewzealand.com/index.php/component/ohanah/cal-ripken-world-series?Itemid=379.

30. Meikle, "Baseball."

Part 4 The Middle East

17

Israel

From the Desert to Jupiter . . . and Beyond

William Ressler

The Israel Association of Baseball started in the 1980s, with fields that were little more than patches of dirt in the desert and with a glaring lack of equipment that meant, in the words of one of the IAB's founders, "living from baseball to baseball."[1] Since then baseball in Israel has grown dramatically. How has that happened and, more important, why? Extensive interviews with IAB officials, supporters, and players provide insight into the passion and the ideals that drive a growing culture of baseball in Israel.

Baseball in Israel: Why?

Not surprisingly, many of the IAB's founders had connections to North America. For them "having a catch" in Israel meant reconnecting with their childhood. Today, however, many IAB volunteers—and even more so many players—grew up having known nothing about base-ball until they crossed paths with the IAB. No longer a predominantly Anglo-Saxon pastime, baseball in Israel is now bilingual and multicul-tural. When asked to explain their broadening and deepening affection for the game, IAB volunteers and players gave two answers: baseball transmits a core set of values that are seen as unique to baseball and invaluable to Israeli society, and Israeli culture includes certain values that can rejuvenate baseball.

"I think [baseball's values] are universal values, not just American values." Although this quote comes from one IAB volunteer, many Israeli players and officials echoed it and emphasized the equal opportunities they see in baseball. Baseball is not just another sport for Israelis to play; it is, as one official said, an "any-kid-who-wants-to-play-can" sport that allows participation regardless of genetic predisposition. As they described what drew them to baseball, volunteers said that they loved the game even more when they saw how playing it reinforces inclusiveness. To one volunteer, inspiration comes "when you see the weaker kids come up and they suddenly make an amazing play that changes the game." As a parent, coach, and league official, this volunteer feels that the fundamentally egalitarian nature of baseball's rules, by which every player must bat and play the field, appeals to Israeli parents, whose children are "miserable in soccer, because no one ever passes [them] the ball" and who learn "if they bring their kids to baseball, they will play."

Inclusiveness creates opportunities. With so many participants who are new to the game, a longtime volunteer noted, "you have this joint experience—everyone is starting at zero." This allows baseball to bring together diverse members of Israeli society: people from big cities, small towns, and rural villages; girls and boys; the very religious and the resolutely secular; Arabic-speaking citizens in Jaffa, Spanish-speaking residents in Be'er Sheva, and Russian-speaking immigrants in Jerusalem. Furthermore, the newness of baseball in the region creates opportunities to build bridges across borders. A veteran coach told a story from Israel's early days of international youth baseball competition. After defeating the Israeli team, the winning country's coaches surprised the Israeli team with an unexpected, magnanimous, and politically implausible gesture: "They said, 'Hey, you guys don't have any equipment. Take our equipment home with you. Just don't tell anybody.' Their coaches gave us their team bags with all their equip-

24. Two players in Baseball for All/Baseball l'Kulanu/Baseball Liljami and Play Global, which bring together Israeli Jewish and Arab boys and girls to learn and play baseball. (Photo courtesy of Margo Sugarman.)

ment, because everybody's helping everybody out at these tournaments. When you see a country who's just starting out, just trying to work hard, they don't have anything, they're wearing stupid uniforms, they're using bats that are likely from the civil war, [you say] 'For us, it's nothing. Here.'"

This illustrates a central IAB tenet: baseball, played right, is "helpfully competitive." Baseball teaches fair play, tolerance, humility, sharing, teamwork, and respect—values, the IAB feels, that are not encouraged by other sports in Israel. IAB coaches and officials teach children that "they're playing to get each other better"—within and between dugouts. One IAB volunteer recounted how "one of my biggest successes" occurred during the early days of Israel's participation in international competition, with his team on the brink of an unaccustomed victory.

Standing in the dugout, one out to go, he began to worry about his players on the field.

> This is the first game they've ever won. What am I going to do? They're going to go crazy, like in soccer. That's not baseball. I have no way to tell them [how to act. But then, after they win,] the whole team, they don't say a word, they run and line it up, shake hands with the other team, come off the field. That was my biggest victory. They learned respect for the game. They learned that the other team wanted to win just as much as they did. That was a very proud moment for me.

To this volunteer and to others in the IAB, baseball's importance for Israel and Israelis lies in its ability to transmit an essential set of values they believe is inherent to the game.

What Israel Gives to Baseball

Just as baseball culture promotes certain values in Israel, many IAB officials and volunteers believe some historical aspects of Israeli culture reinforce the good within baseball. Specifically, they mentioned Israel's classic (some might say archaic) image of the *chevreman*, someone who gets on well with others and keeps calm in stressful situations. This bygone cultural icon captures and affirms five key aspects of baseball.

Friendship. The culture of the *chevreman* emphasizes building relationships through shared experiences. "You start the first grade, you're in the same homeroom class till sixth grade," explained an IAB official. "There's a culture in Israel of forming very strong bonds." Players said baseball, too, is about building relationships. Israeli fans made the same assertion, and thus they root for kids, not teams. One parent concluded, "I don't know if I can root for my own team only."

Fellowship. Chevreman culture carries the expectation that everyone contributes to the success of the group. One official observed, "There's a culture in Israel of inclusion, of saying you're a team, everybody's on the team." Players and IAB officials alike said baseball provides opportunities for a more physically diverse group of individuals to contribute. In Israel, an IAB volunteer noted, "you may not be the fastest, and you may not be able to hit the ball, but you'll be on the team."

Facilitation. In *chevreman* culture competition breeds collaboration— in school, at work, and on the diamond. This follows from Israel's small size and because in Israel, several IAB officials and volunteers noted, "everybody knows everybody." In baseball, one longtime official said, it means that "it's not like they're the enemy—they're the opposing team. And they're working real hard, just like we are. And they're doing everything they can to win, just like we are." Competing players and opposing teams need each other. A volunteer affirmed, "I think that's something that's really strong here. There's a lot of team interaction, people support each other, and it's a nice thing. It's heartwarming."

Flexibility. For the *chevreman*, situations change, new opportunities emerge, and calm focus and perspective keep the individual alert to possibilities. As one founder of the IAB observed about life in Israel, "You gotta be ready for that one time [something] happens." Similarly, he said, in baseball "there's only one pitch that you have to get to 100 percent focus on, and that's this one, right now. You want [to be] intense and focused, but not excited."

Fun. *Chevreman* is also an adjective that means "easygoing." IAB founders' desire to promote baseball began with, in their words, "Having fun! Throwing the ball around with the kids. Helping them out. [Having] a good time." Sharing the fun of playing baseball continues to motivate them. One volunteer said, "For me, it's the kid on the field who hits the ball or catches the ball or throws it correctly, and then he has that big smile on his face."

In short, many people associated with the IAB think and feel that, while baseball offers certain values to Israeli society, certain cultural tendencies in Israel reaffirm aspects of baseball that many IAB members see as essential to the culture of the game, when it is played the right way—beginning with the fact that, to them, baseball is indeed meant to be a game, in which having fun is itself a measure of success.

Baseball in Israel: How?

Israel's baseball players may have always had plenty of fun, but for a long time they did not have decent fields, proper equipment, experienced coaches, or skilled players who could become role models. The IAB believed that attracting children to baseball required addressing all of those needs and debated where to invest its limited capital first. Its eventual choice was counterintuitive yet consistent with the IAB's belief in the inclusive and egalitarian values that baseball teaches: rather than invest heavily in infrastructure to attract players, the IAB decided to focus on getting kids playing baseball and letting kids' involvement in the game attract the fields, coaches, and role models. Thus, when money became available, the IAB hired a director, whose primary responsibility, after making *baseballiyah*, was introducing the game to young prospects in schools and community centers around the country.

Facilities and equipment. IAB officials thought that donors become engaged as they see more children playing and enjoying the game: fun begets funding, at home and abroad. Having more players also leads to more opportunities to participate in European tournaments and more attention. Getting more kids playing baseball in order to attract stadium funding was summarized by an IAB official: "If they come, we will build it."

Coaches. To find good coaches, the IAB first adopted a European system based on clubs, each of which has teams at all age levels. Players grow up together in their club. According to an IAB official, "They see it as a natural progression. They're moving up, and now they're sixteen or seventeen, so they're playing on this team, but they're going to coach the little kids. They stop, they go to the army, they come back, they play in the adult league, the Premier League, then they coach. That's the whole twenty-five-year plan, that these kids come back as young adults, they filter in—logistically, administratively, coaching, umpiring—and then they get their kids to play. It's working out pretty well." The Israeli players and officials interviewed echoed these observations. Success comes from the personal commitment of players and former players and their families and, even more, from the interpersonal bonds forged by a system that emphasizes collective achievement and shared commitment to the game and its values.

Role models. An effort to draw elite ballplayers to Israel, a professional baseball league that began—and folded—in 2007, had very limited success in popularizing baseball in Israel. Instead, it validated the IAB's ideological and pragmatic approach—"quantity begets quality"—that begins with sharing the fun of playing baseball with as many people as possible. A founding member of the IAB summarized this philosophy: "People think you have to have an enrichment program—get the good players and give them extra time. No! Get the *poor* players and give *them* extra time—then everybody's playing baseball." Raising the skill level of the weakest players raises the quality of baseball at all levels, so that as more children begin to play baseball, more children begin to play it well, and the pool of international-caliber players grows. Consequently, Israel has risen steadily in International Baseball Federation world rankings, from fifty-ninth in 2009 to nineteenth in the summer of 2014. As the Senior National Team has enjoyed increasing success, individuals on that team have enjoyed increased recognition; in 2015 a player from the SNT, pitcher Dean Kremer, became the first Israeli selected in Major League Baseball's amateur draft. These players' international success attracts new players and creates incentives for hard work. Advanced instruction can then be introduced to meet growing needs: in 2014 the IAB established Israel's first small academy for elite players. At the same time, the IAB continued to create opportunities for players of all skill levels to play together and learn from each other.

The IAB's egalitarian approach creates a cycle: the large pool of new players yields a growing core of dedicated players, who attract and motivate more players, engage donors, and eventually become coaches and officials. Moreover, these homegrown players can potentially influence baseball beyond Israel. In 2012 the IAB had a chance to test this proposition.

The WBC

The 2012 WBC qualifiers in Jupiter, Florida, united Israel's Senior National Team with "heritage players," Jewish minor leaguers who were eligible for Israeli citizenship and thus, by WBC rules, eligible to play for Israel. This provided an opportunity to see how American professional baseball players would react to the IAB's approach and how they would perceive the mutual influences of baseball and Israeli culture.

The results exceeded expectations. In a series of interviews that included almost all of the players from Israel's WBC team, heritage players reported that playing alongside the Israelis reconnected them to their own cultural identities. One heritage player elaborated: "We're teaching them baseball; they're teaching us Judaism, about Israel." As the heritage players learned about baseball in Israel, they also internalized the IAB mission and, in the process, recalled baseball's core values. "They're enlightening us while we're enlightening them," noted one heritage player. His sentiments were echoed by many of his teammates, who learned, among many things, about that old Israeli icon the *chevreman* and the five aspects of baseball it revives.

Friendship. The WBC took heritage players back to a time when baseball meant playing with friends. In a representative observation, one heritage player reflected, "The most memorable times for me were off the field, getting to know the players and especially getting to know the Israeli guys." Speaking for many of his peers, another heritage player said, "The camaraderie and the relationships we built, the connection we had with each other, [were] what it was all about."

Fellowship. Heritage players noted that playing for Team Israel "was way more of a team atmosphere" than playing professionally in the United States. One explained that the WBC "wasn't just about us, but it was about those guys [from the SNT] sitting on the other side of that clubhouse." Echoing the feelings of many heritage players, another said, "More than any team I have ever been part of, there were no individuals. It was all about the team. It was awesome."

Facilitation. Players were reminded that baseball is about lifting each other up, even from the bench. One heritage player asserted that the willingness of Israeli players to give up their roster spots inspired his fellow heritage players: "It hit home with these guys sacrificing, that can say, 'Take my spot . . . I'm going to let you wear the uniform because you're giving us the best chance to start something that can potentially change the culture in Israel.'" Consequently, after having identified with the aspirations of the Israeli players beside them, when Israel lost to Spain in the championship game, many heritage players felt a sense of having failed their Israeli teammates—their new friends.

Flexibility. Heritage players' feelings went even deeper: "We let down the entire country," said one. One player felt strongly that this feeling was shared by many of his peers: "Everyone just kept saying, 'I've never played in a game that I cared so much about. I've never felt this way about a game, about a team.' I was totally surprised by that, because I thought they were just going to go about their business like they always do, but everyone cared so much." Indeed, another player called it the most "emotionally draining game I had been part of." In true *chevreman* style, however, through flexibility of perspective and an identification with their Israeli peers, success emerged from failure. The following comments from individual players suggest that these heritage players saw success in the very act of playing the game, and success meant something other than winning. Israel benefited logistically: Israelis "were looking for us to really put them on the map, and we did," said one ballplayer. Families benefited emotionally: "I know my grandparents really loved it. It made them really happy." And players benefited socially and culturally: "It was devastating that we lost, but at the end of the day what we all realized after that [was] we've created relationships through that."

Fun. These outcomes, which superseded the final score of the championship game, made the WBC "one of the times where it's more than a game." It was also a reminder, however, that baseball *is* a game. Whether it was the structure of the WBC or the influence of the IAB, Team Israel returned players to the reasons they love baseball. Heritage players said that the Israeli players reminded them of "the way baseball is meant to be played." The Israelis' approaches to baseball redirected prospects' attention away from the cynicism and selfishness that the heritage players perceived as endemic in professional baseball. American professional players are accustomed to the *sotziomat*, the *chevreman*'s polar opposite, who in minor league clubhouses is the salty, self-centered player who cares mainly about his personal stats. One player, reflecting on the enthusiasm of the SNT players, observed, "You see these kids actually enjoying the game, playing it as a game, not a job, hustling on the field, smiling, having fun." Another added, "It was definitely the hardest loss I've ever had in my life, but at the end of the day, it's a game, and you love to play the game and all of those guys do, too." A third heritage player recalled that, in the WBC, "doing stuff like we got to do with the Israeli guys reminds you of how lucky you are to be able to" play baseball. A fourth simply said, "It made me rethink how much I love the game of baseball and how much I love playing it."

Beyond Jupiter

Israel's participation in the WBC has helped to draw more people to baseball in Israel, including more coaches, new role models, and even the donors necessary to help build new fields. It may also have helped to build more international bridges necessary to strengthen the ways baseball gives to Israel and Israel gives back to baseball.

Over the years, the IAB has assisted other nations in trying to build a baseball program. For example, the IAB helped organize an international tournament for the Cyprus Amateur Baseball Federation. This, according to an IAB official, is one example that helps to explain the IAB's popularity within the Confederation of European Baseball: "That's why Israel is big in Europe. We help them do things they want to do."

As baseball in Israel grows and the IAB helps promote baseball in Europe, some within the IAB see Israel as a gateway to increasing baseball's popularity throughout the Middle East, too. For example, the IAB has organized and led an umpiring course in Jordan. "All kinds of things like that," one usually cynical IAB veteran explained, "make everything really"—here he paused and gazed into the distance—"nice."

Nevertheless, children will probably have to lead the way, just as they are leading baseball's growth within Israel. A former Israeli national player recalled an international youth baseball tournament, in 1989: when Jordanian and Israeli teams met off the field, the children enthusiastically and innocently exchanged keepsakes—until Jordan's adult chaperones pulled them apart and forced the children from the Jordanian team to throw the Israeli children's gifts on the ground. More recently, Peter Kurz, president of the IAB and first vice president of the Confederation of European Baseball, was invited to the 2014 World Baseball Softball Confederation meeting in Tunisia, where Tunisian authorities promptly banned him from displaying Israel's flag or from identifying himself as Israeli.[2]

Still, IAB volunteers remain hopeful that baseball has the power to build bridges across even difficult divides, because, as they have noticed, baseball connects people. Although they know that baseball will always represent many things to many people, people in Israel believe that it remains stronger than politics, prejudice, or even big business, for baseball, at its core, is a game. Its emergence in new places, such as Israel, is a reminder of this to baseball fans, executives, and players— including an otherwise jaded cohort of minor leaguers.

The experience of a young American baseball fan, encountering the IAB for the first time, offers one last example of the resilient and rejuvenating character of baseball in Israel. On a 2012 trip to Israel, a group of American college students spent a day teaching baseball to children in Ofakim, an impoverished community in the northern part of Israel's Negev Desert. Because of that encounter, baseball became a regular after-school activity in Ofakim. One of the college students, in a long interview with the author, admitted that the experience changed her view of baseball: "Seeing those kids play [I realized] it's still so much of a game—standings don't matter, batting averages don't matter, salaries don't matter—it's a game. It's something you play in the park." Even if that park started out as a patch of dirt in the desert.

NOTES

1. All quotes in this chapter are from interviews conducted by the author with IAB volunteers, officials, and players and with nearly all of the players on Israel's World Baseball Classic team that competed in the WBC qualifying round in 2012. For more on the IAB, see http://www.baseball.org.il/en/.

2. "IOC Issues Warning over Israeli Flag Incident," July 8, 2014, http://sports .espn.go.com/espn/wire?section=oly&id=11190451.

Part 5 Africa

18

South Africa

The Battle for Baseball

Marizanne Grundlingh

On any given weekend the South African sporting landscape is inundated with people watching, playing, or talking about sport. Sport is ubiquitous in many communities and ranges from grassroots-level participation in schools and clubs to elite-level competition. Sports studies scholars David R. Black and John Nauright accurately describe the role of sport in the country: "There are few national societies in which the cultural significance, indeed centrality, of sport has been more readily apparent than South Africa."[1] The major sports that are played and followed have historically been the male-dominated team sports of soccer, rugby, and cricket. Although these sports are certainly popular in South Africa, many so-called minor sports are also played and appreciated.

This chapter examines baseball in South Africa. Doing so can provide insight into how the global game is appreciated locally. Following anthropologist Alan Klein's proposition that "no matter how recent baseball in South Africa may be, no examination of it can be divorced from the history of apartheid," this chapter considers baseball history in South Africa and the dynamics and politics of playing the game during apartheid.[2] To situate baseball within the country's current developments, I draw on fieldwork at the Bothasig Baseball Club in Cape Town and highlight the meaning that the game has for club members.

History of Baseball in South Africa

Baseball's introduction to South Africa coincided with the unearthing of South Africa's mineral wealth in the late nineteenth century. The discovery of gold in the Transvaal province attracted fortune seekers from all over the world, including Americans who in 1895 brought baseball equipment, created a diamond, and started playing games. The first games were played on mining property and were mostly social affairs. There was enough local interest in the game that an official league was established in 1899, and in 1904 Transvaal's first official baseball body was founded. By the 1930s the game had spread to other parts of the country, as provincial players had moved from Transvaal to Natal and the Western Province and introduced the game to local communities.[3]

The Americans weren't the only ones to introduce the game in South Africa. The Japanese were responsible for introducing baseball in the Eastern Province. In 1934 a Japanese ship, the *Paris Maru*, beached in Algoa Bay. Its sailors had to wait three months for the next ship. With their baseball equipment on hand, they arranged a game with the locals, who worked for American companies, as well as American Mormon missionaries.[4] As a result of World War II, baseball entered a quiet period between 1939 and 1945.

South Africa's first taste of international competition came in 1955, when an American team of "all-star" amateur baseball players toured South Africa on a three-and-a-half-month stint. The American visitors beat the South Africans convincingly, winning thirty-two straight games. Despite the lack of strong competition, the tour exposed South African players to the skill and expertise of the American touring party.[5] The games also ensured a decent spectatorship, and interest was built up around the sport. The largest crowd during the tour was about ten thousand at a game in Johannesburg, while others attracted as many as five thousand spectators.[6] At this point it is worth elaborating on the significant influence that apartheid had on baseball's development in South Africa.

The 1948 election in South Africa is considered to be a watershed moment in South African history, as the newly elected Nationalist Party government, under the leadership of D. F. Malan, developed a grand scheme of racial segregation known as apartheid. Legislation was aimed at segregating the different racial groups in all spheres of daily life, including sport. The 1950 Population Registration Act divided the South African population into four "races": black, white, coloured, and Asian. Legislation was passed to control the movement and interaction of people across different races.

Several antiapartheid sport bodies were formed in South Africa, the first being the South African Sports Association, which was established in 1958 and later replaced by the South African Non-Racial Olympic Committee (SANROC) in 1963. The purpose of these organizations was to spearhead an international boycott against sport. By the middle of 1964 SANROC's leaders were in prison, under house arrest, in exile, or underground, all in the name of a government policy of "keeping politics out of sport."[7]

The pressure of international boycotts on South African sport teams gained momentum, and by 1970 the ruling bodies of more than twenty sports had barred South Africa from participating.[8] By the 1980s South African sport had become sealed off from major international competitions, with only the odd rebel tour taking place in rugby. By the early 1990s the apartheid state had lost political power, and South African sport was reintegrated into the global sports world.

Baseball, like many of the sports practiced during apartheid, was played along racial lines. The South African Baseball Association represented black interest in the game, and most of the baseball traced to black people was centered in Cape Town and dates to the 1950s.[9] The South African Baseball Federation represented white people's interest in the game, and by 1969 a South African national team named the Springboks embarked on a two-month tour of Europe, playing teams in Spain, France, Germany, England, and Belgian.[10] Unsurprisingly, all the members of the touring team were white.

The second international team to tour South Africa, in 1971, was the

"Continental Cavaliers," composed mostly of American, German, and Belgian players. But international pressure and the boycott of South African sport made international competition uncommon. Although strict government regulations were enforced to prohibit interracial baseball games, during apartheid interracial matches occasionally took place. Pet Yuss, the former president of South Africa's white baseball organization, who also played in the white league in the 1950s, noted that there were times when informal interracial games would be organized. It was risky to play such games, and ballplayers were often threatened with arrest for breaking apartheid laws.[11] The end of apartheid allowed the two baseball federations to merge, and the South African Baseball Union (SABU) was established in 1992, under the leadership of anti-apartheid activist Edwin Bennett. This brief historical background on baseball's development in South Africa, and how politics at the time influenced the manner in which the sport was organized and played, allows us to consider baseball in contemporary South Africa.

Baseball in South Africa Today

Baseball in South Africa is played under the direction of the South African Baseball Union and played on an amateur level. In 2008 it was estimated that there were seventy-two thousand registered baseball players in South Africa.[12] Baseball clubs are affiliated with provincial governing bodies, and most clubs are situated in urban areas such as Cape Town, Johannesburg, and Durban. The annual National Inter-Provincial Tournament is where all the provincial teams compete to become the national champion. This tournament is for participants in the age groups of under-fourteen, -sixteen, and -eighteen as well as seniors. In addition to competing for top honors, the selection of players for international tournaments is conducted throughout the tournament by designated selectors. Baseball Western Province (BAWP) is particularly strong, as the majority of the national team that participated at the 2000 Olympic Games came from the province. Three-quarters of the players who competed in the 2009 World Baseball Classic were also products of the Western Province Major League. The president of BAWP, Tommie Norman, explains the region's dominance:

We are the biggest district that plays baseball in this country, both in terms of the number of clubs and the number of registered players. There are currently twenty-two active clubs in the Western Province, and we have more registered clubs than the rest of South Africa together. Traditionally, we have always been strong, and I think it has something to do with the climate in the Cape, because during the summer months, which is the baseball season, we get a lot of game time, whereas the summer months in Gauteng are known for midafternoon showers, which limits the amount of baseball they can play. We have won the national title for something like fifteen years in a row, and it has also happened that our Senior A and Senior B team compete against each other in the finals.[13]

The South African climate also affects the amount of time that the national team can prepare for international competitions. The winter months in the Cape are usually wet and cold, which limits outdoor training. Mike Randall, player-development manager for South African Baseball and Major League Baseball's (MLB) Africa consultant, explains: "A challenge for us on a local and international level is that we always have to prepare in winter, to go play overseas in their summer. The thing is not many clubs have floodlights, and we have to compete for playing fields with soccer and rugby clubs. The Athlone Athletics Baseball Club stadium is the only stadium where hitting and pitching can be played indoors."[14]

Western Province received a major financial boost in 2010 for the development of a baseball infrastructure. A Baseball Tomorrow Fund grant of two hundred thousand dollars, together with funds raised by the club itself and the local municipality, ensured the construction of an indoor sports complex, at the Athlone Athletics Baseball Club. The facility features batting cages, pitching mounds, and a workout facility.

25. The Bothasig Baseball Club diamond. (Photo by Marizanne Grundlingh.)

The Baseball Tomorrow Fund is a joint initiative between MLB and the Major League Baseball Players Association designed to promote and enhance the growth of baseball throughout the world by funding programs, field improvements, and equipment purchases to inspire and maintain youth participation in baseball.

The facilities available to play baseball in the Western Cape are varied. Many clubs share their facilities with other sports. The more affluent, predominantly white clubs, such as Bothasig Baseball Club, Belville Tygers, and Durbanville Baseball Club, have well-maintained fields. The Bothasig Baseball Club, for example, applied for funding from the National Lottery to upgrade its facilities in 2005. In the township areas the availability of practice space is limited.[15] The Phillipi Angels baseball team, which hails from a township on the outskirts of Cape Town, practices on a drained veld area, which the surrounding community sometimes uses as a dumping ground for litter. The

Phillipi Angels, established in 2006 under the guidance of Nyameko Gabada, is the only township team to be affiliated with the BAWP. The dire state of its home ground makes it impossible for the team to host home games. Despite this the Phillipi Angels boast of having eighty children and youth who take part in training sessions, and three members of the club were included on the Western Province team, which took part in the 2014 Inter-Provincial Tournament in Durban. Baseball has also infiltrated local schools in Phillipi, which has an established school league.

Despite the increased interest and growth, baseball in South Africa has yet to establish itself in the sporting public's psyche. The fact that baseball is a minor sport in South Africa resonates clearly when Brett Willenburg, a former Kansas City Royal Minor Leaguer and member of Bothasig Baseball Club, remarks: "Even when I am here [South Africa] and even though I was a professional baseball player, people are like what? You play baseball and they don't even know what it is, and it was so weird because you're representing your country and people don't even know the game exists in the country."[16]

Clearly, baseball is still unfamiliar as a mass participation and spectator sport in South Africa. This despite the national team having competed at the 2000 Sydney Olympic Games and the 2006 and 2009 World Baseball Classic. The South African national team failed to qualify for the 2012 World Baseball Classic. Only a handful of South African baseball players have plied their trade as professionals, in the U.S. Minor Leagues. The most notable is Barry Armitage, who pitched for the Kansas City Royals and is the first South African–born baseball player to make an appearance in Major League Baseball, when he threw an inning for the Royals in an exhibition game in 2005. The South African baseball fraternity is still hopeful that a South African player will make it into the Major Leagues.

A major difficulty in introducing the game to schools has been the reluctance of former Model C schools to promote baseball as a school sport.[17] Cricket has historically been the bat-and-ball sport that boys are exposed to from a young age. An archetypal English game, cricket was historically synonymous with the British upper classes and spread throughout the British Empire as part of the cultural glue that helped to bond the "mother country" with the colonies.[18] The game carried with it "an exaggerated sense of what was considered gentlemanly conduct, and was often thinly disguised elitist snobbery."[19] Baseball was seen as a threat to traditions associated with cricket. Tommie Norman highlights this prejudice: "In the white conservative areas, there is a perception that baseball is an ill-disciplined sport, because it goes hand in hand with chirping and trying to intimidate the player. We teach our boys to be 'ordentlik'[20] and to respect players. Just because people don't know about the game, they compare it to cricket and make assumptions. Look, the game has an American influence, and part of the baseball culture is to embrace that, which makes it positive."[21]

Alan Klein's research on baseball in South Africa also finds that schools are not always receptive to introducing a new sport. For example, Eddie Bennett, SABU's development officer, was chased away at some schools when he attempted to introduce the game.[22] Mark Randall highlights the challenge of introducing baseball at schools: "Our biggest challenge is to established baseball as a sport at schools. There are many players, but the challenge is soccer, cricket, and rugby. They are already established sports, and the schools already have coaches for those sports. They aren't necessarily interested in introducing a new sport, where the coach needs to be trained to be able to teach it."[23]

Nevertheless, providing quality coaching and giving exposure to talented baseball players in South Africa and Africa have been kick-started by MLB, which has organized Africa Elite Training Camps since 2011. Randall has scouted players from African countries such as Uganda, Nigeria, and Ghana to attend an annual training camp where American scouts and coaches extract South African talent. The Boksburg Cardinals Baseball Club in Johannesburg hosted the MLB Africa Elite Camp in 2014.

Baseball in Bothasig

I contacted Patrick Starcke, the marketing and public relations officer for Bothasig Baseball Club, to gain insight into how baseball is appreciated in the country. He invited me to attend the club practices and matches. So I headed twenty minutes north of Cape Town to Bothasig, a predominately white residential area. The club was established in 1974, and the senior team is coached by Raymond Tew, a national baseball team member from 1967 to 1992 and the only South African baseball player to be inducted into the South African Sport and Art Hall of Fame.

Patrick greeted me at the gates of the Abe Sher Stadium. "Welcome to the biggest baseball club in the Western Cape, South Africa and Africa," he said. Patrick's passion for baseball goes beyond the call of duty to get sponsorships, funding, and administrative work done for the club. After attending a few training sessions and matches and speaking to players and parents, I realized that baseball, despite not being a popular sport in South Africa, has significant meaning for its club members. Meaning was attached to winning the Western Province league, but is also epitomized by the family support that players receive weekend after weekend during the baseball season.

A midseason game between the two northern suburb-based clubs, Bothasig Baseball Club and Belville Tygers, culminated in an intense affair, which Bothasig won. The sense of communality brought forth through that win resonates closely with what anthropologist Victor Turner describes as "communitas," a feeling of solidarity and togetherness. A sense of belonging, based on being part of a team or a supporter of a winning team, can be shallow and ephemeral.[24] But for members of the Bothasig Baseball Club, a sense of togetherness was unique in that they were not only victorious against a team with whom they had a long-standing rivalry, but also united in baseball, a game that has to compete against other South African sports.

A strong communal and individual identity is fostered through baseball for members of the Bothasig Baseball Club. Dylan Unsworth, who is under contract with the Seattle Mariners but trains with the Bothasig Baseball Club when in South Africa, explains the sense of belonging he experiences at the club: "Of the thirty guys in the squad, twenty of them I have grown up with and I knew since I have started playing, and that was as an eight-year-old and this was the start. It has been a great journey and one of the best clubs I have been with. I live just around the corner, so that is great, and I enjoy coming home knowing that you have a club where you can slot into and belong."[25]

Baseball was not an exclusively American export to South Africa. The Japanese have been instrumental in growing the game in Asia, while Cubans have been key in spreading the game throughout the Caribbean.[26] In South Africa Eastern Province baseball grew from a Japanese influence, but it would be misleading to think that baseball is completely disassociated from American popular culture in contemporary South Africa.

Historian James T. Campbell has shown how the Americanization of South Africa has a long history, dating back to the mineral revolution in South Africa in the late nineteenth century.[27] In South Africa local baseball clubs have appropriated American team names, such as the Belville Tygers, Goodwood Braves, Westridge Yankees, and Helderberg Pirates, to name a few. Some of these community clubs have not just appropriated American baseball franchise names, but also used baseball as a vehicle to reflect their own nuanced cultural identification with the game. As a coloured baseball player from the Westridge Yankees told me: "I am a Westridge Yankee, because my dad and my grandfather played for them. I never think of my team as imitating the New York Yankees. They are in America; we are here. The baseball we play here has a different meaning for us than the Americans." His disassociation with the American franchise points to how the game has become localized, with family and community ties central to an identity on a local rather than a global level.

Conclusion

Despite the efforts of the SABU and MLB in South Africa, baseball still struggles to get national recognition. The health of clubs is determined by individuals, who volunteer their time and energy to run their clubs efficiently and to promote baseball in South Africa. Mark Randall's dream is to have established baseball academies across the country, where kids can get quality coaching and exposure to the game. Baseball remains a comparatively minor sport in South Africa and does not enjoy the popularity of other national sports, notably rugby, cricket, and soccer. In the words of Tommie Norman, the aim is to make baseball a "good small sport," one that can be played competitive internationally, while also being cognizant of the limitations of growing the game at home. This does not take away from the fact that baseball offers those who play the game in South Africa an athletic identity and sense of belonging to a small but growing and passionate group of baseball players.

NOTES

1. David R. Black and John Nauright, *Rugby and the South African Nation: Sport, Cultures, Politics, and Power in the Old and New South Africa* (Manchester: Manchester University Press, 1993), 1.
2. Alan Klein, *Growing the Game: The Globalization of Major League Baseball* (New Haven CT: Yale University Press, 2006), 197.
3. Josh Chetwynd, "A History of South African Baseball," NINE: *A Journal of Baseball History and Culture* 16 (Spring 2008): 73–79.
4. "History of Baseball in South Africa," http://www.sabu.co.za/index.php /about-us/history-of-baseball-in-sa.
5. *Sport Personalities* (Johannesburg: Special Publications, 1971).
6. Chetwynd, "History of South African Baseball," 75.
7. Rob Nixon, "Apartheid on the Run: The South African Sports Boycott," *Transition* 58 (1992): 77.
8. Nixon, "Apartheid on the Run," 79.
9. Klein, *Growing the Game*, 202.

10. Chetwynd, "History of South African Baseball," 75.

11. Klein, *Growing the Game*, 203.

12. Chetwynd, "History of South African Baseball," 78.

13. Tommie Norman, interview with the author, January 20, 2014.

14. Mark Randall, interview with the author, January 20, 2014.

15. *Township* is the colloquial term used to refer to informal settlements in South Africa. The majority of South Africa's black working-class citizens live in these areas. These areas developed as migrant laborers moved from rural areas to cities in search for jobs.

16. Brett Willenburg, interview with the author, January 20, 2014.

17. Model C schools refers to schools that accepted only white learners, during the apartheid era. These schools became semiprivate toward the latter stages of apartheid.

18. J. A. Mangan, ed., *The Cultural Bond: Sport, Empire and Society* (London: Frank Cass, 1992).

19. Albert Grundlingh, *Potent Pastimes: Sport and Leisure Practices in Modern Afrikaner history* (Pretoria: Protea Book House, 2013), 193.

20. *Ordentlik* is an Afrikaans word that has connotations of gentility, restraint, and self-respect. See Fiona C. Ross, *Raw Life, New Hope: Decency, Housing and Everyday Life in a Post-apartheid Community* (Cape Town: UCT Press, 2010).

21. Norman, interview.

22. Klein, *Growing the Game*, 205.

23. Randall, interview.

24. Daniel A. Nathan, *Rooting for the Home Team: Sport, Community and Identity* (Urbana: University of Illinois Press, 2013), 3.

25. Dylan Unsworth, interview with the author, January 20, 2014.

26. George Gmelch, ed., *Baseball without Borders: The International Pastime* (Lincoln: University of Nebraska Press, 2006).

27. James T. Campbell, "The Americanization of South Africa," in *Safundi: A South African and American Comparative Reader*, edited by Andrew Offenburger, Scott Rosenburg, and Christopher Saunders (Scottsdale AZ: Safundi, 2002), 23–61.

Part 6 Europe

19

Italy

No Hot Dogs in the Bleachers

Peter Carino

Known for Renaissance art, fabulous opera, and unparalleled cuisine, Italy has far less illustriously fielded professional baseball teams for more than sixty years. Baseball had sporadically appeared in the *bel paese* as early as 1884 when two teams of American naval officers staged a game in Livorno. A. G. Spalding's 1889 world tour stopped in Italy to play games in Naples, Rome, and Florence, but baseball was largely forgotten until 1919, when Turin-born Max Ott (né Mario Ottino, 1905) entered the scene. Often called the "father of Italian baseball," Ott had spent his boyhood in New Jersey, and upon returning home as a teenager he began to organize games and teams. By 1923 Ott had assembled three teams. Unfortunately, interest waned when he returned to the United States. Later in the 1920s Guido Graziani formed a couple of teams in Rome with the help of American coach H. Chase Baillou. However, when Graziani had to leave the city for job-related reasons, the game again died. In 1931 the Italian Academy of Physical Education approved baseball as an appropriate sport for youth and sent a contingent of officials to the United States to learn the game. Upon their return several youth teams were formed to put on exhibitions, but this effort was for naught when Benito Mussolini's Fascist government took power and frowned upon anything American.[1]

During and following World War II, the game gained a foothold as American servicemen played and began to form teams with young

Italians in various cities up and down the boot. By 1948 league play began with five teams from Milan and one from Bologna, each playing a game a week in the Lega Nazionale di Baseball, formed by Max Ott, now back in Italy working as a journalist and again advocating for baseball. Meanwhile, Lieutenant Charles Butte was building a cemetery for American war dead in Nettuno, a small seaport town near Anzio, and teaching baseball to locals. Upon completion of the cemetery, Butte secured permission from the United States and land from a wealthy nobleman, Prince Steno Borghese, to build a stadium. Butte and Borghese subsequently formed l'Associazione Italiana Baseball. When Butte returned to the United States in 1949, his replacement, Horace McGarity, embraced these efforts, building a league power at little Nettuno as both a manager and a player.

By 1950 l'Associazione and Ott's la Lega had merged to form the professional league that evolved into today's Federazione Italiana Baseball Softball, with central offices in Rome and several regional offices. With Borghese as director, throughout the 1950s and early 1960s, eight to twelve teams competed in FIBS, playing a game a week through an eighteen-week season. Though a few players received a small fee for their services, the league in those years likely resembled a recreational or semipro league more than the professional organization of teams playing today. By the 1970s each team's schedule increased to thirty or so games a year, and by the 1980s teams played between fifty and sixty games, usually with a three-game series each weekend.

Despite this heritage professional baseball attracts minimal attention in Italian sporting culture, with crowds counted in the hundreds attending regular-season games in ballparks about the size of college or spring-training facilities. The game receives scant coverage in local newspapers; in the country's national sports daily, *La Gazzetta dello Sport*, it is sometimes easier to find scores of American Major League Baseball (MLB) games. This lack of popularity can to some degree be attributed to Italy's status as a single-sport nation, with soccer as the undisputed center of every sports fan's consciousness. Nearly all Italian men (and many women) support a soccer team with the same passion they have for their families. Auto racing (meaning Ferrari on the F1 circuit), basketball, boxing, and even volleyball garner more media coverage and fan interest than baseball, though all lag well behind soccer.

Some signs of progress are evident. With interest from former All-Star catcher Mike Piazza and MLB, a handful of Italian players with experience in the American Minors, as well as in the World Baseball Classic (WBC), the Italians are seeing better coaching and better player development. In addition, the league holds national baseball camps for youth. When Alex Liddi of the Seattle Mariners became the first born and bred Italian player in MLB, the game's popularity spiked. Nevertheless, baseball in the *bel paese* remains a "boutique sport," about as popular as professional lacrosse in the United States. As such it attracts few casual fans. The fans who do follow the game tend to be *appassionati* (diehards). They are knowledgeable about the rules and zealous about their team. While the quality of play certainly falls short of that in the United States, Latin America, or Asia, fans enjoy a game that boasts a strong history of native-born players and teams, attracts a small group of foreign players, and offers a richly satisfying experience at the ballpark.

La Lega Maggiore

Throughout the history and development of Italian baseball, the various changes in the structure of the Italian "major leagues" have been rather Byzantine. During most of its existence the men's "major league" was divided into two levels, A1 and A2. The A1 league, the highest level, fielded ten teams, the A2 usually twenty-four. The length of schedule ranged over the years from as few as ten games with fewer teams the first two years to as many as sixty-six in 1985 and 1990. Through most of the 1990s, fifty-four games made up the A1 regular season, and, since 2000, teams have played in the forties and fifties. Until 2010 the top two teams in A2 each year moved up to A1 the next year, and the bottom two teams from A1 dropped into A2. Until 1985 Italian baseball had no playoffs, but after 1985 the top four teams of the A1 league entered the playoffs (two best-of-seven series) to determine the winner of the A1 championship. The year's best teams from A1 and A2 then contended in a four-team tournament for the Coppa Italia (the Italian Cup). The leagues were reorganized in 2010, eliminating the A1 and A2 designations and consolidating the teams into the Italian Baseball League, composed of eight teams and the now lower Series A with three divisions varying from six to eight teams. Since this last reorganization, the IBL schedule has varied between forty-two and forty-four games to determine the four teams that enter the playoffs. When an Italian team wins the playoff championship, as in soccer, it is awarded the *scudetto*. The word literally means "little shield," for the shape of the patch the champions proudly display on their uniforms.

Below the IBL and Serie A–level league there is a minor league system of sorts, with levels B and C. This is not to say that all teams at these levels are directly affiliated with higher clubs, as in the American system. While a young player can use these lower levels to make a name for himself and perhaps garner a contract from a higher-level team, most teams at B and C are independent. The B-league game is about equivalent to play at the lower divisions of college ball in the United States; C teams would probably be challenged by good American high school teams. The players in B and C are paid, but they also have other jobs. At the C level there are several divisions, arranged geographically to save time and money on travel. These teams also have sponsors, often local, to help meet expenses. But like all pro teams in Italy, from basketball to women's volleyball, baseball teams are subsidized by the government-sponsored soccer lotteries, such as Toto Calcio and its many variations. For baseball, an unpopular sport, these subsidies can provide a sizable piece of a team's budget.

Legendary Players and Teams

The varying number of games in different seasons makes it difficult to assess single-season and career records. For instance, the single-season home run and RBI (runs batted in) leaders came in 1985 and 1990, when the league played its longest schedule. Compounding the problem is the use of wooden bats from 1950 to 1973, aluminum bats from 1974 through 2000, and wood again since 2001. Despite these difficulties Italian baseball, like its American counterpart, marks its history in statistics and legend, with the Federazione maintaining an archive of records in Trieste and now with extensive records on the FIBS and individual team websites.[2] Prior to the Internet league statistician Enzo Di Gesù of Turin compiled weekly box scores and stats and forwarded them to regional league offices. Di Gesù also edited the Italian magazine *Tutto Baseball e Softball*, although finding this magazine on Italian newsstands was harder than finding an ERA (earned run average) under 3.00 on the Colorado Rockies' pitching staff. Because records and statistics have been compiled since the early years, they provide a strong sense of the history and character of the Federazione, its legendary players, and the place of foreign players in it.

While there is no Babe Ruth of Italy, there are players who might be called the Cy Young and Ty Cobb of the Federazione. Giulio Glorioso fills the former role, but since he pitched in the early (and less developed) years of the league, it is difficult to determine the scope of his talent. Dominating Italian hitters from the early 1950s to the late 1960s, Glorioso played most of his career with teams from Rome and perennial powers Parma and Nettuno, except for three years from 1960 to 1962, when he led the Milan team to three *scudetti*. In fifteen seasons from 1953 to 1967, Glorioso topped the league in strikeouts eleven times, averaging more than 150 in seasons that averaged only 18 games. His most phenomenal year had to be 1961, when he whiffed 218, won each of Milano's 18 games, and posted a microscopic ERA of 0.23. In nine of his phenomenal prime of fifteen years, Glorioso led the league in wins, averaging fifteen a season when his teams were playing an 18-game schedule. In the heart of his career, 1961–67, he went 108-8-1.29. Only in the last three years of Glorioso's prime, when the Federazione increased the season to 32 games, was he not responsible for all of his team's wins. As might be expected, Glorioso dominated the ERA statistics, winning the crown seven times, and five times averaging less than one run a game. Following his fifteen-year prime, the glorious Giulio pitched seven more years, posting a record of 49-44, with more than 803 strikeouts, pushing his career total over 2,500. Add to these numbers Glorioso's five no-hitters, and it is easy to see why he was contacted by the Cincinnati Reds for a possible tryout and pitched in Cleveland's spring-training camp in 1953.

As if pitching were not enough, Glorioso played both infield and outfield and won two batting titles, with a .432 average in 1960 and a .444 average in 1961. Despite his prowess at the plate, Glorioso clearly must be measured by his pitching, for his statistics become even more phenomenal since the Federazione has always been and still is a hitter's league. Indeed, it is common for teams to bat more than .300. Some of this output may be attributed to the Federazione's use of aluminum bats from 1974 to 2000, but even in its first decades when wooden bats prevailed, Federazione hitters put up astronomical numbers at the plate.

Among the most prolific of these hitters have been catcher Giorgio Castelli and outfielder Roberto Bianchi. If Glorioso is Italy's Cy Young, Castelli is its Ty Cobb. American teams scouted Castelli, and after his rookie season in 1968 he was offered a contract to be groomed as a backup for Johnny Bench of the Cincinnati Reds. The deal fell apart when the Reds signed talented prospect Bill Plummer. Another version of the story says the Reds were ready to move Bench to first base when Castelli's mother decided she wanted her seventeen-year-old son back home. Either way, Castelli remained in Italy, playing all his seasons with Parma, where he won eight of eleven league batting crowns from 1968 through 1978. His first was shared with another player at, for Castelli, an aberrantly low .324. But then it was his rookie year, and he was seventeen. The remaining seven were won outright, with averages consistently well over .400, two over .500, and a high of .540. In 1974, his best year and maybe the best year ever by a professional player, Castelli won a Triple Crown, hitting .515, with 26 *fuoricampi* (home runs), 79 RBI, and a staggering 1.010 slugging average in a 44-game season. Castelli's prime years were 1968 through 1978, but he played until 1984, remaining one of the Federazione's most potent hitters and finishing with 1,064 hits, a lifetime average of .423, 163 home runs, and 696 RBI in 605 games.

Outfielder Roberto Bianchi, who retired in 1999, was the Federazione's most consistent power hitter. As an eighteen-year-old rookie outfielder for Bologna in 1981, Bianchi served notice on Italian pitchers that he would be a force for years to come, leading the league with 43 RBI in a 40-game season. This marked the first of Bianchi's seven RBI titles, among which are a record 102 over the 66-game schedule of 1985. Though Bianchi led the league in home runs only three times, he is the Federazione's career leader with 288. Six times he has been the league's most potent *bombardieri*, or leader in slugging average. Of his six league-leading figures, the lowest is .741 in 1990, the highest 1.051 in 1987, the year he also won the Triple Crown with 27 homers, 72 RBI, and an average of .474. This league-leading average is the highest of Bianchi's three batting crowns, with the others at merely .460 and .466. Retiring at age thirty-six, Bianchi remained a potent hitter throughout his career, for fifteen years the biggest bat in the lineup of the always contending Bologna and Parma squads, before splitting his last three years with Rimini and Modena. His career line astounds: .384-288-1,170 in 949 games.

In addition to legendary players, the Federazione boasts some storied teams. Nettuno, a small seacoast town about forty kilometers southwest of Rome, is not only perhaps the most important city in the early development of Italian baseball but also home to one of its most storied teams. Along with three European Cup Championships, Nettuno has won fifteen *scudetti* to lead the pack, including several in the 1950s with Glorioso on the mound. Along with winning fifteen, the team has been runner-up in sixteen other seasons, meaning it has participated in nearly half of the league's championships. Given the town's role in the formation of Italian pro baseball and its success he years, it is no surprise that it remains one of the few baseball ⸺eds in Italy. Another strong squad hails from Rimini, an Adriatic resort town known more for its nightlife and beaches. Rimini has won eleven *scudetti* (three of five from 1998 to 2002). Other storied teams in the Federazione's annals are Bologna (ten *scudetti*); Parma, where Castelli played; and, in the early years, Milan. Though Milan no longer fields an A1 team, it dominated in the 1960s.

Nettuno might be called the Yankees of Italy; however, Italian teams are identified not by nicknames but by city and sponsor. For many years, for example, Nettuno was listed as Danesi Nettuno; Danesi is the name of the coffee company that sponsored the team. On the back of the Nettuno jersey, the player's number was imprinted in white against the brown backdrop of a coffee cup labeled "Danesi." Today, a local bank sponsors Nettuno. These sponsorships are necessary to help cover players' salaries and expenses because gate receipts are small and there are no lucrative TV contracts. Sponsors also may change from year to year, so while important financially, rarely do they become part of a team's identity. Some Italian teams will integrate the name of the sponsor with the uniform and logo of an American MLB team without adopting the name of either. For example, Nettuno dresses like Cleveland, but is not known as the Indians. However, fans refer to teams by town or city, rather than sponsors or MLB nicknames. This is fitting given the Italian people's fanatical, at times irrational, pride in their hometowns. Unlike in America, where Major League teams are located in large cities, because of sponsorships and subsidies Italian teams may hail from small towns as well as great metropolises, little Ronchi in the Emiglia Romano region as well as Florence or Rome. Thus, a team in the IBL can be a source of great pride for a small, lesser-known locale.

Americani e Altri Stranieri; or, **Americans and Other Foreigners**

While it is difficult to assess the quality of play in Italy, one measure is the performance of former Major Leaguers who have played in the

Federazione. At one time Italian teams were limited to two foreign players on the roster, but a lawsuit brought by foreign basketball players against their league has relaxed the quotas in all sports. Today the IBL has settled on four foreign players per squad. Some teams do not have any; others will carry three or four. These *stranieri*, usually from the United States or Latin America, are expected to be stars.

Among the most recognizable of the non-Italian players listed in the Federazione's records are journeyman utility infielder Jim Morrison; Lenny Randle, a solid infielder whose best years were with the Texas Rangers and New York Mets; and Jorge Orta, who played most of his sixteen years in the bigs with the Chicago White Sox and Kansas City Royals. In roughly 500 at bats a season during a twelve-year big-league career ending in 1988, Morrison averaged .260 with a high of .304 in 1983. He also hit 112 home runs, belting a career-best 15 in 1980, his only year as an everyday player. In 1990 Morrison turned up in the Federazione, putting up numbers of .390-12-75 in 62 games. Randle is one of a few recognizable position players who spent more than a season in Italy, playing four from 1983 through 1986. In his first year, at thirty-four, Randle won the batting title with a .475 average. In 1986 he led the league in *basi rubati* (stolen bases) with 32. After only 27 home runs in twelve years and 1,138 games in the American Majors, he hit 47 in four seasons and approximately 200 games abroad. Clearly, the success of these two average MLB players, at an advanced age, illustrates the gap between MLB and the Federazione. Not every American, however, has been successful. Jorge Orta, probably the best of the three with MLB career numbers of .278-130-715, signed with Parma during the stretch drive of the 1994 campaign but was a disappointment, batting only .222 with only 1 homer and 4 RBI in 14 games. Perhaps Orta did not have time to acclimate himself to the pitching; then again, he was five years removed from his MLB career and forty-three years old.

Other players with much briefer big-league service or time in the Minors also crop up in FIBS records. Among the briefest but most illustrious tours in Italy is Brad Komminsk's two years in 1994–95.

Never fulfilling the potential hoped for by the Braves and Indians, this hulking outfielder smashed 38 home runs for Rimini in 89 games over two seasons, topping all sluggers with 19 in 1994. In 1994 Komminsk also led the league with 61 RBI and posted the best slugging average in both years with .804 and .848. One of the more interesting short-timers (no pun intended) is Harry Chappas. Other than Eddie Gaedel, Chappas, at five-foot-three, is usually recognized as the smallest man ever to play in the Majors. A shortstop signed by Bill Veeck, Chappas averaged .245 in 72 games over three years with the White Sox. Four years later he hit .319 with 8 homers in 56 games with Grosseto, a long-established and always competitive Tuscan squad.

More than a few pitchers have also tried their hand in FIBS. St. Louis Cardinals right-hander Jason Simontacchi's 11-5 record in 2001 and moderate success over four seasons brought more attention to Italian baseball than it had previously received in the United States. The publicity, however, was not always positive, as commentators used his experience in Italy to underscore that he had seemingly "come out of nowhere" and miraculously learned to pitch all of a sudden. True, Simontacchi had dominated FIBS hitters in the 2000 season, going 15-1 with a minuscule ERA of 1.56 and 136 strikeouts in 133 innings as he pitched Rimini to a *scudetto*. But he himself said that he had learned a change-up in Italy that improved his pitching beyond the mediocrity he had shown in a couple of Minor League seasons prior to going there. Like Simontacchi, Ed Vosberg spent a year in Italy before reaching the Majors. A journeyman reliever in the 1990s, Vosberg is perhaps best (or worst) remembered for scalping his complimentary All-Star Game tickets when he played for Texas. In 1992, pitching for Novara, an also-ran, he won 9 and lost 5, giving up only 2.34 runs per nine innings and striking out 145 in 123 innings, before returning to the United States to put in eight seasons with five teams. The athletic Vosberg also played 35 games at first base and in the outfield, putting up good numbers: .319-9-37.

Unlike Simontacchi and Vosberg, other MLB pitchers surfaced in Italy looking for a last hurrah and a nice paycheck rather than a stepping-stone to the Majors. Starter and Italian American Pete Falcone enjoyed probably the most spectacular of these seasons in 1990. Having retired in 1989 with a 70-90 career record with the Giants, Cards, Mets, and Braves, Falcone went 17-2 with 183 strikeouts in 143 innings and a 1.19 ERA, but he faltered in the playoffs, losing 2 of 3 with an ERA of 3.48 as his Rimini team was edged out by Nettuno for the championship. In 2004 Jaime Navarro, a veteran of twelve seasons with the Milwaukee Brewers and three other Major League clubs, led Grosseto's dominant pitching staff with a 15-2 record. Joining two young Italian pitchers who were a combined 26-2, Navarro went 15-2, with an ERA of 1.76, helping Grosseto edge out perennial contender Bologna for the regular-season championship, the league playoffs, and the European Championship.

Few American players have had long careers in Italy, but there have been exceptions. Craig Stimac, a catcher and third baseman who appeared in 29 games in 1980–81 with the San Diego Padres, played significantly longer than most former Major Leaguers. Stimac's career in Italy spanned six years, during which he accumulated 533 hits and 95 home runs. His first year, 1984, was also his most notable when he nearly won the Triple Crown with a .436 batting average, 74 RBI, and 18 home runs. Fellow American Mark Funderburk beat out Stimac for the home run title, with 23.

Several Americans who spent time in the Minors or on college teams but never reached the Major Leagues chased their baseball dreams to Italy. Career records indicate that though often briefly successful, they returned home after a season or two. The most notable exceptions are Danny Newman and Dave Sheldon, whose career stats, ages, and appearances among career leaders indicate that they found a home in the boot. Both Sheldon and Newman pitched and played in the field. After two unremarkable Minor League seasons, Newman, a Cleveland native, played in Italy until age forty-five, retiring in 2009 after twenty seasons as an outfielder, first baseman, and pitcher. Though never leading the Federazione in any offensive category, his career batting average was a lofty .347, and on the mound he won 146 and lost 100 with an ERA of 3.07. Sheldon, a Californian and former White Sox farmhand, played twenty-three years with nine different clubs, compiling career totals of .293-125-625 before retiring at age forty-seven. Primarily a hard-hitting shortstop, Sheldon was less distinguished as a pitcher. Working mostly in relief after two lackluster seasons as a starter early in his career, Sheldon owns a meager lifetime record of 21-20 with an American Leaguesque ERA of 4.01. Both Sheldon and Newman obtained Italian passports in the late 1990s and were members of Italy's Olympic team at the 2000 Sydney Games.

Quality of Play

Given the success of these players, it is surprising that more aging stars or failed Minor Leaguers have not chosen to play in Italy. Aside from offering the opportunity to develop or extend a career, Italy is a thoroughly modern nation with all the amenities found in the United States, beautiful beaches, and breathtaking landscapes, as well as matchless traditions in culture and the arts (though these last two are not always at the top of most athletes' list of priorities). But there are likely several reasons American players have not flocked to Italy as they have to Japan. First, the Japanese leagues pay far more. In Italy the average player makes only about the equivalent of two to four thousand dollars a month, though he also receives a car and a rent-free apartment. While a former Major Leaguer with solid credentials might earn significantly more, playing in the IBL is not the way to riches.

Second, the lack of depth on most pitching staffs, the resultant prolific hitting, and the sometimes wide gaps between the strongest and weakest players and the best and worst teams detract somewhat from the character of the Italian game when compared to its American or Japanese counterpart. High scores, for instance, result from the fact that the quality of pitching drops significantly from a team's two best starters to its bullpen. Thus, if a starter falters, the middle- or late-inning relievers lack the talent to prevent the game from too often degenerating into a softball-like slugfest. The gaps between the best and worst teams are larger than one finds in American professional leagues. While the league champion often wins 70 or even 80 percent of its games, teams in last often lose the same percentages of games. Rimini, 2002 champs, posted a .722 winning percentage, while cellar-dwelling Paterno won only 7 of 53 for a percentage of .132. In 2004 Grosseto's pitching so dominated the league that the team set a record for winning percentage at .879, finishing 47-7, but just four games ahead of Bologna's 43-11, .796 second-place effort. In the league basement Saim Rho went only 6-48, for a percentage of .111. In 2014 the Grosseto squad, often a contender, hit bottom with a 3-39 record. However, the 1997 Verona team wins the futility award, far exceeding the 1962 Mets by losing all of its games to finish 0-54. This record is hardly surprising given that the ERA of Verona's pitching staff exceeded 11.00.

Despite its problems Italian baseball has produced one Major Leaguer, Alex Liddi of the Seattle Mariners, and several prospects before and after him. In 1997 Claudio Liverziani, then a young outfielder from Juventus Torino and later one of the biggest stars of FIBS, was signed by the Mariners and posted a respectable .262 average with the Single-A Wisconsin Timber Rattlers but slumped the next year and was released. The same year another Italian player, speedster Davide Rigoli, was signed to a Single-A contract by the Montreal Expos but hit only .178 in limited duty and returned to star for the Grosseto club the next year. Andrea Castri, a power-hitting third baseman signed by the Yankees in 1998 and assigned to low-A Oneonta, hit .241 with a couple of homers and 14 RBI in 141 at bats. The next year, at high-A Greensboro, he was released after dropping to .195-4-24. Two players—outfielder Mario Chiarini and first baseman Giuseppe Mazzanti—spent 2000 on the Mariners in the Arizona Fall League. Neither was offered a Minor League contract, but both are continuing long, successful careers in the IBL.

As for pitching, besides Glorioso in the earlier days, Italy has had two prospects: Alex Maestri and Luca Panerati. Maestri spent five years (2006–10) in the Chicago Cubs' farm system, making it to AA and a career record of 24-17 before being sidetracked with a shoulder injury. After a year in the independent Minors and another back home with Rimini, he traveled to Japan in 2012 to join the Orix Blue Wave, where he has become a valuable reliever. His three-year record of 14-9, 3.50, with 130 strikeouts in 160 innings earned him a spot on the 2015 roster. Panerati, signed at eighteen by the Reds in 2008, spent two years in A ball, compiling a 16-14 record before returning to the IBL in 2012.[3] Showing potential in the 2013 World Baseball Classic, at just twenty-four Panerati, a lefty, may yet get another look from MLB clubs.

Of course, Alex Liddi is the pride of Italian fans, having become the first player to grow up in Italy playing baseball to reach the American Majors. The jury is still out on Liddi's fate in MLB. After wowing the Mariners by batting .313 as a seventeen-year-old in the 2006 Arizona Fall League, Liddi enjoyed a productive Minor League career and debuted with the Mariners during a late-season call-up in 2011 based on his stellar power numbers: .266-30-104 at Triple-A Tacoma. He spent significant parts of 2012 and 2013 with the big club, generally struggling at the plate before his contract was sold to the Baltimore Orioles. When he became a free agent at season's end, Liddi signed with the White Sox but was released in May before the Los Angeles Dodgers offered him a contract. As a result, Liddi spent 2014 with three Minor League clubs in three different leagues, falling to AA with his combined season numbers dropping to .207-11-45. It is likely that all of the bouncing around did not help him, but at only twenty-five Liddi could still make the Majors and stick.

It is not surprising that Liddi ended up with the Dodgers, since the team has been quite active in scouting Italy for young homegrown talent. In 2014 Frederico Celli hit .343 for the club's Arizona League team, and more recently the Dodgers signed sixteen-year-old outfield prospect Federico Giordani.[4] Six other players have been signed since 2006 out of MLB's annual European Elite Baseball Academy, but after brief stints in the AZL or low Minors ended up playing in the Italian leagues. These Italian players demonstrate that Italy is consistently beginning to yield MLB prospects. The academy, held in Tirrenia, Italy, in 2014, offers Italian and other European players an opportunity to display their talents as well as have access to coaching from former Major League players and coaches. Developing players the quality of those in the Americas or Japan will take time, but increased MLB interest in Italy could hasten the process.

Though not comparable to American or Japanese baseball, Italian baseball compares favorably with that of other European nations, and even internationally the Italian national team, Gli Azzurri (the Blues), as they are called, have managed to win some games. In the European Championship, a biennial tournament of national teams, Italy has won ten times and finished second sixteen times and third three times in the thirty-three tournaments played. In short, they have finished in the money in all but one tournament. Of the sixteen runner-up finishes, all but one has come against the powerhouse Netherlands, which has won twenty-one tournaments and finished second in seven. However, in the European Cup, the annual tournament of professional rather than national teams, Italian teams have won thirty-three of the fifty-one years the cup has been contested to Holland's twelve. Like other European teams, the Italian nationals have had less success off the Continent, compiling a 52-79 mark in the international World Championship tournament, 8-23 in Olympic matches, and 4-7 in the World Baseball Classic. While these international records are hardly impressive, they are respectable in view of the limited popularity of baseball in Europe.

Italy has qualified for all three World Baseball Classics. In 2006 the Italians started strong, pounding Australia 10–0 in a game stopped after seven innings due to the mercy rule. Italy then lost the next two games, 6–0 and 8–3, to Venezuela and the Dominican Republic, respectively, finishing third in the group. In 2009 the Italian team surprised WBC fans with a 6–2 upset of Canada, while playing powerful Venezuela close in the early innings of their two losses. Though Italian Americans Paul Catalonotto, Nick Punto, and Chris Denorfia anchored this team, the three Italian league players—Chiarini, Mazzanti, and Davide Dallospedale—combined to bat a competitive .267, with Mazzanti leading the way at .357.

The 2013 Classic was a breakthrough for Italian baseball. Not only did the team advance beyond the group stage for the first time, but the roster also boasted seven homegrown players as opposed to just two in the first WBC and five in the second. Two of these were the aforementioned pitchers Alex Maestri and Luca Panerati, both of whom performed well. The former won his first start against Canada, had a no-decision against Puerto Rico despite four and a third scoreless innings, and finished with an ERA of 1.23. The latter pitched three scoreless innings as the starter against the United States and retired two batters in relief to stifle a rally in the Italians' 6–5 victory over Mexico. At the plate Liddi and Mario Chiarini each hit only .235 but contributed 3 RBI each and played well in the field. Finishing 2-3, the Italians led in every game and kept the scores close in their losses, dropping a 6–2 game to the United States in group play, before losing twice by a single run to eventual finalists Puerto Rico and the Dominican Republic. Granted, much of the team's success was driven by Italian Americans—in this case, Anthony Rizzo, Chris Denorfia, and Chris Collabello—yet the homegrown *raggazi* acquitted themselves respectably among the world's baseball elite.[5]

Portarmi Via allo Stadio; or, Take Me Out to the Ballpark

To a baseball-savvy American, Italian baseball, although it is improving, would probably not even look as good as Major League Soccer would to an Italian, but the game offers any fan a pleasant experience at the ballpark. While attendance is often optimistically listed as between five hundred and two thousand, crowds are generally closer to the low end of this average, although playoff games may reach the higher figure. The small crowds are detrimental to league coffers, but they ensure that everyone has a great seat. In addition, the crowd size promotes camaraderie among fans that leads to conversation about the game and

26. Italian National Team playing in the 1978 world championship, Parma, Italy. (Photo by Maurizio Bonazzi.)

allows children to roam freely, never far from their parents' eyes. Most fans are very knowledgeable, and though scorecards are unavailable for sale at the park, usually more than one fan is keeping score in a score book brought to the game. Fans root passionately, often creatively cursing umpires and opposing players, yet the rowdy behavior that mars European soccer and increasingly threatens sporting events in the United States is conspicuously absent.

The lack of rowdyism is likely attributable to the fact that no one at the game is drunk. Italians may be famous for producing wine, but they drink it largely with meals or by the single glass when taking respite in a bar or café. For most people, to become conspicuously drunk is considered a social disgrace and would not be tolerated in the social space of a ballpark. Alcohol is not sold in the stands, but then neither is anything else. No hot dogs, peanuts, or Cracker Jacks. When Italian fans want refreshment or respite, they repair to the small bar in each park. Fans may wander down to the café for a quick espresso, *apertivo*, or *panini*, but the most they will carry back into the stands is a bottle of water or a cone full of gelato. This behavior likely results from cultural attitudes toward eating. Italians tend to view food as something to be savored *a tavola* during leisurely meals, not eaten on the run or in the steady snacking that Americans commonly practice in U.S. ballparks.

The ballparks themselves, as mentioned, are about the size of older A-ball or spring-training venues, with capacities ranging from one to seven thousand. As would be expected, the parks consist of a main grandstand behind the plate, usually covered, with uncovered bleachers extending down each baseline. The grandstands are made of concrete but often without the ballpark chairs common in U.S. parks. Fans sit on the concrete, or at best a small plastic seat without a back. Some fans, however, bring lawn chairs and set them up in the stands. Although small, the parks often have distinguishing characteristics. At Bologna, for instance, a ceramic baseball about three feet tall graces the entry and displays a plaque honoring Gianni Falchi, journalist, baseball pioneer, and the man for whom the park was named. Nettuno boasts an impressive entryway, with *Stadio Steno Borghese* in large sea-blue lettering contrasting with the white facade of the circular home-plate grandstand. Florence's park offers a Lilliputian charm, dwarfed by the nearby home of A. C. Fiorentina soccer, a stadium befitting an NFL team. At Grosseto, though the stadium is a rather shabby concrete affair, it sits in a beautiful city park, adjacent to a café with expansive outdoor seating under bright Cinzano umbrellas. Fans congregate here before and after games, to socialize not just with each other but with the players. One such night when I was there, Jaime Navarro, not long out of the American Majors, was there hanging out with teammates and chatting with fans. To any tourist unfamiliar with baseball, the players would be unrecognizable as they enjoy a pre- or postgame snack and *apertivo*.

More striking than the parks themselves are their settings, with postcard views from the grandstand. In Florence the Tuscan hills rise above the tiled roofs of the small palazzi making up the tidy middle-class neighborhood beyond the outfield fence. Down the left-field line at Bologna's Stadio Gianni Falchi, fans can see high-rise apartments, symbols of modern Italy, above a line of lush greenery, while in center and right olive-tree groves blanketing the hillsides evoke the nation's agrarian roots. B-level Macerata in the Marche region plays in a modest park sloping away from the walled medieval hill town the team calls home; below is a wide valley of green fields ending against the rugged horizon of the Apennine mountains. At Livorno's home field, "I Mori" via Sommati, fans can smell the salt air as they look beyond the outfield fence to see the trains of the Napoli–Torino line wending their way up and down the Tuscan coast.

Transplanted to Italian culture, baseball ultimately suffers a lack of popularity but enjoys a strong commitment from a coterie of devotees. In other words, professional baseball in Italy has exactly the status American Major League team owners fear: it is a game appreciated and supported by a knowledgeable few, a group of what we call "purists" in America, but it has not achieved the status of sport as business, as in the United States. The continued interest of MLB and the increased quality of young homegrown players, some of whom will crack the American Majors, will eventually broaden baseball's small place in Italian sporting culture. Nevertheless, with soccer by far the nation's dominant sport and "national pastime," it will likely be decades before baseball, though increasingly emerging from obscurity, appeals to more than the passionate fan. And therein, perhaps, lies its beauty.

Italian Baseball Terms

> batting average: *media battuta*
> catcher(s): *recevitore, recevitori*
> center fielder: *esterno centro*
> fan(s): *tifoso, tifosi*
> first base player: *primo baso*

home plate: *casa* (literally "house," since the Italian language does not distinguish between house and home)

home run(s): *fuoricampo, fuoricampi* (literally "outside field")

infielder(s): *interiore, interiori* (players are identified specifically by base: *primo baso*)

left fielder: *esterno destra*

outfielder(s): *esterno, esterni*

pitch: *lancia*; wild pitch: *lancia pazza* (literally "crazy pitch")

pitcher(s): *lancitore, lancitori*

player(s): *giocatore, giocatori*

right fielder: *esterno destra*

run: *punti*

runs batted in: *punti battuti in casa*

second base player: *secondo baso*

shortstop: *interbaso*

singles, doubles, triples: all are cognate words resonate with English, *singoli, doppie, tripli*

stolen bases: *basi rubati* (bases robbed)

strikeout: no translation; Italians use the English word

third base player: *terzo baso*

umpire(s): *arbitro, arbitri*

wild pitch: *lancia pazza* (literally "crazy pitch")

NOTES

1. Information on the history of Italian baseball is compiled from Josh Chetwynd's *Baseball in Europe: A Country by Country History* (Jefferson NC: McFarland, 2008) and "La Storia" Federazione Italiana Baseball Softball, http://www.fibs.it/it-it/La-Storia-della-Fibs-aspx.

2. Statistics on Italian players and teams are taken from the current FIBS home page, http://www.fibs.it; the now defunct FIBS website run by Enzo DiGesù, http://monviso2.alpcom.i/.digesu; and *Baseball/Softball '97*, the 1997 edition of *Tutto Baseball e Softball*, edited by DiGesù. Baseball-ref-

erence.com, which is increasingly adding information on international leagues and players, provided stats on homegrown Italians who have more recently played in the American Minor Leagues. I would also like to thank DiGesù for information he provided in a series of emails in the early stages of the initial version of this paper. Other useful websites for information on Italian baseball are Baseball Italia (http://www.baseballitalia.com) and Mister Baseball: All about Baseball and Softball in Europe (http://www .mister-baseball.com).

3. Statistics on Italian players in the American Minors come from baseball-reference.com.

4. Dustin Nosler, "Dodgers Sign Outfielders Yadir Drake and Federico Giordani," September 2, 2014, http://dodgersdigest.com/2014/09/02/dodgers -sign-outfielders-yadir-and-federico/.

5. Statistics and records on Italy's performance in the WBC come from "World Baseball Classic: Italy," http://www.worldbaseballclassic.com/teams /index.

20

Holland

An American Coaching *Honkbal*

Harvey Shapiro

I remember walking to the mound with a runner on second base and a left-handed hitter coming to the plate. I had every intention of walking the batter with first base open, in a one-run game, and facing the right-handed hitter following him. However, Jan Hijzelendoorn, the righty pitcher, and my catcher, Paul Smit, felt we could get the lefty from Team USA out with off-speed pitches away. I reluctantly let Jan Hijzelendoorn pitch to Barry Bonds. We got him out on a grounder to the second baseman. That fall of 1984 I was coaching the Dutch National Team. Would I be the last manager to decide to pitch to Barry Bonds with a base open?

That was not the only major decision I had to make as the Dutch head coach. My role went way beyond calling pitches, making lineups, and giving signs. A more important job was to change the approach and strategies of the Dutch baseball players and baseball community.

Dutch baseball, called *honkbal*, got its start in 1910, and two years later the Royal Dutch Baseball and Softball Association (KNBSB) was founded. The game began to grow during World War I, when American soldiers visited Holland. The American soldiers stationed in Europe played games in Holland, and the Dutch took a liking to baseball. Holland is a small country, and although its favorite sport is soccer, the Dutch people who played and followed baseball became dedicated and passionate about the sport. There are now an estimated thirty thousand baseball and softball members of the KNBSB.[1]

Wanting to improve its status and baseball performance, the Dutch Baseball Federation has long encouraged baseball teams from America to visit and play against Dutch players and teams. My Dutch baseball experiences began in just this way, in the spring of 1975 with the Springfield College baseball team. After I finished my third year as a graduate assistant at Springfield College, working with the legendary college baseball coach Archie Allen, we were invited to Holland to play exhibition games and put on clinics.

The Kinheim Baseball Club of Haarlem and its members hosted the trip. Kinheim played baseball in the *hoofdklasse* (head class) of Holland, which is the highest level of baseball. The Springfield College players and coaches stayed with club members during our visit.

The baseball system in Holland, like other countries in Europe, is quite different from in the United States. In the United States sports such as baseball are played at the interscholastic and intercollegiate school levels. In Holland there are no interscholastic or intercollegiate school teams, though occasionally Dutch schools would have "fun" games between city schools. These games were informal with no qualified coaches to teach or coach baseball. Instead, physical education teachers organized them. In addition, there were no public parks with baseball fields where kids could play pickup or informal baseball. The only way a youngster could play baseball would be in a family club that sponsored baseball. These were private clubs in which a family paid a membership fee to belong.

There were various leagues based on the teams' abilities, with the top league level being the head class. The organization of the leagues was such that every game was significant no matter where a team was in the standings. At the end of the year, the last two teams in the head class were demoted to the first class for the subsequent season. The best two teams in the first class were promoted to the head class. It was a great approach to keep up player and fan interest throughout the season. Because the goal of a team was either to move up in a league classification or stay at the same level, it did not matter if the two best or two worst teams in the league were playing. No team wanted to be relegated to a lower class.

There is a national champion in each class of baseball. After the Dutch baseball playoffs end, a European tournament is held every two years, made up of the champions from the various baseball-playing countries in Europe. Each club team is allowed to have two American or foreign players on its team. The most financially sound clubs would typically sign Americans in order to put the best possible team on the field. Occasionally, there would be an American coach, and I was later fortunate enough to become one of these coaches.

Our Springfield College team spent approximately three weeks in Holland in 1975. We traveled all over the country to play different clubs. The Dutch teams did not have many pitchers on their teams, which meant many high-scoring games for us. We played clubs from the different classes, and we went through the competition pretty easily, undefeated at 7–0, until we lost our last game against the Dutch National Baseball Team, 3–2.

We played several games in the rain until we finished the game or until it was impossible to play. The Dutch were used to rainy conditions, and the weather did not seem to affect them. Their attitude was that the weather could be worse tomorrow, so why not play today?

One significant difference between American and Dutch baseball is the small size of the playing fields. Because land is at a premium in Holland, and the people building the baseball fields did not envision baseball growing in popularity the way it has, the majority of baseball fields are quite small compared to college fields or town fields in the United States. A typical Dutch field may just be 270 feet down the foul lines and 320 to 330 feet to center field. Most fields are not symmetrical because the baseball facilities must be stuffed into the available space.

Compared to American players, the Dutch players were not as strong. Many of our student-athletes played other sports, including

American football and basketball, and did strength training. Though many Dutch players were tall and athletic, they lacked upper-body strength. Most Dutch kids play soccer and cycle for exercise, which do not build upper-body strength. Charley Urbanus, a Dutch player who did graduate work at Springfield College in 1980, took weight training and brought it back to the baseball establishment in Holland, where others followed his example.

The Amstel Tigers

After my first trip to Holland I thought it would be nice to coach there sometime in the near future. In 1979 I got that opportunity when the Amstel Club wanted an American coach. The Amstel Tigers were located in Amsterdam, along the Amstel River, and were one of the strongest clubs in the head class. Two of their board members, Han and Charlie Urbanus, were among the most knowledgeable baseball people in Holland. A very notable baseball player was "young" Charley Urbanus, Han's son.

When I arrived in Amsterdam I went to the Urbanuses' home and met with Han, old Charlie, and young Charley. We discussed the team's strengths and weaknesses and evaluated all the Tiger players. It became apparent at that meeting that I had been brought to Holland to win a championship. The Tigers were one of the most talented teams in the head class with several players on the national team, but the team had not yet won a league championship. The club promoted Dutch baseball and its players and was the only club in the league that did not have American players on its squad. The administrators believed that having Americans in the lineup would hurt the Dutch players' development. The majority of Americans who played in Holland were normally the key positional guys—pitchers, catchers, and shortstops. As I later found a lack of quality Dutch players at these positions, I could understand the Tigers' philosophy. Yet they believed that an American coach was necessary to win a championship.

At the first practice with my new team, I tried hard to put names to faces. I was surprised by how much batting practice the players took. We batted for an hour and a half, which I later learned was normal in Holland. The Tigers also practiced offensive and defensive situations, which most Dutch clubs did not emphasize. This was the influence of old Charlie Urbanus.

My first baseball game was two days later, a Saturday, and I was excited to begin my coaching experience. We won on both Saturday and Sunday. There were a few situations during the weekend that made me realize that coaching Dutch baseball was going to be different from coaching in America.

The Dutch players' approach to the game was more laid-back and less structured than my American college players. It was common for the Dutch to have tea or coffee and sandwiches before they took the field for pregame practice. Many smoked a cigarette in uniform, even when walking around the field. I could not believe that the players would consume food and caffeine before a game. During the seventh-inning stretch, the players would have a snack and drink, such as tea, cola, or coffee for energy. I wanted to change these "bad" habits, but I realized it would take time and much convincing.

After Sunday's game I was feeling pretty good about our two wins. Therefore, I was surprised to be called to an emergency meeting with the team's administrators. They were concerned that I did not play the backup right fielder in either game of the weekend. They thought that he might quit the team if I did not give him one start on the weekends. I reminded the group that they had emphasized how important it was for the Tigers to win. It was the proverbial conflict of "social/ fun versus winning." Oh, well, maybe it was not that different from college coaching.

The league schedule was 36 games spread out over eighteen weeks with 2 games per week. Most teams did not have much pitching, but you did need at least two starters. Later, when I coached the national team, I convinced the Dutch Baseball Federation to play a third league game on Wednesdays. I believed that for the Dutch players to improve, they needed to play more games. After all, it was normal for American college players to play 50 games or more in the spring and another 40 to 50 games in the summer.

The Dutch youngsters, ages eight to fifteen, were similar to American kids. After that American baseball players develop more rapidly than the Dutch because they receive much more exposure to the game. I believed the number of games played per year made a significant difference in how they improved. The Dutch are three or four years behind the Americans. Because there are no collegiate or high school sports in Holland, the only baseball experience for the Dutch players was the league format. It would take a Dutch player three years to play as many games as played by a Division I player in the United States, since a U.S. player typically plays fall and spring baseball on campus and a series of summer-league games.

In spite of their limited playing experience, some Dutch players have succeeded at the highest levels of professional baseball. Wim Remmerswall, a right-handed pitcher, played in the Red Sox organization and was with the Major League club in 1979 and 1980. He had a hard time adjusting to American baseball and left the Red Sox to return to Holland. He later played in the Italian professional baseball league. Another Dutch success was Bert Blyleven, a pitcher with one of the best curve balls in the Major Leagues. Blyleven was a Dutch native, though he moved to the United States with his family as a child. After winning 287 games over his twenty-two-year Major League career, Blyleven was inducted into the National Baseball Hall of Fame in 2011.

Umpiring was another strange facet of Dutch baseball. Many of the Dutch umpires had not grown up playing baseball and did not have a real feel for the game. In club baseball the umpires were basically volunteers, and, as a result, it was difficult to criticize them. They made some of the games an adventure. Some umpires felt they were as important as the players. I thought some bad calls were made by the umpires to bring attention to themselves. The Dutch players would get very upset and emotional over the bad calls, but there was not much you could do. Like the weather, the umpires were just part of the normal baseball landscape in Holland.

That first season, 1979, our Amstel Tigers won their first championship. We finished the season with a 30-6 record and a 14-game winning streak. Considering that games were only played on weekends, we went seven weeks without losing a game. My club was ecstatic, and, as per Dutch tradition, I got dumped in a dirty canal. In the spring of 1980 my family and I returned to Holland, and again the Amstel Tigers were the national champions.

Despite the team's success, the Dutch media could be annoyingly negative. In the United States I was used to reporters being generally positive in their analysis, reporting the outcome and key happenings in the game. At home most reporters realized that my college baseball players were amateurs, and they did not analyze them like professional athletes. In contrast, the Dutch media dealt with their players and teams like we do in the tough media cities of New York and Boston. The Dutch players attend school or maintain regular jobs as teachers, doctors, businessmen, and so forth. They play baseball as a hobby. They are amateurs, not professional ballplayers. Yet the sportswriters were mercilessly critical. I later found that it was easier for our team to play in baseball tournaments abroad, where there were less scrutiny and less pressure on everyone.

The Dutch National Team

In 1983 the Dutch National Baseball Organization was looking for an American baseball coach because the Dutch were going to host the World Baseball Championships for the first time. I was honored when I was hired to coach the Dutch National Team.

The KNBSB thought we should develop a three-year plan geared toward success in the World Championships in 1986. The format of international baseball competition is similar to American football and Major League Baseball (MLB) playoffs and the World Series. International baseball tournaments are short-term affairs, like a World Series, with each game taking on more significance, resulting in a lot of pressure on the players and coaches to perform well.

As I reviewed the results of the previous international tournaments, I noticed the Dutch teams were competitive in most games, but consistently gave up a big inning of three or more runs that took them out of a game. The starting pitchers seemed to go too long. I did not think we would have starting pitchers who could last six or seven innings against countries like the United States, Cuba, Taiwan, and Japan. I thought we should use more pitchers for fewer innings. Bart Volkerijk was probably the best Dutch pitcher with the most international experience. My thought was to make Volkerijk our closer and use the younger pitchers as starters and middle relievers so that they would have less pressure on them. I believe it is easier to start a game than to close a game; the toughest outs are in the seventh, eighth, and ninth innings. Next I had to convince Volkerijk to embrace this new strategy. He agreed to give my idea a try. Nevertheless, I did not anticipate the uproar over this decision—Dutch baseball people, media, and fans thought that Shapiro was crazy or stupid. Take the best pitcher and make him a reliever—what nonsense!

I spent many weekends watching Dutch club baseball in order to select the best players for the national team. I held practices on Wednesday nights with an elite group of Dutch players until the final group of players was selected. The first major event for the national team was the Haarlem Honkbal Week in mid-July. Other than the European Championship, it is the most notable tournament in Europe. The stadium in Haarlem is like an old American Minor League ballpark with seating of approximately seven thousand.

The tournament is a weeklong round-robin event, with the best teams meeting for the championship on the final day. I was anxious to see how my team would perform. I tried to instill a philosophy of unselfish teamwork to the players and encouraged them to play "National League" (American) style baseball—be aggressive on the

27. The Dutch National Team in 1986 in Haarlem. Manager Harvey Shapiro is in the foreground. (Photo courtesy of Harvey Shapiro.)

bases, stealing, hit-and-run, and generally play "small ball." I did not want to sit back and wait to score with just base hits, as I did not think we would hit enough against our international competition. I was especially curious about my new pitching strategy—using two or three pitchers a game with Bart Volkerijk closing for us. The team was young, and I had to be patient, reminding myself that we were looking to the future. I told the players that we wanted to improve with each game and that we had to play the process (nine innings) and not just play for the win. Yes, we wanted to build our team confidence, which comes with winning, but it was more important that we improve and set the stage for the future.

After the festive opening ceremonies, with all the teams parading on the field, we opened the tournament against Taiwan. The Taiwanese hit a home run in the second inning, and then we scored three runs. My starter and midreliever pitched well, and I could have finished the game without using Volkerijk. But I wanted to see how he would handle the closer role. He had an easy one-two-three ninth inning, and we won the first game 3–2 in front of five thousand enthusiastic Dutch fans.

We finished the round-robin play in first place, putting us in the Haarlem Championship game against Team Canada. My first coaching experience with my national team was going well; even the Dutch press seemed to be impressed with the team. That would soon change. In the final game the score was tied 1–1 going into the top of the seventh inning when we fell apart. Canada scored ten runs after two were out and nobody on base. After such a successful week of playing good baseball, that one inning devastated us. In the press conference after the game, the media really gave me a tough time—the reporters wanted to know how I had let it all happen. My six-year-old son, Scott, was with me in the pressroom, and he whispered to me that his T-ball team did not always win either.

In October we traveled to Curaçao for my team's first competition outside of Holland. During our week in Curaçao we practiced and played exhibition games against some of the countries that were going to participate at the Amateur Baseball World Championship. Since there was a gambling casino in our hotel, I gave the team a 2:00 a.m. curfew. As this was the beginning of our trip, I stayed up and oversaw the casino area. I was more exhausted than the players, but they adhered to the curfew, though many did not like having any restrictions placed on them. I reminded the players that there would be no smoking or drinking in uniform. I wanted the players to play and act like national athletes representing their country.

From Curaçao we departed for Cuba. Because of Cuba's tight security, flights arrived and departed from the country only at night so that nobody could see their military installations. Consequently, we arrived in Cuba in the middle of the night. During the two hours it took to get through Cuban customs, we had our luggage meticulously inspected. The customs officers spent more time with my belongings. Was it because I was an American, or was I just a little paranoid?

There was a constant military presence during our visit. Even on the trip to the practice field, our bus was escorted by military police. During practice there were soldiers stationed at the field and on each dugout; one was positioned with a machine gun. About one hundred Cubans watched us practice.

As the Twenty-Eighth Amateur Baseball World Championship began, Cuba was the favorite. Cuba had long been the strongest baseball country in the world, and there was no reason to believe that its dominance would not continue. The Cubans had several players who not only were professional baseball prospects but could probably then play in the Major Leagues. At this time Cuban ballplayers had not yet started to defect to the United States.

The opening ceremonies were held at Guillermon Moncada Stadium in Santiago. The beautiful stadium, which reminded me of an American Minor League park, was filled to its capacity with an estimated twenty-five thousand people. On the following day we won our first game against Taiwan. It was a great win for the Dutch in the World Championship, and I was treated like a celebrity in the postgame press conference. For one day we were tied for first place in world competition, but it did not last. Though we played well at times, my Dutch team finished with a record of 1-8, losing eight straight heartbreaking games. Nevertheless, I was happy with the performance of my younger players in their first year of international competition. Holland is a small country, after all, without a long, rich baseball tradition.

The Cuban team showed its superiority and won the World Championships again. In the final game the Cubans easily handled Team USA. The young American collegians could not compete against the highly skilled Cuban veterans. The Cuban team played an aggressive, intimidating, free-swinging type of baseball, reminiscent of the old St. Louis Cardinals, the Gashouse Gang of the 1930s. They were also similar to the Oakland A's in their championship years in the 1970s, taking the extra base and often sliding with their spikes high. The Cuban pitchers threw inside and sometimes appeared eager to throw at hitters early in the game, to set the tone, not unlike Roger Clemens. The Cuban players had a swagger and cocky nature. They believed that they were the best players and the best team. From the World Championships I learned a good deal about how other cultures approach the game. It seemed that most Latin American countries tried to copy the Cubans but did not have their dominating talent.

The Latin American teams played a very emotional style of baseball. When things did not go well, the players and coaches were vocal and not afraid to yell at each other, the umpires, or the opposing team. The players were somewhat unpredictable and could change their moods from inning to inning. It was difficult to read the opposing team and determine how they were going to compete. Our game against the Netherlands Antilles was a good example—the Antilles players did not seem to be in the game, and we were ahead 7–0 in the seventh inning. Then all of a sudden, with one hit, the Antilles Team got excited, and we could not get them out.

The Americans, who are noted for their good pitching, sound defense, and power hitting, were easier for me to coach against because of their predictability and my own U.S. heritage. One major adjustment players and coaches of American teams have to make when they compete internationally is the intensity of international tournaments. U.S. players are accustomed to playing long college seasons without great pressure until tournament time. In contrast, each international game is magnified in importance. Also, international teams are normally made up of older veteran players, while American teams are college-age players with little or no international experience. It can be intimidating for young Americans playing on foreign soil to compete against the Cubans and good teams from other countries. The American teams are also selected and play together for short periods of time compared to foreign teams, which have years of experience competing together against other countries.

I found the Asian teams—Taiwan, Japan, and South Korea—to be fundamentally sound both at the plate and in the field. Seldom did the Asian players make mental mistakes. Their practice sessions were fun to watch because the teams were so structured and spent far more time practicing than non-Asian teams. No matter how hot, cold, or rainy, the coaches staged long workouts until they were complete-ly satisfied with their players' performance. Offensively, the Asians played a more conservative style of baseball and tended to play for one run at a time. With no outs in the inning, you could bet that the hitter would bunt to advance a base runner or runners. If there was a runner on third base with one out or no outs, the batter was likely to execute a suicide squeeze. Only if their team were a few runs ahead, would they be more aggressive offensively, such as stealing with one runner on base or trying to double-steal.

One area that set the Asians apart was the unorthodox style of their pitching, as most threw sidearm and submarine. Asian pitchers also tended to be economical with their pitches and did not walk many batters. Their coaches were quick to pull a pitcher from the game if his control was a problem. On the other hand, if an Asian pitcher were throwing well, his coach would let him continue to pitch, with-out concern for the pitch count. In addition, if a pitcher was hot, you might see him pitch on consecutive days regardless of the number of pitches or innings he had recently thrown. The health of the player did not appear to be paramount, albeit it is easier for a sidearm or subma-rine thrower to recover and come back the following day. While the Asians were not as physically big or strong as the American players, their teams were tough to beat because of their discipline and sound fundamentals. They were always fun to watch.

The European Championship

As I prepared for another summer with the Dutch National Team, our main goal in 1985 was to beat Italy and win the European Championship. Reflecting on my first year with the team, I was deeply concerned about the mentality and work ethic of some of my players. I believed that it was an honor for a player to be selected for the team, and he should play and conduct himself accordingly. From then on we would select players based on both ability and mental makeup.

The European Championship in 1985 included six national teams—Belgium, Italy, the Netherlands, San Marino, Spain, and Sweden. In reality, only two, Italy and the Netherlands, would be competitive. The others were not yet strong enough to beat us or the Italians.

For our first game against Italy, six thousand fans arrived early to our ballpark in Haarlem and were singing and chanting in unison. They were loud and hostile to the opposition. I thought that their presence might add more anxiety to my players than to the opposition since we could understand what was being said, while the opposing Italians could not. With a home run by my designated hitter and a porous Italian defense (five errors), we took an early lead and won the first game, 5–4. I felt it was important for us to win the first game from a psychological standpoint. Our starter, Jan Hijzelendoorn, pitched six strong innings, giving up four runs. Bart Volkerijk came in the seventh and shut down the Italians. Volkerijk was probably the best pitcher in the tourney coming out of the bullpen. We tried to put a lot of pressure on the Italian pitchers and their defense as we planted the seed in their heads that we were going to run at every opportunity.

In the second game with Italy, in front of seventy-five hundred fans, we jumped out to a four-run lead in the first inning and never looked back. The final score was 6–4. We knocked out their starting pitcher in the first inning. One more win, and the Dutch would regain the European Championship.

The next day we were back at it. I sensed that the Italians were down—their players had the look of guys who did not want to be at the ballpark. If we could take an early lead, it could be an easy game. The stadium was again packed with excited fans. We were ahead 3–2, going into the bottom of the fifth inning, when our team scored seven runs and routed the Italians, 12–4. We were the European champions again!

In the press conference after the game, the Dutch newspapermen appeared confused about what to ask in such a positive setting. They downplayed our achievements by saying the Italians were much weaker this year because, for the first time, their team used only "real Italians" to play. I tried not to mind the Dutch media and just enjoy our victory.

Conclusion

Let me close with a few words about the 1986 Baseball World Championship, which Holland hosted and for which the Dutch National Baseball Organization had initially hired me three years earlier (to build the national team). The event, played in four Dutch cities—Haarlem, Eindhoven, Rotterdam, and Utrecht—was a two-week round-robin competition with ten other qualifying countries (Belgium, Columbia, Chinese Taipei, Italy, Japan, Netherlands Antilles, Puerto Rico, South Korea, the United States, and Venezuela). A new baseball park with lights was built in Eindhoven just for the event, while two other stadiums got new lights.

I knew playing eleven games in a two-week period would test my Dutch players physically and mentally. I was also concerned about the stress on my team playing at home. Although it is normally advantageous to be the home team, the pressure on the Dutch players before a critical hometown media could be difficult.

We completed the tournament with a 5-6 record, tied for seventh place. Cuba was the champion with an 11-1 record. Overall, I was pleased because before the tournament my goal was for our team to place in the middle of the group. In Cuba two years before, we finished in last place, and now we showed that we could compete. From the viewpoint of the Dutch people, our seventh place was disappointing because we were one game behind the Italians.

In Europe today Holland and Italy continue to dominate the baseball scene. The Dutch players are still some of the strongest on the Continent. There are a few players who are in America playing professional baseball at the Minor League levels. In 2004, with professional players now allowed to play, the Dutch baseball team qualified for the Olympics and finished sixth in the tournament of eight teams. Some of the Dutch players were actually pros from the Netherlands Antilles.

How will the Dutch fare in future international competition? Since I coached the national team, the Netherlands has continued to be competitive in world competition. Because it is a small country, with a small pool of baseball players from which to choose, along with inclement weather and the dominance of soccer, Dutch baseball will be hard-pressed to reach higher levels. The availability of Antilles players with professional baseball backgrounds can significantly improve the team's tournament stature, but it would be unrealistic to think that baseball in the Netherlands could reach the echelon of a world baseball power. Nevertheless, those involved in the "American pastime" in the Netherlands have embraced the charm and excitement of baseball.

Epilogue

The Dutch National Team and its place in international baseball have changed significantly since I first wrote this chapter in 2005.

For one, the Dutch team's roster is no longer made up of amateur players from Holland and a few Antillean players who live in Holland. The Dutch National Team is now called the "Kingdom of the Netherlands Team," combining European Dutch with the Dutch Caribbean players who have resided in Aruba, and especially Curaçao, where baseball is very popular. There are also some Americans and other foreigners of Dutch descent on the newly formed Kingdom of the Netherlands Team.

For the most part, the players on the Kingdom of the Netherlands Team are professionals who play or have played Major and Minor League Baseball in the United States. As a result, the Netherlands team is now more competitive on the international level against the likes of world powers such as Cuba, the United States, the Dominican Republic, and Japan, among others.

The Dutch Caribbean influence has significantly changed the Netherlands' place in the world rankings. The Caribbean players, having grown up and lived in a warm climate where baseball is played year-round, have attracted MLB scouts, who follow the development of the players' projected baseball and athletic skills. The scouts sign the best players to American professional baseball teams.

Although there are people in Dutch circles who would have preferred two separate national teams, the winning ways of the combined Kingdom of the Netherlands have reduced the grumbling in Holland, according to Steve Matthew, a former Dutch baseball player, coach, and scout.[2] The Kingdom of the Netherlands Team has brought tremendous baseball success in international tournaments and higher world rankings than ever before.

Well-known Major League Baseball players such as Dutch Caribbeans Andruw Jones, Sidney Ponson, Andrelton Simmons, and Xander Bogaerts have elevated the Kingdom of the Netherlands to a higher baseball status. Among the biggest upset surprises included wins over Cuba in the 2000 Olympics and the 2007 Baseball World Cup Tournament and beating the Dominican Republic twice in the 2009 World Baseball Classic (WBC).

The Dutch also won the 2011 Baseball World Cup, upsetting the United States and Cuba twice. It was the first time since 1951 that a country other than the United States had beaten the Cubans to win an international tournament. It was the best finish ever by the Kingdom of the Netherlands. Winning the 2011 World Cup was looked upon as a great accomplishment by the entire sports world in the Netherlands. Even though *honkbal* still lags significantly behind soccer in popularity and player participation, Dutch sports fans were excited and proud to win the World Cup.

With baseball no longer an Olympic sport, the World Cup and World Baseball Classic are now the two premier world baseball tournaments. Unlike the World Cup with its Minor League players, the World Baseball Classic includes teams with both Minor and Major League players. Because the World Baseball Classic occurs during the Major League spring-training season, Major Leaguers are able to compete and, as a result, raise the level of competition, making the wbc the most prestigious international tournament.

In the last wbc, in 2013, twenty-eight countries competed. Two former New York Yankee players, Hensley Meulens and Robert Eenhoorn, coached the Kingdom of the Netherlands Team.[3] The Kingdom of the Netherlands did not win, but it did reach the semifinals, making it, in the minds of many, an even greater accomplishment, because of the participation of so many Major Leaguers on wbc teams, than winning the World Cup in 2011. Remarkably, the U.S. and Cuban teams finished behind the Kingdom of the Netherlands Team.

In 2009 the International Baseball Federation created a world-ranking system based on international tournament results. After its 2011 success the Netherlands was considered the fifth-best baseball country in the world. Following their 2013 World Baseball Classic finish, the Dutch were considered the sixth best in the world of baseball.

Baseball in the Netherlands is not necessarily more popular today than it was years ago, at least not in terms of the number of people playing or watching the game. But young, talented Dutch *honkbal* players do have more opportunities to develop their baseball skills and to receive more media attention due to Major League Baseball International's outreach in promoting baseball in Europe and Holland's recent success in international baseball competitions. There are now six baseball academies in the Netherlands with skilled professional baseball coaches teaching youngsters how to play the game. Their efforts have promoted the game and produced many talented Dutch ballplayers.

With the continued development of a small number of young Dutch players and the great influence of Dutch Caribbean players participating in American professional baseball, the Kingdom of the Netherlands should continue to prosper and be a significant team on the world's biggest baseball stage, the World Baseball Classic.

NOTES

1. John Tagliabue, "In Netherlands, Soccer Is King, but Baseball Eyes Crown," *New York Times*, May 21, 2008, http://www.nytimes.com/2008/05/21 /world/europe/21dutch.html?pagewanted= print&_r=0.
2. Steve Matthew, email interview with the author, September 21, 2014.
3. Hensley Meulens was the manager, and Robert Eenhoorn was an assistant coach. For many years, Eenhoorn was the manager of the Dutch National Baseball Team and technical director of the Royal Dutch Baseball and Softball Federation. An executive with baseball background, expertise, credibility, and administrative abilities, Eenhoorn has helped elevate Dutch baseball.

BIBLIOGRAPHY

Bloom, Barry M. "Domi-nation: Dr Runs Table en Route to Title." March 20, 2013. http://m.mlb.com/news/article/42998208/domi-nation-dr-runs -table-en-route-to-world-baseball-classic-title.
Royal Netherlands Baseball and Softball Federation. http://www.knbsb.nl.
Stoovelaar, Marco, and Organizing Committee Haarlem Baseball Week. "Haarlem Baseball Week History, 1961–1998." http://home.planet.nl/~stoov /hhwhis.htm.

21

Great Britain

Baseball's Battle for Respect in the Land of Cricket, Rugby, and Soccer

Josh Chetwynd

In 2012, when I sat down in the broadcasters' booth to prepare to do television color commentary for Great Britain's first foray into the World Baseball Classic (WBC), I smiled thinking about how far British baseball had come since I first experienced that nation's version of the game sixteen years earlier.

As a player I joined the Great Britain National Team in 1996, just weeks before the European (B-Pool) Championships. Even though I'd grown up in the United States, I was eligible to join the team by virtue of being born in England. It was truly a different experience. The first game I played on British soil was on a makeshift diamond that doubled as a cricket pitch. The squad, which at the time represented the best Britain had to offer (I was the only player on the team who had never previously played in country) was sturdy: we would win the B-Pool championships that summer, beating the likes of Lithuania and Croatia, despite not having many players with topflight baseball experience.

Fast-forward to 2012 at the WBC qualifier and the GB National Team was now squaring off against the well-established baseball-playing nation of Canada—as well as Germany and the Czech Republic—in a beautiful stadium in Regensburg, Germany. The British squad was nothing like the one I'd played on many years before. Unlike that GB team, this roster was flush with former and current Minor Leaguers as well as four players—Jake Esch (Miami Marlins), Michael Roth (Los Angeles Angels of Anaheim and Texas Rangers), Chris Reed (Miami Marlins), and Antoan Richardson (Atlanta Braves and New York Yankees)—who had or would play in the Major Leagues.[1]

Great Britain's rise to a respectable perch in international baseball has been a long journey. To be sure, for most people the phase *British baseball* sounds like an oxymoron. In fact, before I joined the gb National Team, I would have been one of those guys who asked, "Don't the British just play cricket?"

But to examine the game's British history is to learn a more than century-old story that includes kings, Major League Baseball (MLB) players, captains of industry, and periods of some excellent baseball.

You don't have to look any further than a blustery day more than a century ago to get a taste of the British game's intriguing history. On March 12, 1889, the Prince of Wales settled into his seat at the Kennington Oval, one of England's most famous cricket grounds, to watch baseball. The game between teams of American professionals was part of a tour set up by the great baseball entrepreneur, manager, and former player A. G. Spalding and featured, among others, future Hall-of-Famer Adrian "Cap" Anson. By all accounts the man who would become King Edward VII watched every move intently, staying until the last out as the Chicago White Stockings beat the "All-America" team, 7–3, in a muddy, rain-soaked game.[2]

Following the contest the future king of England began to stroll away when a newspaper reporter caught up to him and asked for his impressions of the game. The Prince of Wales looked the journalist in the eye, thought for a moment, and then asked for the reporter's notebook. He jotted down a small note and walked away. The next day the prince's statement was printed as part of the game account: "The Prince of Wales has witnessed the game of Base Ball with great interest and though he considers it an excellent game he considers cricket as superior."[3]

Since then the British royal has, for the most part, spoken for an entire nation. In fact, the prince may have been more positive than many of his subjects. Nevertheless, some of the characteristics that have helped Britons through the ages—namely, resilience and an abiding optimism—have also ensured that, in down times, British baseball has persevered. And as the country's inclusion in the World Baseball Classic indicates, the British Isles may well be in the midst of a period of promising baseball growth.

In the Beginning

It all started in 1874, when the Boston Red Stockings, winners of America's professional championship the summer before, and the Philadelphia Athletics traveled to England to introduce baseball to Britons. Curious crowds attended these events (July 31–August 25) in such cities as London, Dublin, Liverpool, and Manchester. It was not a success. Newton Crane, a British baseball organizer and former U.S. consul in Manchester, England, wrote in 1891 that the tour failed to spark interest because "the game of baseball was not understood, and in the short hour or two devoted to the exhibition matches but little idea of it could be acquired by the bewildered spectators."[4]

It took fifteen years and one of baseball's great early visionaries, A. G. Spalding, to bring longer-lasting British attention to the sport. Spalding, who played nearly every role in the world of baseball—player, manager, owner, sports equipment manufacturer—organized a world baseball tour in 1888. The magnate took two teams of baseball players—the Chicago White Stockings, the team he managed back in the United States, and a mixed squad of players dubbed the "All-Americas"—around the globe to the Sandwich Islands, Australia, New Zealand, Ceylon, Egypt, Italy, France, and finally to Great Britain.

The Americans arrived in England in March 1889 and played eleven games throughout the country, drawing considerable crowds. Some eight thousand spectators attended the game in London that was attended by the Prince of Wales, and four thousand watched a match in Bristol, despite the weather being "exceedingly unpropitious," according to British baseball organizer Crane.[5]

Overall, the British reaction to the baseball tour was, in the words of historian Peter Levine, "lukewarm."[6] Its efforts to build interest in the game might have failed, like the 1874 tour, if it had not been for a group of young collegians who followed up the Spalding extravaganza by spending their 1889 summer vacation in England. Instead of just playing, they actually taught the game. They also set up matches throughout the country, establishing teams of both American and British players, a marked difference from the previous approach. As there is no substitute for playing, many of the Britons who got a taste of baseball were hooked. In October 1889 a group of enthusiasts formed the National Baseball League of Great Britain and, with the help of Spalding and his associates, planned a professional league to commence play the following season. Four of England's top soccer clubs—Aston Villa of Birmingham, Derby County, Preston North End, and Stoke—decided to start franchises in the new professional baseball circuit. Still, there was one big hitch: very few British athletes had played more than a game or two of baseball before. With that in mind, the organizers supplemented teams with young Americans to serve as instructors and players.

When games began in May, the performance of the players was considered solid, according to *Spalding's Official Base Ball Guide* of 1890. While the Spalding guide was not an objective publication, considering its benefactor's involvement, it is worth pointing out that Jack Devey, a Brit who also played for Aston Villa's soccer team, bested all the foreign imports to win the league batting title with a .428 average.

But there were problems. Many in the media were not keen to accept baseball, fearful that the sport might encroach on cricket's dominance in the summer months. Further, some reporters did not believe that there was genuine interest in the game. "The baseball business is being 'boomed' with a vigour of which is a little too obviously artificial for the average Englishman," said a June 16, 1890, article in the *Birmingham Daily Post*. "The phlegmatic Briton does not care to have a pastime

28. In 1890 Derby was the British baseball team to beat. Run by industrialist Sir Francis Ley, Derby was poised to become the first champion of British baseball, but a controversy led Ley's club to withdraw. Perhaps the club's greatest legacy was that until 1997, Derby's soccer team played at the Baseball Ground, the home of the baseball team. (Photo courtesy of the National Baseball Hall of Fame.)

which has considerable amount of the advertising element about it foisted upon him."[7]

It certainly did not help the game's cause that there was on-field controversy during the season. The Derby team, which was run by a leading industrialist, Sir Francis Ley, had more foreign players (three) than any other club. As a result, within the first month of the season Derby won enough games to clinch the championship. The other teams protested, and Ley agreed to only use his ace American pitcher against Aston Villa, the league's second-best team. When Derby reneged on that promise, however, the other team leaders were furious, and Derby pulled out of the league. Aston Villa was then named the league's champion, while Preston North End won the separate Baseball Association of Great Britain and Ireland Cup competition. Contemporary British baseball historians and organizers regard Preston as the first English champion.[8] Sadly, between the league's high cost and the lack of an immediate attendance boom, Spalding never fully invested in British baseball again, and the circuit folded after just one season.

Still, the circuit did leave a legacy. Most notably, as a result of the initial attention the league generated, the sport made substantial progress as an amateur game during the next twenty years. A number of the country's top soccer clubs followed the lead of the teams from the 1890 season and developed baseball teams for the short summer off-season. Along with Derby County, which continued to be a force in baseball and even played soccer, until 1997, at a stadium called the Baseball Ground, such soccer powerhouses as Arsenal, Tottenham Hotspur, and Nottingham Forest formed baseball teams.

By the start of the twentieth century, baseball had a place in British society. In 1906 the British Baseball Cup attracted around twenty-five hundred fans to White Hart Lane soccer ground to watch the home team, the Tottenham Hotspur Baseball Club, win the national championship.[9]

In British baseball's official history, there are no national champions listed between 1912 and 1933. But during this period, in 1913 and 1914, Major League Baseball did try to spur international interest in baseball with its first world tour since Spalding's 1889 effort. If the Americans had hoped to woo the British public on their London stop, their actions did just the opposite. The London leg of the four-month tour between the New York Giants and the Chicago White Sox was booked for mid-February. Alas, despite plans to play multiple games, the weather limited the visitors—who included future Hall of Famers Tris Speaker, Sam Crawford, and Urban "Red" Faber, as well as former Olympic hero and baseball player Jim Thorpe—to a single contest in London on February 26, 1914.

Even if the tourists had put on an unforgettable show, baseball appeared to lose momentum during this period. No doubt, World War I was a key factor for this diminished interest. As would later be the case during World War II, baseball did not have deep-enough roots to sustain interest during wartime. The influx of Americans into the country during the war did lead to extensive play, but it was almost exclusively among American and Canadian soldiers. In 1918 the Anglo-American League was set up in the London area for the entertainment and recreation of the American and Canadian forces.

Following the war the game had difficulty getting going again. In the fall of 1924 baseball supporters set up a series of exhibition matches between the Chicago White Sox and the New York Giants in London, Liverpool, Birmingham, Dublin, and Paris. Unfortunately, the games did not get a full or warm welcome. In Dublin, for example, an exhibition was scheduled for an afternoon start but was played instead at 11:00 a.m. so as to not conflict with an important cricket match. Overall, the media was dismissive of the tour. As the *Washington Post* reported, "In England they were satisfied with saying that baseball was nothing but glorified [children's game called] 'rounders' and that Henry Chadwick, father of the game, was born in the United Kingdom."[10]

The Golden Age

It took a man who had made his fortune in the world of gambling to facilitate baseball's golden age in Great Britain. Sir John Moores founded the Littlewoods Football Pools Company in 1923, which was a form of legalized gambling. Moores first became involved with baseball in 1933, when he formed the National Baseball Association in response to a challenge by the president of the National League, John A. Heydler, to spur British baseball growth. A skilled organizer, Moores had established eighteen amateur baseball teams in two leagues within a few months of Heydler's dare.

With Moores's business acumen and financial backing, baseball began to flourish. In 1935 Moores decided to form a professional organization called the North of England Baseball League, based around

29. A baseball game in the Liverpool area, ca. 1930. Under the stewardship of businessman Sir John Moores, baseball grew rapidly in Liverpool in the 1930s. Moores started three professional leagues throughout Great Britain, including one league that was made up of teams in and around Liverpool. Note the netting to separate fans on the playing field and the distance at which the catcher positions himself behind the batter. (Photo courtesy of the National Baseball Hall of Fame.)

Manchester.[11] The reaction of some in the baseball community was trepidation. "This is a daring move," wrote the *Liverpool Echo*, on the eve of the pro circuit's debut. "I know that sound judges would have liked such a development to have been deferred until [British baseball was at] a more mature moment."[12]

Undeterred, Moores barreled ahead with the new venture. The players were mostly Americans and Canadians with solid baseball credentials and respected athletes from other sports, such as Jim Sullivan, who is regarded as one of the greatest Rugby League players of all time. Typical of the foreigners was Stanley Trickett, a player for the Belle Vue Tigers, who previously was the captain of the baseball team at the University of Kentucky.

That said, even with the supplement of seasoned players, it was clear that domestic participants wouldn't master the rules of baseball overnight. During the 1935 season officials were concerned that excessive base stealing was leading to extreme scoring (a team scoring twenty runs in a game was common). The promoters considered banning stealing altogether, but the Americans and Canadians protested vigorously. The reason for the high number of steals was not a flaw in the rules, said one experienced player, but rather the result of English pitchers not being able to hold the runners on base. The English pitchers were throwing out of the windup—a no-no with runners on base—instead of the stretch. In spite of such hiccups, most teams in the league drew between one and three thousand spectators, with games between front-runners getting five thousand or more.

The next year Moores formed two new professional leagues—the Yorkshire League and the London Major Baseball League—to go along with the North of England Baseball League.[13] With three pro circuits spread throughout the country, Moores was now covering a tremendous amount of territory.

Owners in the North of England League became more aggressive in terms of recruiting during their second season. The expansion Liverpool Giants had six members with American playing experience, and—between the North of England League and the nascent Yorkshire League—every decent ballplayer in the northern part of the country seemed to be a pro.

While the Yorkshire and North of England leagues were competing for players in the Midlands, which is in central England, and the North, the London Major Baseball League had its pick of top talent in the South. In 1936 there was little doubt that the London league was the best in the country. London's star player was West Ham's Roland Gladu, a French Canadian who had previously played Minor League Baseball for the Montreal Royals. Gladu, dubbed "the Babe Ruth of Canada," would eventually go back to North America and play in the Major Leagues with the Boston Braves in 1944. The London league was so strong that following the 1936 Olympics in Berlin, the U.S. Olympic baseball team traveled to the British capital to play two teams, White City and West Ham. (Baseball had been an exhibition sport at the 1936 Olympics.) Although the Americans prevailed against White City, West Ham beat the U.S. Olympic squad, 5–3.[14]

In 1937 the Yorkshire League became the top circuit, replacing the London Major Baseball League as the place to play. The Yorkshire teams heavily imported American and Canadian players to enhance their squads, and they poached some of the London league's best foreign players, leaving very few British athletes on the field. Yorkshire's Leeds franchise, for instance, had only one English player. British baseball historian Ian Smyth points out that the influx of excellent foreign talent—particularly pitchers—led to some complications in the North, with low-scoring games becoming the norm. For uninitiated baseball spectators, pitchers' duels were relatively boring. Nonetheless, many fans still came out, as evidenced by the eleven thousand who watched Hull win the National Baseball Association Cup against the Romford Wasps, 5–1.[15]

Down in the South, baseball was beginning to fail as a professional sport. Stadium operators in London grew restless when the sport didn't quickly produce sizable dividends, and only the Romford Wasps and the West Ham Hammers had top-caliber players in 1937. After that season the league folded, and teams like the Wasps became amateur clubs. Moores's rapid expansion left too few good players to go around. The London league suddenly had a marginal product.

But even in the North, where interest was much stronger, the sport was also beginning to stumble, as organizers began purging foreign players with dire consequences. In 1938 the Yorkshire League and the North of England League merged to become the Yorkshire-Lancashire League. The major difference with the new circuit was that each club was limited to only two professionals. This was done to allow British players to develop, and it effectively dropped the top level of baseball from professional to semiprofessional.[16] By 1939 attendance appeared to be waning. The loss of professional teams, which certainly lessened the quality of play, probably contributed to the loss of interest.

The professional leagues aside, perhaps Britain's greatest success in the global baseball community took place in 1938, when the country won the first-ever World Amateur Baseball Championship. The story began in August 1938, when the U.S. Olympic baseball team arrived in Plymouth for a five-game "test series" against England. At the time there was no talk of a world championship. The U.S. squad was prepping for the 1940 Olympics in Tokyo. It was composed of high school and college players. As for the English team, it was made up almost entirely of players born in Canada who were playing in Britain at the time.

The series was set for August 13–19 in Liverpool, Hull, Rochdale, Halifax, and Leeds, and attendance was impressive. In front of ten thousand fans in Liverpool, Ross Kendrick defeated curve-ball pitcher Virgil Thompson to lead England to a 3–0 first-game victory. Kendrick threw a two-hitter, striking out sixteen. Two days later England won 8–6 in front of five thousand spectators in Hull. The Americans took the next game, 5–0, in Rochdale, but England won the next two games. In Halifax Kendrick returned to the mound, shutting out the United States for the second time, 4–0, and then England won again, 5–3, in Leeds.[17]

Following the series the International Baseball Federation designated the contests as the first World Championships and named Great Britain the inaugural world amateur champions.

We will never know whether British baseball players would have reached the levels of their North American counterparts because World War II ended the Yorkshire-Lancashire League as players of all nationalities went off to war. During the conflict Allied soldiers played recreational baseball. The London International Baseball League was a highly competitive eight-team circuit that played in front of large crowds of primarily Allied soldiers. In addition to league games, many exhibitions were contested during the hostilities. On August 7, 1943, for example, the U.S. Air Force played the U.S. Ground Forces at Empire

Stadium, Wembley, before more than twenty-one thousand spectators.[18] Still, the game lost its hold on the British consciousness, and a British championship would not be contested again until 1948.

Postwar Baseball

After the war baseball tried to reclaim its place in the British sports landscape. With a huge number of North American soldiers still in the United Kingdom, the sport had enough experienced players to return to minor prominence. In London baseball received solid coverage in local newspapers, and teams in the North—most notably in Hull and in Stretford near Manchester—were also developing capable baseball teams.

Nevertheless, these teams often depended on foreign athletes, a fact not lost on British baseball pundits. The July 16, 1953, issue of *Baseball News*, a British baseball periodical, ran an editorial revealing the concerns about non-British involvement: "The scarcity of 'home-produced' players has led to an increasing demand for the services of visitors to this country who are 'ready-made' ballplayers. Whilst U.S. Servicemen are in England it is natural that there will be a large number of them competing in British baseball, . . . [but] there will naturally be a difference should there be a future decline in the numbers of 'guest stars' available. It is for this fact alone that all teams should concentrate on building up 'local talent' side by side with the experienced men."[19] This concern was prophetic, as the number of military personnel who were seasoned ballplayers diminished through the 1950s and into the 1960s. With the departure of these Americans and Canadians, the quality of baseball suffered.

Another factor that probably contributed to baseball's stagnation was that the sport was becoming regionally fragmented. Signs of this appear as early as 1952. In June a squad from England traveled to the Netherlands to play and was criticized by London's *Evening News* for having a bias against southern players. According to the paper, the Sutton Beavers, which was a particularly strong team in the London area, sent the names of its three top players, but they were rejected. In the end only one player from the South was named to the team. Later in the summer southern organizers retaliated by forming their own squad—dubbed an England team—to play an international game against a Canadian all-star team.

By the late 1960s organizers in the North (centered in Hull) and the South (with clubs mainly in London and the surrounding "home counties") clearly appeared to be focusing on their own areas. Despite winning the silver medal at the 1967 European Championship in Belgium, the country had difficulty putting together a consistent, cohesive national squad. International play in 1969 was emblematic of the factional nature of the game in that period. Representative teams from both South Africa and Zambia traveled to Great Britain to play separate series. Instead of British baseball's governing body forming a single national side, various regions put up all-star teams against the foreign competition. Four areas emerged as baseball centers between the late 1960s and mid-1990s: Hull, Nottingham, Liverpool, and Greater London. During this period teams from in and around these cities won practically every national championship.

British Baseball in the New Millennium

The cycle of optimism and despair about British baseball continues. In 1987 the Scottish Amicable Life Assurance Society, a British-based insurance company, agreed to sponsor British baseball. The three-year sponsorship was said to be worth three hundred thousand pounds. With the funding the British Baseball Federation (BBF) formed the Scottish Amicable National League. Its purpose, according to the organization's official newsletter, was to provide British baseball with a "'shop-window' that gives [the] sport credibility by staging games for the sporting public to the best possible standards."[20]

Many involved with baseball at the time said that the sport was gaining ground on other sports. It also helped that Major League Baseball was being televised by the national network Channel 4 and by Sky Sports. Alas, in 1990, the one hundredth anniversary of organized baseball in Great Britain, Scottish Amicable pulled out. The reasons are unclear. Some suggested that British baseball's leadership misused funds, while others insist that the sponsorship just ran its course. Whatever the case, future sponsors of Great Britain's National League—including Coors and Rawlings—were not as generous as Scottish Amicable.

But today there is hope. In 2000 the BBF joined with the Baseball Softball Federation to form BaseballSoftballUK, an umbrella organization whose aim is to increase interest and funding in both sports. Though there was initially sporadic grousing from some members of the British baseball community about the power BSUK wielded, it is hard to deny the organization's effectiveness. Whereas in the past unpaid part-timers developed the game, BSUK's professional staff has been able to focus full-time on generating resources. For instance, BSUK secured a grant of three hundred thousand pounds in 2005 from Sport England, a public entity that supports athletics in the country. The organization has continued to bring in a steady stream of funding for baseball and softball.

The development body's most notable baseball victory has been the creation of a national baseball and softball complex in southern Britain. In July 2013 the new facility opened at Farnham Park. It includes an adult field featuring proper dimensions (330 feet down the lines and 400 feet to center field), a grass-and-dirt infield, permanent fencing around the field, and sunken dugouts. A second full-sized field was added in 2016. With plans for similar setups elsewhere in the country, this type of infrastructure investment could definitely pay dividends in player development and general interest in the sport.

Internationally, Great Britain has also had some shining moments. In 2007 the British team won a silver medal at the European Championship. It was its first major international hardware since 1967. And the inclusion in World Baseball Classic qualifiers also boosts the nation's baseball profile. While the team finished third at that 2012 event (ahead of the Czech Republic, but behind Canada and Germany), it did bring some worldwide attention to British baseball, as contests were broadcast on MLB.com and Sportsnet in Canada, among other outlets.

In addition, Major League Baseball has maintained a regular presence in London since 1990. Admittedly, MLB's office is responsible for developing the game in Europe, the Middle East, and Africa, but its location in London suggests a certain unique connection to the world's pinnacle league. James Pearce, who is MLB's vice president for international events and the World Baseball Classic, also serves as a tie between the big leagues and Britain. Pearce played on the British National Team in the second-tier European Championship between 1992 and 1996.[21]

Of course, considering British baseball's many moments of boom and bust, it is difficult to tell if the sport is finally ready for sustained growth. Starting in 1997 Major League games were broadcast twice a week on Channel 5, one of the country's five terrestrial television networks. The program featured a London-based studio show that was geared toward the British audience and attracted hundreds of thousands of viewers.[22] The beauty of the setup was that it provided an opportunity for nonfans to happen upon baseball on the television and fall in love with the game. But following the 2008 season the coverage was discontinued, and, while the sport still has a home on pay television, the loss of Channel 5 effectively diminished the chance to expand audiences through television. The reason: only diehard British fans nowadays pay to watch baseball either online via MLB.TV or through the pay channel.

Regardless, while the number of those who actually pick up a bat, ball, and glove regularly in Great Britain is small, their passion is huge. Some of the best athletes have gone to compete at U.S. universities. One British pitcher named Gavin Marshall played two seasons in the Frontier League, an independent professional league in the Midwest. Further good news is that those who just play the game recreationally do so with great joy.

But to prosper baseball in Britain will need more benefactors—like John Moores and A. G. Spalding in the past. Over the years Britons have steadfastly protected their traditional sports. A popular antibaseball chant among detractors is that baseball is "glorified rounders," a child's game that bears a resemblance to baseball. Regrettably, this comparison hasn't changed much in more than a century.

This essay was adapted from *Baseball in Europe: A Country by Country History* © 2008 Josh Chetwynd by permission of McFarland & Company, Inc., Box 611, Jefferson NC 28640. http://www.mcfarlandpub.com

NOTES

1. Fun fact: Richardson scored the walk-off winning run for New York on Derek Jeter's last at bat at Yankee Stadium. Score one for the Brits!
2. Mark Lamster, *Spalding's World Tour: The Epic Adventure That Took Baseball around the Globe—and Made It America's Game* (New York: Public Affairs, 2006), 221.
3. Quoted in Newton Crane, *The All-England Series* (London: George Bell & Sons, 1891), 15.
4. Crane, *All-England Series*, 13.
5. Crane, *All-England Series*, 14.
6. Peter Levine, *A. G. Spalding and the Rise of Baseball: The Promise of American Sport* (New York: Oxford University Press, 1985), 105.
7. *Birmingham Daily Post*, June 16, 1890, 5.
8. See http://www.projectcobb.org.uk/national_champions.html.
9. "Baseball Wins Britons," *Chicago Daily Tribune*, August 19, 1906, B1.
10. "American Players Draw Only 20 Spectators in Dublin," *Washington Post*, November 9, 1924, EF3.
11. The teams in the North of England League included the Oldham Greyhounds, Bradford Northern, Rochdale Greys, Salford Reds, Manchester North End Blue Sox, Belle Vue Tigers, Hurst Hawks, and Hyde Grasshoppers.
12. *Liverpool Echo*, May 4, 1935, 7.
13. The inaugural teams in the Yorkshire League were the Greenfield Giants, Hull Baseball Club, Wakefield Cubs, Bradford City Sox, Sheffield

Dons, Leeds Oaks, Scarborough Seagull, and Dewsbury Royals. The 1936 London Major League Teams were the White City, West Ham, Hackney Royals, Harringay, Romford Wasps, and Catford Saints. The Streatham and Mitcham Giants were also a founding member but folded weeks into the first season.

14. Harold Seymour, *The People's Game* (New York: Oxford University Press, 1990), 288.

15. See Allan Colin, "How Hull Won the Cup in 1937," http://www.projectcobb .org.uk/articles/How_Hull_won_the_cup_in_1937.pdf.

16. An ill-fated renegade league called the International League tried to start up that year but went out of business after only a few weeks. See Ian Smyth, "The Story of Baseball in the North of England," *Leeds Polytechnic Faculty of Cultural and Education Studies* (1992): 1–52.

17. Ian Smyth, "Baseball Put to the Test," *Baseball Research Journal* 24 (1995): 131–33.

18. Gary Bedingfield, *Images of Sports: Baseball in World War II Europe* (Charleston SC: Arcadia, 1999), 73–74.

19. "The 'Overseas' Influence," *Baseball News* (July 16, 1953): 2.

20. Don Smallwood, "The National League," *Touching Base: Official Newsletter of the British Amateur Baseball/Softball Federation* [ca. 1987]: 15.

21. "James Pearce Resigns from the BSUK and BBF Boards," September 28, 2011, http://www.baseballsoftballuk.com/news/view/james-pearce-re signs-from-the-bsuk-and-bbf-boards.

22. Full disclosure: I worked on the show for the better part of eight seasons.

22

Finland

Pesäpallo, Baseball Finnish Style

Mikko Hyvärinen

In the early twentieth century Finland was a country of forests, lakes, and small towns. It was, in other words, much like contemporary Finland. It was also a country with a growing number of sports fans, some of whom experimented with different sports. The Finnish version of baseball—*pesäpallo*—exemplifies this. As most Finns know, *pesäpallo* owes its existence to the Finnish sports expert and proselytizer Lauri "Tahko" Pihkala, who invented the game.[1] In this way *pesäpallo*'s story is atypical. After all, most sports evolve. But just as Dr. James Naismith invented basketball, Pihkala created *pesäpallo*. So although history is (and should be) more than a narrative about a single person, Pihkala is an exception to the rule. Without him *pesäpallo* as we know it would not exist.

The Origins of *Pesäpallo*

In 1958 Martti Jukola, the father of Finnish sports history, wrote, "Finnish ball games from the past are well known. These ball games have been played primarily in rural areas and there have been many versions of them."[2] At the end of nineteenth century, he added, bat-and-ball "games spread across the nation and these could be considered the first widely played team sports in Finland. The most popular among them was king ball," or, in Finnish, *kuningaspallo*.[3] King ball, also sometimes called "four strikes" (*neljä lyöntiä*), had local variations, as it had no official rules. However, certain features of the game were shared nationwide, including that pitchers threw the ball vertically (that is, straight up in the air, like one does to serve a tennis ball), while standing relatively close to the batter; after striking the ball, the batter tried to reach the so-called outer base (the end-of-the-field line) and get back to the batting line; and any runner hit by the ball was called out. After an out the defensive team went to bat, and the offensive team went into the field.[4]

Tahko Pihkala, a top Finnish track-and-field athlete as well as a physical education instructor, made several visits to the United States during the early 1900s. He became interested in baseball during his first trip, in 1907, during which he saw a Boston Red Sox game. At the time there were many stick-and-ball games played across Europe, but Pihkala found baseball the most similar to Finland's king ball.[5] While he considered some aspects of baseball fascinating, he was disappointed by the game's slow pace; in fact, Pihkala was amazed that such a "boring" game could be so popular and bring American spectators so much joy.[6] Returning to Finland, Pihkala had ideas about how to develop a faster-paced and more appealing version of baseball, but it took several years and a few more visits to the United States before he was able to modify the game the way he wanted.

What Pihkala liked about baseball from the beginning was its explicit rules and that the game's winner was determined by which team scored the most runs (not by how many batters it had sent to the plate). In 1914 he wrote the first official rules to his uniquely Finnish version of baseball, a game he also called "king ball." In Pihkala's game there were nine players in the field, a player was entitled to hit the ball three times (including foul balls), and two foul pitches allowed base on balls. After three outs the teams switched from offense to defense (instead of one out in an earlier version of king ball). The field was rectangular, and running took place only between home and the outfield base. Stealing a base was not allowed.[7]

Anxious to improve his version of king ball, Pihkala invented another bat-and-ball game he called long ball (*pitkäpallo*) in 1916. The details of long ball are not important here; the point is that Pihkala continued to innovate. After the First World War, Pihkala's experiments had birthed *pesäpallo*. In *pesäpallo* there were more bases, just like in baseball, but the first, second, and third bases formed a triangle (thus making the base running more challenging).

Pihkala was confident that the first open exhibition game in 1920 would please the Suojeluskunta (a Finnish right-wing militia organization) leadership. He was wrong. Of the more than twenty authorities on a panel assessing the game, only two supported adding it to the Suojeluskunta training program. Undaunted, Pihkala organized another exhibition the next year. The players—some of whom were members of the Suojeluskunta leadership—gave the game highly positive feedback.[8] Pihkala's luck had changed. He found that if people played *pesäpallo*, they loved it.

Ideology behind *Pesäpallo*

It is impossible to understand *pesäpallo* without understanding Tahko Pihkala, who was a typical Finnish sports educator for his era. Politically, he leaned heavily to the right, as did most Finns from the Ostrobothnia region during the early twentieth century. At the time the eugenics movement appealed to many Finnish educators. And thus, like many others, Pihkala was highly concerned with young men's physical fitness in light of the possible degeneration of the Finnish people (alcoholism was considered a widespread social problem). Because Finland, in Pihkala's view, lacked athletic activities that would improve its citizens' health, he started promoting *pesäpallo* to the military and schools. He also emphasized cross-country skiing and swimming, but *pesäpallo* was of special significance to him.[9]

According to Pihkala and others, one of *pesäpallo*'s virtues was that it was less gendered than most Finnish games. That boys and girls could play it together in gym classes made it useful in rural schools with small enrollments. Pihkala also believed *pesäpallo* could challenge soccer's rising popularity in Finland. He did not think soccer provided significant health benefits to young men, especially those old enough to serve in the military. Throwing the ball in *pesäpallo* would make young soldiers better at throwing hand grenades, he argued. He compared hitting to shooting, as both required good vision and fine motor skills. He also suggested that base sliding promoted self-protection for soldiers at the warfront under enemy fire.[10] Under Pihkala's influence, the language of *pesäpallo* became militaristic. When a player is "out," for example, he is "dead" (*kuollut*) or "burned" (*poltettu*). When a fielder catches a ball without its touching the ground, it is not a "fly out"; rather, the hitter is "wounded" (*haavoittunut*).[11]

This terminology reveals Pihkala's militaristic mind-set. He thought that such vocabulary was useful: young men in uniform would not be as frightened at the war front if they were accustomed to hearing about casualties from an early age. Pihkala was convinced that sports and warfare were closely connected. *Pesäpallo* was a form of "pleasant militarism," Pihkala explained in a 1976 radio interview. Pihkala frequently noted that sport is essentially "battle practicing" and warfare in the form of play.[12]

Like all of us, Pihkala was a product of his historical moment. Since the late nineteenth century many Finnish physical education teachers had considered it important and patriotic to make boys and men physically ready for rebellion and war, first against czarist Russia and, after the country's independence in 1917, against the "Red" movement. One of the ideologies informing this nationalism was eugenics and a strong belief in the superiority of the Nordic "race."[13] Athletic success— especially that of Olympian runners such as Hannes Kolehmainen and Paavo Nurmi—contributed to Finnish national self-esteem and confidence in the new nation's ability to defend itself. Pihkala was not the only physical educator to think this, but he was the most important individual behind the glorification of Finnish athletic success.

Pesäpallo's Rules

The rules and the general idea of *pesäpallo* have remained largely intact since Pihkala's patriotic friends approved his game, but there have been some notable changes.[14] For example, base stealing and adding an extra inning in order to avoid a tie have been adopted. Still, as is true of baseball in the United States, the game's largely unchanging nature has been an important factor in *pesäpallo*'s continued popularity.

Just like in the old Finnish bat-and-ball games, the pitcher throws the ball upward while standing close to home plate, which enables the batter to easily hit it. That was Pihkala's first and foremost requirement to create more action and overcome the boredom he saw in American baseball.[15] This kind of pitching is the most significant difference between baseball and *pesäpallo*.

The second notable difference is that when the batter hits the ball, it must always make first contact inside the field (that is, there is no home run like in baseball). In *pesäpallo* there is an out-of-bounds line at the end of field. These field-related rules require hitters to be fast runners. Pihkala, a former track-and-field runner, was deeply concerned with the running speed of Finns, especially of short-distance runners.[16] Again, a pragmatic reason shaped the game's rules.

The field's shape is another significant difference between *pesäpallo* and baseball. Pihkala combined the traditional Finnish field with baseball's diamond shape to make the infield triangular and the outfield rectangular. The bases are also different. There are no bags, as in baseball, only base areas to reach and where a fielder must catch the ball before the runner is safe.

In *pesäpallo*, as in baseball, a home run is made by circling all of the bases. But in *pesäpallo* a batter cannot hit the ball over the fence. So a home run is possible due to the field's large dimensions (it is one hundred meters long), the absence of outfield barriers that would prevent the ball from rolling far away, and the base runner's fleetness. This means there is a lot of running for the outfielders, who are much more involved in the game than in baseball. One modern change to Pihkala's *pesäpallo* rules applies to home runs: unlike in the early game, a home run now only requires a runner to reach third base, after which the player remains on third (and the game can continue like he had just hit a triple). This rule change, which took place in 1986, was prompted by low-scoring games that resulted from the increased skill of pitchers.

High-Level Competition

The first national men's championship was won in 1922 by Helsinki Pallonlyöjät, the most dominant team during the 1920s and 1930s, when a majority of the most successful teams were from the more populous and industrialized southern Finland.[17] The game's strongest promoters were militia groups, national military personnel, schoolteachers, Young Men's Christian Associations, and temperance-movement organizations. Their role in the recruitment of talented athletes to the game cannot be exaggerated. In a country the size of Finland, which then had a population of fewer than 3.5 million, it was almost miraculous that by the end of 1930s there were approximately 40,000 officially registered *pesäpallo* players.[18]

While *pesäpallo* was and remains popular in the rural Ostrobothnia region, Finland's southern teams (that is, big-city teams) dominated the game until the 1950s. No team more than a hundred miles north of Helsinki won a national championship until 1953. When the Vimpeli Veto became the first Ostrobothnia regional team to win the national championship in 1960, it started a long period of northern dominance. These teams were from rural regions and small cities.[19] This was an important shift in *pesäpallo*, as it became heavily identified with a rural culture and small towns. The growing popularity of soccer and ice hockey in nonrural areas, especially among young boys, probably contributed to this development.[20] *Pesäpallo* remained a major sporting event in school gym classes, but otherwise most urban adult Finns lost touch with the game.

There have been many efforts to improve *pesäpallo* since the 1980s and 1990s. The results have been mixed. Several sport organizations have wanted to follow the example of ice hockey and make *pesäpallo* a profitable professional sport and increase spectatorship, especially in the cities. Most of the modern rule changes have been adopted for this

30. Ossi Meriläinen at bat during the 2015 All-Star Game. (Photo courtesy of Jukka Rasimus.)

reason. The Finnish state-owned gambling agency, Veikkaus, has long influenced Finnish society and its sports world, increasing the visibility of several sports, invariably those on which one can bet. Particularly in the 1990s, *pesäpallo* leaders thought that the game needed Veikkaus's support. The idea was that it would stimulate other financial activity. Players' salaries increased drastically, enabling many players to be full-time professionals for the first time. Traditional team uniforms with one or two sponsor logos were all of a sudden almost completely covered by corporate logos, like NASCAR drivers. Investors who wanted to bring the game to Helsinki created a new team (Kaisaniemi Tiikerit) and signed top Finnish players. Yet despite two successful seasons in 1997 and 1998, the Tiikerit owners faced serious financial problems and were unable to pay all the players' salaries on time. *Pesäpallo* was not able to attract large-enough crowds in big cities, and the marketing did not produce significant profits. Tiikerit folded after just two seasons.[21]

Pesäpallo also had its own Black Sox scandal in the 1990s. When

Tiikerit faced Hamina Palloilijat on August 13, 1998, the Tiikerit manager and a few players (including star pitcher Markus Meriläinen) manipulated the game, producing a tie after two four-inning sets. Investigations revealed that at least five games were fixed during the season. All told, fifteen players and seven team officials were found guilty of game manipulation.[22] This not only influenced the teams and men involved. The credibility of professional *pesäpallo* was damaged for a few years, and there are still skeptics who do not believe that all the people involved with the game manipulation were indicted. Professional *pesäpallo* remains under heavy scrutiny by the authorities and the general public. What has remained intact, despite all the problems during the past twenty years, is the northern small-town team dominance at the sport's most elite level of competition.

In the women's highest league the regional variation has been almost identical to the men's top league throughout the game's almost one-hundred-year history. That is, the teams from the southern industrial cities were dominant, with more northern and rural small-town teams coming on strong in recent decades. In fact, no southern team has won a national title since 2002. The last twelve national titles (2003–14) have been divided between two northern teams, Lapua Virkiä (five) and Jyväskylä Kirittäret (seven).[23]

The Meaning of *Pesäpallo* in Finnish Culture

Finns have tried to export *pesäpallo*, but it has never caught on abroad. The only successful cases have been among Finnish immigrants in countries where immigration from Finland has been relatively high, most notably in Sweden and Germany.[24] But even in these countries the number of players remains low, and interest in *pesäpallo* is mostly confined to those of Finnish ancestry and to some who find the game's peculiarities—especially its fast tempo—interesting enough to try it.

Conversely, baseball has never been popular with Finns. There are only a few teams in the entire country, and in general the players are immigrants from countries where baseball is popular or Finns who learned the game while living abroad. And because baseball is only an amateur sport in Finland, the quality of the competition is low.[25]

Why is *pesäpallo* important to Finns? What does it mean? First, *pesäpallo* is probably the only sport that is truly Finnish: most sports played in Finland were imported, and therefore *pesäpallo* represents a unique Finnish tradition. Second, Finns have been justifiably proud of their gender-equity efforts since the early twentieth century, and *pesäpallo* represents better than any other sport in Finland the pursuit of such parity. It can be and is played by boys and girls, men and women. Third, it was the first sport in Finland to have its own summer camps, which were first established in the 1930s. All other sports followed well behind *pesäpallo*'s example in this regard.

Finally, it is also important to understand that *pesäpallo*'s support in Finnish small towns and rural areas is extremely strong. The best teams usually come from small communities, and the attendance figures are often exceptionally high in relation to the local population. Vimpeli, one of the most successful men's teams in recent history, had a regular-season average attendance of 2,118 between 2010 and 2014 and a playoff attendance of 2,960. That may not seem like a lot of people, but Vimpeli has only 3,000 residents. In general, the impact of successful small-town teams in Sotkamo, Koskenkorva, Kitee, Kankaanpää, and Alajärvi— all of which have fewer than 13,000 residents—is hugely important to these communities.[26] Nothing else brings national attention, respect, prestige, and money to these towns like their *pesäpallo* teams. Indeed, in many Finnish communities, especially small ones (and most Finns live in municipalities with fewer than 50,000 people), *pesäpallo* greatly contributes to local identity and cohesion, much as high school football and basketball do in the United States.

NOTES

1. *Tahko* means "grindstone."
2. Martti Jukola, *Urheilun pikku jättiläinen* (Porvoo: WSOY, 1958), 776.
3. Jukola, *Urheilun pikku jättiläinen*, 776.

4. The number of players could be decided by the teams playing, and, most important, winning was based not on the number of runs scored but rather on the number of players who came to bat. Antero Viherkenttä, "Pesäpalloilu," in *Urheilumme kasvot, III, Palloilu,* edited by Risto Rantala et al. (Jyväskylä: Scandia Kirjat, 1973), 1095; Ilkka Heiskari and Erkki Valtamäki, *Seinäjoen Maila-Jussit: Juhlakirja* (Seinäjoki: Seinäjoen Maila-Jussit, 2007), 37.

5. "King ball" itself was the first stick-and-ball game in Finland that had at least some set of rules (made by the gymnastics students at the Jyväskylä Teacher Seminar), although they were not written down clearly enough to avoid confusion among players. Viherkenttä, "Pesäpalloilu," 1095.

6. Noponen Paavo, interview with Lauri Pihkala, *Kansallinen unilukkari,* Yleisradio (Finnish Broadcasting Company), January 3, 1976.

7. Viherkenttä, "Pesäpalloilu," 1095.

8. Viherkenttä, "Pesäpalloilu," 1095, 1097; Lauri Pihkala, *Pitkäpallo pelin säännöt* (Helsinki: Otava, 1921).

9. Pekka Kaarninen, *Murheilua: Eli Suomen sinivalkoiset kyyneleet* (Helsinki: WSOY, 2003), 173–78.

10. Erkki Vasara, "Isänmaan ja sodankäynnin asialla: Piirtoja suomalaisesta urheiluaatteesta 19870-luvulta 1950-luvulle," in *Urheilu katsoo peiliin,* the 1999 Yearbook of the Finnish Society for Sport History, edited by Heikki Roiko-Jokela and Esa Sironen (Jyväskylä: Atena, 2000), 15.

11. See also "Official Vocabulary," Pesäpalloliitto (Finnish Pesäpallo Association), http://www.pesis.fi/pesapalloliitto/international_site/vocabulary/.

12. Paavo, radio interview with Pihkala; Lauri Pihkala, *Nykyhetki ja urheiluväen velvollisuudet* (Lahti: n.p., 1917), 4.

13. Anssi Halmesvirta, "Urheilu lääkkeenä: Eräs terveydenhoitoa, liikuntaa ja kansalaisia yhdistävä tekijä viime vuosisadan vaihteessa," in *Urheilu ja historia: Kansakunnan identiteeksi, yhteiskunnan vaikuttajaksi, joukkojen harrastukseksi,* edited by Vesa Vares (Turku: Turun Historiallinen Yhdistys, 1997), 173–76.

14. The English/international version of the rule book: "Official International Rules," Pesäpalloliitto, http://www.pesis.fi/pesapalloliitto/international_site/rules/; "Pelisääntöjen keskeisiä muutoksia" [Key changes to pesäpallo rules], Pesäpalloliitto, http://www.pesis.fi/@Bin/8802355/Pelisääntöjen+keskeisiä+muutoksia.pdf.

15. Viherkenttä, "Pesäpalloilu," 1097.

16. Viherkenttä, "Pesäpalloilu," 1098. The actual change to the outfield foul line came in 1931 and was one of the last and very few rule changes Pihkala made or proposed.

17. Jukola, *Urheilun pikku jättiläinen*, 795–96.

18. Viherkenttä, "Pesäpalloilu," 1100.

19. Viherkenttä, "Pesäpalloilu," 1101–5.

20. Few cities exist where *pesäpallo* and soccer or *pesäpallo* and ice hockey are both widely popular.

21. Juha Suomela, "Urheiluliiketoiminnan haasteet: Vahva brändi taloudellisen menestykseen edellytyksenä," (thesis, Laurea University of Applied Sciences, 2014), 23–24; "Kansallispelin harhaheitto," *Silminnäkijä Documentary Series*, Yleisradio, May 20, 1999, television; "Pesäpallon jokeri-ilmiö." *Ajankohtainen kakkonen*, Yleisradio, September 3, 1996, television; "Miesten pääsarjatilastoja kautta aikain" [Major history statistics of men's *pesäpallo*], Pesäpalloliitto, http://www.pesis.fi/pesapalloliitto/historia /miesten-superpesis-kautta-aikain/. Suomela has made one of the rare studies of sports marketing in Finland, analyzing the "growing pains" of the Finnish professional sports.

22. Matti Paloaro, *Sopupelien varjot* (Tampere: MC-Pilot, 2001), 11–49.

23. Women's *pesäpallo* medalist teams: "Naiset," Pesäpalloliitto, http://www .pesis.fi/pesapalloliitto/historia/mitalistit/naiset/.

24. "World Cup," Pesäpalloliitto, http://pesis-fi.directo.fi/pesapalloliitto /international_site/world-cup/.

25. Brief history of baseball in Finland: "Historia," Finnish Baseball and Softball Federation, http://www.baseball.fi/fin/liitto_historia.php; statistics on men's national team, "International Tournaments," Finnish Baseball and Softball Federation, http://www.baseball.fi/fin/eng_mjturnaukset .php. Finns have participated in international competition since 1984, but not on annual basis. And unlike *pesäpallo*, baseball has caught on only in Finland's biggest cities.

26. According to the July 2015 Finnish census, Jyväskylä was the 7th biggest municipality in Finland, Kouvola 10th, Vimpeli 233rd (317 municipalities in total). History statistics of men's Superpesis League can be found at http://www.pesis.fi/pesapalloliitto/historia/miesten-superpesis-kautta -aikain; Finnish census of July 31, 2015, http://vrk.fi/default.aspx?doc id=8850&site=3&id=0.

Part 7 World Baseball Classic

23

The World Baseball Classic

Conflicts and Contradictions

Robert Elias

The World Baseball Classic (WBC) began in 2006, and thus far three tournaments have taken place. In March 2013 my son, Jack, and I attended the semifinal and final games at AT&T Park in San Francisco. We saw the Puerto Rican team upset the defending-champion Japanese and then lose to the Dominican Republic in the championship game. While we were there *simply* to watch baseball, there's nothing *simple* about the World Baseball Classic. This isn't just a new tournament, but rather a potentially radical departure for baseball, wrought with conflicts, contradictions, and politics. It makes me wonder: Does the WBC serve the sport's best interests?

Major League Baseball (MLB) announced the founding of the WBC in 2005, one week after baseball was dropped from the Olympics. Obviously, the tournament had been in the works for some time. As far back as the mid-1990s, the former head of MLB International Tim Brosnan wondered: "Why can't there be something that is *ours*: that we could *own*, our *own stage*?"[1]

After the September 11, 2001, terrorist attacks, the world overwhelmingly supported the United States. But the goodwill rapidly vanished in the wake of America's military aggression—even souring people on baseball. According to Mark Lamster, author of *Spalding's World Tour* (2006), "As Americans once again find themselves struggling with their nation's role and image on the world stage, baseball's status as an international sport is at something of a crossroads."[2]

Ironically, MLB had been a cheerleader for the foreign policies that had put America in a bad light, through its endless military rallies, fly-overs, camouflage uniforms, recruitment drives, and God Bless America tributes.[3] Yet its WBC was described as "a welcome relief from American unilateralism and xenophobia."[4] Was it really?

Predecessors

Besides coping with America's responses to 9/11, MLB was contemplating its global role. Other nations focused on regional baseball tournaments, especially the World Baseball Cup—which the International Baseball Federation had sponsored since the 1930s. Held only once in the United States and shut down in 2011 (in deference to the WBC), the World Baseball Cup typically featured fifty or more nations. Cuba dominated the tournament, having won twenty-five World Cups. The United States won only three.

But at least the Olympics might display American baseball prowess. The United States won its first Olympic gold in 2000. Yet in the 2003 qualifying round, America was upset by Mexico and was thus eliminated from the 2004 Olympics, which Cuba won. Former U.S. Olympic coach and Los Angeles Dodgers manager Tommy Lasorda spoke for many in the baseball establishment when he exclaimed, "It's a disgrace. . . . Baseball is America's game. It doesn't belong to the Japanese or the Cubans or the Koreans or the Italians."[5]

When the International Olympic Committee eliminated baseball in 2005, it was the first sport dropped since polo in 1936. Most IOC members were from nations where baseball is not widely played.[6] The IOC insisted on World Anti-Doping Agency testing guidelines, which MLB resisted. MLB was criticized for rejecting the National Hockey League precedent of taking a two-week Olympic break. And some, such as journalist Dave Zirin and scholar William B. Gould IV, traced Olympic baseball's elimination to a backlash against U.S. foreign policies since 9/11 and to MLB's domineering approach to international baseball.

The Olympic announcement shook the baseball-playing nations that relied on it to attract private and public funding. Yet MLB didn't put up much of a fight. Team USA did compete (and place third) in baseball's final Olympic appearance in 2008, finishing behind Cuba and South Korea, but MLB had long since moved in a different direction.[7] It had its own Games: the World Baseball Classic.

Nationalities

In America, the land of opportunity and immigrants, the Major Leagues eventually opened its doors to one nationality after another. Immigrants populated the teams, and their respective ethnic communities championed a few superstars. But as the self-proclaimed national pastime, baseball was widely viewed as an assimilating institution, which *blurred* ethnic backgrounds rather than highlighting them. Yet recently it has become not only acceptable, but apparently even desirable, to pit people of different nationalities against each other in American baseball.[8]

This began most noticeably at the "Home Run Derby" held at each year's All-Star Game. With MLB's encouragement derby contestants began drawing the support of ballplayers defined by their nationality. The *Los Angeles Times* reported in 2006, "No sooner had Bobby Abreu's winning blast cleared the fence than two of his fellow countrymen, Johan Santana and Miguel Cabrera, rushed onto the field to drape him in an enormous Venezuelan flag."[9] Some Americans were offended seeing other nations' flags displayed in the United States at "America's game." But MLB was planning a tournament whose success would rely on precisely such nationalistic fervor.

What Kind of Globalization?

According to anthropologist William W. Kelly, baseball hasn't spread worldwide like soccer because it was quickly professionalized in a league format that created powerful commercial interests, which sought to monopolize the proceeds. And baseball was promoted abroad not merely as a sport but rather as the embodiment of Americanism and often as a surrogate for U.S. foreign policy. Finally, baseball took hold in places where U.S. dominance was resisted, through baseball and other vehicles. Baseball was framed by its relationship to one nation (the United States) and one predominant league (MLB). Different baseball styles have emerged (Japanese, Caribbean, and so forth), but the American center monopolizes authenticity and legitimacy.[10]

These arguments lead me to ask what kind of globalization MLB seeks through the WBC. The tournament was purposely smaller than the Major Leagues' own competition among twenty-nine U.S. teams and one Canadian team ending in the World Series. The WBC was crafted to avoid upstaging the American "championship," intentionally adopting the label "Classic" to distinguish the two. Concerns about the World Series led one owner, George Steinbrenner of the New York Yankees, to oppose the WBC. He was fearful of players getting injured and losing training time.[11]

But Steinbrenner worried not only that the WBC might hamper the Yankees' ability to *win* the World Series, but also that the WBC might—even more seriously—be a threat to the *meaning* of the World Series and the Yankees' dynasty. To further establish the hierarchy between the two, the WBC was scheduled during spring training instead of at the season's end—when it might have been viewed as crowning baseball's real champion.

The baseball commissioner at the time, Allan "Bud" Selig, told owners, "This is a time to put the best interests of the game ahead of your provincial self-interest."[12] But are those "best interests" really for the sake of the game, or was Selig instead chastising shortsighted owners who did not realize that a successful WBC might enhance their profits, even if it occasionally risks some of their players?

Controversies

Some controversies arose. During the first WBC a dose of obsolete Cold War politics led the United States to try to block Cuba's participation. The media, including the sporting press, also objected. ESPN, for example, claimed that Cuba was "the only country here under a dictator."[13] China's dictatorship (and its huge 1.5 billion-person market) was given a "political pass." MLB desperately wanted a Chinese team, but China agreed to participate only if Taiwan was forced to use the name "Chinese Taipei" and was banned from using the Taiwanese flag and national anthem.[14]

In the end Cuba's supporters won. The International Baseball Federation threatened to rescind its WBC endorsement, Puerto Rico vowed to withdraw as a host, and the IOC warned that Cuba's exclusion could jeopardize America's ability to land a future Olympics—with or without baseball. The George W. Bush administration finally relented. Even so, the Cuban team was targeted by right-wing exiles, some of whom held signs at the WBC game in Puerto Rico that read "Down with Fidel!" and "Players Yes, Tyrants No."[15]

Japan sought to run the WBC Asia round, but MLB resisted, saying, "If we allow Japan a separate deal, it would ruin the whole business model."[16] While Japan has protected itself better against MLB raids, it still resents U.S. baseball taking its best players. It claimed the finals and semifinals belonged not in the United States but rather in Japan, where baseball (not football) is *still* the national pastime. MLB wanted Japanese participation without its control, fearing Japan could undermine its operation.

When Japan won the 2006 WBC, outfielder Ichirō Suzuki—a star in two nations—claimed it "probably was the biggest moment of my baseball career."[17] As in Japan the WBC has been a big deal to participating nations because of national pride but also because it is a way to push back against the United States and MLB. Korea had the satisfaction of "beating the U.S. at the game they invented."[18] So valued were the

Korean players for that role that they were exempted from mandatory military service. Some Koreans also used the contest against Team USA to protest the long-term stationing of U.S. troops in their country, to protest MLB treating the Korean League as a minor league, and to protest the Iraq War.[19] So much for keeping politics out of the games.

In both the 2006 and the 2009 WBCs, Japan and Korea turned their attention to each other, replaying old colonial tensions and rivalries—stoked by MLB advertisements to sell more tickets. More than forty-five million people worldwide watched the 2009 Japanese-Korean game, and it broke baseball viewership records in both nations.[20]

The Japanese and Europeans strongly objected to the U.S. war on terrorism, which they viewed as America again ignoring the rules of international law. They accused MLB of doing the same thing with WBC rules, which gave Team USA an advantage. In 2006, for example, twenty-two of the thirty-seven umpires in the Classic were from the United States. That same year the U.S.-Japan game featured three American umpires and none from Japan. To help the U.S. team, a pitch-count limit was imposed, which saved American arms but handicapped other teams. In the first round the United States had two days of rest, while Canada and Mexico had none. Additionally, the U.S. team was scheduled to avoid the tougher clubs until the semifinals. The United States was eliminated anyway, but all of these things understandably rubbed other nations the wrong way.[21]

Team USA

Despite having some advantages, Team USA has not done well in the WBC, and MLB has done only marginally better. The 2006 WBC finalists, Japan and Cuba, had only two Major Leaguers between them, although by the 2013 finals there were several more. But *not* Team USA *itself*. While initially regarding the WBC as celebrating "America's game," some Americans began viewing Team USA's performance as shameful and the WBC as undermining the Americanness of baseball. Many U.S. sportswriters signed on to what scholar Dain TePoel has called

"MLB's traditional, neocolonialist objectives, and its jingoistic business model," whereby the United States must not only profit but also win.[22]

Yet MLB has not seemed troubled by Team USA's performance. In 2009 Selig claimed that "focusing on the U.S. team, frankly, is almost irrelevant."[23] While it might be tempting to seek U.S. dominance to reinforce the "American pastime," doing so might undermine the competition the WBC needs to remain attractive. As *New York Post* columnist Joel Sherman suggested, "MLB—without saying it out loud—is essentially indicating it can tolerate some collateral damage in exchange for winning the war for the hearts, minds and dollars of people all over the planet."[24]

MLB International wanted to create an event that would generate revenue during the tournament and also significant profits year-round. The WBC has been a new opportunity to sell advertising, merchandise, broadcast rights, advanced media (including Internet and cell phone), and sponsorships in cooperation with corporate partners such as ESPN, Intelsat, New Era Caps, MetLife, and many others.

MLB Objectives

Other concerns, about player eligibility and the tournament balls, also arose. But in the end it is important to understand the WBC's *meaning* and *purpose*. Rather than considering what *kind* of globalization strategy MLB wants to pursue (and claims it is accomplishing), we might instead ask whether it is practicing globalization at all.[25] In globalization no local institution controls or dominates its market or endeavor. MLB is international and transnational in its sourcing of players and marketing, but is that really globalization?

Since its earliest days organized baseball has fought off (rather than integrated) league and team challenges from within the United States (such as the Union Association, the American Association, the Players League, and the Federal League) as well as from outside the United States (such as the Mexican League). A possible alternative to MLB dominance, the International Baseball Federation has instead also remained America-centric and, as a result, only a minor organization. Even Little League (now called Little League International) ensures that a U.S. team will always get to the Little League World Series, by separating the teams into U.S. and international divisions.

MLB's dominance of global baseball contrasts sharply with the International Federation of Association Football, the governing body for world soccer. Although it obviously has problems, FIFA seeks to strengthen soccer worldwide. During the three years prior to each World Cup, FIFA runs qualifying rounds for all 207 of its member nations. The thirty-two surviving teams play for the World Cup, held over a month's time and rotated among the member nations. As with Olympic team sports, the FIFA system is decentralized, inclusive, and democratic, notwithstanding its recent experience of corruption among its leadership. No one nation or national soccer league dominates FIFA or soccer.

In contrast, although there are baseball federations in 112 nations, MLB markets *itself* abroad more than it does the sport. Only sixteen teams get to play in the WBC, and they are almost entirely preselected by MLB, based largely on the nation's economy as a potential market and revenue source for organized baseball. The WBC finals are held exclusively in one nation, the United States. MLB, through the WBC, centralizes global baseball under its almost totally unchallenged control, thus undermining international solidarity. One Japanese baseball official observed, "This whole thing smacks of U.S. imperialism on the part of MLB."[26]

Former commissioner Selig claimed that MLB and the WBC seek to "increase global interest, and introduce new players and fans to the game."[27] But this seems more so to ensure MLB control and prosperity than to support the sport at a high level in as many nations as possible.[28] MLB wants to multiply the number of fans who will follow the fortunate few among their countrymen who make it into the U.S. Major Leagues and to whom game tickets, merchandise, and broadcast rights can be sold. It is dedicated to marketing its "product" globally, rather than promoting autonomous zones of baseball and ceding jurisdiction to an independent international body. In *The American Game* (2006), anthropologist John D. Kelly argues that MLB "has positioned itself like the U.S. on the UN Security Council, controlling the commanding heights of intervention."[29]

Kelly further characterizes the WBC as a "separate but equal" system, where one league is more equal than the others, where no leagues matter except for MLB, and where exceptional players have almost nowhere else to go except to MLB. After decades of MLB domination and talent extraction, foreign baseball leagues cannot build themselves up fast enough to keep their homegrown talent at home. They remain separate and second-class institutions. As a player in corporate capitalism, MLB is not just profiting but also controlling the framing and staging of transactions, the terms of trade, and the rules of the game. MLB owns the WBC and subordinates it to its own "World Series," thus making the world safe not for baseball, but rather safe for Major League Baseball.[30]

American Empire

The WBC may also have a meaning beyond MLB objectives, centered on questions of American exceptionalism and U.S. foreign policy in the post-9/11 era. In *Baseball and the Rhetorics of Purity* (2010), Michael L. Butterworth argues that during the war on terror, the WBC helped revitalize America's and baseball's missionary quest. As seen in the HBO documentary *Nine Innings from Ground Zero* (2004), baseball helped the United States recover and reassert itself amid concerns about American preeminence. MLB itself was poised at a crossroads, which invited "interpretations of [an] empire both aging and rekindled with vigor."[31] The WBC was the result.

The WBC served American interests by using nationalism as its rhetorical strategy in producing the games. The tournament was widely hailed by Americans as demonstrating America's and baseball's democratic strengths—baseball for everyone. In the context of the war on terror, in which U.S. foreign policy increasingly returned to "regime change" and "nation building," the WBC was supposed to be a reminder of the purity of the American dream. It rejuvenated baseball's role as a complement to evangelical efforts, dating back to sporting-goods magnate Albert G. Spalding, to show the world the moral superiority of Americans.

As with making the world safe for democracy, it was now America's special role and responsibility to rid the world of terrorism. Much as the Iraq and Afghanistan invasions were rationalized to "liberate" an oppressed people, the WBC was part of a process "to *enlighten* the less baseball-centric nations of the world."[32] "MLB demonstrated," Butterworth suggests, "a pattern of leadership and a global vision consistent with American policy makers who saw the world after 9/11 as one in which an American-led hegemony of neoliberal capitalism needed to exert its influence throughout the world."[33]

Jackie Robinsonization

In any case the WBC gave MLB what it wanted. It did not reproduce the Olympic message of peace and friendship. It did not devise a new diplomatic mechanism. And it did not—despite all the national flag waving—make a statement on nationalism. Instead, MLB's media campaign focused entirely on individual stars. In every venue "trailblazer" films were played on electronic scoreboards, celebrating past Major Leaguers from each nation—except for Cuba, whose ballplayers were intentionally excluded. John Kelly calls this the "Jackie Robinsonization of international baseball."[34] The films told a story: that MLB provides opportunities for worthy individuals and that the pioneers from abroad colonized the Major Leagues and not vice versa. Baseball success stories affirm the American dream, even if it is a fantasy for most players, including those on the low-cost baseball-academy plantations big-league clubs were still running in the Caribbean.

The American media at the WBC told no success stories about national teams and leagues, since there were none to be told. Organized baseball had always kept competing leagues subordinate, if they survived at all. The saga of the Mexican League challenge, for example, was not recounted at the WBC. That would have highlighted the emptiness of the *World* in *World Series*, which should be played not by U.S. pennant winners but rather by the league champions of different nations, as Mexican entrepreneur Jorge Pasquel proposed in the 1940s. Other leagues in the Caribbean and East Asia have not literally become MLB Minor Leagues, nor have their clubs been converted yet into big-league farm teams, but sometimes it seems that way.

When Jackie Robinson broke the MLB color barrier in 1947, it was a triumph for a select group of individuals and a disaster for most black professional ballplayers, their teams, and fans. It destroyed the Negro Leagues. The influx of foreign-born players has had the same effect on their nations' teams and leagues. When Satchel Paige was being mentioned as possibly the first to break the U.S. color barrier, he claimed he would not come alone, but rather only with his whole team. Add a black team to MLB, he argued (and so, too, did Bill Veeck and Paul Robeson).[35] MLB refused, just as it refuses to add foreign teams or leagues to its concept of a World Series. The national champion teams of Japan, Korea, Venezuela, and the Dominican Republic need not apply.

In MLB's empire of baseball nations, each new member gets its own pinnacle league. Teams in these leagues can play each other, enter regional championships, and perhaps participate in the WBC. But they never get real championship games against the New York Yankees or St. Louis Cardinals or San Francisco Giants. If not exactly conquest, then it was nevertheless a kind of exclusion and denial of opportunity. Since foreign ballplayers, on their own teams, had no chance to beat America's baseball champions, they have to leave home to try to join them. That is what MLB sought and celebrated: the individual migration of past trailblazers and the incorporation of new ones (such as Japan's Daisuke Matsuzaka and Yu Darvish and Cuba's Aroldis Chapman) who succeed in the "tryouts" the WBC games provided.[36]

Americanization or Real Globalization?

MLB has been happy to globalize its workforce as long as it retains control and maintains its profits. Former commissioner Selig declared, "Baseball may have been born in America, but now it belongs to the world."[37] Yet while it might be played by (some of) the world, MLB insists it still owns the sport. MLB was even willing to risk losing its mastery on the field to reclaim ownership—a "lose to win" approach, according to a popular Japanese adage. Especially with the Olympics' absence and the World Baseball Cup's demise, baseball-playing nations—in the absence of other international tournaments—have to play in the WBC and by MLB rules. It was as if to say, observes ESPN's Jim Caple, "Cheer up, fellow Americans. Our country might not have reached the final round of the World Baseball Classic, but the best players eventually all wind up here."[38]

With the WBC, MLB controls a tremendously lucrative enterprise, "a vast, high-level tryout camp, and a safety valve for global baseball aspirations."[39] Under this regime the maximum ambition for a baseball-playing nation would be to be chosen, possibly hosting a tournament round, and winning—for whatever meaning it might hold in the still lingering shadow of the World Series. "To call it an empire, or even a monopoly, is to seriously underestimate it," according to John Kelly. "It is to fail to see the form of power it wields in shaping the separateness of its own commodious world."[40]

MLB will inevitably have a role in global baseball. Yet according to the late International Baseball Federation president Aldo Notari, if the WBC permanently supplants Olympic baseball, it will be "a disaster for the development of baseball in the world."[41] Through the WBC, MLB has ensured itself "a highly American style of internationalization" or "Americanization."[42] To pursue any sort of *real* baseball globalization and development of the sport, however, MLB will have to do more than maximize its profits. Its leaders will have to decide whether it will remain "a twentieth century colonialist or rather a twenty-first century democracy."[43]

31. An advertisement for the 2017 World Baseball Classic. (Photo courtesy of htttp://www.baseball-fever.com.)

NOTES

1. Alan Klein, "Globalizing Sport: Assessing the World Baseball Classic," *Soccer & Society* 9, no. 2 (2008): 159 (emphasis added).

2. Mark Lamster, *Spalding's World Tour: The Epic Adventure That Took Baseball around the Globe—and Made It America's Game* (New York: Public Affairs, 2006), 282.

3. Robert Elias, *The Empire Strikes Out: How Baseball Sold U.S. Foreign Policy & Promoted the American Way Abroad* (New York: New Press, 2010).

4. An unnamed MLB official in William B. Gould IV, "Baseball Classic Mirrors World Events," *San Jose (CA) Mercury News*, March 21, 2006, A2.

5. Quoted in Alan M. Klein, *Growing the Game: The Globalization of Major League Baseball* (New Haven CT: Yale University Press, 2006), 238.

6. Chris Jenkins, "New Meaning for Moneyball: Major League Baseball's Globalization of Game Makes Dollars—Billions—and That Makes Sense," *San Diego Union Tribune*, March 18, 2006, 20–22; Christopher Clarey,

"Baseball's New World Order," *International Herald Tribune*, May 16, 2005, 14.

7. In the 2008 Beijing Olympics China's American-coached baseball team won only one game and finished last. The U.S. team finished third, with Cuba second and South Korea taking the gold medal. See Kirsten Jones, "The Game Goes for Gold: A History of Olympic Baseball," *Memories and Dreams* (July–August 2006): 20–22.

8. Jonathan Mahler, "A Whole New Ballgame: The World Baseball Classic Raises Issues of Patriotism and Identity," *Los Angeles Times*, March 5, 2006, M1; John D. Kelly, *The American Game: Capitalism, Decolonization, Global Domination, and Baseball* (Chicago: Prickly Paradigm Press, 2006).

9. Mahler, "Whole New Ballgame."

10. William W. Kelly, "Is Baseball a Global Sport? America's 'National Pastime' as Global Field and International Sport," *Global Networks* 7 (April 2007): 187–201.

11. Murray Chass, "A Sure Sign of Hypocrisy," *New York Times*, March 7, 2006, D2.

12. Quoted in Barry M. Bloom, "Selig: Classic to Get 'Bigger and Bigger,'" March 22, 2009, http://mlb.mlb.com/news/print.jsp?ymd=20090322&content_id=4045676.

13. Dave Zirin, "A Whole New Ball Game," *Nation*, March 15, 2006, http://www.thenation.com/doc/20060327/zirin.

14. Zirin, "Whole New Ball Game"; Roberto Gonzalez Echevarria, "Castro at the Bat," *New York Times*, January 11, 2006, A29; Dave Zirin, "The Bray of Pigs," December 21, 2005, http://alternet.org/story/29878.

15. Daniel Erikson, *The Cuba Wars: Fidel Castro, the United States and the Next Revolution* (New York: Bloomsbury, 2008), 224.

16. Amy Chozick, "World Series; Global Pitch: A World Cup for Baseball? It Isn't as Easy as It Sounds," *Wall Street Journal*, October 18, 2004, R6.

17. Quoted in John M. Glionna, "WBC Has Made a World of Difference to Ichiro and Hideki Matsui," *Los Angeles Times*, March 5, 2009, C7.

18. Craig Simons, "South Korea Boasts New Patriotism, at U.S. Expense: Baseball Victory Reinforces Self-Image," *Atlanta Journal-Constitution*, March 19, 2006, C8.

19. Donald Kirk, "Millions Rally in South Korea—around Baseball," *Christian Science Monitor*, March 20, 2006, 12; Reuben Staines, "Baseball Players Get Military Exemption," *Korea Times*, March 18, 2006; James I. Matray, "Global

Bully: South Korean Perceptions of the United States," in *Proceedings of 5th Annual Conference on War and Media—War and Sports* (Independence MO: Graceland University Center for the Study of the Korean War, 2004), 1–32.

20. Jerry Lee, "Commodifying Colonial Histories: Korea versus Japan and the Re/Productions of Colonial Violence in the World Baseball Classic," *Journal of Sport & Social Issues* 36, no. 3 (2012): 231–44.

21. Gould, "Baseball Classic Mirrors World Events," A2.

22. Dain TePoel, "'We Need to Get the Good Old USA on Board': A Comparison of the 2006 and 2009 World Baseball Classic," paper presented at the North American Society for Sport History conference, May 2013.

23. Quoted in Bill Shaikin, "With U.S. Team Out, Fans Lack Interest," *Los Angeles Times*, March 18, 2009, C5.

24. Joel Sherman, "Interest Growing in WBC, but So Are MLB Concerns," *New York Post*, March 14, 2009, 55.

25. W. Kelly, "Is Baseball a Global Sport?," 187–201.

26. Quoted in Klein, *Growing the Game*, 246.

27. Quoted in Zirin, "Whole New Ball Game."

28. Zirin, "Whole New Ball Game."

29. John D. Kelly, "Making the World Safe for Baseball: Reflections on Internationalism in Cooperstown and the World Baseball Classic," in *American Game(s): A Critical Anthropology of Sport*, edited by Benjamin Eastman, Michael Ralph, and Sean Brown (New York: Routledge, 2008), 94.

30. J. Kelly, "Making the World Safe for Baseball."

31. Alan Klein quoted in Michael L. Butterworth, *Baseball and Rhetorics of Purity: The National Pastime and American Identity during the War on Terror* (Tuscaloosa: University of Alabama Press, 2010), 135.

32. Butterworth, *Baseball and the Rhetorics of Purity*, 156.

33. Butterworth, *Baseball and the Rhetorics of Purity*, 147.

34. J. Kelly, *American Game*, 164.

35. J. Kelly, *American Game*, 170, 101.

36. Peter Bjarkman, *Diamonds across the Globe* (Westwood CT: Greenwood Press, 2005); Mike Marqusee, "World Games: The U.S. Tries to Colonize Sport," *Colorlines* 3, no. 2 (2000): 36; Dave McKenna, "The Washington Nationalists; America: Love It or Leave the Stadium," *Washington City Paper*, July 22–28, 2005, 14.

37. Quoted in J. Kelly, *American Game*, 125.

38. Jim Caple, "The Next Great Japanese Import," March 22, 2006, http:// sports.espn.go.com/mlb/worldclassic2006/columns/story?columnist =caple_jim&id=2377376.

39. J. Kelly, *American Game*, 169.

40. J. Kelly, *American Game*, 170. See also Klein, "Globalizing Sport," 158–69.

41. Quoted in Amy Shipley, "MLB Is Planning a World Cup, While IOC Wants Deeper Commitment," *Washington Post*, May 21, 2003, D1.

42. Gould, "Baseball Classic Mirrors World Events," A2; Tim Brown, "World Baseball Classic: Let's Play Two . . . or More," *Los Angeles Times*, March 18, 2006, D1; Jong Woo Jun and Hyung Min Lee, "Enhancing Global-Scale Visibility and Familiarity: The Impact of the World Baseball Classic on Participating Countries," *Place Branding and Public Diplomacy* 3, no. 1 (2007): 42–52; Robert Lewis, *Smart Ball: Marketing the Myth and Managing the Reality of Major League Baseball* (Jackson: University Press of Mississippi, 2010).

43. Robert Lewis, "'Soft Ball': MLB Shifts from Neocolonizer to Multinational Corporation," in *Cooperstown Symposium on Baseball and American Culture, 2005–2006*, edited by William M. Simons (Jefferson NC: McFarland, 2007), 247.

Afterword

George Gmelch and Daniel A. Nathan

In this afterword we treat the nineteen baseball-playing nations, Puerto Rico, and Tasmania in this book as individual case studies and compare and contrast them to see what patterns emerge in the history and development of baseball globally. Admittedly, the diverse backgrounds and interests of our authors limit how much we can know and say.

Let's start with baseball's diffusion from its birthplace. The game arrived in the latter half of the nineteenth century to most of the countries discussed in this book. Israel and South Africa are notable exceptions. Finland's form of the game, *pesäpallo*, is sui generis. The common belief that Americans are responsible for spreading the game around the world is clearly incorrect. As we have learned, the Japanese took the game to other countries in Asia, while the Cubans spread the game to neighboring Caribbean islands, notably Puerto Rico and the Dominican Republic.

Sometimes a single individual was responsible for introducing the game (or at least was given the credit for doing so). Examples include American teacher Horace Wilson in Japan, lumber-mill worker Albert Adlesberg in Nicaragua, and missionary Philip Gillett in Korea. More often, however, a group of people or an institution, such as the U.S. military in Latin America or Japanese colonial officials in Asia, brought the game. Local people watching soldiers and sailors playing baseball, for example, sometimes took up the game themselves. Locals were often invited to play and form their own teams. In other cases, as in Korea, colonial government policy aimed to encourage the local population to play. Returning students have also been baseball emissaries, bringing back the game after studying in the United States or Japan.

Deliberately attempting to introduce the game is quite different from being an inadvertent catalyst for its growth. In many cases (for example, Australia, Brazil, Cuba, and Puerto Rico), barnstorming foreign teams played an important role in exposing the new sport to the populace. The most heralded barnstormer was Albert Spalding and his 1888–89 world tour, which incited interest in baseball in Australia and Britain.[1] Korean players, returning home from Japan, traveled around Korea playing baseball and developing local interest. The influence of visiting American Negro League players who barnstormed through the Caribbean was a critical force in spreading the game there. These touring teams introduced the sport to many islanders who had never seen baseball before. The 1934 tour of Japan by U.S. Major League players, including Babe Ruth, led directly to the organization of the first Japanese professional league. This wasn't always the case. Of the eight nations visited by Spalding's world tour, Sri Lanka and Egypt never took up the game, and France did not until after World War II, and then only minimally.

In most of our sample baseball's growth as a sport has been glacially slow and spotty, characterized by periods of sound organization interrupted by stagnation, internal strife, and national events such as war and economic crises. The development of baseball in three of our four European cases—Italy, Holland, and Britain—has been particularly stunted. Additionally, the game has grown sporadically in Israel, New Zealand, and Tasmania. Major League Baseball International (MLBI) has spent a great deal of money trying to promote baseball in Europe with little to show for it. True, most European nations have a national team that competes in a Continent-wide competition for the European Cup and for a spot in the World Baseball Classic (WBC), but beyond this there is still only spotty organization.[2] Anthropologist Alan Klein argues in *Growing the Game* (2006) that MLBI should forget about western Europe and put its money into developing baseball in less developed nations, including those in eastern Europe, where athletes would be attracted by the chance to make money playing professional baseball, similar to the way in which poor inner-city African Americans are drawn to basketball.[3]

In Britain and its former colonies baseball faced stiff competition from the entrenched British game of cricket. Even today cricket has a much larger world following than baseball: 106 nations belong to the International Cricket Council, and 10 nations participate in the ICC's Test Championship. In the places where baseball did catch on, it did so primarily as an activity to keep cricketers and other athletes fit during their off-season. In Holland, Italy, and Brazil, among other countries, baseball also had difficulty competing against soccer. George is reminded of baseball's marginal status in these nations when he meets their international students on campus and asks what they know about baseball. Usually they know very little. A few years ago he had a conversation with two young men from England and China; neither one had an inkling that baseball existed in their homelands. The Chinese scholar thought he was confusing his country with some other place like Taiwan. Dan has had similar experiences. On his campus almost a third of the men's basketball team is typically composed of international student-athletes, while the baseball team has none.

In a number of instances, however, a nation's success in international baseball competitions, such as Taiwan's Little League Championships, Korea's winning the Asian Amateur Championship and being cochampions with Japan at the World Baseball Championships, and Australia's better than expected silver medal in the 2004 Olympics, has increased popular interest in the sport and been a source of national pride. Just participating in the WBC's 2013 qualifying round seemed to spur some Israeli interest in the game.

Baseball sometimes becomes a vehicle for promoting nationalism. The Taiwanese, for example, used baseball to assert their identity over their Japanese colonizers, and later, in the 1970s, their numerous Little League Championships fed the country's independence movement and activists used the game to challenge Chinese nationalist hegemony. In Korea baseball played a significant role in constructing an overarching national identity and integrating the country's disgruntled minorities. For patriots in Cuba during Spanish rule, shunning the Spanish-style bullfights in favor of the radical new game of baseball was a bold political statement. When baseball became an official Olympic sport during the Barcelona Olympics in 1992, interest and government funding in Australia, China, Taiwan, and Korea increased. But government support for baseball is precarious and could easily disappear should the International Olympic Committee (IOC) again drop baseball from the Olympic program.[4]

One of the benefits of the diffusion of baseball to other nations is that it gives local people greater choice in the sports they can play and watch. Many people in Asia, in particular, no longer want only traditional sports but yearn for "modern" ones played by Western nations. For many, sports such as basketball and baseball have come to symbolize modernity.

Yet in only 5 of the places examined in this collection—Cuba, Japan, the Dominican Republic, Puerto Rico, and Canada—has baseball developed into a major national sport. If we add Venezuela and the United States to this list, we are talking about fewer than 10 nations in the world where baseball is something like a national pastime. In only 3 of these—Cuba, the Dominican Republic, and the United States—can we genuinely talk about baseball as embodying the nation's character or significant features of it. Nonetheless, baseball today is played in many more nations than ever before. The International Baseball Federation has 124 members. Realistically, however, many of the countries the IBAF counts, such as Armenia, Cameroon, Guyana, Liberia, Mali, and Micronesia, have nothing more than a correspondent and a few club teams in the capital city, and sometimes most of the players are expatriate Americans.

The status of baseball in the 20 countries discussed here hardly adds up to a sport that is truly global, certainly nothing like basketball. Ever since the United States' so-called Dream Team dominated the 1992 Olympics in Barcelona, on the court and in the media basketball has become, in the words of *Sports Illustrated* writer Alexander Wolff, a global lingua franca.[5] NBA league games are now televised in 215 countries. The Los Angeles Lakers even have commentators who broadcast in Farsi. A 1997 survey of western European youth found that 93 percent recognized the Chicago Bulls' logo.[6] The NBA.com website draws more than one-third of its hits from outside the United States. The NBA has eleven offices outside of North America, including one in Mumbai, and in 2009 overseas sales were more than 25 percent of total NBA licensed sales.[7] Among teenagers worldwide the NBA is part of American popular culture, along with fashion, music, movies, McDonald's, Coca-Cola, and Nike. It is doubtful that baseball will ever achieve this kind of international success.

If we compare professional baseball's development in our sample nations with its development in the United States, the differences are staggering. With 30 Major, 240 affiliated Minor, and more than 40 independent professional league teams, the United States dwarfs its competition. Japan, the nation with the next most highly developed level of professional play, has only 12 teams in its Major League with a single Minor League affiliate for each. Korea has 10 Major League teams, and the Dominican Republic league has 6. The talent level of baseball players in most of the nations that have a professional league—China, Taiwan, Korea, the Dominican Republic, Nicaragua, Italy, Holland—rarely equals that of a low-level Minor League in the United States. Except for Japan, where teams play 140 league games, no other professional league even approaches the 162-game regular-season schedule played by MLB and the 144-game schedule of most American Minor Leagues. (In Taiwan they play 120 games, in Cuba 90, in the Dominican Republic 68, and in Italy 42.)

The average attendance at baseball games in all the professional leagues outside the United States, except for Japan, rarely exceeds the number of spectators that the average American Rookie or low Class A Minor League team draws on a typical night.[8] Nowhere do the players' salaries approach the average MLB salary of $4.5 million per season. Nowhere are ball clubs worth anything close to the $625 million (Tampa Bay Rays) to $3.2 billion (New York Yankees) at which MLB franchises are valued.[9] Only in the United States do the Majors and Minors place no limit on the number of foreign or "import" players.

On the other hand, baseball in our sample nations has produced some very talented players, enough that MLB teams are sending scouts all over the world. All have contributed players to the U.S. Major Leagues. Indeed, on opening day of the 2015 season there were 230 players born outside of the United States on MLB club rosters, representing seventeen countries and territories outside the United States. In total, the foreign born made up 26.5 percent of baseball's 868 players listed on opening-day rosters.[10] The largest contingent of foreign players came from the Caribbean and Latin America. The Dominican Republic led all countries with 83 players, followed by Venezuela with 65 and Puerto Rico with 13. The real form baseball "globalization" has taken is not the export of the game from the United States to foreign countries but the migration of baseball labor to the United States.

The presence of so many international players is changing the face of American baseball. For one, the game has become noticeably Latinized. When you walk into a clubhouse today you are as likely to hear Spanish as English, and the food on the clubhouse training table and in spring-training cafeterias often includes Latin dishes. Latin influence is also evident on the field, as Latin players bring a looser and more flamboyant style to the game. Think of David Ortiz pointing to the heavens after hitting a home run or Yasiel Puig running the bases or playing the outfield. Players show exuberance when making a good play or getting an important hit. Such behavior was called "hot-dogging" in the 1960s when there were far fewer Latinos, and it could result in a fastball to the ribs the next time a player came to the plate or a hard slide. Today Latinos have reached the critical mass where such behavior is now a widely accepted part of the game.

Latinos are also influencing how positions are played. Because some Latinos grow up playing on rocky fields, where bad hops make it prudent to protect oneself, Latino middle infielders sometimes field ground balls off to the side instead of getting their bodies directly in front of the ball, as American players are taught to do. Latino infielders sometimes throw sidearm to first base or while their bodies are off balance or on the run, whereas Anglo players are more inclined to plant their feet and then throw. Most baseball people now think that Latin American players have improved the game defensively and made it quicker. The influx of Hispanic players into MLB and their dominance at the top of most statistical categories have shattered the notion for American fans that their baseball players are the best in the world.

Many Anglo players who never learned Spanish in school now know some of the language, and they've learned something about Latin American geography and customs. International players, whether from Latin America or Asia, inevitably also introduce American baseball fans to their countries and cultures, whether it is the customs mentioned by TV color commentators or cultural geography introduced through ESPN specials like the one that followed Hall of Famer Pedro Martínez around his hometown in the Dominican Republic and the ESPN *30 for 30* episode on the Cuban brothers Liván and Orlando Hernández.

What about Asian players? Might they also be agents of change? Because there are far fewer of them (thirteen on MLB's 2015 opening-day rosters), and because they are scattered widely about the two leagues, their influence is certain to be much less than that of Latinos. Years ago, when George asked some of his baseball contacts (that is, scouts and players) what influence Asian players (nine of the thirteen were Japanese in 2015) might have, no one was sure. Several thought, however, that the Asians' highly disciplined approach to the game, healthier diet, rigorous training, and greater respect many have for their equipment—bats and gloves—have already found their way into American baseball (also, most stadiums now have Diamondvision, which was developed in Japan). The unusual hitting style (when swinging the weight is transferred to the front side of the body more quickly than is true for most American players) has, largely because of Ichirō Suzuki's success, been noted and analyzed by many. But it is still too soon to say whether some American players will mimic this.

The essays in this volume raise several interesting questions for future research. Will the international migration of players (for example, Latinos and Asians playing in the United States, Americans playing in Japan and the Caribbean) homogenize baseball, flattening out local versions of the game into a globalized hybrid? Will the World Baseball Classic play a role in this process? We have already seen how the infusion of international talent in the U.S. Major Leagues is producing a hybridized form of baseball, one that exhibits many characteristics of the Latin American game. What is the appeal of baseball for fans in different cultures? The chapters on Japan, Puerto Rico, and Cuba give some clues. How does the experience of being a spectator vary cross-culturally?

Even ten years after the publication of the first edition of this book, there is still much that we do not know about how baseball is transformed abroad, whether it is Korean professional baseball or pickup ball in a Dominican village. The diffusion of baseball is no different from the flow of knowledge, ideas, information, or technology, in that when it arrives in a new society, it is changed as local people adapt the game to fill their own needs and values. This process is sometimes called "glocalization." This term, anthropologist William W. Kelly explains, "captures the sense that local appropriation is seldom simply assimilating and imitating. Rather, it is generally a process of indigenization—of appropriating the foreign objects and practices by recontextualizing them into local matrices of meaning and value."[11] While the chapters in this book give us some insight into the ways in which local people put their own stamp on baseball and in the process create meaning, there is always much more to learn about the game and the people who play it.

1. The underlying purpose of the first expedition/tour, which was limited to locations under European control, was to market Spalding's sporting goods. See Mark Lamster, *Spalding's World Tour: The Epic Adventure That Took Baseball around the Globe—and Made It America's Game* (New York: Public Affairs, 2006); and Thomas W. Zeiler, *Ambassadors in Pinstripes: The Spalding World Baseball Tour and the Birth of the American Empire* (Lanham MD: Rowman & Littlefield, 2006).

2. See Alan Klein's *Growing the Game: Globalization and Major League Baseball* (New Haven CT: Yale University Press, 2006) for an excellent discussion of MLBI's international efforts to promote baseball abroad, such as the envoy and coach-in-residence programs. The latter sends ten to fifteen American coaches to Europe for six to eight weeks during the summer to instruct local youth.

3. Klein, *Growing the Game*, 169–95.

4. In 1981 baseball was granted the status of a demonstration sport for the 1984 Olympic Games in Los Angeles. Another demonstration tournament was held in 1988 at the Olympic Games in Seoul. The International Olympic Committee decided that the first official Olympic baseball tournament would be held in Barcelona in 1992. In 2005 the IOC voted to drop baseball and softball but then, in 2016, reinstated both sports for the 2020 Summer Olympics in Tokyo. Lynn Zinser, "I.O.C. Drops Baseball and Softball," *New York Times*, July 9, 2005, D1.

5. Alexander Wolff, *Big Game, Small World: A Basketball Adventure* (New York: Warner Books, 2002), xvii.

6. Toby Miller et al., *Globalization and Sport: Playing the World* (London: Sage, 2001), 15.

7. Terry Lefton, "Overseas Sales Drive NBA Merchandise Gains," *Sports Business Journal* (November 9, 2009), http://www.sportsbusinessdaily.com/Journal/Issues/2009/11/20091109/This-Weeks-News/Overseas-Sales-Drive-nba-Merchandise-Gains.aspx.

8. See http://www.baseballpilgrimages.com/attendance/minor-leagues-2015.html.

9. Mike Ozanian, "MLB Worth $36 Billion as Team Values Hit Record $1.2 Billion Average," *Forbes*, March 25, 2015, http://www.forbes.com/sites

/mikeozanian/2015/03/25/mlb-worth-36-billion-as-team-values-hit
-record-1-2-billion-average/.

10. See "Opening Day Rosters Feature 230 Players Born Outside the U.S.,"
April 6, 2015, http://m.mlb.com/news/article/116591920/opening-day-
rosters-feature-230-players-born-outside-the-us.

11. William W. Kelly, "Is Baseball a Global Sport? America's 'National Pastime'
as Global Field and International Sport," *Global Networks* 7 (2007): 188.

Source Acknowledgments

Chapter 12, "China: A Century and a Half of Bat Ball," is adapted from "Silk Gowns and Gold Gloves: The Forgotten History of Chinese Bat Ball," by Joseph A. Reaves, which originally appeared in *NINE: A Journal of Baseball History and Culture* 7, no. 2 (Spring 1999), and from a chapter in the author's *Taking in a Game: A History of Baseball in Asia* (University of Nebraska Press, 2002). Copyright 2002 by Joseph A. Reaves.

Chapter 15, "Tasmania: Baseball Struggles to Survive," is adapted from "Baseball in Tasmania," by George Gmelch, which originally appeared in *NINE: A Journal of Baseball History and Culture* 19, no. 2 (Spring 2011).

Chapter 21, "Great Britain: Baseball's Battle for Respect in the Land of Cricket, Rugby, and Soccer," is from *Baseball in Europe: A Country by Country History* (Jefferson NC: McFarland, 2008). Copyright 2008 by Josh Chetwynd. Reprinted by permission of McFarland & Company, Inc., Box 611, Jefferson NC 28640.

Contributors

Carlos Azzoni, one of Brazil's leading economists, served as dean of the Faculdade de Economia, Administracao e Contabilidade, University of São Paulo. He taught at The Ohio State University and the University of Illinois and is the author of many scholarly articles. Like most Brazilians, his first love is *fútbol*.

Tales Azzoni is a journalist and photographer with the Associated Press in Madrid. He writes extensively on sports and played baseball while attending high school in the United States. He worked as a journalist at a daily newspaper in Florida before returning to work for the AP in Brazil. He follows Major League Baseball closely.

Rick Burton is the David B. Falk Professor of Sport Management at Syracuse University and the school's faculty athletics representative to the Atlantic Coast Conference and the National Collegiate Athletic Association. He publishes widely, in books, scholarly periodicals, and the mainstream media, and teaches an honors class, Baseball and American Culture. He is the former commissioner of the Australian National Basketball League and former chief marketing officer of the U.S. Olympic Committee.

Peter Carino is emeritus professor of English at Indiana State University, where his research interests included baseball in literature and culture. For nearly ten years he coordinated the annual Indiana State Conference on Baseball and Literature and edited three volumes of proceedings: *Baseball/Literature/Culture: Selected Essays* (1995–2001, 2002, 2003). He has published articles on baseball novels as well as ballparks. His suffering as a lifelong fan of the New York Mets was somewhat alleviated in 2015 when the team reached the World Series.

Following a career as an NCAA Division I baseball player at Northwestern University and in the independent Frontier League, **Josh Chetwynd** played for the Great Britain National Team from 1996 to 2006. He was inducted into the British Baseball Hall of Fame in 2014. Beyond his on-field experience, he has also had an extensive broadcasting career, having served as an on-air Major League Baseball analyst on both British radio (BBC) and television (Channel 5). As a journalist, he has worked as a staff reporter for publications such as *USA Today* and *U.S. News & World Report*. He has also written seven books. One of them, *The Secret History of Balls*, was named an NPR best book in 2011, and another, *How the Hot Dog Found Its Bun*, was on the *New York Times* best-seller list (ebooks/nonfiction) in 2015.

Robert Elias is a professor of politics and the chair of legal studies at the University of San Francisco. He played baseball briefly at the University of Pennsylvania and semipro ball in western Pennsylvania. He teaches a course called Law, Politics, and the National Pastime. He played baseball on tours in Cuba and Nicaragua. His baseball books include *Baseball and the American Dream* (2001), *The Deadly Tools of Ignorance* (2005), and *The Empire Strikes Out* (2010). He grew up in New York when the city still had the Yankees, Dodgers, and Giants. He follows the Giants now in San Francisco.

David P. Fidler is the James Louis Calamaras Professor of Law at the Indiana University Maurer School of Law in Bloomington and an adjunct senior fellow for cybersecurity at the Council on Foreign

Relations. With Arturo J. Marcano, he has been active since the late 1990s in raising concerns about problems associated with Major League Baseball's operations in Latin America, including through *Stealing Lives: The Globalization of Baseball and the Tragic Story of Alexis Quiroz* (2002) and chapters in *The Cambridge Companion to Baseball* (2011) and *Sport and the Law: Historical and Cultural Intersections* (2014).

George Gmelch is a professor of anthropology at the University of San Francisco and Union College. He played Minor League Baseball in the 1960s while studying anthropology at Stanford University in the off-season. He has done field research on nomads, return migrants, commercial fishermen, Alaska natives, Caribbean villagers, Newfoundland oil workers, and professional baseball players. He is the author of a dozen books, with his most recent being *Playing with Tigers: A Minor League Chronicle of the Sixties* (2016).

Dan Gordon is a freelance journalist who has published extensively on international aspects of baseball. His interest in global baseball grew out of his love affair with the ballpark atmosphere. He has long been fascinated with the subtle differences in how fans experience the game in different cultural settings. Thanks to a Thomas J. Watson Fellowship, Gordon studied baseball culture in Japan, the Dominican Republic, Cuba, and Nicaragua. He is the coauthor of *Haunted Baseball: Ghosts, Curses, Legends & Eerie Events* (2007) and *Field of Screams: Haunted Tales from the Baseball Diamond, the Locker Room, and Beyond* (2010).

Marizanne Grundlingh is a doctoral student in anthropology at the University of the Free State, South Africa. Her research is concerned with the postsport lives of professional athletes and the role of sport heritage. She was an undergraduate student at Southern Methodist University in Dallas, where she held a swimming scholarship. During her sojourn in the United States, she became aware of the popularity of baseball in the country as opposed to its relative minor status in South Africa.

Colin Howell is a professor emeritus (history) and academic director of the Center for the Study of Sport and Health at Saint Mary's University in Halifax, Nova Scotia. A former editor of the *Canadian Historical Review*, he is the author and editor of a number of books on sport history, including *Northern Sandlots: A Social History of Maritime Baseball* (1995) and *Blood, Sweat and Cheers: Sport and the Making of Modern Canada* (2001). For a number of years he served on the selection committee for the Canadian Baseball Hall of Fame.

Mikko Hyvärinen is a records manager of Nokia Corporation and acts as the head of corporate archives in Espoo, Finland. Before his time with Nokia, he was a lecturer and researcher at the University of Tampere, Finland. A devoted Cleveland Indians fan, Hyvärinen has written articles on sports for the annual *Yearbook of the Finnish Society for Sport History* and Finnish university publications. His interests include North American history and sports, and his master's thesis was about Jackie Robinson and the desegregation of professional baseball.

Jorge Iber, a graduate of the University of Utah, is a professor of history at Texas Tech University and associate dean of the College of Arts and Sciences. His research interests include the role and participation of Latinos in U.S. sport history. He is the author or editor of eight books. His most recent work is a biography of Mexican American former Major Leaguer Mike Torrez (he of the infamous pitch to Bucky "bleeping" Dent in the 1978 playoff between the Red Sox and Yankees) that appears in the anthology *More than Just "Peloteros": Sport and U.S. Latino Communities* (2015). He is also editor of the Sports in the American West series for Texas Tech Press.

William W. Kelly is a professor of anthropology and Sumitomo Professor of Japanese Studies at Yale University. While doing fieldwork in rural Japan in the 1970s and 1980s, he occasionally played in a local farmers' baseball league, whose games began at 5:30 a.m. so team members could get to the rice fields afterward. He is the editor of

Fanning the Flames: Fandoms and Consumer Culture in Contemporary Japan (2004), *This Sporting Life: Sports and Body Culture in Modern Japan* (2007), and *The Olympics in East Asia* (2011). He is finishing a book about the Hanshin Tigers, a professional baseball team in Osaka.

Alan Klein is a professor of sociology-anthropology at Northeastern University. His academic interest in baseball research grew out of his love for the game. The convergence of the social scientist and the young man who played the game came about after reading a newspaper account of why the Dominican Republic was producing so many fine Major Leaguers. Twenty-five years later his interest in and defense of Dominicans in controlling their supply of players have deepened, and he has chronicled the power struggle between Dominicans and Major League Baseball. He is the author of *Sugarball: The American Game, the Dominican Dream* (1993), *Baseball on the Border: A Tale of Two Laredos* (1999), *Growing the Game: Globalization and Major League Baseball* (2008), *and Dominican Baseball: New Pride, Old Prejudice* (2014).

Arturo J. Marcano is a Venezuelan lawyer with a master's of law from Indiana University and a master's in sport management from the University of Massachusetts. He is an expert on professional baseball in Latin America, served as the international legal adviser to the Venezuelan Baseball Players Association, and writes on legal and sport management issues for ESPN Deportes. Marcano and David Fidler have published extensively on the topic of baseball in Latin American countries, including the book *Stealing Lives: The Globalization of Baseball and the Tragic Story of Alexis Quiroz* (2002), a chapter in *The Cambridge Companion to Baseball* (2011), and a chapter in *Sport and the Law: Historical and Cultural Intersections* (2014). He lives with his wife, Mary Ann, and daughters, Isabella and Lucia, in Toronto.

Andrew D. Morris is a professor of history at California Polytechnic State University, San Luis Obispo. He is the author of *Marrow of the Nation: A History of Sport and Physical Culture in Republican China*

(2004) and *Colonial Project, National Game: A History of Baseball in Taiwan* (2011) and editor of *Japanese Taiwan: Colonial Rule and Its Contested Legacy* (2015). In the early 1990s he lived two blocks from the baseball stadium in Taizhong, Taiwan. His time spent there led to an interest in questions of colonialism, nationalism, and ethnic identity in Taiwan's national game.

Daniel A. Nathan is a professor of American studies at Skidmore College. The author of *Saying It's So: A Cultural History of the Black Sox Scandal* (2003) and editor of *Rooting for the Home Team: Sport, Community, and Identity* (2013), he has published essays as well as book, film, and exhibition reviews for a variety of periodicals. Nathan has served as the film, media, and museum review editor for the *Journal of Sport History*, is on several editorial boards, and is past president of the North American Society for Sport History.

Franklin (Paco) Otto was born and raised in Puerto Rico. He taught in the U.S. Virgin Islands (St. Croix) from 1970 to 1973 and worked for the New York State Education Department's Office of Bilingual Education from 1977 to 2003. He has published articles on Puerto Rican baseball both on the island and in the United States. His current research is on Major League Hispanic broadcasters. He is the author of *Locutores hispanos: Perspectivas desde las grandes ligas* (2016).

Wayne Patterson is a professor of computer science at Howard University. He previously directed a U.S.-Brazil student exchange program with his coauthor, Carlos Azzoni, which is how he was introduced to *beisebol* in Brazil. He holds a PhD in mathematics from the University of Michigan and does research on computer security and cryptology. His presentation at the 2010 Cooperstown Symposium, "The Cryptology of Baseball," later became the first such symposium presentation to be published in the cryptology journal *Cryptologia*. In addition to many publications in this field, he has also written extensively on baseball, including his recent book, *Category League Baseball* (2014). He became interested in Brazilian baseball on his first trip to the country when he turned on the television in his hotel room and found a live broadcast of a baseball game from Japan. Curious why a Japanese game would be broadcast in Brazil, he began his inquiry into *beisebol*.

Joseph A. Reaves is a former foreign correspondent, Chicago Cubs beat writer, and Major League front-office executive. He lived in seven countries in Europe and Asia for two decades while reporting for the *Chicago Tribune*, *Reader's Digest*, and United Press International. Between overseas assignments, he came home to cover the Cubs and White Sox for four seasons for the *Tribune* and later was national baseball writer for the *Arizona Republic*. He joined the Los Angeles Dodgers in 2007 as director of international and Minor League relations. Reaves is author of *Warsaw to Wrigley: A Foreign Correspondent's Tale of Coming Home from Communism to the Cubs* (1997) and *Taking in a Game: A History of Baseball in Asia* (2002), which won the Jerry Malloy Prize for the best book in baseball in 2001 and the SABR/Sporting News Baseball Research Award.

A communication consultant and scholar, **William Ressler** has taught marketing communication, management, and research. His research explores the ways in which internal and external communications interact. In particular, he studies cultural identification and cultural diversity in Minor League Baseball, the benefits derived by Minor League players and teams performing community service, and the management of strategic creativity when Minor League teams produce innovative promotions.

Greg Ryan is a professor and dean of the Faculty of Environment, Society, and Design at Lincoln University in Canterbury, New Zealand. He has written and edited several books, including the award-winning *The Making of New Zealand Cricket, 1832–1914* (2004). Ryan is an academic editor (Africa, Australasia, and the Pacific) for the *International Journal of the History of Sport* and on the editorial boards of *Sporting Traditions* *and Sport in History.* He is also a member of the New Zealand Tertiary Council for Physical Activity, Sport, and Exercise.

Harvey Shapiro has coached U.S. college baseball for more than thirty years, notably at Springfield College, Bowdoin College, and the University of Hartford. He was hired to coach a club team (Amstel Tigers) in Holland and several years later became the coach of the Dutch National Team. He has given baseball clinics in Zimbabwe, South Africa, Holland, Germany, and the Netherlands Antilles. He has also coached in the Cape Cod Baseball League, the premier summer collegiate league, and in 1996 was named Manager of the Year. Shapiro led the Bourne Braves to their first Cape Cod Baseball League Championship in 2009. With four hundred wins, he ranks among the top coaching leaders in the history of the Cape Cod Baseball League.

Thomas E. Van Hyning was the U.S. correspondent for the Puerto Rico Baseball Hall of Fame from 1991 to 1996. He has written two books on the Puerto Rico Winter League. He has worked as an economist, city planner, and management consultant in Puerto Rico; a tourism and leisure studies researcher at Southern Illinois University; and an assistant professor of tourism at Pennsylvania's Keystone College. Since 1994 he has been the research manager of the Mississippi Division of Tourism.

A writer-in-residence at Johns Hopkins University, **Tim Wendel** is the award-winning author of twelve books, including *High Heat* (2011), *Castro's Curveball* (2012), *Summer of '68* (2013), and *Down to the Last Pitch* (2014). A founding editor of USA *Today Baseball Weekly*, he has served as exhibit adviser to the National Baseball Hall of Fame. He has made three trips to Cuba.

Index

Page numbers in italic indicate illustrations

cessions at, 51; corporate environment of, 50; Diamondvision at, 448
Baltimore Orioles: and Cuba, exhibition series between, 13–14; Wei-Yin Chen playing for, 274, 275
bangqiu (bat ball), 236
Banks, Nicole, 9
Bannatyne, A. G., 61
Barbados, xxix–xxx, 299
los Barbudos, 9–10
Barney, Robert, 58
barnstorming, baseball spread by, 41, 63, 92, 97, 442
Barrios, Francisco, 80
Bartholomew, Professor, 289
baseball: American influence of, 344; commercialization of, 427–28; development of, 57–59; as diplomatic tool, 247, 333; as disreputable, 60, 61, 62, 344; diversity in, 324; as equalizer, 160, 324, 334; as "foreign," 314; as game, 332, 334; growth of, 442–43, 448; homogenization of, 448; long season of, 199–200; as meritocracy, 141; as military training, xxiii, 230, 239, 240, 246–47, 414; as "modern," 444; as off-season sport for cricketers, 307, 313, 315; origins of, xvi, xxxi, 441–42; physical diversity in, 327; slow pace of, 412, 415; status of, 445; values of, 323–26; working class popularity of, 61; world politics affecting, 99, 339, 425–26, 429–30. See also *pesäpallo*
Baseball and the Rhetoric of Purity (Butterworth), 433
Baseball Canada, 70

Baseball for All (Israel), 325
baseball glove, invention of, 59
Baseball New Zealand, xxvi, 318
Baseball on the Border (Klein), 76
Baseball Softball Federation, 406
BaseballSoftballUK, 406
Baseball Tomorrow Fund, 341–42
Baseball Western Province (BAWP), 340–43
Baseball without Borders (Gmelch), xxxi–xxxii
base stealing, 401, 415
basketball: as global sport, 443, 445; in Korea, 207–8; in New Zealand, 317
Bayamón Vaqueros, 44–45
Beeston, Paul, 72
Beezley, William, 76
Beijing International Boys Baseball Tournament, 244
Béisbol (Oleksak and Oleksak), 134
Bell, James "Cool Papa," 78
Beltrán, Carlos, 52
Belville Tygers, 342, 345, 346
Bench, Johnny, 356
Bennett, Edwin, 340, 344
Best, Cal, 68
Bianchi, Roberto, 356, 357
bird dogs, 22, 94
Bissonette, Del, 60
Bithorn, Hiram, 42, 43
Bjarkman, Peter, 76
Black, David, 337
Bloomer Girls, 64
Blue Samurai, 199
Blyleven, Bert, 378
Boca Chica, DR, 27–28
Bogaerts, Xander, 389

between, 274; "traditional Chinese culture" and, 263

36; MLB as escape from, 118; MLB changing baseball culture in, 26–27, 29–32; MLB players from, 17, 21–23, 28–36, 149n2, 446; players from, falsifying documents, 30–31; players from, later careers of, 34; players from, suffering culture shock, 24, 26; political history of, 18–19; remittances to, from MLB players, 33; and the transnational commodity chain, 33–36; U.S. occupation of, 19; and Venezuela, parallels between, 129; and WBC, 36, 425. *See also buscónes* (amateur scouts)

Dominican Summer League, 25–26, 28

Dominican Winter League, 27

Donaldson, Josh, 72

doping, 426

Doubleday, Abner, 58

Doulens, Roger, 241

Du Kehe, 242, 243

Durbanville Baseball Club, 342

Durrant, A. R., 315

Dutch Baseball Federation, 374

Dutch Caribbean, 384, 388, 389

Dutch National Baseball Team, 375, *381; vs.* Canada, 382; changes in, 388–91; in Cuba, 383; in Curaçao, 382–83; discipline in, 382–83, 386; as European champions, 387; in the European Championship, 386–87; *vs.* Italy, 386–87; preparing for World Baseball Championship, 380–82; quality of play in, 380; renamed Kingdom of the Netherlands Team, 388; Shapiro coaching, 373, 379–88; *vs.* Taiwan, 382, 383; in the World Baseball Championship, 379–86

Eastern Europe, 443

East Melbourne baseball club, 290

EC Mailhense, 137

economic slump in Asia, 220

Edward VII (Prince of Wales), 394–95

Edwards, David, 306

Eenhoorn, Robert, 390, 391n3

Efraín Tijerino Stadium, 88

Egypt, 442

Eimei High School, 169

Eindhoven, ballpark in, 387

Elias, Robert, xxix, 112, 425–40

Elite Camp, 144

Enatsu, Yutaka, 219

England. *See* Great Britain

English-language training, 24, 26

la Epoca Romántica, 48

Escalera, Saturnino, 44

Escambrón Stadium, 41. *See also* Sixto Escobar Stadium

Escogido (Dominican team), 20

Escuadron del Panico, 45

Espino, Héctor, 80–81

Espinoza, Lester Hernández, 95

Espolita, Andrés, 97–98, 108n15

Esquina Caliente, 4, 5, 11

Estádio do Bom Retiro, 138

Estrellas Orientales (Dominican team), 20

Ethiopian Giants, 64

eugenics, 413, 414

European Championship, 365, 375, 386–87, 405, 406, 407

European Cup, 357, 365

Korea Amateur Baseball Association, 222

Korea Baseball Organization (KBO), 203, 225–26; company-owned teams of, 215; foreign talent in, 219–21; inaugural season of, 216–17; making baseball outlet for political emotions, 214, 215–16; mercenaries salaries capped by, 220–21; and MLB, posting agreement between, 204, 226n3; player caliber in, 217–18; reaction to mercenaries in, 220; rules of, 215; salaries in, 215, 220–21; Suh Jyong-chul as commissioner of, 214–15; training in, harshness of, 216

"Korean spotting," 218–19

Kōshien (high school baseball tournament), xxi, 154, 254; 1987, 163–68; 2006, 166, 177n15; 2009 summer, 165; 2010 spring, 159, 169; 2010 summer, 169; 2011 summer, 164; 2012 spring, 154; celebration for winning, 156–57; cheering at, 196; injury and illness at, 166–67; Kanō team at, 252, 253; losing, 163, 177n12; oath of fair play and, 161, 163–64; pictures of dead players at, 165; post-tsunami, 178n28; precursors of, 161; selflessness of players at, 163–68; summer, 155–57. See also Japanese high school baseball

Kōshien Stadium, 156, 189, 190; collecting soil from, 154, 156, 163, 176n1; "official entrance" to, 193–94; purity of soil from, 158, 176n2

Krakauskas, Joe, 65

Kremer, Dean, 329

KT Wiz, 221

Kuehnert, Marty, 168, 172

Kuhn, Bowie, 216

kuningaspallo (king ball), 411–12, 420n4, 420n5

Kuo, Hong-Chih, 272, 274

Kurz, Peter, 333

Kuwata, Masumi, 167, 173, 177n18, 179n32, 180n47

labor migration, 22–23, 24, 26, 32–33, 446, 448

LaFrance, David, 81

Lajoie, Nap, 60

Lamster, Mark, 288, 425–26

Lapua Virkiä, 418

Larkin, Barry, 144–45

LaRussa, Tony, 108n15

Lasorda, Tommy, 426

Latino players in MLB. See also specific countries

Lee, Lawrence, 239

Leeds (British baseball team), 402

Lee Kunhee, 216

Lefebvre, Jim, 244

Lega Nazionale di Baseball, 352

Leppard, Brett, 302

Leslie's Weekly article (Shafer), 240–41

Levine, Peter, 396

Ley, Francis, 397, 397–98

LG Twins, 223

Liang Dunyan (Liang Tun Yen), 233, 234

Liang Fuchu, 242

Liang Pixu (Liang Cheng), 236–38

Licey (Dominican team), 20

Liddi, Alex, 353, 363, 364, 366

Liddle, Don, 48

118, 124; colonialism of, 18, 21, 32–33, 118, 119–25, 427, 429, 430–31, 436; competing for media coverage, 188; and Cuba, 6–7; cynicism in, 332; Dominican Office of, 34–35, 37; Dominican players in, 17, 21–23, 28–36, 149n2, 446; draft threatened by, 31, 32; exploitation and abuses by, 118, 119–25, 199–200; globalization by, 32, 111, 114–25, 427–28, 431–33, 436; as governorship, 32–33; Great Britain and, 394, 398–99, 401, 407; hegemony of, 431–33; international flavor of, 133, 446–48; Italian players in, 353, 364, 365; Japanese players in, 175; Korean players in, 203, 204–5, 218, 219, 226n3; Latinization of, 446–47; marketing itself, 432; Mexico and, 79, 80, 149n2; New Zealand players in, 318; Nicaragua and, 93–97, 108n19; players from, in Italy, 358–59, 360–61; Puerto Rican talent in, 51–52, 446; pulling out of Venezuela, 126–27; racism and discrimination in, 11–12, 20–21; restricting players from WBC, 125; salaries, 446; San Juan team, 52; South Africa and, 341, 342, 344; televised abroad, 97, 275, 307, 405–6, 407; U.S. foreign policy supported by, 426, 428; Venezuela exploited by, 118, 119–25, 129, 130; visiting Puerto Rico, 41; WBC as marketing for, 124–25, 431, 434–35; and Winter League Agreement (WLA), 119–23; World Series of, 428, 433, 435. *See also* academies; World Baseball Classic (WBC)

Major League Baseball International (MLBI), 33; on Brazil's potential, 148; coach-in-residence program of, 449n2; promoting baseball in Europe, 390, 442–43
Major League Baseball Players Association (MLBPA), 32, 122, 125, 342
Malan, D. F., 339
Manatí Atenienses, 45
Manchester, England, 399–400
Man-Dak League, 68
Manifest Destiny, 285–86
Manitoba, 60–61
Manzanillo, Ravelo, 262
Mao Zedong, 241, 242, 243
Maple Leaf (Hongye) Elementary School, 257–58, 271, 274, 278n12, 278n15
Marcano, Arturo, xx–xxi, 111–32
Marchildon, Phil, 65–66
Maronde, Nick, 318
Marshall, Gavin, 407
martial arts, baseball's similarity to, 155, 158, 159–60
Martin, Freddie, 67, 68
Martin, Russell, 72
Martínez, Dennis, xx, 46, 86–87, 109n22; academy founded by, 94–96, 107n10
Martinez, Ibsen, 128
Martínez, Pedro, 29, 36, 447
Matos, José, 53
Matsui, Hideki, 175
Matsumoto, Yoshitsugu, 153–55, 161–62, 168, 169, 174, 176
Matsuzaka, Daisuke, 166, 222, 435
Matthew, Steve, 389

Shanghai: eight-club league in, 240–41; foreign influence in, 241

Shanghai Base Ball Club, 230, 235–36

Shapiro, Harvey, xxvii–xxviii, 373–91, *381*; coaching Amstel Tigers, 376–79; coaching Dutch National Team, 373, 379–88; first game of, in Holland, 377

Shapiro, Scott, 382

Sheldon, Dave, 361, 362

Sherman, Joel, 431

Shimabukuro, Yosuke, 169

Shimoda, Takeso, 216

Shimomura, Hakubun, 172

Shizuoka High School, 156

Showalter, Buck, 273

signings: increase in bonuses for, 107n11; million-dollar, 28

Simmons, Andrelton, 389

Simontacchi, Jason, 360

Simpson, Harry, 290–91

Sino-Japanese War, 208, 212–13, 230, 236, 241

Sinon Bulls, 279n19

Sixto Escobar Stadium, 39, 41–42, 50–51

Skydome, 72

Smit, Paul, 373

Smith, Hilton, 64

Smyth, Ian, 402

soccer: baseball competing with, 99–100, 174–75, 198, 311, 388, 443; development of, 57–58; FIFA's role in, 432; as ideal pick-up game, xx, 79, 86, 100; in Italy, 352–53, 369, 443; and *pesäpallo*, 413

social class: baseball and, 41, 61, 304, 313–14; cricket and, 344

softball: New Zealand, 316, 317, 319; in Tasmania, 302, 310n8

Somoza Debayle, Anastasio, 87

Somoza García, Anastasio, 89, 98

Soroka, Mike, 73

South Africa, xxvi–xxvii, 337–48; 1948 election in, 338–39; academies and training camps in, 344, 347; Americanization of, 346; antiapartheid sports organizations in, 339; apartheid and, 337, 338–40, 348n17; ballparks in, 341, 342; baseball's meaning in, 345; boycotts of, 339, 340; climate of, 341; coaches needed in, 344; cricket in, 343–44, 347; funding baseball in, 341–42; gold rush of, 338, 346; history of baseball in, 338–40; identity in, 345–46, 347; infrastructure of, for baseball, 341–43; international tours of, 338, 339–40; Japanese influence in, 338, 346; MLB and, 341, 342, 344; Nationalist Party of, 339; at Olympics, 340, 343; organization of clubs in, 340–41; origins of baseball in, 338, 441; racial and class distinctions enduring in, 342–43, 348n15; school sports in, 343–44; sports in, 337; team names of, 346; townships of, 343, 348n15; and the WBC, 340–41, 343; Western Province dominating baseball in, 340–41

South African Baseball Association, 339

South African Baseball Federation, 339

South African Baseball Union (SABU), 340, 344, 347

South African Non-Racial Olympic Committee (SANROC), 339

baseball in, 112–14; players from, in Minor Leagues, 116–17, *117*; players from, in MLB, *115*, 115–16, 427, 446; politics and economics of, 111–12, 118–19, 125–28, 129; poverty in, 119, 125, 128, 129; teams of, 113; U.S. military presence in, 112; Winter League season canceled in, 126; and World Baseball Classic, 124–25

Venezuelan Baseball Players Association, 118; and Winter League Agreement, 123

Venezuelan Professional Baseball League (LVBP), *113*, 113–14, 126, 128

Venezuela Summer League, 117, 128

Venezuela Winter League, xx, 119, 126

Veracruz Azules, 78

Verona, Italy, 363

Vieira, Thyago, 150n11

Vietnam, xxix

Vilar, Yasiel Cancio, 105

Vimpeli Veto, 416, 419

Virgil, Ozzie, Sr., 21, 149n2

Virtue, John, 79

Volkerijk, Bart, 380, 381, 386

Vosberg, Ed, 360

Votto, Joey, 74n11

Walker, Larry, 69, 74n11

Wang, Chien-Ming, 272, 274–75

Ward, John Montgomery, 289

War on Terror, 430, 433–34

Waseda University baseball team, 138, 211

Wawryshyn, Evelyn, 65

weather. *See* climate and weather

Webb, Cyrus, 312

Weichuan Dragons, 261, 270

Wei Te-Sheng, 276

Wellington, New Zealand, 312, 313–14

Wellington Baseball (Softball) Association, 316

Wellington Baseball Club, xxv, 312

Wellington Baseball League, 312

Wen Bingzhong, 234

Wendel, Tim, xvi–xvii, 3–16

Western values, Asians adopting, 211, 235

West Ham Hammers, 401, 402

Westridge Yankees, 346

Wetherell, Donald, 62

White City (British baseball club), 402

White Rose club, 90

Whiting, Robert, 177n16, 219, 221–22, 224; on Koreans in Japanese baseball, 218; on Kōshien, 167; on purity, 158

Whitt, Ernie, 71

Wilcox, Chester, 302

"Wild Ball," 27

Wilding, Frederick, 313

Willenburg, Brett, 343

Williams, Ted, 12

Williamsport. *See* Little League

Wilson, Alfred, 64

Wilson, Bill, 316

Wilson, Horace, 441

Wilson, Travis, 318

Wilson, Woodrow, 19

Winnipeg, MB, baseball teams, 60–61

Winter League Agreement (WLA), 119–23

Winter Leagues: history of, 119–20; MLB declaring players exempt

CPSIA information can be obtained
at www.ICGtesting.com
Printed in the USA
LVOW11s1932110117
520602LV00003B/186/P

9 780803 276826